CW00762134

ROYAL HISTORICAL SOCIETY

STUDIES IN HISTORY 64

THE VICTORIAN POST OFFICE

THE VICTORIAN POST OFFICE

THE GROWTH OF A BUREAUCRACY

C. R. Perry

THE ROYAL HISTORICAL SOCIETY
THE BOYDELL PRESS

© C. R. Perry 1992

All Rights Reserved. Except as permitted under current legislation
no part of this work may be photocopied, stored in a retrieval system,
published, performed in public, adapted, broadcast,
transmitted, recorded or reproduced in any form or by any means,
without the prior permission of the copyright owner

First published 1992

A Royal Historical Society publication
Published by The Boydell Press
an imprint of Boydell & Brewer Ltd
PO Box 9 Woodbridge Suffolk IP12 3DF UK
and of Boydell & Brewer Inc.
PO Box 41026 Rochester NY 14604 USA

ISBN 0 86193 220 X

ISSN 0269–2244

British Library Cataloguing-in-Publication Data
Perry, C. R.
    The Victorian Post Office: The growth of a
    bureaucracy. – (Royal Historical Society studies
    in history)
    I. Title   II. Series
    383
    ISBN 0–86193–220–X

Library of Congress Cataloging-in-Publication Data
Perry, C. R. (Charles Richard), 1946–
    The Victorian Post Office : the growth of a bureaucracy / C. R.
Perry.
    p. cm. – (Royal Historical Society studies in history, ISSN
0269–2244 ; 64)
    Includes bibliographical references (p.   ) and index.
    ISBN 0–86193–220–X (hardback : acid-free paper)
    1. Great Britain. Post Office – History – 19th century.   I. Title.
II. Series.
HE6935.P47   1992
354.410087'3–dc20   91–32889

This publication is printed on acid-free paper

Printed and bound in Great Britain by
Woolnough Bookbinding Ltd, Irthlingborough, Northants

Contents

The Society records its gratitude to the following whose generosity made possible the initiation of this series: The British Academy; The Pilgrim Trust; The Twenty-Seven Foundation; The United States Embassy's Bicentennial funds; The Wolfson Trust; several private donors.

Preface

'Nobody ever notices postmen, somehow,' he said thoughtfully;
'yet they have passions like other men'. – G. K. Chesterton, *The
Invisible Man*

I began this study convinced that at least as far as historians were
concerned Chesterton was correct. The Post Office had not been noticed. To be sure Howard Robinson had investigated the department.
But his work, as valuable as it was, appeared before the explosion of
scholarly interest in the nineteenth-century revolution in government
and the emergence of the modern corporate state, and inevitably it did
not address the questions raised by these topics. As a result any mention of the Post Office in general histories – when the department was
mentioned at all – was usually limited to a few vague words about
improvements in communications. Fortunately this neglect has begun
to be redressed, as the work of several individuals mentioned in this
preface demonstrates. What this book proposes to do is to continue
this process by moving the expansion of the Post Office closer to the
centre of our understanding of the role of the Victorian state and the
origins of a mixed economy in Britain.

During the course of writing this book I have incurred a large number of debts. I wish to thank the archivists and librarians who maintained the records on which this study is based. These include the staffs
at Widener Library, Harvard University, Wilson Library, the University
of North Carolina, Heard Library, Vanderbilt University, and duPont
Library, the University of the South. In England the British Library,
the Public Record Office, the Bodleian Library, the archives of University College, London, the Union of Communication Workers Library,
and the House of Lords Record Office, whose clerk gave permission to
consult the Samuel Papers, should be mentioned. But above all I am
indebted to the staff at St Martin's le Grand, especially Celia Constan-
tinides, for their generous help during my extended research trips
there.

Many others have also contributed to the evolution of this book.
H. J. Hanham continued to encourage and admonish long after he was
under any statutory obligation to do so, while the late John Clive
kindly, but firmly asked me to raise my intellectual horizons.

Conference papers at various points in the gestation period benefited from the insights of Paul Lazarsfeld, Nathan Glazer, and John Cell. Robert Sullivan scrutinised the penultimate version of the manuscript with his fine eye, and Russell Snapp and Charles Miller tracked down references. Richard John pointed out a fruitful line of inquiry. Henry Parris, Jill Pellew, Alan Clinton, and Douglas Pitt discussed my work and theirs. From our first meeting in 1981 in what he later described as the Dickensian basement search room of St Martin's le Grand, Martin Daunton has helped me in too many ways to recount here. I remain profoundly grateful to him.

Research was facilitated by a Harvard University travelling fellowship, a Whiting Foundation fellowship, and a grant from the Mellon fund of the University of the South. I also wish to thank the Royal Historical Society for undertaking the publication of this book. I happily acknowledge the support of my departmental colleagues at Sewanee, especially that of Brown Patterson, Edward King and Susan Ridyard. Christine Linehan proved a most helpful trans-Atlantic editor. Cathy Young and her capable secretarial staff miraculously deciphered my handwriting, while Minnie Childers patiently handled word-processing headaches.

My greatest debt is to Dana for reasons which touch upon this book, but which go far beyond it.

C. R. Perry
Sewanee
November 1990

PART ONE
ADMINISTRATIVE CONTEXTS

1

The World of St Martin's le Grand

[O]wing to its extent and the variety of work it embraces, it furnishes in itself a series of the examples of most of the difficulties which are experienced throughout the civil service, and an inquiry into it involves the necessity of considering nearly all those measures which have been separately suggested in the cases of other offices. – *Report upon the Post Office* (London, 1854), p. 1.

If the Treasury was the department of departments, the Post Office was the bureaucracy of bureaucracies. In 1914 its staff accounted for almost one third of all the men and women employed in the civil service.[1] Moreover, until the consolidation of the railway companies in 1922 the Post Office, handling a dauntingly wide variety of responsibilities from the management of long distance telephone communication to the sale of licences for armorial bearings, comprised the largest business operation, public or private, in Great Britain. The headquarters of this vast enterprise was located in the City of London north of St Paul's on St Martin's le Grand. There the department had in 1829 moved into a new building designed by Robert Smirke. Resembling the architect's more famous work at the British Museum, the General Post Office was an impressive neoclassical structure with a Portland stone facade and Ionic columns across the front. The building from all accounts was the focus of considerable interest and activity. Londoners and visitors from the rest of the country as well as dignitaries from abroad, such as the Queen of Saxony, came to inspect the complicated processes involved in conveying mail. The building also provided a seemingly endless supply of amusing statistics – the relative savings habits of the Irish and the Scots – and bizarre stories – £50,000 found derelict in a letter box or jars of leeches sent through the mails – to stimulate the pens and brushes of Victorian writers and artists. Thus, Dickens commented on

---

1 David Butler and Jennie Freeman, *British Political Facts* (New York, 1963), p. 157. The figures were 240,000 in the Post Office versus approximately 810,000 in the entire civil service. The latter figure includes industrial and non-industrial staff. The latter figure has also been raised by 31,000 to adjust for Butler and Freeman's underestimation of the size of the Post Office staff.

the excitement of 'Valentine's Day at the Post Office', and G. E. Hicks captured some of the drama of 'The General Post Office: One Minute to Six'.

From a departmental point of view there were, however, two great drawbacks to Smirke's building. The first was its location. Like their fellow civil servants at the Customs Office, Post Office administrators always somewhat resented their exile in the City. St Martin's le Grand was simply too far from the more fashionable, more lively West End haunts frequented by clerks from the elite Whitehall departments. One Post Office man complained that the headquarters' location alone reduced the department to second-class status. According to F. E. Baines,

> The headquarters of this department lie too far east of Whitehall for its permanent officials to be closely in touch with the governing bodies of the realm, a condition which may have lent strength to the tendency . . . to rate the revenue-earning branches, and therefore, this one on a lower scale than the spending branches of the State.[2]

The second problem was that, while the building was attractive from the outside, its interior was not well-designed. Rooms were so badly arranged that odours from water closets wafted into the kitchens. Activities requiring extensive lighting were consigned to poorly illuminated areas, and the combination of inadequate ventilation and effluvia from gas lights often caused nausea among the workers. Moreover, as the demands of departmental business grew, the building – planned for the more leisurely pace of the ancien régime – began to burst at the seams. As The Times noted in 1860, 'Rooms have been overcrowded, closets turned into offices, extra rooms hung by tie rods to the girders of the ceiling.'[3] Sadly, parts of the structure rivalled Bentham's Panopticon in sheer dreariness, as detectives in a six-sided observation booth closely watched letter-carriers to prevent theft.

From St Martin's le Grand the Post Office controlled a huge administrative network, and it would be misleading to omit the other essential parts of what has been called 'a great and ubiquitous machine'.[4] There were metropolitan offices in Edinburgh and Dublin which oversaw the operations of the department in those countries. (The latter has undoubtedly gained more historical notice from its role in the events of Easter 1916 than from the intrinsic reason for its existence.)

---

[2] F. E. Baines, Forty Years at the Post Office, vol. 1 (London, 1895), p. v.
[3] The Times, 29 March 1860, p. 5.
[4] J. W. Hyde, The Royal Mail (Edinburgh, 1885), p. 118.

The system extended far into the British countryside. Major post offices in cities such as Liverpool and Glasgow and smaller sub-post offices, operated on a part-time basis by shopkeepers, were linked together to facilitate communication. The constantly increasing number of these offices is in itself a reflection of the administrative expansion which is the basic characteristic of Post Office history during the nineteenth century. In 1855 there were 920 head offices in the larger towns and 9,578 smaller sub-offices. By 1913 there were 1,098 offices in the larger towns and 23,256 sub-offices.[5] Even these offices did not constitute the boundaries of the Post Office's realm, since from the London headquarters administrators also organised mail channels for foreign and imperial communication.

Given the magnitude and the complexity of the ever-widening range of tasks taken on by the department, it is not surprising that Smirke's building was joined by others on St Martin's le Grand. In 1874 the G. P. O. West was opened to accommodate the recently acquired telegraph operations. In 1895 the G. P. O. North, built from the designs of Sir Henry Tanner, began to provide offices for the Postmaster General and other senior administrators. Of course, these additions did not represent the totality of the expansion of the department, which was forced to seek space elsewhere in London. For example, in 1880 a Savings Bank Office, subsequently to move to South Kensington, opened on Queen Victoria Street, and seven years later a new sorting facility was established at Mount Pleasant. At times the experience of growth was less than happy, as the Money Order clerks who suffered in temporary quarters at Cold-bath Fields Prison could testify.

At the top of this empire of stone and mortar was the Postmaster General, and some account of the men who served as, to use Bagehot's term, the dignified symbol of the department is necessary. These politicians, representing the party in power in Westminster, fall into two broad categories. For one group, St Martin's le Grand was merely a convenient spot where one might pause before moving on to more important and more responsible positions. Viscount Canning after serving as Postmaster General 1853–5 went out to India where, as First Viceroy, he earned the nickname of Clemency. The Marquess of Hartington, known to generations of schoolboys as the last Whig, was Secretary of State for War after leaving the more peaceful territory of the Post Office, and Austen Chamberlain, although he never reached the top of the greasy pole, did become Chancellor of the Exchequer. For another, larger class of politicians, the office did not function as a stepping stone to greater opportunities. Rather it was a reward for past services to party and country, a means by which the government might

5   *Report of the Postmaster General on the Post Office* (London, 1913), p. 30. ✳

5

keep these individuals active without placing them in a crucial spot. Men belonging to this group included Disraeli's friend Lord John Manners and the former Liberal Chief Whip and Patronage Secretary Arnold Morley. For politicians in either category, the Post Office with its reputation for a certain dull earnestness, only partly deserved, was certainly not a goal toward which they had worked during their entire careers. Henry Cecil Raikes, for instance, was probably not exceptional in the bitter disappointment he felt in 1886 when he was passed over for the job he actually desired, Home Secretary, and was forced to accept the more humble position at St Martin's le Grand.[6] A circumstance which further diminished the prestige of the office was that the Postmaster General was not necessarily a member of the Cabinet. Of the twenty-eight Postmasters General between 1835 and 1914, only sixteen sat in their government's cabinet. Questions of Post Office policy were only infrequently a central concern for the more important ministers, and the attractiveness of the office of Postmaster General suffered as a result.

The generally low appraisal of the position's importance was demonstrated by periodic attempts to abolish it altogether. As Ward Hunt bluntly argued, 'the only object in keeping up the office was to pay a compliment to some person of high rank, and give him a salary [of £2,500] for doing nothing'.[7] In 1835 a report to the Treasury had recommended the elimination of the office of Postmaster General and its replacement by a board, a system which Inland Revenue and Customs already employed. It was hoped that through this change the growing tendency to place the entire burden of administration on the permanent Secretary would be avoided. Arguing that the postal system of Great Britain made it 'the laughing stock of our continental neighbours', The Times supported the report's proposal.[8] Although the campaign for this alteration in the department's decision-making structure initially failed, the idea was periodically revived. Rowland Hill in 1847 and then again in 1861 sought to convince Whitehall that a board – in a revealing phrase – 'with myself for Chairman, would work well', but to no avail.[9] Thus, throughout the nineteenth century the pinnacle of the department's administrative hierarchy continued to reflect its pre-industrial origins as a patronage position despite the fact that the department had become a massive, modern enterprise. In 1866 one constitutional change concerning the office did occur when a bill allowing the Postmaster General to sit in the House of Commons was

6 Henry St John Raikes, *The Life and Letters of Henry Cecil Raikes* (London, 1898), pp. 246–8.
7 *Hansard's, Third Series*, vol. 182, 1079, 11 April 1866.
8 *The Times*, 13 July 1835, p. 4.
9 Post, Hill's Journal, 1 May 1847 and 23 April 1861.

passed.[10] This provision was intended to make the Post Office more responsive and accountable to the public. Thereafter, when the Postmaster General sat in the House of Lords, the Post Office was represented in the House of Commons by the Financial Secretary to the Treasury.

Given the fact that the position of Postmaster General was not abolished, the more important question to explore is how the official actually functioned in the decision-making process. Men with firsthand experience at St Martin's le Grand have reached different conclusions on this issue. Herbert Samuel, who in the late Edwardian period twice served as Postmaster General, gave perhaps the expected answer.[11] He emphasised the point that the permanent Secretary and his staff handled a large part of the administrative burden. For Samuel there was much time left after he had fulfilled his duties at St Martin's le Grand for more exciting political activities in Westminster. Taking a different position, Sir Evelyn Murray, who was permanent Secretary from 1914 to 1934, believed that as 'the Post Office is seldom responsible for controversial legislation, and is not directly concerned in the major items of the Government programme, the Postmaster General has more time than many ministers to devote himself to departmental work'.[12] In regard to the Postmasters General who served during the period 1835 to 1914, Samuel's assessment is much more accurate. The holders of this position were men with wider interests than the functioning of the department. Indeed, only a handful, among them Lord Stanley of Alderley, Henry Fawcett, and Henry Cecil Raikes, can be said to have left any distinct impression of their administrations. Without doubt, most did make policy decisions and modest contributions, such as Manners's revocation of free addresses on telegrams. However, there is not one Postmaster General whose contributions approach even distantly those of great Victorian departmental chiefs such as the third Earl Grey as Secretary for War and Colonies or Sir Richard Cross as Home Secretary. The nature of the department simply did not raise the kinds of issues with which most politicians were concerned. One can imagine, furthermore, how quickly a Postmaster General might tire of the oppressive volume of detail, which was endemic in his office and extended down to the approval of the erection of individual letter boxes. Hill once asked the Marquess of Clanricarde how an expenditure of less than £4 should be recorded in the accounts, and Edmund Yates related how irritated Lord Stanley became when bothered about

---

10 The bill was 29 and 30 Vict., c. 55.
11 Herbert Samuel, *Memoirs* (London, 1945), pp. 62, 77.
12 Evelyn Murray, *The Post Office* (London, 1927), pp. 178–9.

departmental business at home.[13] Another reason for the ineffectiveness of Postmasters General was their relatively brief tenure of office in comparison with the long years of service of the permanent officials. This situation, of course, was found in all government departments, but there was a complicating circumstance at St Martin's le Grand. There the somewhat technical nature of much of the business simply did not allow Postmasters General to muddle through on generalities, which might suffice in other offices. While Secretaries such as Sir John Tilley were masters of detail, few of their superiors were.

Yet a Postmaster General could be more than a figurehead. He could make policy, if he demonstrated the necessary perseverance. As will be seen in chapter six, Henry Fawcett refused to endorse his Secretary's recommendation for an active Post Office role in the development of the telephone, and as a result the history of the invention in Britain was fundamentally altered. Moreover, in industrial relations a Postmaster General's political outlook was especially important. The Edwardian Liberals Sydney Buxton and Herbert Samuel, for example, adopted a much more accommodating stance toward staff demands than had some of their Conservative predecessors. Courage was also a quality that was often needed in the office, for permanent officials did not lightly regard interference by a Postmaster General. In 1858 when Tilley was only an assistant secretary, he had no hesitancy about disagreeing with a Postmaster General as to the best course of action to follow in dealing with employee unrest.[14] Another such difference of opinion arose between Lord Stanley of Alderley and Sir Rowland Hill. From the beginning of Stanley's term at St Martin's le Grand in 1860 the two had not got on. Hill was accustomed to a succession of weak chiefs, but Stanley had no intention of being so pliable. They quickly argued about Stanley's intention to raise the wages of letter-carriers and his transfer of Hill's brother Frederic out of the Savings Banks Department. In May 1861 Hill recorded in his journal that 'The P.M.G. has . . . interfered with my Department.'[15] Hill, of course, had been the most important advocate of the Penny Post, which was established in 1840 and which dramatically increased the department's social and economic usefulness. By the time Hill and Stanley quarrelled, however, Hill's sense of self-importance had grown almost as rapidly as the Post Office. It was predictable, then, that Hill did not hesitate to go over the Postmaster General's head to plead his case before Gladstone, then Chancellor of the Exchequer, and even before

---

13 Post 100, Hill Papers, Hill to Clanricarde, 28 December 1847; Edmund Yates, *Recollections and Experiences*, vol. 1 (London, 1884), pp. 104ff.
14 Post 101, Tilley Papers, 27 August 1858.
15 Post, Hill Journal, 24 May 1861.

Lord Palmerston the Prime Minister. Palmerston summarily rejected Hill's appeal and confirmed that Stanley, not Hill, should exercise ultimate authority at St Martin's le Grand. As Palmerston explained,

I clearly perceived from what he [Hill] said to me that he entirely misunderstood the relative positions of a Secretary and the head of the department. He appeared to imagine that he ought to be Viceroy over his chief, and the substance of his complaint was that Stanley acted upon his own opinions instead of being invariably governed by his. I told Sir Rowland Hill that I consider Stanley quite right in the matter and that I have always acted myself on the same principle. That I have served in several offices, and that in each of them I have always been willing to hear and consider the opinions of my subordinate officers when they differed from my own, but that as I, and not they, must be held responsible for what was to be done, I acted upon my own decision when deliberately taken. Rowland Hill had no doubt the merit of suggesting penny postage, but he seemed to me to be the spoilt child of the Post Office, and he ought to make up his mind to be what he really is, a subordinate officer, or retire from a post which his own notions of his personal importance make it unpleasant for him to hold. As to leave of absence, if I was Stanley, I would give it to him *sine die*.[16]

Palmerston's words offer a classic statement of the case for the constitutional precedence of a political chief over his departmental subordinates. In this particular skirmish Stanley emerged the victor. Hill resigned in 1864 at the age of sixty-nine, and Stanley remained Postmaster General for two more years.

However, a significant feature of such disagreements was that one victory by no means signalled the end of the war. Over twenty years after Palmerston chided Hill, a similar disagreement arose between Raikes the Postmaster General and his Secretary, Stevenson Arthur Blackwood.[17] In February 1887 a vacancy had occurred among the first class clerks in the Secretary's Office. Blackwood, who believed in promotion on the basis of merit alone, felt that the man fourth in seniority was best qualified and recommended him. Raikes, who favoured promotion by seniority if the senior man was qualified, promoted the man second in seniority instead. The ensuing argument spilled beyond the walls of St Martin's le Grand into the pages of *The Pall Mall Gazette* and *The Daily News*. Blackwood's fellow permanent officials offered him a

16 Palmerston to Gladstone, 21 May 1863 quoted by Henry Parris, *Constitutional Bureaucracy* (London, 1969), p. 129.
17 Raikes, pp. 224ff.

formal address of sympathy for his rude treatment by Raikes. Both the Postmaster General and G. J. Goschen the Chancellor of the Exchequer considered Blackwood's acceptance of the address a grave case of insubordination. The matter was even discussed on the floor of the House of Commons. In the end the authority of the Postmaster General was confirmed, and Blackwood backed down. Still it was not clear how far the power of the political chief extended. Two years later in December 1889 Raikes asked Blackwood not to preside at an Evangelical prayer meeting at Exeter Hall. Critics of Blackwood believed that his zealous religious convictions bordered on anti-Catholic bigotry, and the government did not want to expose itself to criticism from Irish MPs. However, Blackwood refused to give way and attended the meeting. It is evident, then, that the exact allocation of power between the permanent officials and the Postmaster General had to be established anew upon each change of government. There was no manual accurately outlining the exact limits and prerogatives of the various officials. Descriptions in establishment books were general to the point of being uselessly vague. Therefore, each Postmaster General faced the difficult task of getting the feel of the office. Some never caught on. One such chief, Lord Hardwicke Postmaster General 1852–3, was a

> blunt, eccentric mannerless person with an overwhelming sense of the importance of his position; he had previously served in the navy, which fact, coupled with the peculiarity of his ways, caused him to be known among us as the 'Bosun'. His genial inquiry on his appointment, when the list of officers of the department was submitted to him was 'Now, can I dismiss all these men?' And his general idea was that late attendance, or any other shortcomings on the part of the clerks, should be punished by Keel-hauling or the cat.[18]

In contrast to the overbearing Hardwicke, other Postmasters General, William Monsell being the most egregious example, delegated too much authority.[19] It was a rare individual who, as Tilley described Lord Hartington, knew which matters of detail to leave to the permanent officials and which cases to handle personally.[20]

Immediately below the Postmaster General in the hierarchy was the permanent Secretary. Earning a maximum salary of £2,000 per year, the Secretary was the lynchpin of the administrative system at St Martin's le Grand. This circumstance was the natural result of the fact that all

[18] Yates, vol. 1, 103.
[19] See chapter five for Monsell's role in the Scudamore scandal.
[20] Post 101, Tilley to Hartington, 2 January 1871.

policy decisions normally flowed through him. Sir Edward Hamilton, Joint Permanent Secretary to the Treasury 1902–7 and a perceptive observer of the British bureaucracy, considered the Post Office Secretaryship the most important position in the whole of the civil service.[21] Although Hamilton's appraisal was perhaps inflated, it is understandable how he could have come to such a conclusion. Simply managing the army of departmental employees – 10,000 in 1839, almost 250,000 in established and unestablished positions by 1914 – was a mammoth job.[22] Moreover, as table one shows, the Post Office secretariat came to dwarf its rivals in other government offices.

Table 1
Civil Service Secretariats
1913

Department	Higher division clerks		Second division clerks	Assistant clerks
Post Office	80	(including 21 on surveying staff)	1,022	745
Treasury	29		14	–
Home Office	26		34	47
Colonial Office	37		43	–
Board of Trade	47		262	145
Local Government Board	60		183	87
Customs and Excise	38		166	48
Inland Revenue	42		538	322
War Office	43		144	48
Admiralty	37		101	219

Source: Post 33/729, M 1247/1922. Evidence prepared for the Royal Commission on the Civil Service, 1913.

Nine men served as Secretary between 1835 and 1914, but it is difficult to find very many common characteristics among the group. For example, their interest in the work varied enormously. Colonel William Maberly the Secretary from 1836 to 1854 represented much of the essence of the pre-reform Post Office. Edmund Yates has graphically described how Maberly, an absentee Irish landlord,

[21] Algernon West, *Private Diaries* (London, 1922), p. 203.
[22] Figures on the number of employees before the late nineteenth century are difficult to analyse, as part-time workers were often not included in the totals. Hence, the figure of 10,000 for 1839 is an underestimate.

11

used to arrive about eleven o'clock, and announce his arrival by tearing at the bell for his breakfast. This bell brought the head messenger whose services he arrogated to himself, who, being a venerable-looking and eminently respectable personage, probably well-to-do in the world, was disgusted at having to kneel at the Colonel's feet, and receive the Colonel's dirty boots into his arms with the short adjuration, 'Now, Francis, my straps!' The custom was for certain clerks of recognised status, who had a distinct portion of the official work in their charge, to submit the reports . . . to the Secretary. . . . The Colonel, a big, heavily-built, elderly man, would sit in a big chair, with his handkerchief over his knees and two or three private letters before him. Into a closely neighbouring seat the clerk would drop, placing his array of official documents on the table. Greetings exchanged, the Colonel, reading his private letters, would dig his elbow into the clerk's ribs, saying, 'Well, my good fellow, what have you got there – very important papers, eh?' 'I don't know, sir, some of them are perhaps –' 'Yes, yes, my good fellow; no doubt you think they're very important: I call them damned two penny-ha' penny! Now, read, my good fellow, read!' Thus adjured, the clerk would commence aloud one of his documents. The Colonel still half engaged with his private correspondence, would hear enough to make him keep up a running commentary of disparaging grunts, 'Pooh, stuff! upon my soul!' etc. Then the clerk, having come to the end of the manuscript, would stop, waiting for orders; and there would be a dead silence, broken by the Colonel who, having finished his private letters, would look up and say, 'Well, my good fellow, well?' 'That's all sir.' 'And quite enough too. Go on to the next!' 'But what shall I say to this applicant, sir?' 'Say to him to go and be damned, my good fellow!' And on our reading of those instructions we had very frequently to act.[23]

Yet one should not assume that the Secretary's Office was merely a branch of the Circumlocution Office which happened to be located on St Martin's le Grand. In contrast to Maberly's often indifferent attitude, Rowland Hill worked so hard that he suffered from headaches, diarrhoea, and nosebleeds.[24] And John Tilley, who was as much a product of the ancien régime as Maberly, showed more concern for the Post Office's service to the public than did Maberly. As Tilley lectured one of his subordinates in 1865,

23 Yates, vol. 1, 97–8.
24 Post, Hill's Journal, 8 January 1848 and 18 August 1853.

I think you have got yourself into what I may call a bad line of doing your work; and your morbid desire to get rid of papers seems to show this. It seems to show that you dislike the work, that you think the public unreasonable when they desire to be better accommodated, and that any demand for further information from us is a personal offence.[25]

Furthermore, it would be difficult to find a more conscientious Victorian civil servant than Stevenson Arthur Blackwood, Secretary from 1880 to 1893. Reportedly the most handsome man of his generation, 'Beauty' Blackwood had undergone a religious conversion in the Crimea. Accordingly, he unselfishly devoted his life to public service, the temperance movement, and Evangelical proselytising.

There were also significant differences in the quality of mind which individual Secretaries brought to the position. Consider the contrast between two men who entered the civil service after the Northcote-Trevelyan reforms and rose through the ranks to the Secretaryship at St Martin's le Grand. One, Sir Henry Babington Smith, who took a Double First at Cambridge and was a member of the Apostles, has been cited as a member of England's intellectual aristocracy.[26] The other, A. F. King, had little drive and few intellectual pretensions. As King once wrote to Matthew Nathan, 'I shall be glad to see you in charge here . . . because I don't care for the chief post. I have no ambition and am naturally lazy; at any rate mentally.'[27] Furthermore, the social and educational backgrounds of the nine Secretaries and their career patterns do not conform to a particular model. Maberly had been an MP in the pre-1832 House of Commons and a soldier. Hill, who grew up in a Birmingham family deeply influenced by radical Utilitarianism, had a background which included work as an inventor and educational and colonial reformer before he rode the wave of improvement into the Post Office at the age of fifty-one. Tilley who succeeded Hill was the son of a London merchant and entered the department at the age of sixteen through the patronage system. Maberly, Hill, and Tilley had not attended a prestigious public school or university. Later in the century the typical background included a public school education – Blackwood, Walpole, and Smith were old Etonians, Murray an Harrovian – and a university degree – Blackwood and Smith were Trinity College, Cambridge graduates, while Murray was a Christ Church, Oxford man. Only two of the Secretaries, Tilley and King, spent their

[25] Post 101, Tilley to Newman, 28 November 1865.
[26] Noel Annan, 'England's Intellectual Aristocracy' in J. H. Plumb (ed.), *Studies in Social History* (London, 1955), p. 256.
[27] Nathan Papers, King to Nathan, 4 December 1909.

careers solely concerned with Post Office business. Maberly had been Commissioner of Customs. Blackwood began his government career at the Treasury before being forced on St Martin's le Grand in the wake of the Scudamore telegraph scandal of 1873. Walpole had been Inspector General of Fisheries and Lt. Governor of the Isle of Man. Murray had a truly distinguished background at the Foreign Office, Treasury, and Board of Inland Revenue. Smith had also been at the Treasury as well as serving as Private Secretary to the Governor-General of India. Nathan, always something of an outsider in the establishment because he was a Jew, had been Governor of Hong Kong as well as a colonial administrator in Africa.

Of course, the fact that these Secretaries had experience outside St Martin's le Grand did not necessarily prevent them from becoming effective advocates of Post Office policy. Blackwood, for instance, was a vigorous adversary against his old friends at the Treasury when disagreements arose. Of greater importance in shaping the administrative effectiveness and outlook of the Secretaries was the fact that between 1893 and 1914 the length of tenure for these officials dropped dramatically from its earlier level. The typical Secretary before 1893 served an average of fourteen years. Between 1893 and 1914 the average time in office was only slightly longer than four years. Instead of remaining in harness until retirement or death, three of the Secretaries went on to other administrative posts. Murray became Permanent Secretary to the Treasury; Smith President of the National Bank of Turkey; and Nathan Chairman of the Board of Inland Revenue.[28] It may be argued that the shorter tours allowed an infusion of fresh ideas and approaches into the bureaucracy. Two negative results, however, should also be mentioned. For one, the lack of focus in Post Office policy during much of this period – particularly the difficulties over employee unrest and union agitation – must in some part be attributed to the inexperience of the Secretaries. Secondly, the constant stream of outsiders must have been galling to able departmental servants such as John Lamb who, after entering St Martin's le Grand at the age of nineteen and working hard, was passed over when vacancies at the top occurred.

Immediately below the Secretary in the departmental hierarchy were the undersecretaries and various levels of clerks who formed the backbone of the bureaucracy. The organisation of this body depended less on any abstract theory of administrative procedure than on the pressing demands of the moment and the particular individuals avail-

---

[28] An analogous blurring of departmental identity has been noted in the Colonial Office: R. C. Snelling and T. J. Baron, 'The Colonial Office and its Permanent Officials' in G. Sutherland (ed.), *Studies in the Growth of Nineteenth-Century Government* (London, 1972), p. 166.

able for assignments. Thus, when Frank Ives Scudamore was involved in the nationalisation of the telegraphs from 1868 to 1875, there was a second secretary. However, upon his retirement there was not another second secretary until 1897. When Lamb was promoted to third secretary in 1896, he brought his old responsibility of supervising the telegraph and telephone operations to his new position. The telegraph business, which required a certain expertise, was at various times managed by a second secretary, a principal clerk, an assistant secretary, and a third secretary. As table two indicates, the size of the Secretary's Office mirrored the growth of the department.

Table 2
The expansion of the Secretary's Office

Superior Establishment in 1839

Position	Length of service	Salary
1 assistant secretary	less than 5 years	£700
	more than 5 years	750
	more than 10 years	800
1 chief clerk	less than 15 years	530
	more than 15 years	630
2 senior clerks, 1st class	less than 15 years	350
	more than 15 years	500
6 senior clerks, 2nd class	less than 15 years	350
	more than 15 years	440
6 junior clerks, 1st class	less than 3 years	110
	more than 3 years	140
	more than 7 years	180
	more than 10 years 3 first	240
	3 last	230
11 junior clerks, 2nd class	less than 3 years	90
	more than 3 years	110
	more than 7 years	150
	more than 10 years	200

Superior Establishment in 1881

Position	Salary range
1 financial secretary	£ 1,500
3 assistant secretaries	1,000 x 50 x 1,200
1 chief clerk to secretary	900
5 principal clerks, upper section	625 x 25 x 800
9 principal clerks, lower section	500 x 20 x 600
9 clerks, 1st class	400 x 20 x 500
19 clerks, 2nd class	260 x 15 x 380
26 clerks, 3rd class	150 x 10 x 250

in addition to 19 lower division clerks, 36 copyists, and an assortment of other officials.

Superior Establishment in 1915

Position	Length of service	Salary range
2 joint 2nd secretaries	less than 3 years	£ 1,250
	more than 3 years	1,400
6 assistant secretaries		1,000 x 50 x 1,200
10 principal clerks		700 x 25 x 900
18 clerks, first class		550 x 20 x 650
25 clerks, second class		200 x 20 x 500
supplementary establishment:		
6 staff officers		500 x 20 x 600
31 clerks, 1st class		350 x 15 x 450
54 clerks, 2nd class		260 x 10 x 340
136 clerks, 3rd class		100 x 10 x 250

Source: Post Office establishment books. The figures in this table represent the authorised numbers and do not reflect any temporary vacancies or additions.

These clerks were grouped into smaller sections, usually headed by an assistant secretary to handle the different kinds of problems faced by the Secretary's Office, establishment, home mails, foreign and colonial mails, buildings, discipline, and after 1870 telegraphs.

In addition to the Secretary's Office there were numerous other specialised branches. The Receiver and Accountant General's Office, as it was known for most of the period under survey, was the bookkeeping branch. It alone employed over 1,000 clerks by 1915. The Solicitor's Department was responsible for advising the Postmaster General on legal matters and the wording of Parliamentary acts. There were also Money Order, Medical, and Savings Banks Departments. As the Post Office nationalised industries, a Stores Department, consisting of several hundred employees by 1915, was developed to handle the necessary materials. The Surveyors, a group familiar to the readers of Trollope's autobiography, were the eyes of the Secretary out in the countryside. Numbering fourteen in 1915, these men travelled from one provincial post office to another where they checked local procedures and enforced regulations and discipline. This list of departments beyond the Secretary's Office could be further extended, but little purpose would be served. The centre of Post Office administration remained the Secretary's Office and its upper echelons at that. It was this office which constituted the mind of St Martin's le Grand. It was there that decisions dealing with issues from the most complicated railway contract to the salary of a foot messenger at an insignificant receiving house were made. Moreover, the Secretary's Office was by far the most fertile source for new ideas in the department. In contrast to some other government offices where inspectors or 'field executives' – to use Professor MacDonagh's term – were active proponents of an expanded role for the state, the Post Office Surveyors were a profoundly conservative group, usually hesitant to countenance change in the existing system.[29] Rather it was the clerks in the central bureaucracy at St Martin's le Grand who led the way in proposing and accepting new responsibilities.

To what extent did this administrative machine change under the onslaught of increased business and new burdens? It would not be difficult to picture the history of the nineteenth-century Post Office in stark black and white tones, contrasting the sloth and inefficiency of the pre-reform clerks jobbed in by patronage hacks with the strength and vigour of civil servants endowed with Gladstonian virtues, who were chosen by open competition after the famous order in council of 4 June 1870. Certainly St Martin's le Grand in the 1820s and 1830s and even afterward was poorly administered. The accounting procedures were archaic, and payments were frequently in arrears. For example, in 1836 only £204 out of £31,000 owed by Irish deputy postmasters since 1831 had been collected.[30] With this situation one could contrast the improvements brought about by the final implementation of double-entry bookkeeping in 1847 and the reorganisation of the Receiver and Accountant General's Office in 1854.[31] Much could be made of the growing standardisation of procedures and salaries. In the pre-reform period the pay structure was a warren full of incongruities and surprises. Many clerks received less from the government than from side earnings associated with their jobs. One individual had an annual official salary

29 Oliver MacDonagh, *A Pattern of Government Growth* (London, 1961), p. 340.
30 BPP, 1836, vol. 50, Returns of the Post Office, Dublin.
31 T1/5430A/4396, Post Office to Treasury, 22 February 1847.

of £170, but took home an additional £540 from a half-penny fee paid on each newspaper posted after six o'clock at night. Clerks also ran the Money Order service and sold the packet lists for their own profit, not for the public purse. This practice was eliminated, and slow progress was made toward making the pay scale more uniform. Other areas in need of overhaul were the registration of memoranda and the flow of paperwork. In 1847 Hill complained that 'the registration clerk . . . says if he were to die no one else could find the papers. To me the practical evil is this – I read to a certain point, and am then stopped for want of a paper which requires hours, and occasionally even days, to find.'[32] Not only were there improvements in the methods of handling minutes, but more importantly Hill increased the responsibility of clerks in the decision-making process.[33] It had formerly been the custom for clerks in the Secretary's Office simply to select those cases requiring the judgement of the Secretary and then await his instructions before minuting them. Hill instructed each clerk to form his own opinion and draft a proposed course of action before presenting the case to the Secretary.

In addition to these procedural difficulties of the early period, one could point to the somewhat indifferent habits of officials at even the highest levels of service. As he was more occupied with his duties as Lord Liverpool's private secretary, Robert Willmot, a Receiver-General in the 1820s, went to the Post Office only two or three times a week.[34] Trollope also has emphasised the relaxed atmosphere of St Martin's le Grand where young clerks were apt to 'come late to their office, and impatient to leave it when the hour of four drew nigh' and Yates, who entered St Martin's le Grand in 1847, fondly recalled that it was the pleasant custom to have lunch brought in from a local tavern and that men bearing foaming pewter pots wandered through the lobbies.[35] In contrast to such images one could emphasise the growth of standardised procedures and work discipline, even if a seven-hour day for clerks was not fully established until 1893.[36] Overtime, especially when new enterprises were launched, became a regrettable fact of life at St Martin's le Grand. Indeed, there were occasions when pressure of busi-

---

[32] Post, Hill's Journal, 15 April 1847.
[33] G. B. Hill, *Life of Sir Rowland Hill and History of Penny Postage*, vol. 2 (London, 1880), p. 266.
[34] BPP, 1836, vol. 28, Fourth Report of Commissioners, p. 6.
[35] Although there are references in Trollope's *Marion Fay* to specific events in the year 1879, the novel evokes the atmosphere of an earlier generation at the Post Office: Anthony Trollope, *Marion Fay* (1882, rpr. Ann Arbor, Michigan, 1982), p. 48. Yates, vol. 1, 118.
[36] Post 30/4368, Blackwood to Morley, 1 August 1893. See also Post 72, Reorganisation of the Secretary's Office.

ness became so oppressive that mutinies occurred in the ranks. In 1891 243 clerks in the Savings Banks Department refused to continue working long, monotonous hours of overtime, and C. D. Lang the head of the department suspended them. As Lang stated, 'It was a painful experience, but without firmness and a certain amount of severity it would have been impossible to have restored discipline and a healthy condition of affairs.'[37] Such evidence of change, modernisation, and regimentation is not completely misleading, and it would be incorrect to assert that the Post Office did not attempt to reform itself. For example, the Money Order Office was redesigned in 1870, and the Secretary's Office restructured in 1872.

Yet it would be equally incorrect to assume that the Post Office of 1900 or 1910 was a fundamentally different organisation from that of fifty or so years earlier. The overwhelming impression one receives from departmental records is that of continuity in the mechanics of decision-making. Administrative problems and bureaucratic obstacles to change were certainly not confined to the years before Hill and Northcote-Trevelyan. For example, in 1873 Tilley wrote to the Postmaster General concerning the possibility of a new surveying organisation in Ireland. But the Secretary was not optimistic that needed improvements could be carried out in the face of personnel difficulties:

> You must get rid of Mr Cornwall. You must get rid of two English and one Scotch surveyors who are redundant. You must be sure that the Irish surveyor to be transferred would be useful in England. Mr Barnard certainly would not be, and you must be prepared to do what has never yet been done – order a Surveyor arbitrarily to break his home in Ireland and to move to England however much he remonstrated. I would not like to say that the Scotch plan can be introduced into Ireland in the next twenty years.[38]

Moreover, one should be cautious in claiming too much for the effectiveness of civil service reform in quickly bringing a more efficient type of employee into public service. It was not until 1893 that men entering the civil service through competitive examination began to predominate at the highest levels in the Secretary's Office. As late as 1890 only two out of the top six permanent officials in the department had passed entry examinations. The average length of service for the other four was over forty years. Too much also can be made of the rhetoric concerning the increased pace of work in the Secretary's Office. There is much accuracy in the *Spectator*'s 1882 judgement that 'The position

37 B. V. Humphreys, *Clerical Unions in the Civil Service* (London, 1958), p. 45.
38 Post 101, Tilley to Monsell, 19 April 1873.

of the Postal Clerk is of the good, middle-class order. . . . His work – although the besom of reform has left less time for fly-hunting and lounging over *The Times* in St Martin's than in any government office – is not too hard.'[39] After all, even an ambitious administrator like George Murray, Secretary 1899–1903, enjoyed wasting an hour each day before lunch in idle gossip.[40] Furthermore, the Northcote-Trevelyan reforms by no means opened the highest levels of administration to men of ability regardless of social class. There was still, as Trollope never ceased to point out, the need to be a gentleman. In 1886, two decades after Trollope's retirement from the Post Office, another civil servant argued in a similar vein that

> it is found that men of the ordinary stamp if promoted from the lower grades of the service are of much less use than men of a better class socially. It was stated that such men are not and cannot be trusted with an important portion of the . . . duties – such as for instance seeing persons of position and influence and dealing with Chief Postmasters. The Staff . . . are very quick to observe defects of manner and breeding and resent interference from such persons which they accept willingly from others.[41]

Under ideal circumstances it would be possible to make a definitive appraisal of the quality of those senior clerks recruited under the old patronage process and those who entered after open competition and rose to the top through the levels of bureaucracy on the basis of merit. Those circumstances do not exist. For one thing, the meritocracy did not function in practice. Appointments to positions where in theory ability was the determinative criterion were influenced by considerations of seniority. The difficulty of arriving at some clear verdict as to the quality of departmental administrators is further heightened by the conflicting stories, incidents, and examples of inefficient time-servers as well as exceptionally able men from both the pre- and post-reform eras. Throughout the period from the 1830s to the Great War there were frequent complaints concerning the quality and diligence of the staff. In 1847 the Money Order Office clerks were categorised as being of a 'very indifferent capacity'.[42] Five years later Tilley predicted that,

---

[39] Post 16/20, *Spectator*, 7 October 1882.
[40] Edward David (ed.), *Inside Asquith's Cabinet from the Diaries of Charles Hobhouse* (New York, 1977), p. 72. By this point Murray had taken this habit from the Post Office to the Treasury.
[41] Post 30/507, E9036/1887, Lewin Hill's memorandum, 4 October 1886. For an analysis of Trollope's views, see R. H. Super, *Trollope in the Post Office* (Ann Arbor, Michigan, 1981).
[42] T1/5321/28256, Barth to Maberly, 2 November 1847.

because of a series of unwise appointments in the Secretary's Office, it would soon become impossible to conduct any business whatsoever.[43] In 1896 the middle and upper ranks of the department were said to be 'overloaded with duffers'.[44] A similar point was made by A. F. King who in 1912 noted that the class of principal clerks, in many ways the core of the Post Office's mind, had deteriorated to the point that only three out of ten clerks could be regarded as truly able and mature enough to accept additional responsibilities. In short, it can never be known how many clerks were similar to one individual who entered the department in 1873 after receiving his civil service certificate and who was described as 'genuinely anxious for the welfare of the Post Office' but 'deficient in power of thought. He lacks rather markedly the capacity for thinking out a complicated problem. Upon committees he has no fresh view and as a rule no useful contribution to offer, and [he cannot] recognise and distinguish those cases most likely to cause trouble from those which he might properly dispose of on his own authority.'[45] Despite this assessment, the clerk was promoted to assistant secretary in 1912, with the understanding that he seek early retirement in a year or two.

Still one should not forget that in the same department there were men of first-rate ability such as Frank Ives Scudamore and George Murray. Moreover, the civil servants at St Martin's le Grand did manage to handle the ever-increasing flow of paperwork and committee assignments which the expansion of the Post Office entailed. By 1902 there were over 600,000 papers registered annually in the Secretary's Office. One somewhat biased observer supported the *Spectator*'s assertion that Post Office clerks were the most efficient in government, even if they did not work as hard as counterparts in private firms. (See table three.)

Table 3
An estimate of work performance in private and government offices

Office	Amount of work performed in a day
Clerk in the City	100 points
Clerk in the Post Office	75 points
Clerk in Somerset House	60 points
Clerk in Customs Office	40 points
Clerk in the Foreign Office	30 points

Source: Charles Marvin, *Our Public Offices* (London, 1882), pp. 324–5.

[43] Post, Hill's Journal, 6 January 1852.
[44] Post 30/738, E11598/1896, Murray to Walpole, 17 October 1896.
[45] Post 30/4528, E5067/1920, King's memorandum, 23 September 1912.

In the final analysis, perhaps the only certain statement that can be made concerning the quality of the department's clerks is that the Post Office did about as well as offices of a comparable stature in recruiting. An examination of men entering St Martin's le Grand with those joining the Board of Trade and the Local Government Board between 1897 and 1908 is the basis for this conclusion.[46] In 1899, for example, the Post Office attracted men finishing fifth and sixth on the civil service examination, while the Board of Trade had to go all the way down to men finishing fifty-second and seventy-first. Similarly, in 1904 a candidate finishing twelfth joined the Post Office versus sixteenth for the Local Government Board.

If the mixed quality of clerks was one feature of continuity throughout the nineteenth century, so was the feeling of inferior status displayed by many of the department's leaders. The Victorian civil service was by no means a homogeneous mass with individual departments of equal prestige and power. Like the greater hierarchical society outside, government departments evidenced considerable concern for their image, their rank, and the degree of deference displayed by others toward them. The Foreign Office gloried in its position at the pinnacle and recruited men who could function effectively in a socially as well as politically rarefied atmosphere. The Post Office even after Rowland Hill's tenure languished much farther down the list of desirable departments. Besides the admittedly boring nature of much of the work – a prospect which led Leonard Woolf after receiving low scores on his civil service examination to choose Ceylon over St Martin's le Grand – there was also the problem of the low salaries received by Post Office clerks.[47] This was, of course, another aspect of continuity throughout the nineteenth century. As Yates pointed out, 'When I first entered the service, the Post Office was one of the worst paid of the public departments and one of the lowest in rank. There seemed to be a general acceptance of the idea that duties there were entirely confined to sorting letters.'[48] The reputation of the office as measured by its pay scale did not rise. In 1860 the average annual salary paid to a Post Office clerk in the upper establishment was £305 as compared with £420 in the Colonial Office.[49] By 1885 the Post Office had dropped

[46] Post 30/2015, E23763/1915, File 9.
[47] Leonard Woolf, *Sowing* (New York, 1960), p. 211. See Jill Pellew, *The Home Office, 1848–1914* (East Brunswick, New Jersey, 1982), p. 35 for other comments on the relative status enjoyed by government departments.
[48] Yates, vol. 1, 122.
[49] Post 30/738, E11598/1886, Appendix A. The Postmaster General shared this problem, earning only half as much as the £5,000 received by the Presidents of the Board of Trade and the Local Government Board.

back on its list of rival departments even farther, ranking eleventh behind Colonial, Home, Admiralty, India, Customs, Exchequer and Audit, War, Board of Trade, Inland Revenue, and the Local Government Board. The average salary for Colonial Office clerks was £623 per year as opposed to £363 per year for the Post Office. It was bad enough to be paid less than more prestigious departments, such as the Colonial Office or the Admiralty, but what was even more galling was the fact that Post Office clerks earned less than those in the other revenue departments. (See table four.)

Table 4
Revenue department salaries in 1885

Department	Average salary including principal clerks	Average salary excluding principal clerks
Customs	£507	£336
Inland Revenue	410	326
Post Office	363	280

Source: Post 30/738, E11598/1886, appendix a.

By 1894 the disparity had grown to the point that in the case of two clerks entering the civil service on the same day, one in Customs or Inland Revenue and another in the Post Office, the former would receive after ten years of service £170 more per year than the latter. It was not until 1912 that the Treasury was worn down by years of pleading into approving a £200 starting salary for second class clerks in the Secretary's Office, thus bringing St Martin's le Grand into line with many other departments.[50] The fact that the Post Office was near the bottom of the government hierarchy could lead to unanticipated consequences. For example, it helps partly to explain why administrators were at times overzealous. One gets the frequent impression that men such as Scudamore and Raikes were convinced that their department and the vital functions it fulfilled were not properly appreciated by the public at large, who followed the intricacies of diplomacy or the exploits of the Army much more closely. Elements of departmental chauvinism crept into the official pronouncements of Post Office leaders. Accordingly Scudamore could trumpet that 'there can be but few intelligent persons, who will not take an interest in . . . an establishment,

[50] Post 30/2615, E2934/1912, Treasury to Post Office, 17 February 1912.

which has risen from such small beginnings to be so vast and powerful, and which . . . has grown to be essential to the well-being of the people, whose wealth it increases and whose intellectual culture it promotes'.[51]

Beyond low salaries and insecure status the most important element of continuity in the nineteenth-century Post Office, as well as a source of frequent difficulty, was the excessive centralisation of decision-making. Despite the fact that the department experienced dramatic growth as new services and enterprises were taken on, authority and initiative remained the prerogative of only the officials at the top. The commissioners appointed to study the Post Office in 1854 had favoured such a centralisation of power. In their view, 'The business of the Post Office is of a kind which peculiarly requires centralisation, and to what ever extent the subordinate Departments may be divided and sub-divided; it is essential that the whole should in the last resort be brought together and placed under the direction of a single Secretary.'[52] This fact of centralisation was the predominant characteristic of Post Office administration in the nineteenth century and after. At all levels officials made decisions and handled tasks which could have easily been dealt with at lower echelons. For instance, postmasters drawing salaries of £600 or £700 had to ask for higher authority to hire a bicycle temporarily and were required to submit expense accounts of a very trifling nature for approval. Similarly the Secretaries in Scotland and Ireland were required to submit questions to London where they were settled by men of no higher rank than the original clerks handling them. The department's excessive fondness for statistics, including for a time an annual tally of dog bites on duty, further clogged administrative channels and discouraged local resolution of issues out of concern that a particular decision might diverge from the national standard.

The logical conclusion to this trend was that the Secretary's Office in London faced a growing burden of casework. Maberly's reaction to many matters of business as 'damned two penny-ha' penny' is perhaps more understandable if one remembers the flood of insignificant matters as well as issues of some importance, which came across a Secretary's desk each morning. The day after Nathan became Secretary in 1910, he considered the suitability of motor vans for Post Office work, the possibility of increased payments to the Northwestern Railway, the terms of a South African packet contract, telegraph arrangements for the first night of a general election, and a scheme for reorganisation of the Post Office.[53] Nathan's later correspondence further reinforces this

51 *Report of the Postmaster General* (London, 1855), p. 51.
52 *Report upon the Post Office* (London, 1854), p. 5.
53 Nathan Papers, 18 January 1910.

impression of excessive centralisation, as he handled requests ranging from polite inquiries as to the promotion prospects of employees to a demand from one outraged individual that suffragettes cease tampering with her letters. To be sure, there had been a certain amount of decentralisation of authority throughout the nineteenth century. Rowland Hill's decision to let clerks prepare their own minutes on questions was a major example of this trend. By 1913 Edward Crabb, who had entered the Post Office in 1876, could see a dramatic transformation in the nature of the work falling upon the upper establishment.

> Circumstances have changed so greatly that the classes of Ass't Secretaries, Principal, and First Class Clerks [do] work of a character and difficulty which could formerly be met only by exceptional men of those classes and fell in their way only rarely is now part of the daily task; and men who twenty years ago could hold those positions without loss of credit to themselves or the Dept., if with no brilliant success, would now be counted a dangerous impediment to the work. Moreover, it is my personal opinion that the new volume of work falling on the individual is much greater.[54]

It was felt that at St Martin's le Grand, in contrast to many other government departments, the work of the higher division clerks was of a supervisory nature from almost the very beginning of their service. Yet the pattern of permitting clerks at lower levels to make decisions and take action which Crabb noted was never carried far enough. As new responsibilities were added, the department did not react swiftly to changing situations. For example, over 27,000 hours of extra duty, the equivalent of a year's work for fourteen full-time clerks, were performed by members of the Supplementary Establishment in 1897 to handle problems associated with the transfer of the long distance telephone lines. Centralisation remained the primary characteristic of decision-making in the Secretary's Office as well as its primary problem. By 1914 fourteen different clerks and officials, ranging from the second secretary to the chief medical officer, reported directly to the Secretary.

A 1909 departmental report cited several reasons for the slow pace of decentralisation.[55] The tendency of MPs to ask questions on all points of administration, large or small, encouraged the Secretary's Office to retain in its control many matters that could have been handled more conveniently at a lower level. This constant scrutiny of all parts of Post Office operations by Parliament was certainly an irritating phenomenon. Austen Chamberlain estimated that fully one-

---

54 Post 30/2615, E30965/1913, Crabb's memorandum, 3 November 1913.
55 Post 30/1953, E5692/1911, Report of the Decentralisation Committee.

third of the time of upper officials of the department was occupied in preparing answers to MPs' questions.[56] Such inquiries ranged from is-sues directly connected to the department's business – working condi-tions in the Mount Pleasant office – to trivia – the number of unclaimed postal orders over a ten-year period – to matters far distant from the usual concerns of administrators – claims that the Irish Post Office was a hotbed of Masonic, i.e. Protestant, activity. All required time to answer, and all encouraged the Secretary's Office to maintain a firm grip over every aspect of administration. Another reason cited for the highly centralised system was the involvement of the Treasury in Post Office affairs. The 1909 report contended that, as items of expen-diture had to be approved by the Treasury, delegation of authority was impossible in many aspects of administration. Here a certain degree of scepticism may be in order for, as will be seen, Treasury control was by no means unduly restrictive in the middle of the nineteenth century. Moreover, by 1903 the Treasury had delegated much of its authority over minor items of expenditure to the Post Office. There was, how-ever, a rather indirect way in which the Treasury had unintentionally fostered centralisation. This arose from the process by which the Treas-ury patronage secretary chose all postmasters between 1821 and 1854 and the less important ones from 1854 to 1895.[57] The party in power, upon the recommendation of MPs, often appointed men with no pre-vious postal experience. Thus, it was necessary that Surveyors closely supervise all aspects of their work and that the local postmasters not be entrusted with any major decisions. As the committee report of 1909 noted,

> Thus, the Surveyor became the officer by whom all matters of im-portance were decided, or referred to higher authority, as the case might be; and a system grew up under which the Postmasters were not encouraged, or allowed to take any serious responsibility, and even the Surveyors were to refer many matters of purely routine character to the Secretary.[58]

A final circumstance contributing to centralised control was the growth of unionism and its active criticism of Post Office procedures, which began in earnest in the 1870s. Some administrators feared that decentralisation would lead to a lack of uniformity in the application of rules and practices and that such deviations would only open the

[56] *Hansard's, Fourth Series*, vol. 66, 733–4, 18 April 1902.
[57] H. J. Hanham, 'Political Patronage at the Treasury, 1870–1912', *The Historical Journal*, 3 (1960), 80–2.
[58] Post 30/1953, E59692/1911.

department to additional complaints and increase the leverage exercised by the unions.

By the close of the Edwardian period the administrative bottleneck in the Secretary's Office had become a matter for real worry. As Murray described the situation, 'the tightly centralised system under which the P.O. administration has hitherto been carried on has been breaking down for some years, and things cannot go on as they are much longer'.[59] As a result of the recognition of this state of affairs, the 1909 departmental committee recommended sweeping changes in the delegation of authority on numerous matters ranging from the appointment of postmen to the extension of savings banks to sub-post offices. The entire list of suggestions ran to twelve pages and proposed the most far-reaching revolution in administration in the history of the department. However, it is instructive to note that the major resistance to the key proposal of the committee, the creation of six Surveyors-General with extensive authority, did not come from the Treasury, the supposed villain in such confrontations. In fact, the Treasury was in favour of changes even more extensive than those proposed. Rather the opposition came from Herbert Samuel the Postmaster General. Once again, a political chief was proving himself more that a figurehead. Samuel inquired 'I should like to know why it is thought desirable and whether there would be any great advantage in having work done in these [six] districts which is now done here.'[60] The Postmaster General strongly supported the traditional model of centralisation, which had shaped, or misshaped, the nineteenth-century Post Office. After much internal wrangling, in August 1910 a compromise was reached whereby the delegation of authority recommended by the committee would be put into effect without creating a new structure to handle it. New powers were grafted onto the traditional structure of Surveyors, independent postmasters in large cities like Birmingham and Leicester, and ordinary postmasters in smaller towns. These changes were not drastic enough. Thus, in the 1920s the same complaints of overwork and petty detail were heard inside the Secretary's Office. Outside St Martin's le Grand Viscount Wolmer and the Bridgeman Committee of 1932 further criticised the stratified bureaucracy which ran the department.[61]

---

[59] T1/11424/22563, Murray to Hobhouse, 16 December 1909.
[60] Post 30/1953, E5692/1911, meeting of 26 July 1910.
[61] Viscount Wolmer, *Post Office Reform* (London, 1932). BPP, 1931–2, vol. 12, Report of the Committee of Enquiry on the Post Office. The Post Office was, of course, not the only British bureaucracy resistant to change. See T. R. Gourvish, 'British Business and the Transition to a Corporate Society: Entrepreneurship and Management Structures', *Business History*, 29 (1987), 40–1.

Without question, there was a pronounced tension in the history of the Victorian Post Office. In many ways the agency was transformed by the acceptance of new responsibilities. Moreover, its administrators' vision of the proper goals for the department and their attitudes toward growth evidenced considerable change. In these aspects the Post Office was a major participant in the nineteenth-century revolution in government. Yet the administrative channels through which these innovations flowed did not so dramatically evolve. Change came both rapidly and slowly in the tight, highly centralised world of St Martin's le Grand.

2

The Role of the Treasury

I know of no Department where the work is more technical and
complicated than the Post Office. The Treasury work is supposed
to be hard to learn, but [mastering] the technicalities of the Post
Office is about the most difficult job I ever had. – R. W. Hanbury,
Financial Secretary to the Treasury, *Hansard's Parliamentary
Debates, Fourth Series*, vol. 66, 1550, 20 February 1899.

The history of the Victorian Post Office cannot be understood without
reference to the Treasury. The Post Office, with Inland Revenue and
Customs, was a revenue department and, therefore, a tax-collecting
bulwark of the Exchequer. Critics of St Martin's le Grand, when not
castigating the department, often turned their attention to the Treasury and its reputedly excessive concern for revenue as an explanation
for the failure to institute reforms, expand services or lower postal
charges. As one letter-writer to *The Times* complained in 1890, 'It is a
most indisputable fact that the Treasury does interfere down to the
smallest and most petty details of expenditure.'[1] Indeed, by the end of
the nineteenth century conventional wisdom held that the power of
the Treasury over the Post Office was so intimidating that independent
action on the part of St Martin's le Grand was almost an impossibility.
Such was the view of A. L. Lowell, who published his authoritative
work on English government in 1908.[2] Viscount Wolmer, who having
served as Assistant Postmaster General from 1924 to 1929 had an
insider's knowledge of the question, agreed with Lowell and lamented
that the Post Office had become only an 'appendage of the Treasury'.[3]
One can easily understand how Lowell and Wolmer could have
arrived at such conclusions. There was undoubtedly a close relationship between the two departments, as the dozens of Treasury letter
books in the Post Office archives remind us. To a politician such as A.
J. Balfour, serving as First Lord of the Treasury in Lord Salisbury's Third
Cabinet, it was self-evident that 'Every question of Post Office policy

[1] *The Times*, 25 January 1890, p. 7.
[2] A. L. Lowell, *The Government of England*, vol. 1 (New York, 1908), p. 112.
[3] Viscount Wolmer, *Post Office Reform* (London, 1932), p. 14.

29

was really a question of Treasury policy.'[4] After all, St Martin's le Grand provided the Treasury with a mass of statistical and miscellaneous information on subjects ranging from the number of letters delivered to descriptions of furniture placed in offices. Moreover, by the end of the century the dominance of Whitehall appeared secure. Treasury approval was required to alter postage rates, to make additions to the staff, and to enter into contracts with railway companies, to cite only a few of the more important examples. However, it remains an open question as to whether 'approval' constituted 'control' in the restrictive sense implied by Lowell, Wolmer, and Balfour. Maurice Wright and Henry Roseveare have shown that the power of the nineteenth-century Treasury to limit expenditure and to dictate policy to other government departments has been greatly overestimated.[5] Furthermore, one should be cautious before assuming that the degree of Treasury influence over Post Office policy remained constant over decades regardless of the issue under consideration. Post Office–Treasury relations were never that simple or static.

The validity of this statement becomes even more apparent if one remembers that in the continual round of give-and-take neither department played a stereotyped role, the Post Office constantly clamouring for new programmes and larger expenditures and the Treasury always responding with a resounding veto. There was usually a good deal of middle ground shared by administrators at St Martin's le Grand and clerks in the Fourth Division of the Treasury, where Post Office requests were initially considered. Post Office officials were acutely aware of their fiscal responsibilities to the Exchequer. In opposing a request for a more rapid, and hence a more expensive, Scottish mail service in 1866, Tilley advised the Postmaster General, 'Whatever . . . may have been the intention of the legislature when the penny post act was passed, I cannot help thinking that to give up the revenue which it now produces would not . . . confer a benefit on the community at large.'[6] Twenty-two years later another Secretary, S. A. Blackwood, was equally insistent that his department 'endeavours to reduce expenditure and declines to extend services, to accelerate trains, or establish new services wherever they do not appear likely to be remunerative'.[7] Such statements were not simply rhetoric hiding spendthrift agenda. The department's commitment to economy and efficiency was recognised even by hypercritical observers such as Sir Ralph Lingen,

---

[4] Hansard's, Fourth Series, vol. 51, 321, 16 June 1897.
[5] Maurice Wright, Treasury Control of the Civil Service (Oxford, 1969); Henry Roseveare, The Treasury (London, 1969).
[6] Post 101, Tilley to Montrose, 18 November 1866.
[7] BPP, 1888, vol. 18, Select Committee on Revenue Department Estimates, p. 70.

Permanent Secretary to the Treasury 1869–85. Lingen, who had the reputation of enjoying bitter disputations even more than Robert Lowe and whom Gladstone once described as a 'ferocious economist', was forced to admit that the Post Office deserved some credit for the manner in which the department conducted its affairs. As he phrased it,

> My impression of the P.O. is that as fast as it grows, almost any other Dept. would grow faster, and cost more under the same circumstances. I have considerable confidence in their desire to do their best and in their attention and skill. They have to work always against time, and in direct contact with the public.[8]

If the Post Office was not indifferent to its responsibilities as a revenue department, the Treasury was also not always the inhibiting villain in battles for change. Certainly the most famous instance of Treasury advocacy of sweeping reform against Post Office advice involved the establishment of the Penny Post in 1840. Three years before Hill had joined a campaign for changes in the system for charging letters. The Post Office resisted Hill's suggestions as 'utterly unsupported by facts and resting entirely on assumption'.[9] Yet Hill won the support of the Whig government, especially that of Sir Francis Baring the Chancellor of the Exchequer. As a result, the Post Office was forced to give way. Moreover, as will be seen, there was essentially no Treasury resistance to the proposal to launch out on the course which led to the nationalisation of the telegraph industry. In addressing such issues Whitehall often ignored abstract considerations of the merits of laissez-faire versus state intervention or at least cast them in different terms from the way they are sometimes pictured. The Treasury, and this was especially the case during the middle third of the century, could demonstrate a notable flexibility when considering Post Office requests to expand its services and, thus, widen its role in the economy. Supporting the rationale for a Money Order system, one Treasury clerk in 1860 pointed out

> The fact is that abstract principles are generally fallacious in the mixed and complicated questions of practical conduct. The real test whether the State ought or ought not undertake any branch of business on behalf of the community can only be found in the balance of practical advantage and disadvantage of its doing so. The only thing like a principle . . . is that the State ought not to interfere

8 T1/8637D/1225, Lingen's memorandum, 27 January 1885. See Roseveare, pp. 209–10.
9 W. L. Maberly quoted by M. J. Daunton, *Royal Mail* (London, 1985), p. 22.

with ordinary branches of business when it possesses no peculiar advantage over private traders.[10]

Even if the Post Office and the Treasury shared many of the same assumptions concerning the proper role of government, it was inevitable that disagreements over policy and specific details would arise. When such problems occurred, St Martin's le Grand was by no means defenceless before its more prominent Whitehall adversary. There were elaborate strategies of appeal open to the Post Office. For example, in a letter to a departmental Surveyor, Tilley cautioned against asking the Treasury for any permanent additions to his staff, but rather advised requesting only temporary help. Later, Tilley believed, the Treasury would agree to make the auxiliaries a permanent part of the force.[11] The Treasury, of course, was not unaware of this tactic. As one exasperated clerk wrote beside a Post Office request for more staff, 'The old story. Apply piecemeal, and use the last concession to gain the next.'[12] Furthermore, the degree of control was weakened by the sheer volume of requests and trivial detail with which the Treasury was forced to deal in the process of oversight. Treasury approval was required for minor expenditures such as the costs of washing Post Office windows or compensating the unfortunate Tewkesbury family (pregnant wife, five children) of a one-armed mail carrier who, having become intoxicated on duty, stopped beside a ditch to 'ease himself', as a departmental letter officially stated, fell in and died of exposure.[13] Vital issues rubbed side-by-side with petty matters in the jumble of requests for Treasury approval. On the same day the Post Office made a crucial request for the extension of the telegraph system, it also wrote the Treasury concerning a £15 payment to an individual whose eye had been injured when some telegraph messengers threw bread crumbs out the window of a departmental building. Not surprisingly in 1886 Reginald Welby the Permanent Secretary to the Treasury bemoaned the fact that it was 'almost impossible to fight a Dept. like the Post Office on detail'.[14] Another aspect of departmental operations which inhibited tight Treasury control was the complicated, sometimes highly technical nature of much of Post Office work. Not only were establishment questions involving numerous classes of employees and various kinds of jobs somewhat arcane to the uninitiated – for example, the difference between a sorter and a sorter tracer –, but the Treasury was often called

10 T1/8637D/14367, J. L. Laing to Hamilton, 15 September 1860.
11 Post 101, Tilley to F. Abbbot, 24 January 1865.
12 T1/11316/13(58).
13 T19, Treasury to Post Office, 12 September 1850. Post 1/393, Post Office to Treasury, 24 February 1908.
14 T1/8260A/17544, Welby's note, 22 November 1886.

upon to consider engineering matters about which it had no practical knowledge. As one Treasury clerk studying a Post Office request for maintenance charges confessed, 'This is highly technical. . . . I have heard of "tees", but I have not the slightest notion as to the nature of "plumbers' wiped joints" or "solidly filled in potheads".'[15]

Such complications – sophisticated strategies of appeal, a flood of minor details, and the technical nature of its operations – were not unique to St Martin's le Grand. Admiralty letters to the Treasury, for example, must have been full of confusing data. Indeed, on one level Post Office–Treasury relations corresponded closely to a wider governmental pattern which has been accurately described as at 'best . . . a kind of indoor sport with recognised rules and minimal stress [and] at worst . . . a rather bitter conflict with political repercussions'.[16] However, there was one critical characteristic of Post Office operations in which it was unique. St Martin's le Grand was the only government department to operate a profit-making business. Yet it also provided essential social services to the public and often held a monopoly of those same services. Which should have the higher priority, the Exchequer or the public? In theory there was no tension between the two. Proponents of reform and expansion always predicted that new services would pay their way, benefit the public, and yield a surplus. In practice such claims were not always realised. Hill's 1840 Penny Post required a much larger establishment than he had anticipated, and as a result it was not until 1873 that departmental net revenue recovered and consistently maintained its pre-reform level of £1.63 million. Scudamore's telegraphs, as will be seen, also never achieved the financial results predicted. When deficits and losses arose, the public nature of the department's responsibilities placed it in a fundamentally different position from that of private firms. As Blackwood explained the Post Office's quandary,

A commercial undertaking . . . if it finds that a branch house in the provinces is conducted at a loss, can close it, or again, it can discontinue the production of a certain item of its wares. The Post Office cannot do that. It cannot close a post office because it is unproductive, or discontinue a part of the business to which the public has been accustomed, because it thinks it is not remunerated.[17]

One aspect of this dilemma manifested itself in 1876. The Treasury attempted to peg salary increases for Post Office clerks on the basis of

15 T1/10945/21, Treasury memorandum, 4 January 1906.
16 Roseveare, p. 203.
17 BPP, 1888, vol. 18, Select Committtee on Revenue Department Estimates, p. 70.

the profitability of the particular office in which they worked. Salaries in the Money Order Office, which barely made a profit, were to be lower than salaries in the Savings Banks Office, which yielded a good surplus. St Martin's le Grand successfully protested this approach by pointing out that the clerks had passed the same qualifying examination and worked side-by-side.[18]

No consensus ever emerged among the most directly interested parties, politicians, Post Office administrators, trade union leaders, and Treasury officials, as to precisely where the line should be drawn between revenue and public service considerations. In 1855 Lord Palmerston pronounced that the 'main duty of the Post Office is not to collect revenue for the public, but to effect easily and readily the cheap transmission of correspondence of the public, and for the commercial interests of the country'.[19] Five years later Gladstone, whose vision of public policy emphasised the utility of government programmes in support of private initiative and capitalist organisations, argued that any profit made by the Post Office 'was well made, and referring to an ancient story, it was a profit which "smelt sweet in the nostrils" compared with the produce of general taxes'.[20] A select committee sitting in 1888 was even more adamant on the point. It concluded that the Post Office, as a government business, was most likely to be operated satisfactorily if ultimate profits were the primary consideration.[21] Inside St Martin's le Grand there was a similarly wide range of opinion, which varied according to personality, ideology, and the particular expenditure under consideration. Rowland Hill and the small gang of relations which he placed in the department always argued that services should pay their way and in the same manner wages as far as possible should be established by the market. Furthermore, there should be no 'cross-subsidies' in the department, i.e. profits from one operation should not be used to offset losses in another area. As Hill testified before a Parliamentary committee, 'if we were to depart very widely from the rule of requiring that . . . [new projects] should be self-supporting, then we think we should make a mistake, inasmuch as we should in effect tax the community at large for the advantage of a single locality'.[22] This rather strict emphasis on 'economical reform' was successfully challenged in the decades after Hill's retirement in 1864 by men such as Frank Ives Scudamore who, while never denying the importance of profits, placed

18 Post 30/305, E7827/1876, Blackwood's draft, 22 December 1876.
19 *Hansard's, Third Series*, vol. 139, 888, 16 July 1855.
20 *Ibid.*, vol. 157, 1082, 11 April 1860.
21 BPP, 1888, vol. 18, Select Committtee on Revenue Department Estimates, p. vii.
22 BPP, 1854–5, vol. 11, Select Committee on Postal Arrangements, p. 1. See also Daunton, *Royal Mail*, pp. 84ff.

a higher premium on service to the public, even if in certain instances this necessitated losses. Still another approach was voiced by certain department unions, which regarded large profits not so much as an occasion to lower rates or to extend new services, but rather as an opportunity to raise salaries. As Charles Durrant of the Fawcett Association testified before a Parliamentary committee,

> The Postmaster General has no competition to face. He can fix his own prices, and the public must deal with him whether they like those prices or not. He makes an immense annual profit, and therefore can afford to employ the pick of the working class and pay high wages.[23]

Where did the Treasury stand on this question? No single answer will suffice for the entire nineteenth century. The Treasury could and did choose varying points on the continuum of policy options which ran between concern for the Exchequer and commitment to service to the public. However, at the end of the day it always recognised that the Post Office was an essentially different enterprise from the other revenue departments. Welby summed up his department's view when he wrote

> The Post Office is a speculative Dept. and comparing the proceedings of the Customs and Inland Revenue with that of the Post Office is very much like supposing that the regulations under which business is conducted at Drummonds and Coutts's is the same as that under which some new speculative business is conducted.[24]

An examination of the contributions of the three revenue departments to the Exchequer confirms Welby's point that Post Office operations were different both in scale and in kind. (See table one.)

Table 1
The financial record of the revenue departments

	Net receipts	Charges of collections	Net produce
1869–70			
Inland Revenue	£45,758,339	£1,666,586	£44,091,753
Customs	21,381,326	1,000,760	20,380,566
Post Office	4,982,744	3,547,296	1,435,448
1879–80			
Inland Revenue	48,368,860	1,916,406	46,452,454
Customs	19,171,086	1,005,556	18,165,530
Post Office	8,273,928	5,220,794	3,053,134

23 Quoted by Alan Clinton, *Post Office Workers* (London, 1984), p. 44.
24 T1/7425B/1630, Welby's memorandum, 19 February 1888.

	Net receipts	Charges of collections	Net produce
1889–90			
Inland Revenue	58,241,648	1,872,000	56,369,648
Customs	20,460,154	929,963	19,530,191
Post Office	11,993,047	8,486,964	3,506,083
1899–1900			
Inland Revenue	85,218,234	2,115,000	83,103,234
Customs	23,364,425	928,911	22,435,514
Post Office	16,808,531	13,424,110	3,384,421
1909–10			
Inland Revenue	43,680,676	1,643,000	42,037,676
Customs*	60,756,148	1,899,789	58,856,359
Post Office	23,125,715	19,845,746	3,279,969

* Excise under Customs

Source: BPP, 1880, vol. 40, n. 356; BPP, 1890, vol. 51, n. 267; BPP, 1900, vol. 47, n. 289; BPP, 1910, vol. 59, n. 263.

As these figures indicate, between 1870 and 1910 Post Office expenditures rose approximately 5.6 times, while net produce (or profit) rose less than 2.3 times. Put another way, profit as a percentage of net receipts – approximately 14 per cent in 1910 – was less than the 29 per cent achieved in 1870. (And neither figure distantly approached the 68 per cent earned in the last year before Penny Post.) Given the drift of these figures, one might assume that the degree of Treasury control over the Post Office had diminished markedly in the decades after 1840. In point of fact, a rather more complicated history stands behind these statistics.

As early as 1837 the Post Office began to submit monthly schedules of proposed increases in its expenditures to the Treasury. Control nonetheless was minimal, and two further changes in 1855 did little to affect the situation. That year St Martin's le Grand began to submit expenditure estimates for consideration by the House of Commons and to pay its gross receipts into the Exchequer. (Previously the department had paid its operating expenses directly from revenue.) During these years the usual response from Whitehall to a departmental request was positive. Yet in the late 1860s the harmonious relationship between the Post Office and the Treasury broke down for legislative as well as political reasons. In 1866 the theory of Treasury control was strengthened by the Exchequer and Audit Departments Act, which created for the first time an effective system of annual, retrospective audits of government offices.[25] This shift of direction was confirmed two years

[25] Roseveare, p. 141.

later in 1868 when Robert Lowe became Chancellor of the Exchequer. As his most recent biographer has written, 'From the moment Lowe came to the Treasury, the department gained a reputation for tactlessness and discourtesy.'[26] Tilley, with over thirty years' experience at St Martin's le Grand, would have readily agreed. In 1872 he complained that until 'the present Government came into power . . . there was a manifest desire on their [the Treasury's] part to consider our propositions favourably and after requiring explanation where explanation was necessary to approve them if they possibly could'.[27] Tilley further observed that the old practice of informal discussions between Post Office and Treasury clerks, in which problems could be solved in an amicable fashion, had been replaced by a pattern of icy correspondence in which St Martin's le Grand was thrown on the defensive. 'I am not very thin skinned in official matters,' Tilley wrote, 'but these rude scolding letters from the Treasury are a little too bad. We attempt to make improvements and we are told we are idiots and don't know our business.'[28]

Less than one year after Tilley made these charges, Post Office–Treasury relations reached their lowest point in the nineteenth century. In March 1873 Gladstone's government was shocked and Lowe's Treasury angered by the revelation of what was termed the gravest administrative scandal since the Crimean War. The crisis originated from the zeal of a Post Office manager. As will be seen in chapter five, Frank Ives Scudamore the second secretary at St Martin's le Grand had spent over £800,000 on the expansion of the telegraph system without Treasury or Parliamentary approval. A twenty-one month interdepartmental war quickly broke out, as the Treasury sought to chastise the wayward Post Office, to set effective internal accounting checks, and to weaken the proclivity for independent action by establishing a beachhead in St Martin's le Grand. Treasury strategy called for the creation of a new position in the Post Office, a financial secretary equal in salary and rank to the second secretary. The financial secretary was to report on all proposals involving expenditure increases before any final sanction by the Postmaster General. In this manner a dual check at the Post Office and at the Treasury would be established. (Of course, Scudamore could not have operated in the manner he did if internal accounting procedures at St Martin's le Grand and, indeed, the individual in charge of them, George Chetwynd, had been more effective.) The War Office and the Admiralty, it was pointed out, already had such administrators, and, given the fact that the Post Office handled

26 James Winter, *Robert Lowe* (Toronto, 1976), p. 252.
27 Gladstone Papers, Add. MS. 44512, fol. 157, Tilley to Monsell, 16 October 1872.
28 Post 101, Tilley to Monsell, 16 March 1872.

almost £40 million annually, firmer control was necessary. As the Treasury insisted,

> It is hardly to be expected that able and zealous officers, who are devoting their best energies to the conduct of a service in which they feel so keen an interest, should at the same time exercise vigilant control over its finance which an independent financial critic would do. Parliament, while encouraging the Post Office authorities to undertake more and more work, looks to the Treasury for criticism which is necessary to prevent extravagance.[29]

The vigour of the Post Office's response to this proposal is a reminder of the strong defensive positions subordinate departments could adopt against the Treasury. St Martin's le Grand opposed the appointment of a financial secretary on two principal grounds.[30] First, it argued that such an officer would inevitably discourage departmental initiative through a niggardly approach to questions of expenditure. Secondly, the interposition of a financial secretary would disrupt the decision-making process by interfering in the close relationship between the Postmaster General and his permanent officials. The fact that the reports of the financial secretary would go directly to the Postmaster General and then to the Treasury would, in Tilley's opinion, weaken the Secretary's authority beyond repair.

As the war continued, Gladstone's government was replaced by Disraeli's second cabinet, which included a much less combative Chancellor of the Exchequer, Sir Stafford Northcote. In an effort to improve relations between the two bickering departments in August 1874 Northcote privately wrote Scudamore, the Post Office administrator most offended by the Treasury proposal, to praise him for his accomplishments with the telegraphs. Northcote tactfully urged that a financial secretary would help, not hinder, the department in the fulfilment of its wider social service obligations and that

> while you have been doing all this to develop your Dept, you have been creating the necessity for a more systematic and thorough financial machinery; and it is this necessity which has forced itself upon our attention. . . . The work has grown to be too great for you without assistance and we are endeavouring to supply that assistance.[31]

[29] Post 30/269, E2160/1877, Treasury minute, 31 July 1874.
[30] For the following, see Post 101, Tilley to Manners, 4 April 1874 and Post 30/269, E663A/1875, Tilley's memorandum, 5 August 1874.
[31] Iddesleigh Papers, Add. MS. 50052, fol. 38, Northcote to Scudamore, 25 August 1874.

The Treasury also sought to smooth ruffled feathers by stressing the point that the financial secretary would by no means supersede the Secretary at St Martin's le Grand. He would simply serve as an advisor for the Receiver and Accountant General's Office and would attempt to stay out of policy considerations as much as possible. Furthermore, the Treasury admitted that the Postmaster General would have to consider several points of view, not simply the financial secretary's, before submitting proposals for approval by Whitehall. The Post Office accepted these clarifications and concessions with one important proviso. The Postmaster General, not the Treasury, was to exercise the ultimate authority in determining whether a particular case should be considered at all by the financial secretary. The matter appeared closed when in October 1874 Stevenson Arthur Blackwood, Treasury clerk and author of Evangelical tracts, became the first financial secretary of the Post Office. As one wag commented, the Treasury, having tried all other means of disciplining St Martin's le Grand and having failed, had decided to test the efficacy of prayer.[32]

In this case prayer proved less efficacious than the Treasury would have wished. Blackwood, as an outsider, encountered a very hostile atmosphere at the Post Office, and he quickly became involved in a procedural squabble with the permanent officials there. At first glance the particular issue appears trivial. Upon the absence of the Secretary and the second secretary, who was in charge of the department – the assistant secretary or the financial secretary? Nonetheless, the answer was crucial as to the role Blackwood would play. If the assistant secretary, an insider, took charge of the department, it would mean the isolation of Blackwood in a weak position. If the financial secretary took charge, it was feared that Blackwood, and by extension the Treasury, would dominate St Martin's le Grand. The issue was considered so important that Scudamore, in order to prevent Blackwood from assuming command, refused to take a much needed holiday and remained at the office instead. To Scudamore, 'it would be without precedent that a gentleman, who is wholly unacquainted with the general business of the Department and who is by the terms of his appointment restricted to one part of that business, should take the entire charge of it'.[33] In this dispute Lord John Manners the Postmaster General and Tilley supported Scudamore in his aim to lower the financial secretary to the position of a glorified bookkeeper, checking the accuracy of accounts, but making no comment on the wisdom of the expenditures themselves. The Treasury was incensed by this strategy. Northcote pointed out that the Post Office effort to diminish Blackwood's effectiveness

---

32 H. Buxton Foreman, 'Sir Arthur Blackwood', St Martin's le Grand, 4 (1894), 3.
33 Post 30/269, E663A/1875, Scudamore to Blackwood, 22 October 1874.

and authority by placing him below the assistant secretary in the departmental hierarchy resembled the actions of the Eton masters who did not allow the French master to wear cap and gown or to sit in the masters' seats at chapel. But Northcote was doing more than simply engaging in old boy pleasantries. As he correctly pointed out to Lord John Manners, a Postmaster General's first loyalty should be to his government, not to his particular department. Political chiefs stood, according to Northcote, in a fundamentally different position from that of the permanent civil servants. We 'must look at the matter ministerially as well as departmentally'.[34]

At this stage Tilley shrewdly suggested a compromise. The financial secretary should abandon his role as overseer of the Receiver and Accountant General's Office and become a full-fledged member of the Secretariat, taking precedence over the assistant secretary and communicating not only with the Postmaster General but with the other senior secretaries as well.[35] All minutes, not only those concerned with finance and expenditure, would circulate through him. The Treasury, undoubtedly fatigued by the months of argument, was content with this proposal and in a rather circular statement agreed that 'it may be better to dispense altogether with the detailed regulations as to the position of the financial secretary and merely leave him to take in the Department the position which the title of his office indicates that he was intended to hold'.[36] Tilley's compromise was intended to draw Blackwood into the heart of the Secretary's Office, involve him in policy questions, and transform him from an outsider concerned with the Exchequer into an insider sensitive to the ambitions of St Martin's le Grand. Tilley's goals were more than fulfilled. In less than two years after his appointment as financial secretary, Blackwood had adopted the prevailing Post Office ethic that expenditure proposals should not be judged solely on their impact on revenue.[37] This outlook was maintained by the next financial secretary, Algernon Turnor, who took up the post in 1880 after having earlier served in the much more interesting job of private secretary to Disraeli. Like his predecessor, Turnor was constantly bogged down in administrative detail, such as selecting the subjects suitable for the Parcel Sorters' examinations, and never exercised any real restraint on spending.

Upon Turnor's retirement in 1896, Spencer Walpole the Secretary at St Martin's le Grand suggested to the Treasury that the post of financial secretary be abolished. Walpole, who had held down both

---

[34] *Ibid.*, Northcote to Manners, 15 December 1874.
[35] *Ibid.*, Tilley's memorandum, 30 December 1874.
[36] T1/7408B/1854B, Treasury to Post Office, 28 January 1875.
[37] Post 30/305, E7827/1876, Blackwood to Manners, May 1876.

positions for one period, claimed 'as Secretary, I have saved the country many thousands of pounds any year I have been here. While as financial secretary, I do not think I have ever had the opportunity of saving the country as many shillings.'[38] The Treasury reluctantly agreed and sought more effective control through the appointment of an independent officer with responsibility for financial issues only. Hence, an idea proposed and rejected twenty-two years earlier was revived. Unfortunately, J. J. Cardin the individual chosen to fill the new position of Comptroller and Accountant General was as ineffective in limiting spending as Blackwood and Turnor had been. He was simply too old and too set in his ways to adapt to the regimen that strict control of expenditure entailed. As one Secretary described Cardin's approach, 'The check that he applied would better be termed "arithmetical" than "financial".'[39] Thus, Cardin simply performed his former bookkeeping duties at an additional £200 per year in salary. When Cardin retired in 1901, no suitable replacement could be found to fill the position, and a twenty-seven year attempt to impose Treasury control inside St Martin's le Grand was abandoned.

The ineffectiveness of the financial secretary did not, however, necessarily preclude the development of other means for increased Treasury supervision during this period.[40] In 1884 the Post Office was required for the first time to submit contracts with railway companies for sanction by the Treasury. In 1890 the departmental schedule for salary changes was separated from the schedule for rents and other expenses, a change which enhanced the effectiveness of Treasury scrutiny. Two years later the system was further streamlined with the separation of the salary schedule into two parts, one covering routine, minor changes and another outlining major revisions requiring close consideration by Whitehall. At this same time a further modification came with the development of the work unit system, which compared the amount of work done at various post and telegraph offices and eliminated much of the previous imprecision in allocating salaries from one town to another. By 1903 the Treasury was so confident of its authority that it permitted the Post Office wider authority over normal salary increases. Moreover, the limits on capital expenditure for the telegraphs and the telephone which could be spent without Treasury approval were raised. The net effect of these changes was to eliminate much of the unnecessary detail which had previously hampered the exercise of Treasury oversight.

[38] Post 30/2615, E23763/1913, Walpole to G. H. Murray, 22 October 1896.
[39] Post 30/943, E6347/1901, Murray to F. Mowatt, 18 February 1901.
[40] For the following, see T1/11515/525, Treasury Report on Post Office Periodical Returns, 1905.

Still there is reason to doubt that the Treasury was in absolute control of Post Office policy in the years before 1914. On questions of reductions in postage St Martin's le Grand could wear down Treasury resistance. When proposals for Diamond Jubilee concessions were discussed, for example, Sir Michael Hicks Beach the Chancellor of the Exchequer initially opposed any reduction in the inland letter rate. Nonetheless, he was swayed by the Post Office argument that the senders of such letters provided the whole of the departmental surplus, offset losses in other areas, and were, therefore, 'morally entitled to . . . prior consideration'.[41] As a result Post Office net postal revenue dropped over £160,000 the year of the concessions. Even in matters where it was deeply and more influentially involved, the nationalisation of the telephone being the most obvious, the Treasury's was only one of many voices. Indeed, the fact that the acquisition process in this case was delayed and then carried out in a rather jerky, piecemeal fashion can only be fully explained if one takes into account the fundamental disagreements over proper telephone policy which existed in the wider society and the fact that by the 1890s the Post Office itself had begun to lose much of its former optimism and zeal for expansion.[42]

The inability on the part of the Treasury to control policy precisely or to determine exactly the financial record at St Martin's le Grand is perhaps best illustrated by a consideration of the pattern of rising salary scales there. As a labour-intensive industry, the Post Office needed to keep personnel expenses low in order to return a large surplus. However, salaries accounted for an increasing proportion of departmental budgets, as the table two illustrates.

Table 2
The place of wages in Post Office budgets

	Wages as percentage of total revenue	Wages as percentage of total expenditure
1860–1	29	33
1880–1	31	45
1910–11	50	61

Source: Annual reports of the Postmaster General.

---

[41] Post 30/774, E7306/1897, Walpole to Norfolk, January 1896. The rate was lowered from 1 oz. for 1 d to 4 oz. for 1 d.
[42] See chapters seven and ten for analysis of these developments.

In part this outcome was the paradoxical result of the department's own success. The more it earned, the more its employees believed they should be paid. In part it was the result of an important evolution in the power of staff associations.[43] Although there is evidence of nascent departmental labour unrest in the 1840s, it was not until the 1870s that such discontents became a matter of serious concern to the department's leaders, as a series of developments altered the relationship between staff and management at St Martin's le Grand. In 1868 legal restrictions which had previously denied Post Office workers the right to vote, if otherwise qualified, were lifted. In 1870 the nationalisation of the telegraphs brought into the department a particularly militant (and self-important) group of employees, who first formed an association in 1871 and who reorganised it a decade later. They were joined by the United Kingdom Postal Clerks' Association in 1887; the Fawcett Association, a union of sorting clerks, in 1890; and a Postmen's Federation in 1891, to cite the more important examples. The strength of these unions must be assessed on two levels. By many objective criteria they were poorly organised, under-financed, and naively led. The collapse of the July 1890 strike of London postmen is a case in point. However, despite these weaknesses the Post Office unions managed to evoke a response from the department's leaders and Parliament out of proportion to their actual power. At times the response of the department was one of calculation. Hence, the 1872 establishment of Good Conduct Stripes, which held out periodic pay raises to those postmen who adapted themselves to strict standards of military loyalty. (Good Conduct Stripes were intended, of course, to discourage more than unions. Three-fourths of the stripes lost in 1903 were forfeited because of intemperance.) At times the response of the department was one of paternalism. Hence, Blackwood's anguished description of the 1890 strikers as 'Christian men . . . led wrong'.[44] At times the response was one of outrage. Hence, Austen Chamberlain's 1903 complaints as to the lobbying tactics of the unions.[45] At times the response was one of resistance. Hence, Lord Stanley's rejection of the recommendations of the 1904 Bradford Committee on the grounds that the committee, in supporting requests for salary increases of over £1 million, had ignored its original terms of reference.[46]

For the most part, however, the response of the leadership at St

[43] See Clinton, chapter 6.
[44] Harriet S. Blackwood, *Some Records of the Life of Stevenson Arthur Blackwood* (London, 1896), p. 492.
[45] Hugo Meyer, *The British State Telegraphs* (New York, 1907), p. 209. Meyer subtitled this book A *Study of the Problems of a Large Body of Civil Servants in a Democracy*.
[46] Post 30/1185, E6980/1905, Post Office to Treasury, 8 March 1905.

Martin's le Grand was slow, but steady concession and compromise. More and more rights and privileges were granted to the staff and to their unions, as the chronology of policy changes found in appendix, table four indicates. In part – and this is especially true for the decades after Blackwood's death in 1893 when the upper echelon of the department was opened to an influx of generalists with no previous Post Office experience – the changes came as the result of a conviction that the employees had been unduly restricted in their political and trade union activities. (Such shifts, of course, were more likely to occur when a sympathetic Postmaster General was in office. Sydney Buxton, for example, held that the 'Post Office cannot fail to have an influence for good or bad on the labour market . . . and that influence ought to be for the good'.[47]) It was also their eagerness to serve the public which occasionally encouraged departmental leaders to accept a policy of accommodation. Faced with a choice between on the one hand higher salary costs and lower net revenue and on the other hand stationary salary costs and the possibility of labour trouble and reduced service, Post Office managers frequently chose the former. Thus, after a strike in the telegraph department in 1871, Scudamore tried to convince Gladstone of the necessity for salary increases. If 'we have another strike, I shall not be able to put it down. The men will strike in such numbers that it will be impossible for me to supply their places. [The] . . . result of a successful strike in the Government service will be an endless succession of strikes'.[48] In light of Scudamore's penchant for hyperbole, one might discount such a prediction. Yet after another strike occurred the next year at Huddersfield, Tilley – who was once described as being as unimpressionable as an oyster and who was never accused of overstatement – advised Lingen of the Treasury that 'The letter carriers won't strike [again]; but nonetheless [it] should . . . [be] remembered that if they did you would simply have to give them any wages they choose to demand.'[49] Five decades later Charles Hobhouse the Postmaster General equally pessimistically recorded in his diary worries concerning the possibility of a Parliamentary defeat for his Liberal party on the issue of departmental wages 'so strongly had the Postal associations been canvassing all parties and so little moral courage have MPs when an election is in sight'.[50]

Given these attitudes, and given the fear which the unions peri-

47 *Hansard's, Fifth Series*, vol. 4, 198, 26 April 1909.
48 Post 30/215, E274/1872, Scudamore to Gladstone, no date, probably January 1872.
49 Gladstone Papers, Add. MS. 44152, fol. 170, Tilley to Lingen, 19 November 1872. Given the relative tightness of the labour market at this time, Tilley's assessment should not be dismissed out of hand.
50 David, p. 169. The date was 1 May 1914.

odically could evoke among the public at large – *The Times* in December 1913 used the phrases 'Syndicalist Activity' and 'Extremist Proposals' in a headline describing a Post Office union rally – it is not surprising that an extended series of major salary revisions was approved by Postmasters General, inter-departmental conferences, and Parliamentary select committees.[51] (See table three.)

Table 3
The pattern of Post Office wage adjustments

Revision	Year	Estimated annual increase in cost
Fawcett	1881–2	£320,000
Raikes	1890–1	406,000
Tweedmouth	1897–8	388,000
Stanley	1905	372,000
(in reaction to Bradford Committee)		
Hobhouse	1908	707,900
Holt	1914	772,000

Source: Annual reports of the Postmaster General and Post 60/118, General Revisions in the Post Office.

It should be pointed out that these figures refer only to the cost of providing salary improvements and other benefits to the staff in place during the first year of change. In reality the magnitude of the ultimate cost to the department was significantly greater, for when new employees were hired, they also received the benefit of higher wages. For example, in 1911 the department estimated that it was paying over £3.3 million more per year as a result of the cumulative effect of the salary increases since 1881. The significance of this sum may be more clearly understood if a further point is made. In 1911 the entire departmental expenditure on wages was £12.5 million. Hence, the revisions represented over one quarter of the total expenditure on salaries.

Quite obviously, such statistics are open to a number of interpretations. It is true that the general pattern of Post Office wages falls into two distinct phases in the period before 1914. (See table four.)

51 *The Times*, 16 December 1913, p. 5.

Table 4
Departmental salaries in the context of wider economic trends

Postmen and sorters	Percentage change in money wages	Percentage change in real wages
1875–97	+ 32.4	+ 71.9
1897–1914	+ 12.7	– 4.2

Source: Daunton, *Royal Mail*, p. 233.

It is true that between 1897 and 1914 Post Office wages in real terms slipped more rapidly than the average national decline of 2 per cent, despite the efforts of union leaders. It is equally true, however, that a widespread perception in the entire 1875–1914 period held that government employees in general and Post Office employees in particular were better paid and enjoyed more job security than comparable workers in private employment. Arthur L. Baxter reached this conclusion as part of the Charles Booth survey of London economic and social conditions, and he went on to argue that the 'chronic agitation which exists almost throughout the civil service for better conditions of employment may be traced in part to the tendency of all men to magnify the importance of their position and duties'.[52] Similarly, in 1911 *The Times* pointed out that 'the position of all the important sections of postal servants has been rapidly and substantially improved by successive Governments' and published figures to substantiate the claim. (See appendix, table five.) Statistics were often cited to demonstrate the enviable situation enjoyed by department workers. For example, postmen averaged 28s 8d for a 48 hour week versus an average of 26s 7d for railway signalmen for a 57 hour week.[53] A London sorter averaged £131 10s 1d per year versus £121 13s 2d for warehousemen in wholesale firms and £106 15s 5d for clerks in retail firms. The department also insisted that its women employees were better off than their counterparts in other institutions. Women counter clerks and telegraphists, in addition to looking forward to a higher maximum salary than similar staff in private employment, worked shorter hours and enjoyed longer holidays and more generous sick leave arrangements. Post Office employees also had a non-contributory pension plan, a benefit which many other workers did not enjoy during the decades before 1914.[54] Two additional points need to be kept in mind

[52] Arthur L. Baxter, 'Civil and Municipal Service' in Charles Booth (ed.), *Life and Labour of the People in London*, vol. 4 (London, 1903), p. 12.
[53] These figures were compiled by the department for consideration by the 1912–13 Holt Committee. Post 60/116.
[54] See Daunton, *Royal Mail*, pp. 246–7.

in considering these issues. First, the leadership of the unions consistently and loudly rejected such comparisons as misleading and invalid.[55] Secondly, there was no doubt whatsoever at the Treasury as to the accuracy of these comparisons. As one memorandum put it, 'Speaking very generally, Post Office employees are probably a privileged class. . . . Given two brothers of equal capacity and opportunity, it is probably true . . . that A who enters the P.O. service does better than B who adopts an outside career.'[56]

In light of these assumptions, what was the Treasury's role in the handling of wage disputes and salary allocation at St Martin's le Grand? Without question evidence can be easily produced to portray the Treasury as an unmovable line of resistance against the appeasers in the Post Office. Thus, Lingen responded to Tilley's analysis of the 1872 labour situation with the following blast:

> Were I Postmaster General, I should return this memorial to the gentlemen from whom it proceeds, and let them know pretty plainly what I thought of their conduct in presenting it. I cannot understand your proceedings at the Post Office. You appear to regard yourselves as the mere delegates of your establishment, instead of being the advanced-guard bulwarks of the Treasury, as the ultimate guardians of the public purse.

> Your men speak and write as if they had no masters.[57]

This rather disdainful attitude remained something of a constant at the Treasury throughout the years before 1914. Reacting to complaints from Post Office employees, Sir Edward Hamilton in 1907 insisted 'There are classes of men (as I saw myself in early days in the Admiralty) who spend all their spare time discussing such questions and who seem never happy unless they are writing memorials.'[58] One year later a Treasury clerk lamented the Post Office's 'tendency to give everyone the benefit of the doubt' in labour disputes.[59] The impact of such statements, nonetheless, was more rhetorical than substantive, as the Treasury did not play an effective role in reversing the cycle of higher and higher salary settlements. Perhaps the clearest answer why this was the case can be found in an important memorandum drafted in 1914 by Roland Wilkins, a principal clerk in the Treasury. Wilkins painted a gloomy picture of recent trends in the process of pay allocation. Ac-

---

55 See, for example, *The Post*, 22 August 1903.
56 T1/15125/525, Wilkins's memorandum, no date, probably 1913.
57 Gladstone Papers, Add. MS. 44152, fol. 180, Lingen to Tilley, 25 January 1873.
58 T1/11057/15657, Hamilton's memorandum, 3 June 1907.
59 T1/10888/180083, J. W. Cawston's memorandum, 11 April 1908.

cording to Wilkins, the old system in which the Chancellor of the Exchequer weighed the relative merits of expenditure proposals against available financial resources was breaking down under the onslaught of external pressures. This was especially serious, given the fact that in 'public service there are no economic forces to govern the settlement of wages'.[60] Rather the outcome was now the result of political struggles fought in select committees, which meant that the determination of salary scales was regrettably not a matter for Treasury control. Condemning certain MPs for their oversensitivity toward employee grievances and their equally unmanly fear of losing their seats, Wilkins in a telling admission concluded 'The battle being between the departments and Parliament, it is no good the Treasury trying to step in with an attempt to out-Herod Herod.'

Thus, when proposals for major salary revisions came forward, the Treasury like the Post Office somewhat unhappily accepted accommodation over confrontation. The fundamental decisions having been made elsewhere, the best Whitehall could hope for was that sanctioning such revisions might allay future labour unrest. When Sir Francis Mowatt the Permanent Secretary, for instance, examined the recommendations of the 1895–7 interdepartmental committee headed by Lord Tweedmouth, he regarded them as open 'to some criticism in detail'. Yet he recognised that, if the Treasury failed to approve the entire package of recommendations, 'the fact will be used as the basis of a new agitation which will cost us more than we had temporarily saved'.[61] What should be made of these clerks' attitudes? Wilkins was perhaps too pessimistic about the future role of his department in the settlement of wages throughout the civil service. Mowatt was undoubtedly too optimistic in his belief that concessions would quiet unrest among the staff in the Post Office. Yet the crucial point remains that both men accepted the reality that the role of the Treasury was a limited one on salary issues as was the case with many other matters.[62]

Hence, an analysis of labour issues helps to place Post Office–Treasury relations in the period before 1914 in a clearer perspective. Without question Whitehall by 1914 knew more of the day-to-day, internal operations of the Post Office than it had fifty years before. Without question the Post Office by 1914 was less expansionist in its drive to provide new public services than it had been fifty years before. However, there was no necessary causal relationship between these two

[60] For the following, see T1/11928/13311, Wilkins's memorandum, 13 June 1914.
[61] T1/9213A/18855, Mowatt's memorandum, 4 March 1897.
[62] The above analysis should be considered in relation to the somewhat different picture of Treasury control drawn by Roger Davidson, *Whitehall and the Labour Problem in Late-Victorian and Edwardian Britain* (London, 1985), pp. 176–7.

conditions. Treasury control, as described by Lowell and as condemned by Wolmer, cannot be said to have unilaterally determined the course of events at St Martin's le Grand. In some instances the Treasury could influence decisions. In others it could only slow the pace of growth or slightly change the direction of Post Office affairs. This was evident to John Kempe, a principal clerk in the Treasury, surveying the relationship in 1889 after over twenty years' experience,

> Should we be prepared to alter the P.O. policy if they are unable to produce clear evidence in support of it? On the whole . . . our duties and responsibilities in regard to the P.O. are best discharged without attempting any positive policy; our relations to them should rather be in the nature of a drag than of active direction; that our function should be to ensure that proposals are carefully considered by the Post Office themselves, which we shall do by making them feel that they will have to make out a good case to us.[63]

In conclusion, to conceive of the story of the nineteenth-century Post Office as a tug-of-war between the two departments which the Treasury invariably won is incorrect. As subsequent chapters will demonstrate, Post Office history was shaped by a much larger number of players in a much more complicated arena.

---

[63] T1/8394A/2898, Kempe's memorandum, 16 February 1889. For further elaboration of his thinking on Treasury control, see J. A. Kempe, *Reminiscences of an Old Civil Servant* (London, 1928), pp. 205–14.

PART TWO
NEW RESPONSIBILITIES

3

The Encouragement of Thrift

There can be no doubt that the Post Office Savings Banks which
Mr Gladstone is proposing to establish will be beneficial, if any
National Savings Banks are beneficial. – *The Economist*, 16
February 1861, p. 172.

That the Victorians proclaimed the virtues of hard work, self-help and
frugality is a cliché known to all students of the period. That the
Victorian state undertook an active, public role in the promotion of
these private virtues is, however, a less familiar phenomenon. In large
measure this arises from the tendency of many historians to concen-
trate their attention on the unemployed and the very poor and the
poor law system designed to ameliorate their all too real problems. As a
result the complex range of ranks and orders stretching upward into
the lower middle class and the equally complex range of credit and
thrift institutions serving these groups have only begun to be properly
studied.[1] A consideration of the place of the Post Office in this network is valuable for at least two reasons. First, it illuminates the process
through which a bureaucracy designed for one purpose took on a radically different one. Secondly, it serves as a reminder of the very mixed
record of success and failure which this same bureaucracy achieved in
pursuit of the encouragement of thrift.

As one might expect, the gestation period of a state-sponsored system of savings banks was lengthy. Many social thinkers had long
viewed prudence and savings, instead of welfare relief from the government, as the proper cure for poverty. Daniel Defoe, for example, concluded in 1704 that neither the work-house nor handouts would
answer the needs of the poor. Instead Defoe called for an act of Parliament which would 'make drunkards take care of wife and children;
spendthrifts lay up for a wet day; idle, lazy fellows diligent and thought-

---

[1] The following should be cited: Geoffrey Crossick, *An Artisan Elite in Victorian
Society* (London, 1978); Takao Matsumura, *The Labour Aristocracy Revisited: The
Victorian Flint Glass Makers* (Manchester, 1983); P. H. J. H. Gosden, *Self-Help*
(New York, 1974); Paul Johnson, *Saving and Spending* (Oxford, 1985); and H.
Oliver Horne, *A History of Savings Banks* (London, 1947).

ful; sottish fellows, careful and provident'.[2] The modest response of the late eighteenth century to this sweeping challenge was a variety of private philanthropic institutions, such as Friendly Societies and Trustee Savings Banks. These were organised on a somewhat haphazard basis to inculcate the virtues of thrift among the lower classes and to provide an outlet for saving to a group not well served by middle-class institutions. As with other attempts at social betterment, government at first was content to rely upon the energy and initiative of private citizens to originate and administer these efforts.

Nevertheless, the line between private management and state control was never completely clear or distinct, as Parliament indirectly supervised the operation of these private bodies. The Friendly Societies were officially recognised in 1793, and the Trustee Savings Banks came under government scrutiny in 1817. In 1828 another Savings Bank Act, consolidating all previous legislation, was passed. There were specific ways in which the state became directly involved with these private institutions. For example, the government invested the money collected by the trustees. It also established limitations on the size of each account. Accordingly, an individual could deposit up to £30 in one year and £150 total. Interest was allowed to compound to £200. As table one indicates, Parliament also set the rate of interest.

Table 1
Interest rate structure of Trustee Savings Banks

Year	Percentage rate payable to trustees	Maximum percentage rate payable by trustees to depositors
1817	4–11–3	——
1828	3–16–0½	3–8–5
1844	3–5–0	3–0–10

Source: Post, Report of Committee on Savings Banks Funds, 1896, pp. 2–3.

As these funds were invested with the National Debt Commissioners, it was natural for the average citizen to assume that the state was somehow responsible for the sound management of the entire system. In fact, the state took on responsibility for the funds only when they were received in London. It had no liability for fraud or mistakes committed by the trustees. Nevertheless, to many this legal distinction appeared sophistical. Hence, an 1858 select committee concluded, 'It

[2] Daniel Defoe, *Giving Alms No Charity* (London, 1704), pp. 56–8.

is difficult . . . to maintain that Parliament . . . should not be bound to provide some guarantee for the money of depositors, who have no share themselves in the management of their Bank.'[3]

There was no shortage of critics who argued that the Trustee Banks stood in need of improvement. Jeremy Bentham, never a man to tolerate disorder, believed that the private system fell short of its goal of providing an outlet for the savings of the poor. The banks were subject to embezzlement or inaccurate bookkeeping. Frequently funds were collected at public houses where the temptation to spend a little of one's savings on drink was almost irresistible. A preferable location, to Bentham's thinking, would be a vestry-room where on Sundays thrift would be endowed with religious virtue. As Bentham argued, 'Money transactions are neither ill-suited nor foreign to the main business of the day.'[4] He proposed that a private company should be chartered to handle the savings accounts of the poor in a regular, safe manner in all areas of the country. Others believed that government management offered the best means to improve the situation. In 1807 Samuel Whitbread, the only son of a prosperous brewing family, elaborated in great detail a scheme for one great national bank, which would collect the savings of the poor and safely invest them.[5] In 1827 George Taylor, Secretary to the Commission on the Poor Law, suggested in the *Quarterly Review* employing the Post Office as the medium of collection and even went a step further to advance the proposal that such saving should be compulsory.[6] In 1852 George A. Hamilton, Vicar of Berwick-upon-Tweed and later Archdeacon of Lindisfarne, contacted a relative at the Treasury, G. H. Hamilton, to suggest a system of Post Office Savings Banks. Four years later John Bullar, an attorney, submitted a similar plan, which cited the 'want of perfect security to depositors [in private banks]: risk of loss of trustees by defaulting clerks, and want of opportunities for the labouring classes to make deposits as soon as they have anything to deposit'.[7] The Post Office was a suitable choice to handle a savings banks operation for two reasons. First, it constituted, as a letter-writer to *The Times* noted, 'the only real piece of administrative centralisation existing among us'.[8] There was simply no other

3 BPP, 1857–8, vol. 16, Report from the Select Committee to Inquire into the Acts relating to Savings Banks and the Operation thereof, p. x.
4 John Bowring (ed.), *The Works of Jeremy Bentham*, vol. 8 (New York, 1962), p. 414. For studies of the wider context of Bentham's thought, see David Roberts, 'Jeremy Bentham and the Victorian Administrative State', *Victorian Studies*, 2 (1959), 193–210 and L. J. Hume, *Bentham and Bureaucracy* (Cambridge, 1981).
5 William Lewins, *A History of Banks for Savings* (London, 1866), pp. 270–7.
6 George Taylor, 'The Substitution of Savings Banks for Poor Laws', *Quarterly Review*, 36 (1827), 488–9.
7 Lewins, pp. 280–1.
8 *The Times*, 12 April 1861, p. 9.

national bureaucracy as wide in scope as St Martin's le Grand. Secondly, the department had been involved in the sale of money orders since 1792.[9] In the beginning the Post Office did not handle the business officially; but rather the six clerks of the road, seeking their own profit, financed the operation from private sources. In 1838 the Money Order Office was placed under firm public control. The system worked efficiently, operating costs were kept low, and in 1860 over 7 million orders amounting to over £13 million were issued. Hence, the factor of momentum in government growth emphasised by many students of bureaucracy was not absent in this case.

By far the most important private citizen campaigning for government savings banks was Charles W. Sikes, a Huddersfield banker. Sikes had become interested in the issue of elevating the condition of the poor through thrift as early as 1850. Subsequently he published a pamphlet on the subject which fused the Victorian cult of domesticity with the morality of thrift, 'Good Times, or Savings Banks and the Fireside'. Six years later he began to pressure G. Cornewall Lewis the Chancellor of the Exchequer on the issue. Before a select committee in April 1858, Sikes presented compelling evidence that the labouring poor lacked confidence in the Trustee Banks, especially because of the failures of banks of which the 1849 Rochdale case was perhaps the most infamous. Only a national system under strict central control could allay the fears of the public. Only a national system would be extensive enough to meet the needs of the public. Sikes, using language which might have been applied to any number of cases of government expansion, stated 'I wish the State to step in and merely do that which private individuals cannot do.'[10] Since the idea of a state-managed system of savings banks was by no means unique to Sikes, the crucial question to consider is why Sikes succeeded where others had failed. Due credit should go to Sikes himself, who was much more diligent and systematic than earlier proponents. Nonetheless, one should not neglect the changing situation within the government, both at St Martin's le Grand and at higher levels.

By the 1850s there was much more receptivity to new ideas and much more social concern among the civil servants at St Martin's le Grand than there had been two or three decades earlier. Instead of confronting a bureaucracy bound to routine, Sikes encountered a group of men who envisaged the Post Office as a medium of social betterment. Rowland Hill, who had succeeded Maberly as Secretary in 1854,

[9] *Historical Summaries of the Post Office Services to 30th September 1906* (London, 1906), pp. 32–9.
[10] BPP, 1857–8, vol. 16, Select Committee on Savings Banks, p. 181. See also Lewins, p. 256.

appeared enthusiastic. He advised Edward Baines, MP for Leeds, that 'if carried into effect, the plan would in my opinion prove highly useful to the public, and in some degree advantageous to the revenue'.[11] Yet Hill's support for the proposal was ultimately limited by both ideological and personal considerations, considerations which ran so closely together in his mind that it is impossible to determine where the one ended and the other began. On the ideological level Hill and his familial supporters at St Martin's le Grand strictly adhered to two working principles. First, the conveyance of mail was the chief business of the department, and, therefore, other tasks and responsibilities should be undertaken only if they did not divert attention from the primary task at hand. Secondly, as was explained earlier, in the view of the Hills each departmental enterprise should operate at a profit. Thus, to Rowland's brother Frederic interest rates and deposit regulations in a departmental banking system should be structured with an eye toward profit and with a healthy fear of government lurching too far into competition with private enterprise and existing institutions.[12] On a more personal level the Hill faction adopted an ambivalent view toward the proposals for a savings bank system because such a system was enthusiastically supported by other departmental administrators whom they despised. St Martin's le Grand was a bureaucracy, like all bureaucracies, beset by rivalry and animosity. The Hills always liked to portray themselves as men of pure virtue and honest principle, fighting the laziness of time-serving drudges. Hence, even at the height of Hill's power as Secretary, in the proud words of his daughter, 'the old hostility to . . . reform and the reformer did not die out'.[13]

In this instance, however, there was no hostility to the particular programme of reform, only distrust of the self-serving rhetoric of Hill the reformer. Indeed, on the savings banks question Hill was by no means in the vanguard of the movement. At the Post Office that more advanced position was occupied by George Chetwynd and Frank Ives Scudamore. An analysis of the careers and outlooks of these two administrators demonstrates the complexity of the forces which were shaping government expansion in the mid-nineteenth century. Both men had spent their entire adult lives within the bureaucracy of St Martin's le Grand. Neither man held an especially exciting position. Chetwynd worked in the Money Order Department, while Scudamore was the Receiver and Accountant General. Judged merely on the basis of their job titles, both men were no more than somewhat stodgy bookkeepers. Yet they had developed an ideological outlook which was

11 Lewins, p. 256, Hill to Baines, 2 August 1859.
12 Daunton, *Royal Mail*, p. 87.
13 Eleanor C. Smyth, *Sir Rowland Hill* (London, 1907), p. 277.

highly critical of faults and shortcomings in certain private institutions and which confidently proposed that the state should play a more active role in fulfilling necessary social and economic functions. Of the two, Scudamore was without question the more important and the more interesting. Having entered St Martin's le Grand in 1840, he never gained much experience of the mail side of the department's operation, which was the more usual route to promotion and greater responsibility. Rather he rose partly on the basis of his remarkable grasp of the statistical and accounting aspects of the department's operations. (Trollope, complimenting and criticising his rival with the same phrase, once described Scudamore as 'a great accountant'.[14]) But Scudamore was more than simply a manipulator of figures. He was a man of some humour who, when not labouring on esoteric departmental matters, wrote light pieces for *Punch*, the *Comic Times*, and other periodicals. More to the point, by 1860 Scudamore was in the process of nurturing an outlook which idealised the concept of a mixed economy so well planned and managed by technocrats such as himself as to ensure maximum efficiency and maximum benefit for everyone. Thus, Scudamore should be regarded as standing left of centre on the ideological spectrum between earlier Utilitarian thinkers with their somewhat restricted conception of government usefulness and later advocates of state intervention in virtually all aspects of economic activity. Like his enemy Rowland Hill, Scudamore was always eager to present his ideas to the widest audience possible. Moreover, as was the case with Hill, it is equally difficult to determine where the line separating the promotion of Scudamore's schemes for social improvement and the promotion of his own career actually lay. Certainly he, and this is true of Chetwynd as well, does not conform to a typology outlined by Kitson Clark who once hypothesised that men who entered the civil service at an early age were likely to be anonymous, neutral, and docile.[15] These aspiring statesmen-in-disguise were anything but that.

In November 1860 Chetwynd on his own initiative submitted to Lord Stanley the Postmaster General a detailed plan which outlined a departmental savings banks system.[16] Chetwynd had read of Sikes's idea in the newspapers and had devoted many hours to working out an elaborate prospectus – even down to the point of suggesting one shilling as the minimum deposit – as opposed to Sikes's proposal of £1 – which could be profitably accepted by the department. Furthermore, Chetwynd proposed a one penny fee per transaction, instead of the

---

[14] Anthony Trollope, *An Autobiography* (1883, rpr. New York, 1950), p. 279.

[15] G. S. R. Kitson Clark, 'Statesmen in Disguise', *The Historical Journal*, 2 (1959), 34–5.

[16] Post 30/145, E2572/1861, Chetwynd to Stanley, 30 November 1860.

higher money order charges suggested by Frederic Hill, further increasing the attractiveness of the programme. To Chetwynd a Post Office banking system would meet the needs of 'that large and deserving class whose efforts to save ought to be encouraged'.[17] After studying Chetwynd's proposal, Scudamore quickly supported the idea and, in fact, seized the planning initiative from Chetwynd. In a characteristically optimistic phrase Scudamore predicted that a chain of government-operated banks would remove from the labouring classes 'any pretext for improvidence'.[18] Boldly going further than Chetwynd in proposing a departmental system which would be independent from other existing administrative programmes, Scudamore envisaged a wide network of offices which would be open at much more convenient hours under Post Office management than was currently the case. In 1861 there were only 638 private Trustee Banks in the whole of the country, and many working-class people were as far as an entire county from the nearest one.[19] Over one half the banks were only open once a week, and fifty-four were open only once a fortnight. Not only would a Post Office system eliminate these problems, encourage thrift, and lower the expenses of poor-law relief, but Scudamore also claimed it could accomplish these goals more cheaply through a unified approach in which the money order operation and the savings banks would be effectively merged. He estimated that the department could administer its system for almost £50,000 less a year than the private trustees could.[20] As Scudamore was later to write, 'I am sure that this arrangement will be for the advantage of the public, and I have many reasons for thinking it will be equally for the advantage of the Post Office.'[21] The proposal seemed to offer that ideal combination of social service and administrative expansion so revered by ambitious bureaucrats of any age. Clearly Scudamore's competitive spirit had been aroused by the prospect of a system which would attract customers who had never before made use of a savings bank as well as former depositors in Trustee Banks seeking the convenience and security of the Post Office system.

Scudamore and Chetwynd were not the only men in the government who supported the idea of state-managed savings banks. From the very beginning Gladstone was closely associated with the scheme. As early as 1853 he had considered the appointment of government receivers of the savings of the poor in areas where trustees could not be

[17] *Ibid.*
[18] Post, Reports relating . . . to Savings Banks, Scudamore's report, 7 January 1861.
[19] Lewins, pp. 238–9.
[20] Post, Scudamore's report, 7 January 1861.
[21] Post 30/145, E2572/1861, Scudamore to Tilley, 1 February 1861.

found. Thus, the leap to the idea of a government-operated network was not a broad one. In November 1859 Sikes had approached Gladstone, then Chancellor of the Exchequer, on the subject. Gladstone further discussed the topic with Sir Alexander Spearman who, as Commissioner of the National Debt, was involved in the investment of public funds. Gladstone was hesitant to plunge ahead immediately because of complex questions relating to accounting procedures and interest rates. Still he was generally impressed with the idea. As he wrote Sikes, 'there is so much of promise in the plan on the face of it, that we are unwilling to let it drop without a most careful examination'.[22] The next year Scudamore and Chetwynd, of course, provided exactly the required examination and, perhaps more importantly, the required encouragement. It is impossible to reconstruct exactly the nuances of the developing relationship between Gladstone and Scudamore during this period from accounts such as the following entry in Gladstone's diary for 17 December 1860: 'Gov. and Dep. Gov. Bank 12–2. – Mr Stephenson – Mr Scudamore'.[23] What is clear, however, is that in the months before introduction of the savings banks legislation to Parliament this Post Office official was deeply involved in the forging of the bill and at the same time was gaining Gladstone's attention. Scudamore had begun to play a crucial role in the emergence of Gladstone's great – undoubtedly excessively great – admiration for the management at St Martin's le Grand. By 1866 Gladstone was to insist that 'I am far from thinking very highly of our rank as a nation of administrators, but if we could be judged by the post office alone, we might claim the very first place in this respect.'[24]

The debate on the Post Office Savings Banks bill, which was introduced in February 1861, helps to display the fault lines of mid-Victorian attitudes toward government expansion. The proponents of the measure were convinced that an unacceptable situation existed in regard to outlets for working-class thrift. (This first stage of argument, of course, corresponds to what MacDonagh once termed 'the exposure of a social evil'.[25]) There were 15 counties in England not served by Trustee Banks, and many towns with as many as 30,000 people lacked them. Moreover, the fact that such banks were often administered by local businessmen was said to discourage thrift. As one MP put it, 'Workingmen were often very much afraid to let their masters know they were saving money from a notion it would lead to a reduction of

22 Lewins, p. 288, Gladstone to Sikes, 30 November 1859.
23 H. C. G. Matthew (ed.), *The Gladstone Diaries*, vol. 5 (Oxford, 1978), p. 539.
24 John Morley, *The Life of William Ewart Gladstone*, vol. 2 (London, 1903), p. 182.
25 Oliver MacDonagh, 'The Nineteenth-Century Revolution in Government: a Reappraisal', *The Historical Journal*, 1 (1958), 58.

their wages, and under the present system the masters were often concerned with these banks and could know exactly how each man's account stood.'[26] Another difficulty involved the exact allocation of responsibility between the trustees and the government in the event of mismanagement or fraud. As the issue was so hazy in the mind of the average citizen, it was only right and proper that the government should actually shoulder the responsibility by opening its own system of banks. The financial advantages of the plan were also emphasised by the bill's supporters. In the past the Trustee Banks had been a drain on the Exchequer. Between 1817 and 1844 the rate of interest paid by the government to trustees was so high that a £2 million deficit accumulated, as the government was unable to invest the funds at comparable rates.[27] Although the situation had improved after 1844 when the rate of interest paid out to trustees had been lowered, Gladstone was still uneasy about the prospect of indirect government subsidies to depositors. Gladstone proposed to pay only 2.5 per cent to depositors in Post Office Savings Banks versus slightly more than 3 per cent paid in the Trustee Banks. In this way the danger of any loss would be reduced. Moreover, a government-operated system would, in Gladstone's words, 'provide the minister of finance with a strong financial arm, and . . . secure his independence from the City by giving him a large and certain command of money'.[28] All in all, the Post Office with its network of over 2,000 Money Order offices was pictured as the ideal medium to provide an efficient, extensive system to collect the savings of the poor.

Still the case pleading the inadequacies of the old, private system and the advantages of a Post Office operation was by no means universally accepted.[29] Lord Clanricarde, a former Postmaster General, believed that the excursion of the department into this new field of responsibility was unwarranted and that it would interfere with the proper function of the Post Office, the conveyance of mail. Sotheron Escourt doubted that the provincial employees of the department were sufficiently dependable to be entrusted with the savings of others. The real opposition, however, came from those who viewed the proposition of government encouragement of thrift as a dangerously centralising proposal. Like the supporters of Trollope's kindly Mr Harding in *The Warden*, they feared a grab for control by the state which would upset the delicate balance between local, private management of philanthropy and the central government in London. In the House of Lords

26 *Hansard's, Third Series*, vol. 161, 265, 8 February 1861.
27 Post, Report of the Committee on Savings Banks Funds, 1896, p. 3.
28 Morley, vol. 2, 52.
29 *Hansard's, Third Series*, vol. 162, 889, 22 April 1861 and vol. 161, 2189, 18 March 1861.

Lord Monteagle who, as Thomas Spring-Rice, had been Chancellor of the Exchequer in Melbourne's second cabinet, voiced this sentiment when he opposed 'interference with local management of our local charitable institutions'.[30] In the House of Commons A. S. Ayrton, whose adamant opposition to any extension of national government programmes was to win him a certain notoriety, couched his argument in similar terms:

> the present savings banks, with all their imperfections, were infinitely preferable to a great Government institution. It was desirable that the country gentlemen of England should take an interest in the welfare of the labouring population by which they were surrounded, and to supersede their exertions by the services of mere stipendiaries of the State would weaken that social system on which the liberties of the people were mainly founded.[31]

For these politicians the fundamental issue raised by the bill involved competing visions of the proper means toward social policy – the local, personal *ad hoc* paternalism exercised by private managers of the Trustee Banks as opposed to the national, more anonymous and systematic organisation administered by government clerks in the Post Office system. (The continuing importance of paternalism in shaping political and economic attitudes can hardly be overstated. As Roberts has cogently argued, in 'early Victorian England no social outlook had deeper roots and wider appeal than . . . paternalism'.[32]) The debate, then, was not so much over the merits of a particular social policy, the encouragement of thrift, but rather over who was to control and direct it. Scudamore later went so far as to claim that the motivations influencing the supporters of the Trustee Banks were less philanthropic than psychological. As he put it, 'Many benevolent people cling to the little show of authority, the little appearance of influence, the slight kind of control over their humbler neighbours which this exercise of their benevolence brings to them. . . . If it had not been for this feeling, there would not have been in this country at this moment one single old Savings Bank remaining.'[33] Given the magnitude of Scudamore's own ambition, it is open to question whether his support for the state system was as disinterested as he liked to believe. What is beyond question is that both advocates for and opponents of the bill were not deeply concerned with the specific issue of individual responsibility

---

[30] *Ibid.*, vol. 162, 884, 22 April 1861.
[31] *Ibid.*, vol. 162, 270, 8 April 1861.
[32] David Roberts, *Paternalism in Early Victorian England* (New Brunswick, New Jersey, 1979), p. 1.
[33] Post 30, E1139/1874, Scudamore's memorandum, 23 January 1873.

which was raised by *The Economist* when it regretted that 'the Government, by promising to take their [the working classes'] money, should have relieved them from the educating responsibility of finding natural as well as safe investments for it'.[34] After all, such a statement wrongly implied that individual members of the working class existed autonomously without the support of philanthropic institutions. A different set of circumstances was involved, for paternalistic intervention in the form of the Trustee Banks was already an established fact. Was an alternative type of intervention necessary or even preferable? For the MPs and civil servants debating this question, considerations of laissez-faire versus intervention as they are sometimes simplistically portrayed were not germane.

In order to convince opponents that a new approach was wise, supporters of the Post Office plan emphasised the tentative nature of this experiment in government growth. Gladstone, for example, pointed out the fact that the state was not seeking to establish a national bank or even to drive the existing Trustee Banks out of existence. After all, the Post Office banks would offer interest at a lower rate than the private banks. Furthermore, no patronage openings would be created, since no new army of clerks would be necessary, at least at first. As he said, 'It was not proposed to create a large and new establishment under highly-paid officers. The framework already existed, and everything would fall in with the existing machinery of the Post Office.'[35] Finally, the point was made that the savings banks programme adhered to conventional concepts of fiscal responsibility and probity. The government would be able to turn a profit by investing the money at a higher rate than it paid. It is not surprising that Gladstone, who in 1863 was to propose taxing the endowments of private philanthropic organisations, was intransigent on this issue. In his words, 'It would be absurd for the Government and Parliament, even for the purpose of encouraging provident habits among the poor, to make the working classes of the country pensioners on the Exchequer.'[36] Arguing along these lines, Gladstone was able to convince his colleagues in Parliament of the wisdom of the proposal. On 17 May 1861 the Post Office Savings Act (24 Vict. c. 14) received the Royal Assent. The department was authorised to establish a network of savings banks where deposits as low as one shilling could be made. (At this time only a few Trustee Banks accepted deposits this small, but the supporters of the bill hoped that this feature would enhance the system's attractiveness.) A £30 annual limit and a maximum limit of £150

---

[34] *The Economist*, 17 February 1861, p. 19.
[35] *Hansard's, Third Series*, vol. 162, 273, 8 April 1861.
[36] *Ibid.*, 272.

per depositor were also set. These were the same limits enforced by the Trustee Banks, and in this way it was assumed by many that the Post Office banks would serve essentially the identical clientele.

At St Martin's le Grand the real work now began. As the Savings Banks essentially constituted a huge bookkeeping operation, the implementation of the legislation demanded large amounts of manpower. Despite Gladstone's confidence that the existing establishment at St Martin's le Grand could accommodate the programme, another bureaucracy quickly emerged. By December 1862 the Savings Banks Department in its upper echelons consisted of one controller, one assistant controller, ten first-class clerks, eighteen second-class clerks, twenty third-class clerks, eight messengers, and twelve temporary clerks.[37] Moreover, without the benefit of modern business machines it was a deadly boring job, which mainly consisted of checking the accuracy of an ever-growing number of accounts. By 1866 when there were over 643,000 accounts, the number of established officers had risen to 52 in addition to 153 temporary clerks. The Savings Banks Department was one where women later came to be widely employed. They were found to be efficient as well as less expensive than male clerks. In 1915 there were almost 2,000 women employees.[38] The Savings Banks Department remained one of the most overworked in the Post Office. Morale among lower-level clerks was at times poor, as many felt their work was not properly appreciated by the Secretary's Office. As one clerk complained in 1868,

At Canon Street we poor clerks were worked like cab horses, treated like city dogs, and paid like British soldiers! Nine a.m. to seven p.m. were frequently my office hours. The rooms were crowded and badly ventilated, the work was tedious in the extreme, and the treatment of the 'officers' by their 'chiefs' was at once annoying and ridiculous. We wretched ones were often addressed as if we were unruly schoolboys or impertinent apprentices. It is scarcely an exaggeration to say that if the Pall Mall bureau was Paradise, the Post Office in comparison was something worse than Purgatory.[39]

In fact, the department was nicknamed 'The Cinderella of the Post

---

[37] Post, Reports . . . relating to the Post Office Savings Banks, Stanley to Treasury, 15 December 1862.

[38] For an analysis of the problems faced by women in such positions, see Meta Zimmeck, 'Jobs for the Girls: the Expansion of Clerical Work for Women, 1850–1914' in Angela V. John (ed.), *Unequal Opportunities: Women's Employment in England* (Oxford, 1986), pp. 153–77.

[39] Post, *The London Review*, 18 May 1868.

Office' because of the treatment it received from its older, more prestigious departmental sisters.

However, one should not assume that the Savings Banks were of little interest to senior civil servants at St Martin's le Grand. Indeed, it is important to realise that these managers began to push for a much more extensive system than that envisaged when the bill was passed. In promoting the bill, Gladstone had not adopted an aggressive or competitive stance against the Trustee Banks. When Scudamore and Chetwynd initially studied the proposed distribution of the Post Office banks, they took Gladstone's outlook into consideration. If a particular county was already well served by the Trustee Banks, they refrained from setting up a competing Post Office operation. Other towns were eliminated because the local postmasters were untrustworthy. Yet Scudamore and Chetwynd still felt an obligation to 'leave no considerable district of the country without the required accommodation'.[40] In a matter of weeks they began to forget the tentative emphasis of Gladstone. They started ambitiously to pursue the goal of planting departmental savings banks all over the country. For example, in October 1861 the two complained to Tilley that the expansion of the system in London had been too limited and hesitant. Although nineteen offices had been opened there since the act's passage the previous April, much more could be done. They proposed to expand the system into 'the neighbourhood of Railway stations and of Large Factories, the densely populated shores of the river, and the great tracts and suburban villages inhabited by the Wealthier classes in which are a vast number of Domestic Servants in receipt of good wages'.[41] Clearly these administrators had a remarkably acute sense of the system's potential.

During the first nine months after the passage of the bill the Post Office requested expansion of the system into hundreds of towns and villages. In December 1861 alone the Treasury approved new postal savings banks in 184 places.[42] In January of the next year Scudamore and Chetwynd proposed to open 300 banks in Ireland, 44 of which would be located in towns already served by Trustee Banks. The bureaucrats at St Martin's le Grand gloried in this competition with the private savings banks. They believed that such a struggle would help to eliminate all the clichés about bumbling inefficiency in government. Elaborate statistics were maintained to illustrate the superiority of the Post Office system. In January 1862, for instance, it was calculated that, while the Trustee Banks had suffered an almost £1.85 million

40 Post, Reports . . . relating to the Post Office Savings Banks, Report Of G. Chetwynd and F. I. Scudamore, 26 July 1861.
41 T1/6327B/1350, Scudamore and Chetwynd to Tilley, 10 October 1861.
42 T1/7232/14428, Treasury to Post Office, December 1861.

decline in deposits, the departmental accounts had increased by over £1.6 million. Hence, the conclusion to be drawn was that the government system was draining funds away from the private system. In its 1863 annual report the Post Office took the closing of thirty-six Trustee Banks as 'proof of the fact that the Post Office banks are generally considered to have been efficiently conducted, and they have provided savings banks accommodations in a manner satisfactory to the public'.[43] The one great advantage which the Post Office system possessed over its rivals was its absolute security. After irregularities were uncovered at a private bank in Bilston in 1862, *The Times* hoped for the day when all Trustee Banks would be replaced by departmental banks.[44] For a time it appeared that this hope might be fulfilled. Between 1861 and 1868 the deposits in Trustee Banks fell from £41.5 million to £36.9 million, while the departmental accounts grew to £11.7 million.[45]

However, administrators at St Martin's le Grand were neither satisfied with the pace of growth nor pleased with their share of the savings of the country. As a result in January 1869 Scudamore planned a two-pronged attack against the opposition. First, he sought to make the Post Office system more attractive by raising the maximum limits for annual deposits to £100 and total deposits per account to £300. Secondly, he suggested a reduction in the maximum rate of 3.04 per cent interest which the Trustee Banks were allowed to pay in order that the Post Office with its lower rate would be more competitive. (Many Trustee Banks paid only 2.75 per cent interest.) In a letter which clearly illustrates his disdain for the private system Scudamore wrote to Sir Alexander Spearman, 'This reduction will give the old banks a gentle push and will slightly accelerate their extinction.'[46] Scudamore's thinking on this matter also serves as a reminder that he was not solely influenced by considerations of social improvement. He displayed a very real concern for revenue and efficiency considerations as well as public betterment. Raising the maximum limit to £300 would increase the earnings of the department without proportionally increasing its expenses. Using the same logic, he opposed raising the annual limit to £300, because such an alteration would lead people to open drawing accounts, which would be much more expensive for the Post Office to manage.

Scudamore's projected changes came under violent attack. By March 1869 he had decided to drop any proposal for reducing the

---

[43] *Ninth Report of the Postmaster General on the Post Office* (London, 1863), p. 16.
[44] *The Times*, 17 January 1862, p. 8.
[45] B. R. Mitchell and P. Deane, *Abstract of British Historical Statistics* (Cambridge, 1962), p. 413.
[46] Post 30/216, E4188/1877, Scudamore to Spearman, 22 January 1869.

interest allowed by the Trustee Banks. Yet, when he pressed on with plans to raise the deposit limits, the banking community of the country rose in opposition. As a group of Leeds bankers pointed out to Lord Hartington the Postmaster General, their industry had no real objections to the government's encouragement of thrift among the lower classes. However, by raising the limits on deposits, the Post Office seemed to be transforming a social policy aimed at the working classes into an outright bid to lure middle-class customers away from their traditional banks. Such a change was an infringement of their prerogatives which could not be tolerated. In April 1869 *The Birmingham Daily News* was equally disturbed by this

> thinly disguised attempt to destroy all the private banking establishments of the country. One certain result of such a measure would be the draining from country banks of vast sums of money now deposited with them; and this enormous aggregate – which is now usefully employed in support of the agricultural, manufacturing, and mining interests in the provinces – would be *permanently* withdrawn by Government.[47]

In some ways the issues raised were similar to those in the original 1861 struggle – public versus private, national versus local. Yet in 1869 the relative strength of the opposing sides had changed. Then it had involved the fairly weak and disorganised Trustee Banks versus the Gladstone–Scudamore coalition. Now Scudamore without much help from his superiors was challenging a much more powerful interest, the larger banking community. The results were also predictably different. In May 1869 the government dropped its effort to alter the Post Office Savings Banks limits.

In 1873 Scudamore tried once again to enhance the competitiveness of the department's banks.[48] Although he was then deeply immersed in the administration of the telegraphs, he had not forgotten the savings banks project. By this point approximately 160 Trustee Banks had closed, and Scudamore thought the moment ripe to make the government's banks even more attractive. Therefore, he proposed to lower the minimum deposit from one shilling to one penny. The Society of Arts had been especially interested in such a change, which would enable children to set up their own savings accounts. He also proposed raising the deposit limits to £50 annually with £500 as a maximum. In order to buttress these suggestions, Scudamore prepared impressive tables to underscore the fact that the Post Office was more

47 Post, *The Birmingham Daily News*, 29 April 1869.
48 Post 30/249, E1139/1874, Scudamore's memorandum, 23 January 1873.

efficient than the Trustee Banks. He also emphasised the fact that the Trustee Banks continued to cost the Exchequer money (over £3 million by 1871), while the departmental system earned a profit. It should be further noted that Scudamore's memorandum outlining these proposals is a typically idiosyncratic blend of attention to the most mundane of details – questions of how sub-postmasters would be paid if the changes went through or considerations of bookkeeping problems arising from carrying pence in several accounts – and deep concern with wider social policy. If the deposit limit were not lowered to a penny, 'We should lose all the persons, young and old, who if they could put a penny into a bank would deposit it and follow it up by other deposits. . . . We should not be giving facilities for frugality to those who need to be most frugal.'[49] Moreover, there were reminders of Scudamore's pronounced dislike of local establishments, controlled by 'the principal employers of labour or the parochial authorities' and statements of his preference for national systems such as the 'Post Office Bank, which is perfectly free from local supervision or observation'.[50] Scudamore's fears of outside interference in such enterprises were by no means unfounded. In 1863 the department had rejected a suggestion that lists of depositors and information on their accounts be furnished to Poor Law Guardians, who could then deny those named relief.[51] Finally, as befitted a civil servant who believed in the virtues of an expanded government which could harmoniously link all social groups together through their use of a common set of public institutions and a writer who allowed his fondness for vivid imagery free rein, Scudamore could picture 'The working classes who migrate from town to town in search of work, commercial travellers, travelling actors, singers, and showmen, tourists, and generally all who are led by business or pleasure to move much from place to place in the United Kingdom, avail[ing] themselves largely of the facilities which the Post Office affords them for, as it were, carrying their bank with them.'[52]

The Times was in favour of Scudamore's proposals, when it argued that the only losers as a result of the change would be publicans.[53] Lyon Playfair the Postmaster General also supported Scudamore's recommendations, although he realised that the banking community would object. Hence, Playfair believed it prudent to wait until the 1874 Report of the Friendly Societies Commission was available before

49 *Ibid.*
50 *Ibid.*
51 Post, Tilley Papers, Tilley to Stanley, 25 March 1863.
52 Post 30/249, E1139/1874, Scudamore's memorandum, 23 January 1873.
53 *The Times*, 2 January 1874, p. 9.

pressing ahead.[54] By this time, unfortunately, the telegraph scandal had broken in the spring of 1873, and as a result Scudamore's effectiveness as an advocate was severely weakened. The matter was once again tabled. It is significant, however, that even after Scudamore's 1875 retirement the department retained his appraisal of the private trustee banks as unworthy competitors. In 1878 C. H. Davey, a clerk at St Martin's le Grand, was authorised to study the condition of the Trustee Banks, not a subject technically under the purview of the Post Office. Davey was decidedly critical in his report. He found insufficient margins to provide for mistakes in a system too dependent on the frequently inadequate abilities of local treasurers. St Martin's le Grand also continued to be angry that the Trustee Banks were allowed to pay a rate of interest too high for what was commonly held to be their 'decaying condition'.[55] After all, depositors in the profitable Post Office system were indirectly subsidizing the depositors in the Trustee Banks.

At times the Treasury was sympathetic to the department's predicament. In 1878 Sir Stafford Northcote the Chancellor of the Exchequer looked forward to 'the gradual absorption of the smaller banks in [to] the Post Office system'.[56] There were fears both in and outside of government that the Post Office Savings Banks might evolve into a general banking system. C. Rivers Wilson of the National Debt Commissioners spoke for the former when he pointed out that 'The Commissioners have reason to believe that even at the present time the Post Office Savings Banks system is largely used by Tradespeople and others, especially for the collection of debts, an evasion of the Spirit if not the letter of the act.'[57] Such frequent use of the system, of course, raised operating costs as well as fears at the Treasury over the system's profitability. The economist W. S. Jevons writing in *The Contemporary Review* espoused the views of the financial community. Jevons pictured the departmental savings banks as a *'deus ex machina . . . called from above to help a thriftless residuum out of the mire of pauperism'.*[58] This was all fine and well. Jevons, who by no means was dogmatically opposed to all suggestions of government expansion into the private economy, nonetheless criticised the new proposals which he described as a 'settled design on the part of the Post Office to become a vast banking corporation'. Given such opposition, it is understandable, then, that legislative attempts to enhance the Post Office system's competitiveness were withdrawn in 1880, 1884, and 1887.

54 Post 30/249, E1139/1874, Playfair to Scudamore, 12 February 1874.
55 Post 30/337, E1878, Davey to A. C. Thomson, 17 October 1878.
56 Post 30/337, E6258/1878, Northcote to Blackwood, 5 June 1878.
57 Post 30/510, E11318/1878, Wilson to Post Office, 29 April 1878.
58 W. S. Jevons, 'Postal Notes, Money Orders, and Bank Cheques', *The Contemporary Review*, 38 (1880), 156.

In the long run, nevertheless, the victory lay with St Martin's le Grand.[59] In 1880 a stamp scheme was instituted by Henry Fawcett the Postmaster General in order to allow individuals with a penny or two available for savings to accumulate stamps in a book until the required one shilling deposit was available. This plan was especially popular among school children, and after the Education Act of 1891, the department began to send clerks to schools to collect deposits. Over 6,000 schools were participating by 1894. In 1888 the interest rate paid by the Trustee Banks was lowered to 2.5 per cent, the same as that paid by the Post Office. (This alteration was made as much to reduce the Trustee Banks deficit as to increase the attractiveness of the government banks.) Finally, the deposit limits were slightly increased. The maximum deposit was raised to £200 in 1891, and the annual deposit limit to £50 in 1893. As table two illustrates, the Post Office system grew rapidly and surpassed the Trustee Savings Banks.

Table 2
The record of deposits in POSBs and Trustee Banks

(£ millions)

Year	Post Office Savings Banks	Trustee Savings Banks ordinary depts.	special investment depts.
1861	——	£41.5	£ 0.2
1865	£ 6.5	38.7	0.3
1870	15.1	38.0	0.3
1875	25.2	42.4	1.1
1880	33.7	44.0	2.0
1885	47.7	46.4	3.3
1890	67.6	43.6	4.4
1895	97.9	45.3	4.7
1900	135.5	51.5	4.5
1905	152.1	52.7	5.6
1910	168.9	52.3	11.0
1915	186.3	51.4	15.4

Source: Mitchell and Deane, *British Historical Statistics*, pp. 453–4.

Moreover, it is significant that the department outstripped the Trustee Banks in 1886 *before* interest rates between the two were equalised.

---

[59] Post, Committee on Savings Banks Funds, 1896, p. 2ff.

Measured in terms of the number of accounts and as a percentage of the total population, the results were similarly successful. (See table three.)

Table 3
The growth of the POSBs

Year	Number of Post Office accounts open at end of year	Number of accounts as percentage of total population
1862	176,569	0.604
1870	1,183,153	3.785
1880	2,184,972	6.311
1890	4,827,314	12.878
1900	8,439,983	20.508
1910*	8,373,789	18.708

* Before 1909, the department did not distinguish between active and dormant accounts. Thus, the figures prior to that date are significantly inflated, perhaps by as much as 20 per cent.

Source: Annual reports of the Postmaster General.

What kinds of people had opened these accounts? In 1865 a survey of 11,000 depositors from all parts of England was taken, and in 1896 another survey conducted over a three-month period revealed a similar pattern. (See tables four and five.)

Table 4
The profile of POSB depositors, 1865

Females, Male Minors, and Trustees	55%
Males of independent means or of no stated occupation, Professional Men, and their Clerks or Assistants	6%
Tradesmen and their male Assistants, Farmers, and Clerks of all kinds except Clerks to Professional Men and Clerks in General Offices	10%
Mechanics and Artisans, Domestic Servants, Farm Servants, Railway Servants, Policemen, Labourers, Pensioners, Fishermen and Merchant Seamen	27%
Persons employed in Revenue Departments or by the Army or the Navy	1%
Males engaged in Education	1%

Table 5
The profile of POSB depositors, 1896

Professional	1.55%
Official	2.81%
Educational	1.01%
Commercial	3.88%
Agricultural and fishing	1.83%
Industrial	18.43%
Railway, shipping, and transport	2.96%
Tradesmen and their assistants	8.14%
Domestic service	8.61%
Miscellaneous	0.37%
Persons describing themselves as married women, spinsters, widows, and children	50.41%

(The department estimated that women and children represented 61 per cent of the entire 1896 sample.)

Source for tables four and five: Annual reports of the Postmaster General.

Given the relatively imprecise categories used in these surveys, the significance of the above percentages is open to debate. As Johnson has correctly pointed out, the predominance of women and children as depositors, the presence of white-collar depositors – almost 10 per cent in each table – and the relatively large size of the average account – £20 2s 7d in 1910 – reinforce the hypothesis that the Post Office Savings Banks were not reaching the 'poorest ranks of the working class'.[60] Still three other points need to be kept in mind. First, the system was attractive to large segments of the upper lower class, as demonstrated by the fact that at least 40 per cent of the depositors in each table came from this background. Secondly, the fact that the system appealed to middle-class depositors may be explained by noting its efficiency and ubiquity and by remembering that at certain times, as in the mid-1890s, the rate of interest offered by the Post Office banks was quite competitive with that offered by other institutions. The system is by no means the only instance of a government programme ostensibly established for the good of one class or group, which came to be used by other classes. Thirdly, the efforts of Scudamore and other department managers to widen the appeal of the banks demonstrate that they at least never narrowly defined its potential clientele. While

[60] Paul Johnson, 'Credit and Thrift and the British Working Class, 1870–1939' in Jay Winter (ed.), *The Working Class in Modern British History* (Cambridge, 1983), p. 167.

earlier advocates of a government savings bank were concerned, in the words of Samuel Whitbread, with a system for 'the use and advantage of the labouring classes alone', St Martin's le Grand sought, as the 1897 *Report of the Postmaster General* put it, to make its banks 'familiar and acceptable to all classes of the people'.[61]

Apart from the question of the obvious public support of the savings banks among the upper working and middle classes, how well did the Post Office internally administer the programme? By several standards it was efficiently managed. When Scudamore first studied the idea of departmental savings banks, he predicted that the Post Office could handle each transaction at a lower cost of 7d as opposed to the 1s or more average in the Trustee Banks. As table six shows, with the exception of the period around 1880, Scudamore for once erred on the side of caution:

Table 6
Management costs of the POSBs

Year	Average cost per transaction in pence
1862	5.57
1870	5.58
1880	8.68
1890	6.71
1900	5.74
1910	4.87

Source: *Report of the Postmaster General on the Post Office* (London, 1913), p. 71.

Another measure of the system's success lay in the fact that after expenses and interest were paid there remained a small annual surplus until a deficit appeared in 1896 as the result of a fall in the yield of the government securities in which the deposits were invested. (See table seven.)

[61] *Forty Third Report of the Postmaster General* (London, 1897), pp. 32–3.

Table 7
The financial record of the POSBs

	Total investment income	Interest credited to depositors	Administrative costs	Surplus+ or deficit−
1876	£ 908,441	619,331	156,184	+ 132,926
1880	1,119,381	777,985	188,891	+ 152,505
1885	1,416,523	1,092,112	256,402	+ 68,009
1890	1,948,867	1,553,355	326,394	+ 69,118
1896	2,884,110	2,460,645	429,627	− 6,162
1900	3,644,019	3,145,978	487,025	+ 11,016

Source: BPP, 1902, vol. 7, Select Committee on Savings Banks Funds, p. 197.

Indeed, so competitive had the rate of interest paid by the department become that the net inflow of funds increased from £2.3 million in 1891 to £7.7 million by 1896. Whitehall was alarmed by the prospect of annual losses, and Sir Edward Hamilton at the Treasury proposed a reduction in interest rates as the solution to the problem. Writing to Walpole of the Post Office, Hamilton accurately outlined the opposing views of the two departments: 'You want to extend your business; we wish to see it curtailed, as it is becoming unmanageable.'[62] In this case the Post Office emphasis on the social benefits of the programme and wider political considerations overrode fiscal concerns. As *The Sheffield Independent* put it, 'To tamper with it at its present stage might make it more profitable for the moment, but the ultimate results would be not only financially, but morally injurious.'[63] The interest rate was not lowered, and by 1911 after a period of deficits the system once again began to yield a surplus.

Clearly the Post Office was well suited to run what became the largest banking system in the country. There were over 14,000 branches by the turn of the century. The operation did not demand special technical or engineering expertise, as did the telegraphs and the telephone. Rather the experience of managing the bookkeeping procedure of the Money Order Office served the department well enough. The savings banks also did not demand a heavy investment in plant and equipment. As the business grew, more clerks were simply hired to tally the figures and verify the accounts. Further, the programme did not necessitate the purchase or nationalisation of a private industry. The Trustee Banks were allowed to coexist with the competing departmental system. Moreover, the department was energetic in explaining the

[62] Post 30/704, E16988/1895, Hamilton to Walpole, 25 March 1896.
[63] Post 16/36, *Sheffield Independent*, 4 January 1897.

system to the public. Over 1,250,000 copies of Fawcett's *Aids to Thrift* were distributed free of charge, and leaflets explaining the system were translated into Welsh. Earlier assessments of the system have tended to minimise the significance of the Post Office Savings Banks. W. L. Burn concluded that the act was 'not a real exception to the rule that the State rarely took the initiative in encouraging the habits by which it set so much store', and Barry Supple has described the programme as by no means 'minatory or positively interventionist'.[64] While these judgements perhaps apply to the original legislation of 1861 and the attitudes of politicians such as Gladstone, they do not fully take into account the vigorous manner in which the system was expanded and administered by men such as Scudamore and Fawcett. Such assessments equally fail to deal with the sense of pride and triumph felt within the walls of St Martin's le Grand when a Trustee Bank closed as a result of Post Office competition, as did the Birmingham Savings Bank with capital assets of almost £600,000 in 1863. Especially for someone like Scudamore, who more than anyone else determined the direction of the department's policy, the Post Office Savings Banks were founded on a radically different ideological basis than that of the old Trustee Banks – one which was national, public, perhaps more bureaucratic, but at same time one which was also less class bound. As with so many other aspects of government growth, the actual historical importance of the idea of government encouragement of thrift only developed a mature form in the process of implementation in the decades after 1861. Clearly the Post Office banks did not remove every pretext for improvidence, as Scudamore had originally dreamed. Yet they remain an example of a most successful case of government expansion into an area previously served primarily by local, private paternalism. After all, if only 40 per cent of the depositors in 1914 came from the upper lower class, over 3.7 million such individuals had been drawn into the state system. As one deeply aware of the problems of the working classes had earlier observed,

I have been asked by several MPs and others what I thought of Post Office Savings Banks. I have answered them, that I know no measure of late years affecting the condition of the working and the lower middle classes which appeared to me so excellent in principle. I am disposed to say, as Sir Robert Peel said with reference to the Encumbered Estates Act, that it is 'so thoroughly a good measure, he wondered how it ever passed'.[65]

[64] W. L. Burn, *The Age of Equipoise* (New York, 1965), p. 152; Barry Supple, 'Legislation and Virtue' in Neil McKendrick (ed.), *Historical Perspectives* (London, 1974), p. 252.
[65] Lewins, p. 346. Chadwick, of course, had long been interested in savings

The speaker was Edwin Chadwick.

In contrast to the Savings Banks, another departmental attempt to encourage working-class thrift proved an abysmal failure. Indeed, the history of the Post Office Life Insurance and Annuity Programme demonstrates that two ideas with a common origin can take very divergent paths. Like the proposals for savings banks, the idea of government insurance had long been in existence. In 1807, for example, Whitbread advanced a scheme whereby the poor could insure their lives with the government. This plan was approved in 1834 when the National Debt Commissioners were authorised to sell government life insurance policies for sums not exceeding £100. However, little use was made of the programme because, as a prerequisite to taking out a policy, the insured also had to take out a deferred annuity. By the 1860s there were only 6,500 annuities in force. By that stage the programme had reached a stage familiar to administrative historians, namely the point at which additional legislation is required to remedy weaknesses in an original plan and its operation. What is striking about this case is that the demand for reform did not come from an outside pressure group or even an individual humanitarian, such as Sikes, but rather from within the bureaucracy of St Martin's le Grand. In an 1861 report to Lord Stanley, Scudamore and Chetwynd argued that the department should seize the opportunity provided by the establishment of Savings Banks to expand into a related field, the sale of annuities and life insurance. The thrust of their thinking emphasised the public character of the Post Office and the potential of its national network in the encouragement of thrift. If

> the Post Office Banks were to become agencies for the purchase and payment of government annuities, there would be a considerable increase in the number of annuities purchased. The Post Office could not undertake the duty without making that undertaking public, and in so doing, it would of necessity inform a larger number of people than are now acquainted with the circumstances, that they might, for a fair price, purchase annuities, secured by the government, exempt from income tax, and payable to the doors of the annuitants.[66]

The two were particularly concerned that an alternative should be offered to 'bubble insurance companies' which often collapsed, with disastrous consequences. These fears were compounded when several

institutions as bulwarks of society. See his 'Life Assurances', *Westminster Review*, 9 (1828), 408.
[66] Post, Scudamore and Chetwynd's Report upon the Progress of the Post Office Savings Banks, 1861.

failures occurred in the autumn of 1863 to which *The Times* and *The Daily Telegraph* devoted leading articles. Hence, once again, it was being proposed that the state take a more active role in the promotion of self-help. Annuities sold by the department would serve as pensions in old age, and life insurance would ease the burden of death on the relatives of the insured.

Gladstone, who had come to consider Scudamore an 'indefatigable and most able public servant',[67] was receptive to the suggestion. (After all, as Chancellor of the Exchequer, he had in 1853 lowered the tax duty on life insurance in order to increase its attractiveness.[68]) In February 1864 a bill to sell government life insurance and annuities through the Post Office was introduced in the House of Commons. As in the case of the Savings Banks legislation, the subsequent discussion offered Scudamore the opportunity to present his ideas and his abilities to Gladstone in the best possible light. Over the course of the next three months Gladstone read Scudamore's pamphlet on life insurance, met with him on at least seven occasions, and wrote to him five times.[69] What differentiated the life insurance discussion from the earlier consideration of government encouragement of thrift was that the tone of debate over the question was much more acrimonious and the amount of Parliamentary time consumed by speeches much longer. In part this was the result of the fact that the government had more difficulty marshalling statistical information on the condition of Friendly Societies and private insurance companies than it had experienced with the Trustee Banks. The difference is further explained by the technical nature of life insurance and annuities which perplexed many MPs. There was also a personal aspect to the 1864 opposition. During the course of heated argument Gladstone virtually accused the Liberal MP H. B. Sheridan of fraud in his dealings with the British Provident Association. Not surprisingly Sheridan emerged as one of the leading critics of the bill.[70] But the main circumstance involved was that the bill seemed to threaten much more powerful adversaries, the Friendly Societies and the private insurance companies, than the Savings Banks proposal had challenged. The opposition was able to rally support outside Parliament in the form of petitions, meetings at Exeter Hall, and letters to the press. For example, one writer in *The Times* argued 'if Mr Gladstone must go into business, he had better take an easy business first, and have Government ginshops at one corner of the street, and Government tobacco-shops at the other, and leave the

67 *Hansard's, Third Series*, vol. 173, 1558, 7 March 1864.
68 Morley, vol. 1, 462.
69 See H. C. G. Matthew (ed.), *The Gladstone Diaries*, vol. 6 (Oxford, 1978) for references to these contacts.
70 *Hansard's, Third Series*, vol. 173, 1574, 7 March 1864.

delicate matters of assurance for the present'.[71] Inside the House of Commons a dissenting voice was again that of A. S. Ayrton, accurately described as 'a fairly able and very pertinacious man with a limited outlook and small mind'.[72] Ayrton had opposed the Savings Banks, and now the insurance bill provoked his wrath. Carrying the banner of local control, Ayrton proposed that 'The Government would pursue a much better plan if they were to encourage the establishment of associations among the people themselves; for it was through the exercise of local administration that a nation became most fitted for the enjoyment of political rights.'[73] Ayrton evoked the spectre of a gigantic bureaucracy creeping across the land and prying into the private affairs of every citizen. J. A. Roebuck further predicted that, if government continued to take on such tasks, the people would become 'a set of helpless imbeciles, totally incapable of attending to their own interests'.[74]

In order to counter such rhetoric, supporters of the bill adopted three basic strategies. The first was to emphasise that, given the fact that approximately one hundred companies and Friendly Societies failed each year, the proposal met a definite need. (The plan was shown to be financially and actuarially sound since the government proposed to be much stricter in accepting applications for life insurance than private companies were.) The second approach was to stress that, although private institutions were usually superior to public agencies, a doctrinaire adherence to this position was unwise. In support of this argument in a speech which was his second longest of the 1864 session, Gladstone offered an intriguing line of thought which posited a hierarchy of degrees of state intervention. The highest form was a positive order requiring something to be done, such as the provision of sanitary facilities. A lesser form was a simple prohibition of a certain activity, such as child labour. The proposed bill fell into the mildest category of state intervention. As he explained, 'you enjoin nothing and you prohibit nothing, but you offer to such numbers of the community as may be disposed to avail themselves of your proposal certain facilities for what I may call self-help'.[75] Thirdly, Gladstone went on to point out that the cries of interference from the opposing forces were ill-founded because government was currently subsidizing the Friendly Societies by grants from the National Debt Office. As in the case of the Savings Banks, the government was already involved in the promotion of a certain social policy. Thus, the bill did not represent an innovative

71 *The Times*, 18 February 1864, p. 7.
72 Burn, p. 119.
73 *Hansard's, Third Series*, vol. 174, 797, 11 April 1864.
74 *Ibid.*, vol. 173, 1595, 7 March 1864.
75 *Ibid.*, 1553ff.

attempt to interfere with sacrosanct 'private trade and private enter-prise'. That line had already been crossed.[76]

It is questionable to what extent these arguments would have won over opponents if the government had not decided to reduce signifi-cantly the scope of its proposal. Gladstone originally had favoured selling life insurance in amounts ranging from £5 to £200.[77] However, the Friendly Societies had protested that such a minimum amount would compete with their burial policies, while the upper limit seemed to infringe upon the preserve of life insurance companies which sol-icited business from the middle class. In the late spring of 1864 the government bowed to this pressure and altered the limits to £20 and £100, excluding a huge range of potential customers. Annuities rang-ing from £4 to £50 were also to be sold. Thus, the legislation as it emerged represented a compromise, which fell far short of the original hopes of its departmental backers, Scudamore and Chetwynd.

After the bill received the Royal Assent on 14 July 1864, Scuda-more was put in charge of the programme, and he displayed his usual energy as he took up the task.[78] In April 1865 he wrote to other government departments and railway companies in an effort to stimu-late business. The next year he pressed for extension of the scheme to the major cities of Scotland and Ireland. In pursuing such a policy it is notable how far Scudamore diverged from the hackneyed image of the timid government clerk. He was completely confident that the Post Office was more efficient than many private organisations, and he had no compunction in stating publicly that he would welcome the failure of one or two Friendly Societies, as his departmental system would only gain more customers as a result. He suggested employing a team of government-sponsored lecturers who would stump the country extoll-ing the merits of Post Office Life Insurance. As a means to expedite the payment of premiums, he proposed allowing postmen to collect the sums as they made their daily rounds. In effect, Scudamore was, of course, seeking means by which the rather restrictive provisions of the original bill might be circumvented. The precision which characterised Scudamore's approach to such questions of departmental expansion was remarkably sharp, and it belies any images of bureaucrats blunde-ring forward in an *ad hoc* manner without first considering broader issues. On the one hand, he believed that health insurance should not be provided by the central government. He reasoned that the state simply lacked the means to verify whether the insured was actually ill.

---

[76] *Ibid.*, 1555–6.
[77] BPP, 1873, vol. 22, Friendly Society Committee, pp. 156–7.
[78] For the following see *ibid.* and Post 30/470, E1788/1885, Scudamore to Stanley, 10 August 1865 and memorandum of 21 March 1866.

Thus, any system of health insurance should be managed on a local level. On the other hand, life insurance was unquestionably suitable for a national operation. In his view of the economic order,

> I think the government has a peculiar right to get the insurance business, for this reason, that insurance business deals with the remote future; and although the future of no Government is absolutely secure, the future of this Government is a great deal more secure than that of any private institution, for something which is to occur at a remote period of time.[79]

The use of the word 'right' is especially revealing for the light it throws on his strategy on questions of social policy. For Scudamore this 'right' was not established by any prescription or custom passed down from time immemorial. Instead logic should weigh the utility of any programme. In this instance the security enjoyed by government would lead any rational man to buy Post Office insurance rather than that sold by a necessarily more unstable private company.

Unfortunately, Scudamore and the ideology he espoused came up against a world which was influenced by more than rigorous logic. The Post Office Life Insurance and Annuity programme never fulfilled his hopes, as table eight demonstrates.

Table 8
Post Office insurance contracts

Year	Number of insurance contracts granted	Amount insured
1865	547	£40,649
1870	385	31,254
1875	370	32,022
1880	258	20,378
1885	457	34,768
1890	468	25,466
1895	720	38,358
1900	617	35,511
1904	517	28,629
1911	426	20,039
1915	389	25,808
1920	242	16,115

Source: Post 30/1200, E14099/1909; Post 30/2512, E11588/1924.

[79] BPP, 1873, vol. 22, Friendly Society Committee, p. 159.

The sale of annuities was equally low. Between 1865 and 1884 immediate annuities numbered 13,897, while deferred annuities totalled 1,043. Comparison with the millions of savings banks accounts opened during the same period only compounded the magnitude of the failure. Moreover, the annuity business usually ran at a small annual deficit.[80] In part this dismal record may be attributed to the fact that from the autumn of 1865 on Scudamore, the driving force behind the programme, was deeply immersed in the question of the nationalisation of the telegraphs and, thus, was not able to give his full attention to life insurance and annuities. However, there were also serious structural flaws. An 1882 Select Committee cited four basic weaknesses in the programme as explanations for the unattractiveness of Post Office life insurance among the artisan classes.[81] In contrast to the large number of savings banks, only 2,000 offices conducted life insurance business. Taking out a policy was also a much more complicated procedure than opening a savings account, and the formalities involved often dissuaded potential customers. Of course, the fact that the department did not resort to personal solicitations by 'touting Agents' as Gladstone once described them was a definite handicap, because private insurance companies relied upon such canvassers to get business. The minimum and maximum limits on policy size, a problem Scudamore had noted years earlier, were also criticised. Not mentioned by the committee, but nonetheless a difficulty of fundamental importance was the absence in the Post Office system of what has been called mutuality.[82] Whereas the public, somewhat anonymous character of the Savings Banks contributed to their success, the sale of insurance was a very different matter. Here the Post Office had nothing to offer which compared with the warm sense of camaraderie sought and enjoyed by the working classes in their Friendly Societies. As one MP had stated when the programme was originally debated, 'I do not believe that those classes enter into Friendly Societies or clubs for the sake of the benefits of such societies so much as companionship.'[83]

In a rather feeble attempt to improve the situation, the Government Annuities Act of 1882 authorised the merging of the postal life insurance operation with the Savings Banks Department.[84] This money-saving idea had originally been suggested by J. J. Cardin, a depart-

80 Post 30/756, E18609/1896 and Post 30/470, E909/1885, Treasury minute, 18 December 1880.
81 BPP, 1882, vol. 12, Select Committee on Annuities and Life Insurance, iv–vii.
82 Daunton, Royal Mail, pp. 105, 109.
83 Hansard's, Third Series, vol. 174, 238, 17 March 1864.
84 Post 30/1700, E14099/1909, Report of the Departmental Committee Appointed to Consider the Question of Encouraging the Life Insurance System of the Post Office (Farrer Committee), pp. 1–2.

mental bookkeeper. Moreover, limits for life insurance policies were lowered to £5, while annuities between £1 and £100 could now be purchased. These changes did not dramatically reverse the pattern of slow growth. In 1885, one year after the arrangement took effect, only 457 contracts were issued as opposed to 348 in 1884. Even a reduction of the rates in 1896 did not improve the programme's attractiveness. Thereafter, the Post Office entered into almost ritualistic examinations of the reasons for the continuing failure of the programme. In 1907 a committee headed by Lord Farrer took up this task, and in 1922 Sir Alfred Watson the Government Actuary led another inquiry. The Watson Committee's report was especially damning. It found, among other problems, rates for whole life insurance which were based on outdated mortality tables and, hence, were substantially more expensive that those charged by private companies. The report, in reference to the fact that the Post Office required the insured to pay all premiums before the age of 60 whereas private companies usually lowered the annual cost by spreading the payments throughout the entirety of the insured's life, further noted a somewhat priggish departmental desire to provide 'what is thought to be more suitable to the public needs' instead of 'what the public requires'.[85] This had contributed to the fact that less than 12,000 Post Office insurance policies were in force in 1922 in comparison to over 2 million endowment policies on the books of the industrial assurance companies. At the other end of the market the department's programme was overwhelmed by the large number of policies, over 25 million in 1907, sold by commercial insurance firms to cover the cost of funerals.[86]

Given the fact that the weaknesses in the Post Office programme were apparent to all observers, why were more drastic remedies not applied? Apart from the obviously effective opposition from private companies and Friendly Societies, real doubt had developed inside government as to the wisdom of Post Office involvement with life insurance. Such misgivings manifested themselves in Treasury resistance to the idea of paid canvassers, which appeared unseemly to some senior civil servants. In 1894 the Treasury adamantly rejected a request from St Martin's le Grand to establish such a system of paid agents. The Treasury preferred to offer the service to the public on a take-it-or-leave-it basis. Such was the attitude of Sir George Murray, who had served as Secretary to the Post Office before becoming Permanent Secretary to the Treasury. When the state engaged in competition with private enterprise, in Murray's words, 'it should confine itself to making

---

[85] Post 30/2512, E11588/1924, Report of the Departmental Committee on the Post Office System of Life Insurance (Watson Committee), p. 3.
[86] Ibid. See also Daunton, Royal Mail, p. 109.

the fact known, and then should sit back and wait for people to avail themselves of the facilities offered'.[87] Others at St Martin's le Grand were equally uninterested in nurturing the growth of the system. H. B. Smith the Post Office Secretary from 1903 to 1910 adopted essentially the same attitude as had Murray toward canvassing when he wrote:

> It is unsatisfactory and expensive to have a branch of business which gives a good deal of trouble and does very little good. On the other hand there are obvious objections to a Government Department competing by means of commissions with Companies which meet the public need for industrial insurance and cover the ground pretty completely. I, therefore, should not advise any extension of the commission system unless from the financial point of view it is thought desirable to encourage the deposit of savings in the hands of the Government in this particularly permanent form.[88]

As will also be seen in the case of the telephone, administrators in St Martin's le Grand as well as Whitehall had come to believe that government should take up new programmes only if it safely enjoyed a monopoly in that particular area. Outright competition between government and private enterprise was much too uncertain. Given such attitudes, it is not surprising that extensive advertising for Post Office life insurance was rejected on grounds of expense and of 'the need to avoid provoking the opposition of the powerful interested companies and societies'.[89] In the period following the First World War St Martin's le Grand sought to extricate itself from what it more and more viewed as a regrettable Victorian mistake. Hence, the 1922 Watson Committee was specifically prohibited by the terms of reference established by the Postmaster General from even considering new methods of canvassing and collecting premiums. Not surprisingly the sale of life insurance was discontinued in 1929.[90] In the end, the history of the life insurance programme demonstrates that not all examples of bureaucratic innovation grow indefinitely in almost a self-perpetuating manner.

Much has been written about a supposed failure of entrepreneurial spirit in Britain before 1914 as a factor in her relative economic decline

---

87 Post 30/1699, E14099/1909, Murray to H. B. Smith, 13 May 1905.
88 Ibid., Smith to Murray, 6 May 1905.
89 Post 30/1700, E14099/1909, Jay to E. Murray, 5 May 1920.
90 Post 33/2514, M39/1929, E. Murray to Postmaster General, 20 February 1926. When the scheme closed, there were 9,956 contracts in force, insuring £494,536. At the same time there were over 73 million contracts insuring over £1.1 billion on the books of the industrial life companies. Johnson, *Saving and Spending*, pp. 35–6.

in comparison to Germany and the United States.[91] The debate over this wider question continues to rage among historians as well as social commentators. In what ways does a consideration of the failure of this Post Office programme, a government programme not normally linked to business history, contribute to the controversy? Without question, administrators such as Murray and Smith – given the strength of the competition, the existence of alternative systems such as old age pensions after 1908, and their own conceptions of orthodox political economy – were making 'rational' decisions in their refusal to push the sale of life insurance and annuities. As such they cannot be faulted. However, it is equally true that these same 'rational' decisions were not made by administrators operating from a position of strength. At St Martin's le Grand there was a marked decline in self-confidence and in eagerness to grow and take on new programmes by the end of the nineteenth century. (Indeed, one of the purposes of the rest of this book is to explain why such a decline occurred.) The proper role of the Post Office in the larger society as defined by Scudamore or Chetwynd was regarded as unacceptably grandiose by many of their successors. Victorian zealots had given way to Edwardian civil servants, who were much less committed to departmental expansion. It was these men who were content to watch programmes such as Post Office life insurance wither on the vine.[92]

---

[91] See these recent surveys of the controversy: L. G. Sandberg, 'The Entrepreneur and Technological Change' in R. Floud and D. McCloskey (eds.), *The Economic History of Britain since 1700*, vol. 2 (Cambridge, 1981); and D. Coleman and C. MacLeod, 'Attitudes to New Techniques: British Businessmen, 1800–1950', *Economic History Review*, second series 39 (1986), 588–611. The work of Martin J. Wiener, *English Culture and the Decline of the Industrial Spirit* (Cambridge, 1981) bears directly on this controversy and vice versa. For an article which raises the debate to a higher level of sophistication, see M. J. Daunton, ' "Gentlemanly Capitalism" and British Industry', *Past and Present*, 122 (1989), 119–58.

[92] Lazonick has made use of Schumpeter's distinction between managers and entrepreneurs. The former tend to work within the constraints of a situation. The latter seek to transform those same constraints. Without pushing the analogy too far, it might be argued that Murray and Smith were successful enough managers, while Scudamore in his handling of life insurance was an entrepreneur who failed. See William Lazonick, 'Competition, Specialisation, and Industrial Decline', *The Journal of Economic History*, 41 (1981), 37–8.

4

The Nationalisation of the Telegraphs

There are some ways in which the fifty years of Victoria cannot be
said to mark an unquestioned advance over some other half centuries. What they have been signalled by is an unprecedented
command over natural forces; steam and the telegraph are the
most conspicuous examples of this. – *The Times*, 28 July 1887, p. 9.

Beyond government regulation of industries and injunctions to local
authorities lay the most intrusive form of state expansion into the
private economy, nationalisation. During the course of the nineteenth
century reformers proposed land, coal mines, and railways as ideal
candidates for government take-over. However, when all was said and
done, the Victorians, as Professor Perkin has correctly reminded us,
preferred to talk of nationalisation rather than actually attempting it.[1]
There were two major exceptions to this proclivity, both of which
involved the Post Office. The first was the acquisition of the inland
telegraphs, 1868–70. Unfortunately the history of this purchase has not
been properly linked to the larger question of government growth in
the nineteenth century. Indeed, the only modern study of the telegraph
industry tended to treat its history and the roles of the important
individuals behind the take-over in isolation, thereby missing the opportunity to establish connections to wider, more significant issues.[2]
This is not the way many Victorians regarded the nationalisation of the
telegraphs by St Martin's le Grand. As *The Economist* pointed out in
1868, a consideration of the debate over this proposed extension of
government power would provide a clue

how far the current opinion on the subject of State 'interference
with private enterprise' has really ebbed during the last few years.

1 Harold Perkin, 'Individualism versus Collectivism in Nineteenth Century
Britain: a False Antithesis', *The Journal of British Studies*, 17 (1977), 116.
2 J. L. Kieve, *Electric Telegraph* (Newton Abbot, 1973). Kieve, for example, does
not cite the voluminous literature on the debate over the nineteenth-century
revolution in government. In fairness it should also be stated that Kieve's work
presents a solid analysis of many of the economic aspects of the subject.

Twelve or fourteen years ago, it would have been useless for any Chancellor of the Exchequer to prepare such an operation.[3]

In order to explain why the telegraphs, unlike other industries, fell victim to government expansion, some account of their early history is required. The technological and economic development of the telegraphs paralleled the expansion of the railways in the first three decades of Victoria's reign. From the very beginning there was a close relationship between the two industries. As early as 1836, for example, William Fothergill Cooke pointed out the potential of the telegraph for signalling and other safety measures along railway track.[4] He was commissioned by the Great Western Railway in 1838 and by the Blackwall Railway in 1840 to construct telegraph lines for this purpose. These successful experiments, along with the use of the telegraph in the 1845 capture of the criminal John Tawell, led to an enlarged interest in the value of the instrument for commercial and social purposes. The first fruit of this activity was the Electric Telegraph Company, which was provisionally registered in 1845. The Electric, as it came to be known, developed its lines principally along railway wayleaves. It remained the largest of the telegraph companies, and its first directors included John Lewis Ricardo, MP for Stoke and a leader in the free trade agitation of the 1840s, Samson Ricardo, the famous economist's brother, and Cooke.

For the next twenty years the telegraph industry developed solely through the initiative of private joint-stock companies. By the 1860s there were five principal firms in the United Kingdom. The Electric and International Company, formed in 1855 by a merger of the Electric and the International, dominated England and Scotland. The British and Irish Magnetic Telegraph Company, also formed by a merger in 1858, was the leader in Ireland. Until 1861 the rates charged by these two companies were based on the distance a message was sent in addition to the number of words it contained. Organised in 1860, the District Company sought to reap the profits of the lucrative London market through a cheaper tariff of 4d for 10 words or 6d for 15 words for messages delivered within a small radius. The United Kingdom

---

[3] *The Economist*, 11 April 1868, p. 412. Part of the explanation of the lack of interest in Victorian ventures into nationalisation arises from the tendency of some historians to link nationalisation with Labour party history and, therefore, to dismiss those cases of government expansion which are not part of that tradition. Thus, for Morgan 'The real history – as opposed to the prehistory – of public ownership began in 1931': Kenneth O. Morgan, 'The Rise and Fall of Public Ownership in Britain' in J. M. W. Bean (ed.), *The Political Culture of Modern Britain: Studies in Memory of Stephen Koss* (London, 1987), p. 279.
[4] For the following, see the account in Kieve, chapters 2–3.

Telegraph Company, which began operations in 1860, represented an effort to break the hold of the Electric and the Magnetic on the trade of the nation. The company was organised by Thomas Allan, who hoped to win business by means of a uniform tariff of 1s per 20 words regardless of the distance which the telegram was sent. The fifth major company was the Universal Private Telegraph Company, incorporated in 1861. This firm used the Wheatstone's universal or ABC telegraph, which as it did not require a code could be worked by any literate person. The Universal constructed and maintained wires between places of business and homes. In addition to these five major firms, certain railway companies also operated telegraphs for public as well as their own use, as is shown in table one.

Table 1
The structure of the telegraph industry on the eve of nationalisation

Telegraph companies	Miles of line	Miles of wire	Total messages inland and abroad
Electric	10,007	50,065	3,676,666
Magnetic	4,696	19,235	1,743,725
UKTC	1,692	10,001	807,155
District	345	345	183,304
UPTC	139	400	27,542
	16,879	80,046	6,438,392

Railway companies

Lancashire and Yorkshire	432		Figures not available
South Eastern	351	Figures	123,283
London, Brighton and South Coast	284	not	86,937
London, Chatham, and Dover	140	available	83,410
Other railways	3,664		Figures not available
Total	4,871	11,022	360,924
Grand total	21,750	91,068	6,799,316

Stations open to public

Telegraph companies		2,155
Railway companies		
England and		
Wales	904	
Scotland	270	
Ireland	52	1,226
Total		3,381

Source: BPP, 1867–8, vol. 41, Returns of the Names of All Railway Companies and Kieve, pp. 73 ff.

Assessing the history of the first two decades of the industry, Kieve has concluded that 'in spite of the risks involved and the very real cost of being the pioneers, private enterprise had by 1868 developed a system of communication within the British Isles which brought every town of any importance in contact with any other part of the country and with all parts of the world'.[5]

Yet even while 'private enterprise' was developing the system, tracts both criticising the service offered by the companies and emphasising the benefits of nationalisation began to circulate. In 1854 in the *Quarterly Review* Andrew Wynter, a physician who had devoted much attention to the treatment of the insane, bemoaned the dominance of the Electric over its competitors and vaguely broached the idea of government intervention.[6] That same year the first detailed plan for the nationalisation of the telegraph industry by the Post Office was brought forward. Its author was Thomas Allan, the inventor and electrical engineer who had been working for four years to establish the UKTC. He was particularly struck by the economies of scale which would result if the telegraphs were centralised under the Post Office. These savings would further allow the charging of a standard rate of 1s per 20 words regardless of distance, the rate later tried by the UKTC. Adopting the same line of reasoning which Rowland Hill had earlier espoused, Allan argued that telegraph traffic would expand in a geometric progression as a result of lower rates.

> It may be assumed that a general and more extended use of the electric telegraph will follow the same general laws as the working of the penny post and cheap literature, and, from the wonderful development of these principles in the instance of the penny postage, the

5 *Ibid.*, p. 100.
6 Andrew Wynter, 'The Electric Telegraph', *Quarterly Review*, 95 (June, 1854), 150–1.

hypothesis became reduced to an anticipated fact. . . . Hitherto, in this country, there has been no fixed principle adopted in telegraphing, arising from the want of system and experience, in the first instance, great costs in the construction of works, and fragmentary or isolated arrangements; yet wherever a reduction of charge has been made, a marvelously corresponding increase in quantity [of telegrams] has been the result.[7]

A certain degree of self-interest, however, was also present in the proposal as Allan hoped that the Post Office would use his new invention in its system.

As in the case of the savings banks, there were also those within St Martin's le Grand who were eager to move into new fields. In 1856 such a scheme was put forward by F. E. Baines, a clerk in the Home Mails Branch, who had previously worked for the Electric. Baines's ideas, which were forwarded to the Treasury for consideration, did not differ radically from Allan's. The Post Office would nationalise the private companies and operate a unified system on the basis of a tariff which did not vary with the distance the message travelled. Baines proposed a rate of 6d per 20 words or half as expensive as Allan's. Where Baines advanced over Allan was in his clear analysis of the financial condition of the telegraph industry, its capital and rate structure, and the path which the Post Office should follow in expanding the telegraph network. Moreover, it is significant that in this case of government growth as with so many others civil servants such as Baines were committed to an imprecise, if nonetheless real, belief that the goal of government was social betterment. He was particularly troubled by the high rates charged by the private companies which were 'sufficient to place the telegraph within the reach of only the more opulent classes, whereas it is of the highest importance that the facilities afforded by its use should be readily available to all classes'.[8] The thrust of the argument is especially striking, if one remembers that only two decades earlier communication by letter had been regarded by many as a luxury appropriate for only the wealthy. Baines, however, felt that the almost instantaneous speed of the telegraph was an essential service which should be offered to all. If private initiative did not provide this, the next recourse was the state. The fact that Baines anticipated that the Post Office would make a profit of at least £50,000 per year from the telegraphs, of course, served to strengthen his argu-

---

7 BPP, 1867–8, vol. 41, Thomas Allan's Reasons for the Government Annexing an Electric Telegraph System to the General Post Office, p. 40.
8 *Ibid.*, p. 42, F. E. Baines to Treasury, 1 March 1856.

ment, as he realised that this aspect would be of vital concern to the Treasury. He felt that the Post Office, functioning in the best of all economic worlds, could provide an important social service as well as fulfil its role as a revenue department.

Criticism of the telegraph companies continued to rise. The next important broadside was issued in 1861 by J. L. Ricardo and William Burchell, who had also promoted the original Electric Telegraph Company as well as the Croydon and Metropolitan Railways. Ricardo and Burchell submitted a memorandum advocating nationalisation to Gladstone, then Chancellor of the Exchequer in Palmerston's second cabinet. By this point these two advocates had severed their connection with the industry, although Scudamore later claimed that the memorandum had actually been composed earlier in 1858 when Ricardo was still Chairman of the Electric.[9] In any case, it should be noted how far they went in criticising the 'individual and irresponsible hands' which directed the private companies and in claiming that government acquisition could remedy the existing evils. After all, in a nationalised system public-minded statesmen, not managers chosen by profit-minded shareholders, would direct the telegraphs.[10] The memorandum also cited the examples of continental countries where state-owned telegraph systems had helped to increase the invention's commercial, military, and diplomatic usefulness. (Clearly Englishmen long before Lord Beveridge were looking across the Channel in search of ideas regarding the improved operation of an expanding government bureaucracy.[11]) As with Baines's analysis, Ricardo and Burchell stated that the Post Office could turn a profit on the telegraphs. The probable purchase cost of the private companies was estimated to be £2 million. If this amount were raised at 3.25 per cent, the anticipated annual profit of £60,000 per year would adequately cover the sum necessary to establish a sinking fund.

Ricardo's strong support for nationalisation is of further interest in light of the fact that he had been active in the campaigns for the repeal of the Corn Laws and the Navigation Acts. Kieve found it 'difficult to account' for this apparent disavowal of free trade on the part of Ricardo, and in an effort to explain this apparent contradiction he relied on Clapham's contention that Ricardo was fearful of growing

9   BPP, 1867–8, vol. 11, Select Committee on the Electric Telegraph Bill, p. 1.
10 BPP, 1867–8, vol. 41, Memorandum In Support of the Expediency of the Telegraphic Communication being Placed in the Hands of Her Majesty's Government, pp. 48ff.
11 Of course, there was no necessary assumption that all such continental experiments should be imitated in England. See, for example, E. P. Hennock, *British Social Reform and German Precedents* (Oxford, 1987).

competition within the telegraph industry.[12] This is a less than complete explanation. A more useful approach would emphasise the fact that free trade in a strongly capitalist system and government intervention in that same system were not mutually exclusive ideals. As Supple has persuasively argued, 'extensive institutional reform was perfectly compatible with a commitment to individualism and market forces, and was indeed a prerequisite of a competitive society'.[13] After all, Richard Cobden had welcomed the Penny Post, certainly an example of government expansion, as a means to facilitate free trade.[14] Moreover, if one examines Ricardo's analysis of the shipping industry under the Navigation Acts and his description of the telegraphs before nationalisation, the parallels are remarkable. In each an oligopolistic system caused unnecessarily high prices and inhibited the expansion of the economy. Only his solutions differed. In the case of the shipping industry, free trade was the remedy; for the telegraphs, nationalisation.

By 1861 the major arguments for nationalisation – a lower as well as uniform scale of tariffs, greater economies of scale, the successful operation of continental state-owned systems, and the importance of vital communications being in public hands – had all been clearly enunciated. Yet the proposals in and of themselves were not sufficient to spark the Postmaster General into action. As late as 1865 Lord Stanley of Alderley, although a firm believer in the merits of nationalisation since his days at the Board of Trade, acquiesced in Tilley's rejection of a scheme for government take-over.[15] The department had only recently accepted the burdens of managing the packet services as well as the savings banks and life insurance programmes. Furthermore, there were doubts as to exactly how much use the public would make of the telegraphs whether run by the state or private initiative. It was certainly the case, as Scudamore vividly portrayed, that only a limited clientele currently availed itself of the services offered by the companies:

Whoever could make money on a turn of the market, whoever could advantageously place a few pounds when 'Bumble-bee' went below 'Dulcibella' in the betting, whoever had it at heart to let Thames Street know that there was a large take of herring at Wick, rushed cheerfully to the telegraph office, and would have submitted to any

---

[12] Kieve, pp. 120–1; J. H. Clapham, *An Economic History of Modern Britain*, vol. 2 (Cambridge, 1932), p. 208.
[13] Supple, 'Legislation and the State', p. 212.
[14] See Cobden's evidence in BPP, 1837–8, vol. 20, Select Committee on Postage. See also Nicholas C. Edsall, *Richard Cobden Independent Radical* (Cambridge, Massachusetts, 1986), p. 350.
[15] Post 30/489, E7036/1886, Frederic Hill to J. Gostick, 15 July 1865.

inconvenience, and paid any charge, to get his message through in time. But, the general public, puzzled by a variable and complex tariff and disheartened by the distance of the telegraph offices from their doors, had got to regard the telegraph as a medium of communication which they might use in times of sore necessity, and then only, and to look upon a telegraph message with a feeling amounting to fear.[16]

The campaign for nationalisation might have remained stalled, if it had not been for a crucial miscalculation on the part of the major telegraph companies. In July 1865 the uniform tariff of 1s for 20 words between certain major cities was withdrawn, and a higher scale substituted.[17] There was an immediate backlash against the companies. Moreover, the change in tariffs demonstrated that the patchwork of government legislation which had been enacted to regulate the industry was inadequate. Quite obviously the stimulus which deficient legislation could give to further demands for government intervention was at work in this situation. Two small, but powerful pressure groups, first the Chambers of Commerce and then the press, were galvanised into action by the increase in telegraph charges.

The Edinburgh Chamber of Commerce quickly appointed a committee to examine the condition of the telegraph industry and to make suggestions for its improvement. The committee found three main areas for complaint.[18] Inevitably, the first was the high cost of sending a telegram. The complicated rate structure was held to inhibit the convenience and growth of the industry. Using statistics gathered from foreign countries, the committee concluded that Great Britain lagged behind other nations in the use of the telegraph. In the United States, for example, per capita use of the telegraph was three times higher than in Britain. The second area of complaint involved delays in delivery and inaccuracies in transmission of messages. Although no statistical information was offered relating to this problem, the report emphasised the 'serious consequences which have sometimes resulted from unwarrantable blunders, [of which] almost every person using the telegraph had had reason to complain'.[19] The third deficiency in the privately operated system lay in the relatively small number of offices, which provided communication between approximately one thousand cities

[16] Forty-First Report of the Postmaster General on the Post Office (London, 1895), p. 34.
[17] Kieve, p. 125.
[18] BPP, 1867–8, vol. 41, Report of Committee appointed by the Chamber of Commerce to consider the present condition of Telegraphic Communication throughout the United Kingdom.
[19] Ibid., p. 53.

and towns in contrast to the Post Office's network of over twelve times as many offices. The committee was well aware of the range of alternatives available to remedy the abuses in the telegraph industry. One solution considered in the committee's report was the formation of a private monopoly, along the lines of the Edinburgh Water Company with maximum rates of tariffs and dividends established by acts of Parliament. Another alternative was a system of complete free trade such that any person or company could erect telegraph lines along the public wayleaves. However, the proposal which most intrigued the committee was purchase of the private companies by government and the institution of a uniform tariff of 6d for 20 words. The committee envisaged no major obstacles to this course of action. The capital value of the companies, estimated to be £2.5 million, could be easily covered by Post Office revenue, and no powerful opposition to nationalisation, such as the railway interest, had surfaced. Moreover, as the committee urged, 'The time has passed when every action of Government was looked upon with suspicion.'[20] Although the committee did not take a definitive stand on any of the three possible solutions, it did call for the appointment of a royal commission to survey the state of the telegraph industry.

It should be further noted that these problems in the telegraph industry coincided with a particularly propitious moment in the development of the Post Office. In the mid-1860s the reputation of St Martin's le Grand was perhaps at its highest point in history. The past achievements of Penny Post and the Savings Banks stood as unmistakable proof of the department's efficient ability. The future problems of deficits and labour unrest had not yet emerged to tarnish its image. An astute observer of the economy such as W. S. Jevons could argue before the Manchester Statistical Society in April 1867 that

> To other Government establishments . . . the Post Office presents a singular and at first sight an unaccountable contrast. We are here presented with a body of secretaries and postmasters alive to every breath of public opinion or private complaint; officials laboriously correcting and returning the property of careless letterwriters; and clerks, sorters, and postmen working to their utmost that the public may be served expeditiously. No one ever charges the Post Office with lavish expenditure and inefficient performance of duties.[21]

---

20 *Ibid.*, p. 54.
21 W. S. Jevons, 'On the Analogy Between the Post Office, Telegraphs, and Other Systems of Conveyance of the United Kingdom, As Regards Government Control' in *Methods of Social Reform* (London, 1883), pp. 278–9.

Equally convinced that nationalisation under the Post Office represented 'our only hope of obtaining a complete and cheap system of telegraphy' was George Harrison, who was to become Chairman of the Edinburgh Chamber of Commerce in 1866.[22] His correspondence with the President of the Brussels Tribunal of Commerce on the results of the state-owned system there only served to confirm his belief in the advantages of such an arrangement. Under Harrison's guidance, a petitioning campaign was organised by the Association of Chambers of Commerce of the United Kingdom. A total of thirty cities initially joined together to ask the House of Commons to investigate the question of Post Office acquisition and operation of the telegraphs.[23]

To what degree these lobbying efforts influenced thinking within St Martin's le Grand remains a cloudy issue. As early as September 1865, two months after he had blocked a plan to consider nationalisation of the telegraphs, Lord Stanley reversed his prior decision. It was later claimed that the Postmaster General made the decision 'of his own motion'.[24] There is some justification for this view. The Edinburgh chamber's report was not published until October, and the petitioning drive organised by Harrison did not get fully underway until the next year. Nonetheless, Stanley could not have been unaware of the groundswell of opinion against the telegraph companies, and he was also subject to pressure exerted by Gladstone that the Post Office should take up the question.[25] Hence, the Postmaster General found himself in the happy position of being able to satisfy his own inclinations as well as external demands when he wrote to a departmental administrator:

> The Post Office possesses many advantages and facilities for working it [the telegraph system], very superior to any that can be obtained by private Companies and I should think the acquisition of all the Electric Telegraphs now at work in the Kingdom would not impose any very heavy pecuniary burthen [sic] on the nation if they could be obtained at their present value. As this subject has probably received some consideration at your hands, I would like to know your views upon it and whether in your opinion the Electric Telegraph Service might be beneficially worked by the Post Office and

[22] BPP, 1867–8, vol. 41, Extract from the *Edinburgh Evening Courant*, 12 January 1866.
[23] BPP, 1867–8, vol. 11, Select Committee on the Electric Telegraph Bill, p. 32. Two other cities later joined the campaign.
[24] Post 83/47, H36A, Scudamore to Monsell, 20 March 1872.
[25] H. C. G. Matthew (ed.), *The Gladstone Diaries*, vol. 8 (Oxford, 1982), p. 184, Gladstone to Scudamore, 25 July 1872.

whether it would possess any advantages over a system worked by private companies, and whether it would entail any very large purchase of existing rights.[26]

The recipient of this charge was, of course, Frank Ives Scudamore. He was the natural choice. In March 1864 he had been appointed to the second highest civil service position in the department, thus triumphing over his rival Anthony Trollope who was six years senior to Scudamore in the Post Office and at the same time angering the departmental Surveyors who believed that Scudamore lacked experience out in the field. Yet his vision and drive were held to compensate more than adequately for any such shortcomings. Indeed, Scudamore with his successful advocacy of savings banks and life insurance now a matter of public record was well along in the process of establishing his reputation as a rising bureaucratic star, a image which went far beyond the walls of St Martin's le Grand and the corridors of Whitehall. As the *Spectator* would put it in 1867, 'we have noticed for some years past that whenever Government intends to construct anything, to step out of the routine of sweeping paths clear, a notice has appeared that Mr Scudamore is engaged in the matter, and the ultimate scheme comes out large, simple, and efficient'.[27] (Scudamore was without question fortunate to have friends at the *Spectator* which subsequently described him as 'perhaps the very ablest [civil servant] in the service of the crown' and 'the single human being in England who seems competent to construct anything'.[28] Still, such comments were not confined to this one periodical. Favourable, if less glowing, stories throughout the press followed his career, even after the revelations of maladministration in 1873.)

Scudamore later liked to claim that he accepted Stanley's commission reluctantly, as he was then deeply involved in the management of the savings banks and did not wish to take on another responsibility. It is, however, difficult to resist the conclusion that Scudamore was being disingenuous in making such statements. After all, he was a committed spokesman for the expansion of the Post Office's role in social betterment, and he was already familiar with the general issues involved in the telegraphy question, even if he had no technical training as an engineer. Scudamore quickly immersed himself in a study of the condition of the telegraphs, travelling to the continent to inspect state-operated systems there as well as examining the situation at home. He brought to this task a dedication and resolve which

26 Post 30/488, E7036/1868, Stanley to Scudamore, 13 September 1865.
27 Post 16/10, *Spectator*, 23 November 1867.
28 *Ibid.*, *Spectator*, 16 December 1871 and 13 April 1868.

impressed colleagues and friends alike. As one clerk described Scudamore's routine, 'To work all day, all the evening; to go to bed for an hour or two and then arise, to labour throughout the ensuing day was no uncommon thing with him. His energy knew no bounds.'[29]

One result of this energy was Scudamore's report on the telegraph question, which was ready for consideration in July 1866.[30] His analysis deserves close inspection, as it served as the basic document in the later government campaign for nationalisation. After surveying the previous studies on the issue by Allan, Baines, and others, Scudamore briefly summarised the complaints concerning the existing situation in the United Kingdom. Tariffs were too high, and telegrams were either often delayed in transmission or inaccurately sent. Also, general facilities were not widely available for public use. Some towns or entire districts were without telegraph offices, while in other places the offices were located inconveniently in train stations away from business or residential areas. Scudamore had conducted a survey of over 475 towns in England and Wales with a population of 2,000 or larger in which he compared the location of each telegraph office and its hours of operation with the location and hours of nearby Post Offices. He concluded that 30 per cent of the towns were well served by the telegraph companies, 40 per cent indifferently served, 12 per cent poorly served and that 18 per cent had no service at all.

He next contrasted the chaotic situation in Britain with the smooth operation of the Belgian and Swiss systems. To Scudamore the former, which had been controlled by the state since 1850, was a model endeavour. The tariffs had been reduced twice until the charge for ordinary inland telegrams was approximately 5d for 20 words. Furthermore, delays and inaccuracies were very rare. In Belgium telegraph use had grown rapidly from one telegram for every 218 letters in 1860 to one for every 73 in 1865. On top of this 'conclusive proof' of the success of the system, the government had still managed to earn a 16 per cent profit from its gross receipts. The Swiss system, likewise, was held to be superior to the British network, which made it much more attractive to customers. Hence, there was much more frequent use of the telegraph – one telegram for every 69 letters in Switzerland versus one for every 151 in Britain. Switzerland also had just begun to realise a profit from its industry. After making complicated adjustments to compensate for

[29] Baines, vol. 2, 12.
[30] BPP, 1867–8, vol. 41, A Report to the Postmaster General Upon Certain Proposals which have been made for Transferring to the Post Office the Control and Management of the Electric Telegraphs Throughout the United Kingdom.

what he considered the wasteful competition in England, Scudamore produced statistics to demonstrate the inadequate service provided by the private British companies. (See table two.)

Table 2
Private versus state management of the telegraphs in three European countries

	Belgium	Switzerland	United Kingdom
Miles of telegraph line to every 100 square miles of territory	17.75	13 .7	11.3
Number of telegraph offices to every 100,000 persons	6.34	9.9	5.6

Source: BPP, 1867–8, vol. 41, A Report to the Postmaster General, p. 20.

As he summarised the situation,

> We have, in short, in the telegraphic system of the United Kingdom precisely what we had in the postal system . . . before 1840, when the receptacles for letters were few in number, when the charge for transmission was excessive, and when the limits of free deliveries were so narrow that large numbers of letters were subjected to additional taxation before they reached the hands of the addressees.[31]

Having examined the three systems from the standpoint of public service, Scudamore next turned to the question of the management of the public and private systems. Of particular concern were the relative costs of constructing and maintaining telegraph facilities in the three countries. He was aware that such comparisons were difficult because of the varied terrain, climate, and labour costs in each country. However, he boldly produced the following figures to prove that 'the cost of providing telegraphic facilities in this country [the United Kingdom] is not such as to necessitate a restricted provision of such facilities, or a high charge for their use and enjoyment'. (See table three.)

[31] *Ibid.*

Table 3
Comparative working costs for the telegraphs in three European countries

	Belgium	Switzerland	United Kingdom
Cost per mile of constructing, maintaining and working telegraphic lines from beginning of operation to 1865	£41 16 18	£65 19 2	£64 11 10
Average annual cost of working and maintaining per mile of wire 1862–5	£5 1 5	£4 19 7	£4 9 7

Source: BPP, 1867–8, vol. 41, A Report to the Postmaster General, p. 22.

Yet, with comparable operating costs, the British companies had been able to turn a profit of 33 per cent on gross receipts, which greatly exceeded the percentages earned in the continental countries. To Scudamore this figure was not a sign of success, but rather evidence of the exploitation of the public. At this point in the report Scudamore abandoned his consideration of statistics and continental comparisons and began to argue in an even more committed manner against the private companies and by implication, at least in this instance, against the merits of private enterprise. He predicted that 'little or no improvement can be expected so long as the working of the telegraphs is conducted in a wasteful competition with each other'.[32] Not only had competition failed to ensure efficiency, but there was also the problem of false priorities in the minds of company directors. The directors 'have of necessity thought rather of the interest of their stockholders than of the interests of the whole community'.[33] The remedy for this problem was, not surprisingly, nationalisation under the aegis of the Post Office. Once again Scudamore considered the question of government expansion into the business sector from the perspective of a technocrat, emphasising the advantages of the Post Office bureaucracy. He cited, for example, the smooth operation of the Savings Banks system as evidence of the growing efficiency in government endeavours. He further argued that more obligations and duties, not fewer, were the way to improve operations, as a better grade of employees could be hired to handle the growing volume of business.[34]

[32] Ibid., p. 8.
[33] Ibid., p. 18.
[34] Alfred Chandler's scale/scope distinction has a certain applicability here. Economies of scale result from a reduction in unit cost from 'increased volume of a single product or service through a single set of facilities'. Economies of scope

Scudamore proposed eighteen detailed improvements in his nationalisation scheme. Fortunately, they can be summarised quickly. Telegraph offices would be opened in all central cities as well as in the money order offices of all towns of at least 2,000 population. The tariff would be set at 1s for 20 words with free delivery, within certain limits. In this way the telegraph would be available at lower rates for longer hours each day at more convenient locations. The single remaining matter was the estimated cost of nationalisation and the system's future profitability to the Exchequer. After studying the annual reports of the companies, Scudamore concluded that the maximum purchase price for all property and rights should not exceed £2.4 million. Moreover, officers of the private companies whom the Post Office did not hire should be compensated by the former, not the latter. With an additional £100,000 to cover the cost of new extensions, construction, and fittings, the government could finance the total amount at an annual interest charge of £81,250. He further estimated an annual total of 11.2 million telegrams which would yield £676,000 in gross receipts. After deducting the interest charges and £456,000 for maintenance and operating expenses, he predicted a net profit of £138,750.[35]

The impact of Scudamore's report did not stem from its original vision of the subject, as he readily admitted. He was indebted to previous writers both for his general approach and for specific proposals on the subject. Allan had earlier considered the wasteful nature of competition among the private companies. Baines had also surveyed the quality of telegraph services in post towns. Ricardo and Burchell had drawn examples from the continent. Originality, however, was less a virtue in this campaign than thoroughness. Scudamore had provided a convenient summation of the case against the private companies. He had added, with apparent accuracy, detailed estimates of the cost and

result from the 'use of a single set of facilities to produce or process more than one product or service'. Rowland Hill with his advocacy of the Penny Post was, thus, seeking to exploit economies of scale, while Scudamore always eager to move into new fields was in an almost intuitive manner looking for economies of scope. Both Hill and Scudamore would have benefited from a further point of Chandler's that such economies are less likely in labour-intensive industries. See Thomas K. McCraw (ed.), *The Essential Alfred Chandler Essays Toward a Historical Theory of Big Business* (Boston, 1988), pp. 475, 503. In a wider context Chandler's work has helped to open a new line of debate over the relatively poor performance of smaller 'competitive capitalist' firms in Britain as opposed to that of larger 'corporate capitalist' firms in the United States and elsewhere. See Bernard Elbaum and William Lazonick (eds.), *The Decline of the British Economy* (Oxford, 1986) and Joel Mokyr, 'On the (Alleged) Failures of Victorian Britain', *The Journal of British Studies*, 28 (1989), 89–95.

35 BPP, 1867–8, vol. 41, A Report to the Postmaster General upon Certain Proposals, p. 38.

probable revenue under Post Office management. The most important aspect of the report was perhaps that in its preparation an increasingly influential civil servant, driven as he claimed by the 'mere force of facts', had been convinced of the wisdom of nationalisation.[36]

The report was submitted to the Treasury in the transition period between the end of Russell's second, and last, government and the formation of Lord Derby's third cabinet in the early summer of 1866. This circumstance, and the generally unstable economic outlook of that year, precluded any immediate action on the report. Nonetheless, Scudamore began a vigorous and extensive lobbying campaign to win the support of political leaders on the nationalisation question. A letter of July 1866 to Gladstone is typical of the charm, if viewed in a positive light, or sycophancy, if viewed more negatively, which Scudamore could display in the advancement of a cause and his own career. After reminding Gladstone of their association on the Savings Banks question, he wrote

> in the midst of all your labour and anxiety, you might very easily have forgotten me. I should still have felt myself repaid by the pleasure of working for you, and by the knowledge that I had gained your good opinion. In the course of a few days you will have a copy of a report which I am now finishing on the proposal to transfer the telegraphs to the Post Office. It is not very probable that much progress will have been made in the matter before your return to office and I hope that when you do return you will be willing to employ me in that, or any other matter in which I can be useful, as I shall be delighted to be employed.[37]

Scudamore was mistaken in his appraisal of the chances of nationalisation under the new Derby administration. The Tories grasped the merits of the idea as quickly as the Liberals had. Indeed, the appeal of Scudamore's proposal appeared to transcend the limits of party ideology. The arguments seemed reasonable, the logic sound, and the matter was carried forward through the Treasury to the highest levels of government. In December 1866 Sir Stafford Northcote, then Secretary of the Board of Trade, wrote to Disraeli, who was Chancellor of the Exchequer:

> I hope you will be able to manage the purchase of the Telegraphs; it will be a great move, and I see no reason why it could not be made. As a general rule one looks doubtfully on proposals that the Govern-

---

36 *Ibid.*, p. 39.
37 Gladstone Papers, Add. MS. 41411, fol. 94, Scudamore to Gladstone, 7 July 1866.

ment should carry on business on its own account; but I think this is an exceptional case. The Telegraph is treading on the heels of the Post Office, and it is quite possible that a few improvements of detail might make it a formidable rival. Moreover, the work is entirely . . . [comparable] to the Postal Work which we have learnt to do, and to do well. I have not time to look minutely into the calculations, but I have great faith in Scudamore, and his general line of argument appears to me to be sound.[38]

It mattered little that Northcote favoured nationalisation not because of the inefficiency of the private companies condemned by all their critics, but for exactly the opposite reason, i.e., they were becoming so formidable as to threaten the Post Office. Rather it is indicative of the respect which Scudamore could evoke that Northcote did not trouble himself to examine closely the statistics presented, but simply relied on the civil servant's advocacy of what was rapidly becoming the conventional view: the state should purchase and manage the telegraphs.

It was to be almost sixteen months before the bill authorising nationalisation of the telegraphs reached the floor of the House of Commons, which was in the meanwhile occupied with the more critical matter of electoral reform. During this time Scudamore was officially engaged in further study of the question and preparation of a draft bill. He drew up another prospectus on the state of the industry, which did not vary from the basic assessment developed in his report of July 1866. He did, however, raise his estimate of the purchase price to £3 million in order to compensate for a change in the market price of the companies' shares. Even with this increase, he still anticipated a £77,750 annual surplus.[39] A draft bill accompanying the second report was submitted to the Treasury in February 1868. The limited scope of the bill should not be overlooked, for Scudamore was acutely aware of the need to appear conciliatory and prudent in his proposal. No monopoly would be granted to the Postmaster General. Scudamore believed that this concession would help to disarm any feeling that government operation would inhibit technological progress in telegraphy. Furthermore, the Postmaster General would not possess any rights over private property companies. As Tilley pointed out, if the bill became law, it would simply enable the Post Office, as any newly established competitor might, to negotiate satisfactory terms with the

---

[38] Iddesleigh Papers, Add. MS. 50015, fols. 173–6, Northcote to Disraeli, 24 December 1866.
[39] BPP, 1867–8, vol. 41, Supplementary Report to the Postmaster General upon the Proposal for Transferring to the Post Office the Control and Management of the Electric Telegraphs Throughout the United Kingdom, pp. 146–7.

telegraph companies.[40] Of course, the precise definition of 'satisfactory' remained ambiguous. The main features of Scudamore's bill can be briefly described. A uniform rate of 1s for 20 words, irrespective of distance, was to be established. The Postmaster General was to be authorised to buy part or all of any telegraph company. If one company were purchased, other firms could demand that they also be purchased, an arrangement intended to prevent unfair competition by the Post Office. An arbitrator, selected by the Board of Trade, would settle any disputes between parties.

During these same months Scudamore with great skill continued to promote unofficially the cause of nationalisation. He formed an alliance with Edwin Chadwick, who was at that time in the midst of what has been termed his third career, i.e. a somewhat unhappy retirement from his earlier public health crusades.[41] Chadwick had long been concerned with the waste found in certain large industries and was prepared to resort to, in his phrase, 'authoritative intervention' by government to prevent such inefficiency.[42] As Chadwick was to argue, 'The saving of time; the stuff of which business as well as life is made and which increases in importance with the rise now going on in wages, [depends on] . . . the cheapness of communication and its completeness in pervading the whole country.'[43] As early as 1866 he had sent a proposal on telegraph nationalisation to Gladstone. Thus, the association between Chadwick and Scudamore was a natural, if never very warm, one. Its first public fruit was borne at a meeting of the Society of Arts on 27 February 1867, where Scudamore spoke briefly and atypically in a rather subdued manner. Chadwick also read a paper 'On the Economy of Telegraphy as Part of a Public System of Postal Communication'. The paper did not actually advance the argument from the earlier position outlined by Scudamore. The usual complaints of inadequate service, slow delivery, and high tariffs were aired. In an argument for what might today be called a mixed economy, Chadwick urged that nationalisation of the telegraph industry should be understood as part of a wider scheme which would promote efficient competition and free trade in other private industries. It is a point worth remembering that Chadwick, like Scudamore, approached the question of nationalisation as fundamentally an issue of political economy and, thus, ignored any of the technological complexities involved. As

---

[40] *Ibid.*, p. 119, Post Office to Treasury, 14 February 1868.
[41] S. E. Finer, *The Life and Times of Sir Edwin Chadwick* (London, 1952), p. 483.
[42] *Ibid.*, p. 476.
[43] Chadwick Papers, 'On the Economy of Telegraphy as Part of a Public System of Postal Communication'. This was later published in the *Journal of the Society of Arts*, 15 (1867), 222–6.

he later admitted, 'I do not pretend to knowledge of more than the economical elements and little or none of the scientific elements.'[44]

During this same period the telegraph and railway companies were not idle, as they had launched a counter-attack. The telegraph opposition was led by the Electric. As early as December 1867 Henry Weaver, its Secretary, wrote to a number of MPs, especially those in the railway interest, in hopes of gaining their support.[45] The Chairman of the Electric, Robert Grimston, both by letter and in a personal interview with Ward Hunt the Chancellor of the Exchequer on 5 March 1868 urged the abandonment of the proposal.[46] Grimston, moreover, took his case to the public in two polemics.[47] The argument in both pamphlets was essentially the same. He ridiculed Scudamore's reasoning and statistics on a wide number of points. Grimston charged that the Post Office would lose money on the telegraphs, if it extended the system to a large number of small towns. He questioned the ability of village postmasters and other personnel to operate the equipment and predicted breakdowns and delays as a consequence. Moreover, Grimston argued that the Belgian state-owned system, so lauded by Scudamore, lost money on inland telegrams and only earned a profit because of a large volume of foreign messages. He suggested that an amalgamation of the existing companies under private ownership would be a better alternative to Scudamore's unwise nationalisation proposal.

The opposition of the railway companies involved in the telegraph system presented a much more serious threat to the prospect of nationalisation. Not only did several companies operate their own lines, but there existed a complicated relationship between the railways and the telegraph companies, especially the Electric, on matters of wayleaves and reversionary rights. Moreover, as Chadwick pointed out, the railways also feared the nationalisation of the telegraphs because to them it represented the 'thin end of the wedge', i.e. a preparatory step toward the possible take-over of the railways themselves.[48] Given the strength of the railway interest, if it staunchly resisted Scudamore's proposal, then he and the government faced a formidable obstacle. The leading companies, including the Great Western Railway, the Midland, and the London and North Western, met in February 1868 to consider how to face the challenge posed by the bill.[49] Like the telegraph companies,

---

44 Chadwick Papers, Chadwick to Scudamore, 22 November 1867.
45 Kieve, p. 141.
46 Post 30/488, E7036/1886, Grimston to Disraeli, 3 December 1867.
47 These were 'A Review of the Leading Principles involved in the Proposed Transfer of Electric Telegraphs' and *Government and Telegraphs*, the latter published in May 1868.
48 Chadwick Papers, Chadwick to Scudamore, 22 November 1867.
49 Kieve, p. 139.

a group of railway spokesmen also met with Ward Hunt to express their supposedly complete opposition to the Post Office nationalisation of the telegraphs. The principal points which concerned the railways were the prospect of Post Office interference in wayleave rights and the internal management of their own telegraphs as well as the issue of adequate compensation for the loss of their partnerships with the companies. Some idea of the tenor of railway rhetoric during this stage of the struggle may be gleaned from the following statement of *The Railway Times* painting a less than pleasant picture of nationalisation. It would result in 'the abandonment of further telegraphic enterprise in the stagnation and [the] dreary routine inseparable from official regulation [and] in the interference by Government with commercial business'.[50]

Still the Conservative government continued to support Scudamore's proposal, and the bill was read for the first time on 1 April 1868. The resolve of the government was undoubtedly strengthened by the fact that the telegraph companies had antagonised the press, especially the provincial newspapers which did so much to shape public opinion in Victorian Britain. As *The Economist* summarised the situation, 'There is, probably, no interest [the telegraph companies] which is so cordially disliked by the press, which, when united, is stronger than any interest, and which has suffered for years under the shortcomings of the private companies.'[51] The telegraph companies were under contract with the provincial press for the gathering of news as well as its transmission. There were frequent complaints about the handling of the stories sent by the companies. Hence *The Glowworm* claimed that transmission by the private companies was so poor that 'in nine cases out of ten much more accuracy and equal speed can be obtained by the penny post'.[52] For example, the announcement of Lord Brougham's death in Cannes in May 1868 had never reached certain country papers. Led by John Edward Taylor of the Manchester *Guardian*, a number of provincial papers had formed a cooperative news agency, the Press Association, in November 1865. However, the telegraph companies refused to release the newspapers from their existing contracts. The result was a stalemate, which to Francis Finley of *The Northern Whig* 'placed in the hands of Telegraph companies a power which they have used in a despotic and arbitrary manner'.[53] The provincial press strongly supported the campaign for nationalisation of the telegraphs

[50] *The Railway Times*, 11 April 1868, pp. 428–9.
[51] *The Economist*, 11 April 1868, p. 412.
[52] Post 16/10, *The Glowworm*, 26 September 1866.
[53] BPP, 1867–8, vol. 11, Select Committee on the Electric Telegraph Bill, p. 102. See also David Ayerst, *The Manchester Guardian Biography of a Newspaper* (London, 1971), p. 144.

less as an end in itself than as a means to break the monopoly held by the telegraph companies. St Martin's le Grand cooperated with the press through a departmental proposal for an approximately 40 per cent reduction in the transmission fees as opposed to those charged by the private companies.[54] (Of course, the newspapers would have to bear the cost of gathering the news, as the Post Office would not do that.) After all, Scudamore viewed the issue as a tactically important one in his nationalisation campaign as well as another opportunity for the Post Office to fulfil a proper social function. 'It seems to me, indeed', he wrote Taylor of the *Guardian*, 'that the transmission of news to the press throughout the kingdom should be regarded as a matter of national importance and that charge for such transmission should include no greater margin of profit than to suffice to make the service fairly self-supporting.'[55] In point of fact, the rate established was much too low for the department to break even, and for years the Post Office indirectly subsidized the provincial press in its competition with the London dailies.[56]

With a powerful press participating in the rising chorus of criticism, the telegraph companies were clearly on the defensive. Some idea of their relative position in the public mind may be gathered from the number of petitions submitted to the Post Office on the proposal. (See table four.)

Table 4
Petitions submitted to the Post Office on the issue of nationalisation

Petitions against nationalisation

telegraph companies	railways	shareholders	miscellaneous
11	10	329	6

Petitions in favour of alterations in the private system

public bodies	Chambers of Commerce	shareholders
4	2	2

Petitions in favour of nationalisation

Chambers of Commerce	general public	press	public bodies
32	24	297	64

Source: Post 30/488, E7036/1886.

54 BPP, 1867–8, vol. 11, Select Committee on the Electric Telegraph Bill, p. 92.
55 Ayerst, p. 147.
56 See Kieve, chapter 11. For an overview of some broader connections between politicians, journalism, and new forms of technology such as the telegraph, see H.

No exact statistical inferences can be drawn from the figures in table four. Predictably, the telegraph companies had pressured their shareholders to submit petitions. On the other side, many of the petitions calling for nationalisation were instigated by supposedly neutral civil servants. Local postmasters encouraged newspaper editors to join in the campaign. Scudamore was the most important agent involved, as he established a semi-private network of supporters throughout the country. Thus, writing to Chadwick in May 1868, he had counselled

> I send you two copies of a petition in favour of the Bill. Do you think that you, without letting it be known that the petition is prompted by us, could set it going in one or two large provincial towns. I can manage Liverpool, Hull, Birmingham, Southampton, and Glasgow and Edinburgh but I know no discreet person in Manchester, Bristol or Newcastle.[57]

Scudamore further sought to calm the opposition through indirect persuasion. He sent the presidents of the Edinburgh and Liverpool Chambers of Commerce lists of stockholders of the private companies and asked 'if you find in it names of any with whom you have influence, you may be able to satisfy them that further opposition is not in their interest but merely for the interest of Parliamentary lawyers and agents'.[58] In spite of manipulation by both sides, the overwhelming predominance of petitions in favour of nationalisation was nonetheless an accurate indication of the public mood in the late spring of 1868. Scudamore certainly had not manufactured discontent with the service provided by the private companies. Rather he had helped to channel prevailing opinion into a form which would be apparent to all those interested in the future of the government's proposal.

Given the state of public opinion, it is not surprising that the central focus of the nationalisation question began to shift. The contest became less a debate between advocates and opponents of nationalisation and more a struggle over what the terms and purchase price would be. Negotiations had begun on 21 April 1868 at the chambers of the Parliamentary agent R. H. Wyatt at 28 Parliament Street, Westminster.[59] Although the companies professed to be fundamentally opposed

---

C. G. Matthew, 'Rhetoric and Politics in Great Britain, 1860–1950' in P. J. Waller (ed.), *Politics and Social Change in Modern Britain* (London, 1987).

[57] Chadwick Papers, Scudamore to Chadwick, 14 May 1868.

[58] Post 83/53, Scudamore to Presidents, Liverpool and Edinburgh Chambers of Commerce, 20 June 1868.

[59] Post 30/488, E7036/1886, Brief in Support of the Bill. For an account of the work of such men as Wyatt, see D. L. Rydz, *The Parliamentary Agents* (London, 1979).

to nationalisation in principle, they did offer the following proposals. All companies or none should be purchased. Provision should be made for compensation to the officers of the companies. Terms should be settled on the basis of the precedent of the 1844 Railway Act, i.e., twenty-five years' purchase of profits. The Post Office issued a set of counter-proposals at a meeting on 5 June 1868. The government offered to use the highest price that each company's shares reached on the Stock Exchange until 25 May as the basis of purchase. As one might expect, the shares had risen as a result of speculation over impending nationalisation. (See table five.)

Table 5
The rise of telegraph company stock prices

Company	Amount paid up per share	Market Price	
		1 Nov 1867	8 May 1868
Electric	£100	£143–148	£164–169
Magnetic	100	97–102	124–129
United Kingdom	5	1¼–1¾	3–3½
London District	5	¾–1¼	2–2½

Source: Post 30/488, E7036/1886, Brief in Support of Bill.

The government also agreed to give compensation to officers of the companies not hired by the Post Office, if they had been employed at a yearly salary for five years or more. This proposal represented a reversal of Scudamore's earlier position that the companies should be responsible for such compensation and marked the beginning of the massive erosion of the anticipated savings under Post Office management. Despite this exchange of proposals, the matter remained unresolved when the House of Commons took up the second reading of the bill on 9 June.

The fact that the telegraph companies and the railways were still united in the struggle for generous terms was symbolised in the person of their chief spokesman in the debate, George Leeman, a Liberal MP from York and later Chairman of the North Eastern Railway. Leeman attempted to revive latent fears concerning the expansion of government into industry. He strongly criticised the effort to 'slur over . . . this great question, whether it was the duty of the Government to conduct business which had hitherto in this country been left solely to private enterprise'.[60] Accordingly, he raised the issue of government spying on

---

[60] *Hansard's, Third Series*, vol. 192, 1307, 9 June 1868.

individuals and businesses by reminding the House of Commons of Sir James Graham's opening of Mazzini's mail. He was also concerned with the over 250 complicated railway–telegraph companies agreements. What would happen to these, if the state stepped in? He went on to claim that the Post Office could not work the lines as safely and efficiently as they were presently operated. Leeman's ultimate line of argument, however, proved feeble in that he contended that the existing tariff structure – criticised by others as much too high – was fair. Yet in the end he was forced to admit that less than one man in a thousand used the telegraphs as they were presently operated.

The House of Commons was unmoved by Leeman's oratory. As the *Saturday Review* noted, 'it is remarkable that, with the single exception of the avowed advocates of the Companies, not a single member ventured to say that he was opposed to the object of the Bill'.[61] Indeed, the relatively easy, somewhat pragmatic acceptance of the idea of nationalisation in this case stands as a reflection of a point made earlier by Jevons when he had considered the case for nationalisation. To Jevons, no 'abstract principle, and no absolute rule, can guide us in determining what kinds of industrial enterprise the State should undertake and what it should not'.[62] Thus, Jevons favoured the nationalisation of the telegraphs, while opposing the nationalisation of the railways. The Manchester *Guardian* evidenced a similarly flexible outlook when it reminded its readers that the usually sound dislike of 'needless centralisation' was misapplied when it prevented government from taking up suitable responsibilities and tasks.[63]

The lack of controversy over principle, nevertheless, did not assure automatic passage of the bill, although the government wanted to push ahead with the matter as fast as possible. Its desire for haste is understandable. The Conservatives had been defeated on the Irish Church Bill two months earlier, and Parliament was soon to be prorogued. The Tory party now under the leadership of Disraeli naturally wanted to be able to cite nationalisation of the telegraphs as one more achievement of its administration in the coming election. A consideration of both this political motivation and Scudamore's energetic commitment to the cause helps to explain the lengths to which the government went to accommodate the companies in the early summer of 1868. Even though the estimated purchase price had risen almost £1 million over the February estimate of £3 million, there was no slackening in the government's campaign. Continued efforts were made to appease the opposing parties. Hence, the railways were informed that they would

---

61 *Saturday Review*, 25, 13 June 1868.
62 Jevons, 'On the Analogy' in *Methods of Social Reform*, p. 278.
63 Post 16/10, the Manchester *Guardian*, 18 March 1868.

continue to enjoy a privileged position under a nationalised system. Either the government would supply the necessary safety and signalling lines or the railways would be allowed to work telegraphs for their own use.

If the Conservative government wished to go forward with the bill, the attitude of the Liberals was much more ambiguous. Certainly the idea of nationalisation of the telegraphs was well supported on the opposition side of the House. Gladstone described the system operated by the private companies as 'maimed and crippled in every point, from want of independent and effective means for distribution of messages'.[64] He was confident of the Post Office's ability in general, and Scudamore's in particular, to overcome the problems inherent in nationalisation. Moreover, there was the pressure of Scudamore's lobbying among the Liberal ranks. On 19 February of that year, for example, Scudamore had written Gladstone a long letter marked private contending that 'the question should be settled now'.[65] Gladstone's diary does not reveal the details of his immediate reaction, but a later letter of July 1872 illuminates what had been differing positions as to the principles which should guide nationalisation.[66] Scudamore in his eagerness to move ahead with the take-over believed that the process would be facilitated if the government did not insist on establishing a monopoly. For the slightly hesitant Gladstone, a monopoly was 'vital', to use his word, if the plan was to succeed. Behind this relatively minor issue lay a larger disagreement. Gladstone, who always stood rather to the right of Scudamore on economic issues, had never completely abandoned the assumption that private institutions were normally superior to public authorities. By extension, Gladstone had never lost the fear that a government system might suffer, if private alternatives continued to exist. Such considerations were not germane for Scudamore, who confidently assumed that his Post Office could conquer any competition in a fair economic contest. In addition to the monopoly issue, there were also unresolved questions in the minds of other Liberals as to whether the specific terms and conditions of the acquisition had received sufficient consideration. George Joachim Goschen, whose meteoric rise to a directorship of the Bank of England at the age of twenty-seven and whose work on foreign exchange had won him wide respect as an economic expert, emerged as the most effective critic of the scheme in this area. Goschen was especially concerned by the haste and lack of rigorous examination of

---

64 *Hansard's, Third Series*, vol. 192, 1331.
65 Gladstone Papers, Add. MS. 44414, fol. 105, Scudamore to Gladstone, 19 February 1868.
66 Matthew, *The Gladstone Diaries*, vol. 6, 577 and vol. 8, 184, Gladstone to Scudamore, 25 July 1872.

Scudamore's projections of cost and profits. As he put it, 'It was scarcely possible that a Bill dealing with such vast private interests should pass into law in the course of six weeks or two months.'[67]

Hence, the exact outcome of the proposal remained uncertain, even if the opposition was inclined to a degree of cooperation. As Scudamore wrote to Chadwick six days before the all-important debate of 18 June, 'we shall win or lose, and we must do all in our power to make matters safe. It is very desirable indeed that leading liberals should be secured'.[68] During the course of that debate the Liberals successfully pressed for the appointment of a select committee to study further the question of nationalisation. The terms established for the inquiry underscored the fact that the debate on the issue of nationalisation had now been reduced to a narrow discussion of the terms under which nationalisation should take place. The committee was to consider the issues of establishing a Post Office monopoly on telegraphy, the working of cables to foreign countries, the granting of the discretion to the Post Office to set reduced rates for news transmission, and the drafting of regulations to ensure the secrecy of messages. It was also to hear any petitions from the telegraph companies and the railways.

Before the committee could convene, however, the opposition of the telegraph companies and the railways evaporated, as purchase terms were agreed upon by the government and the private industries.[69] The basis of the agreement was that the telegraph companies would receive twenty years' net purchase of profits. (It will be remembered that in the meeting of 21 April the companies had asked for twenty-five years' purchase.) The shift from valuing the companies in terms of their shares to their profits represented another major concession on the government's part. For example, the Electric's price, if calculated on the basis of its shares, would only have equalled seventeen and one-half years' purchase of profits.[70] The District and the UKTC, because of their late start in the business, would receive compensation based on the market value of their stocks. Agreements on the purchase of the railways' telegraph profits, wayleaves and other reversionary rights, and the operation of the system under the Post Office were also reached. Given this understanding the role of the select committee in hearing complaints from the companies was effectively vitiated. In the nine days of testimony, no important voice was raised against the principle of nationalisation. Scudamore instead was allowed yet another opportunity both to outline his statistical analysis

---

[67] *Hansard's, Third Series*, vol. 192, 1321.
[68] Bateman-Chapman Papers, Scudamore to Chadwick, 12 June 1868.
[69] Post 30/488, E7036/1886, Scudamore to Postmaster General, 27 June 1868.
[70] BPP, 1867–8, vol. 11, Select Committee on the Electric Telegraph Bill, p. 222.

of the telegraphs question and to expound his views on the social utility of efficient systems of communication. As he stated in one characteristic answer, 'a mere beggar in the street, who does not write a letter in a year, would be a more wretched beggar than he is if the correspondence of the country were cut off'.[71] Repeatedly and expansively, Scudamore urged that the proposal offered unmistakable benefits in comparison to the current situation. If, through its smoothly running bureaucracy, the Post Office by managing the telegraphs could provide a social service and 'at the same time lay by something in aid of the national budget, would anyone say that was not a great advantage'?[72] Previous supporters, such as Taylor of the *Guardian* and John Patterson of the Liverpool Chamber of Commerce, were brought forward to confirm the wisdom of the plan. Not surprisingly, Scudamore was directly and deeply involved in the orchestration of witnesses, as his correspondence with a Post Office administrator in Manchester reveals.[73] By this point no dissenting voice arose from the companies, as even former opponents recanted after the terms of purchase had been agreed upon. E. B. Bright, Secretary of the Magnetic, when questioned about his company's earlier petition against the bill, admitted 'We push arguments very far, when we are in opposition.'[74]

Thus, it was left to the members of the committee, chiefly Goschen and Leeman, to provide a critical perspective. The central topic of concern was the purchase price and its effect on the future profitability of the Post Office telegraphs. This matter had grown in importance, as Scudamore now estimated that the new purchase costs could be as high as £6 million or £2 million more than the figure earlier given by the Chancellor of the Exchequer during the course of debate. Scudamore, whose testimony occupied almost one-half the committee's time, was subjected to a close interrogation on all aspects of the plan, his use of statistics from continental countries, and his projections of future results in England. He withstood this scrutiny quite effectively. After all, he had been diligently studying the question for three years and knew more about the telegraphs than any other man in government. In contrast the MPs had only recently taken up the issue, and, thus, they were always slightly on the defensive in the game of give-and-take. Still there were MPs who remained unconvinced of the accuracy of Scudamore's analysis and predictions. Goschen held that Scudamore had overestimated both the number of telegrams which would be sent in England and the savings which would be achieved by amalgamation

71 *Ibid.*, p. 133.
72 *Ibid.*, pp. 229–30.
73 Post 82/53, Scudamore to Beaufort, 30 June 1868.
74 BPP, 1867–8, vol. 11, Select Committee on the Electric Telegraph Bill, p. 179.

of the private system into a unified whole. He feared that these errors would cut the profits of the Post Office telegraphs by £150,000 a year. The remaining margin would barely be sufficient to meet the interest charge of 3.5 per cent on £6 million. Goschen, moreover, argued that twenty years' purchase of profits meant that the government would pay £6 million to buy a system, which it could build for around £2 million. The government, therefore, was 'to pay £4,000,000 more for good-will for the buying up of interest, and . . . for the eagerness to do the thing in a hurry'.[75] As table six shows, the Post Office in the end did pay significantly more than the capital value of the companies.

Table 6
Comparison of companies' capital and government purchase price

Company	Estimated capital and debenture debt	Price paid by government
Electric	£1,240,000	£2,938,826
Magnetic	534,000	1,243,536
UKTC	350,000	526,000
Reuter's	266,000	726,000

Source: T1/9133B/4495, R. Hunter's memorandum, 17 December 1896.

Nonetheless, it would be a mistake to make too much of the immediate impact of these criticisms, however accurate they later turned out to be. The overwhelming impression at the time was how effectively Scudamore had done his job and 'how well-natured the project' was in the judgement of *The Economist*.[76] Gladstone, although still somewhat troubled by certain aspects of the proposed purchase agreement, 'attached very considerable authority to the opinion of that Department when he considered upon how many great and seemingly doubtful enterprises it had entered during the last thirty or thirty-five years, and how much the results of those enterprises had tended to sustain the judgement of those by whom the public mind had been led'.[77] And even the hypercritical Goschen was forced to admit that the Post Office had successfully quelled any doubts about its ability to operate the system, to avoid possible breaches of secrecy, and to resolve any difficulties with the railways.[78] This confidence in the basic soundness of the proposal for nationalisation was reinforced by repeated govern-

---

[75] *Hansard's, Third Series*, vol. 193, 1574, 21 July 1868.
[76] Post 16/10, *The Economist*, 18 April 1868.
[77] *Hansard's, Third Series*, vol. 193, 1583–4, 21 July 1868.
[78] *Ibid.*, 1568–9.

ment insistence that twenty years' purchase represented a fair price for both the government and the telegraph companies. The effectiveness of this argument was demonstrated when an amendment introduced by Hugh Childers, who supported the principle of the bill, to substitute arbitration for the previously negotiated terms was easily defeated. The principle of nationalisation, 'a step in a direction quite new to the Government of the country – an undertaking founded upon an opposite principle to that which had been hitherto acted upon by them – namely, the principle of leaving all such operations to private enterprise'[79] was approved and received the Royal Assent on 31 July 1868.

Nevertheless, an escape route remained. The act also provided that, if no money were allocated by the end of the next session of Parliament, it would be considered void. By the time the money bill came under consideration the following year, Gladstone's first administration was in office. During the interim, the Post Office had been involved in an intensive audit of the telegraph companies to determine as accurately as possible the size of each firm's profits for the year ending 30 June 1868. Through close scrutiny and negotiations the Post Office was able to reduce the profits claimed by the telegraph companies from £7,036,037 to £5,715,407.[80] With another £700,000 for the railways and £300,000 for extensions, Scudamore's final estimate of the cost of nationalisation reached over £6,715,000 or more than £4,000,000 above his original estimate in 1866. In the end the government allocated £7,000,000 for expenditures before the transfer of the telegraphs to the Post Office. In spite of the increased costs, Scudamore still believed that the government would make a small profit. (See table seven.)

Table 7
Scudamore's final projection of telegraph profits

Estimated annual gross revenue	£673,838
Estimated annual working expenses	− 359,484
Net profit	314,354

Source: Post 30/489, E7036/1886, Scudamore's memorandum, 3 July 1869.

Hence, the anticipated net profit would cover interest charges – £280,000 if the £7 million were borrowed at 4 per cent – and leave a small surplus.

---

79 *Ibid.*, 1589.
80 For the following figures, see Post 30/489, E7036/1886, Scudamore's memorandum, 3 July 1869 and *Hansard's, Third Series*, vol. 197, 1217ff., 5 July 1869.

What must be emphasised, however, is that revenue was not the primary consideration in the minds of the proponents of nationalisation. Lord Hartington the new Postmaster General made this clear when the issue came up for reconsideration in July 1869:

> the Government did not expect this undertaking would be unremunerative. Indeed, he hoped that in time it would be a source of considerable revenue to the Government; but in resolving to enter into this matter the Government had been much more influenced by a regard to the advantage and convenience of the public than by a desire to make profit.[81]

Such statements demonstrate that the broad, optimistic vision of the department's proper social goals as advocated by administrators such as Scudamore was in the ascendancy at St Martin's le Grand by the late 1860s, as the alternative emphasis on economy dramatically slipped away in the years after Rowland Hill's 1864 retirement. Still the fact that the government was instituting a beneficial service did not satisfy the worries of those who felt the costs involved were simply too high. In a crucial debate on 26 July an attempt was made by Sir Robert Torrens, Liberal MP for Cambridge, to refer the bill back to select committee for further examination of Scudamore's estimates and the terms granted to the companies. Torrens argued 'it was better to reject the Bill than squander much public money'.[82] The rapid rise in the price of the companies' shares was cited as irrefutable evidence of the overly generous terms. For example, the Electric's stock had gone from £132 in January 1868 to £255 by July 1869. Even Robert Lowe, serving as Chancellor of the Exchequer in a cabinet now supporting nationalisation, complained of 'the immense price the Government was called upon to pay – a price of which he, at all events, washed his hands altogether'.[83]

Nevertheless, the general feeling of the House of Commons was one of confidence in the Post Office to fulfil the promises made by Scudamore. Hartington's vision – that reduced rates and the extension of service to outlying areas would ensure a steady growth in the use of telegrams by the public and, therefore, Post Office revenues – appeared reasonable to others. Torrens's amendment was defeated 148–23. The enthusiasm of the House of Commons was further strengthened by the fact that the cabinet had decided to establish a government monopoly in the industry, thus going against both Scudamore's thinking and the

[81] *Hansard's, Third Series*, vol. 197, 1223.
[82] *Ibid.*, vol. 198, 751, 26 July 1869. Torrens's family was connected to Rowland Hill's through marriage.
[83] *Ibid.*, 767.

recommendation of the 1868 select committee. The government's basic reasoning was that no firm should be allowed to exploit the lucrative business of densely populated regions, while the Post Office provided service to less profitable rural areas. As Lowe put it,

The country was buying not merely the plant connected with these telegraphs, but the whole of the business, and why were they not to get that for which they paid? They paid, and dearly too, for the whole of the business, and those engaged in it now ought not to be allowed at any future time to recommence operations.[84]

The Economist, abandoning its usual economic outlook to favour a Post Office system, put the issue in a slightly different way: 'We certainly prefer the Government which is wholly under control, to a company which is not and which has an interest conflicting with the community. We can hardly conceive . . . a better agency than the Governments of civilised countries for the development of a physical power.'[85] In the end, the House of Commons was no more reluctant to establish a state monopoly than it had been earlier to sanction the principle of government operation of the telegraphs. The monopoly clause was approved 123–27. With this obstacle overcome, the bill went forward smoothly, and the Royal Assent was obtained on 9 August 1869. Thus, the nationalisation of the telegraphs had been approved for a second time.

The government's handling of the nationalisation of the telegraphs, particularly Scudamore's central role in that same process, has been the subject of much criticism. The most recent student of the question reflected this negative outlook when he urged that the 'whole inquiry was conducted with a haste not commensurate with the important interests and large sums of public money involved'.[86] Undoubtedly mistakes were made by Scudamore and other civil servants. For instance, the closely intertwined relationship between the railways and the telegraphs was initially overlooked by Scudamore, whose first estimate of the purchase cost included only the four major telegraph companies. Moreover, M. H. Foster, Principal Officer of the Treasury's Financial Division, later admitted that even he had not closely examined Scudamore's analysis of the railway situation. Indeed, he testified that he was not really certain what Scudamore had included in his railway estimates.[87] Foster had assumed the amount necessary to settle with the railways would be relatively small. In the end payments to the

---

[84] *Ibid.*
[85] Post 16/11, *The Economist*, 18 July 1869.
[86] Kieve, p. 175.
[87] BPP, 1867–8, 11, Select Committee on the Electric Telegraph Bill, p. 199.

railway companies totalled almost £2 million.[88] Furthermore, the fact that the Post Office eagerly sought to come to an agreement with the telegraph companies instead of seeking arbitration has also been singled out as a costly error. This line of argument is found, for example, in an 1869 *Edinburgh Review* article by Arthur Hill who criticised the government for having 'dealt with the petitioners against the Bill much as an anxious traveller in danger of losing his steam packet deals with a boatman – paying whatever is asked'.[89] (Rowland Hill, sulking in retirement, had prompted his younger brother to make this attack.[90]) Perhaps the most serious of all the errors was that many of Scudamore's estimates, especially those for the working expenses of the system, proved to be sadly inaccurate. As will be seen, a nationalised system under central control ultimately did not save as much money as had been hoped. After all, Scudamore had only been able to project a profit in 1869 because his final estimate of working expenses, £359,484, was almost 20 per cent less than his original estimate of £425,250.

Nonetheless, in seeking to understand the dynamic of nationalisation one should not ignore the ideological and practical assumptions as well as the changing historical context which determined the ultimate passage of the two bills. Many contemporaries firmly supported Chadwick's contention that Scudamore's preparations for take-over were 'complete and his exposition . . . full, clear, and conclusive'.[91] The Treasury agreed with Chadwick's assessment, believing Scudamore's estimates to be accurate and cautious almost to an extreme. He had, after all, factored a number of variables into his statistics in an effort to anticipate later contingencies. Moreover, Gladstone did 'not doubt at all that the promises made in Mr Scudamore's report would be realised and fulfilled'.[92] Regarding the repeated increases in the estimated purchase cost as calculated by Scudamore, it should be remembered that the earlier, lower figures addressed only the four major companies. The final purchase price represented a much larger capital acquisition by the government, as the nationalised system in the end included the plant of the railways and other telegraph companies. The government was paying more, but it was also getting more. Furthermore, Scudamore had been handicapped in his early estimates by the absence of accurate information on the exact condition of the British private system, which was the result of an understandable hesitancy on the part of the

88 T1/9133B/4495/97, Hunter's memorandum, 17 December 1896.
89 Arthur Hill, 'Government Telegraphs', *Edinburgh Review*, 129 (January, 1869), 160.
90 Post, Rowland Hill's Journal, 15 January 1869.
91 Post 16/11, *Western Times*, 10 July 1868.
92 *Hansard's, Third Series*, vol. 192, 1331.

companies to make much of their internal operations known to the public and to the government. Until some settlement was reached with the industry Scudamore had, in his own words, 'been in some respects merely groping in the dark'.[93]

As for the charge that the take-over was rammed through in undue haste, it is true that Scudamore's correspondence for these months is replete with statements on the need to move ahead. To a degree this may accurately be attributed to Scudamore's ambitious desire to add another territory to his empire. However, most proponents of nationalisation inside and outside of government believed that delay would not only have allowed the continuation of the existing system of high rates and poor service, but in the end would have increased the final purchase price paid by the government. As Harrison of the Edinburgh Chamber of Commerce said in 1868, 'every day, every month, every year that was passing was rendering it [nationalisation] a more costly experiment to undertake'.[94] Setting the number of years' purchase at twenty was also held by many to be only fair and just. The consensus was that it would be improper and unfair for the Post Office to construct its own telegraph system without compensating the existing private companies. In this regard a government industry was in a fundamentally different position from that of a private company. As Scudamore expressed it, 'I will not say that they [the companies] have no right to expect that the Government shall not compete with them, but they have a fair right to say, if the Government by competing threatens to destroy their trade, it is actually compelling them to sell it.'[95] In other words, for Scudamore Goschen's claim the the government was paying much more than the capital value of the companies' plant was not directly relevant. The Times was in agreement with this argument when it pointed out

But apart from the fact that the State always buys dear, we do not grudge the purchase money. The companies had done good service as pioneers, and we are stepping into the fruits of their work. We have not the slightest doubt that, even at this price paid, the country will find that it has made a good bargain. No apprehensions need be entertained for the revenue, but pecuniary profit to the government is the least of the advantages to be expected.[96]

In sum, the ground-breaking aspect of the telegraph purchase should not be forgotten. The government was doing something completely

93 BPP, 1867–8, vol. 11, Select Committee on the Electric Telegraph Bill, p. 124.
94 Ibid., p. 140.
95 Ibid., p. 218.
96 The Times, 5 February 1870, p. 9.

new. Years later when Scudamore was advising Lord Hartington on the possible nationalisation of the Irish railways, he pointed out that Hartington might be able to come to better terms with the railways than he had with the telegraph companies. As Scudamore wrote, 'Admitting that the Government paid more in a sense than a fair price for the Telegraphs, they still paid no more than the novel and exceptional circumstances of the case required them to pay. . . . You must remember the proposal for the purchase of the Telegraphs was the first of its kind.'[97]

There is even evidence to indicate that the Post Office was not paying much more than might have been anticipated. Twenty years' purchase, the figure finally agreed upon, was less than the twenty-five year standard established by the Railway Act of 1844 for that industry. Moreover, the volume of trade of the two largest companies, the Electric and the Magnetic, was growing at the annual rate of 18 and 32 per cent respectively. Therefore, twenty years' purchase of profits was by no means a bad bargain in these cases.[98] W. H. Smith, who it must be admitted was a director of one of the companies, insisted that with the rising profits of the companies the government was actually paying only sixteen, not twenty, years' profits. Indirect support of the wisdom of the terms granted by the government came from the business community. One firm, Stern Brothers, offered to pay the Post Office an annual royalty of 4 per cent on the capital raised for the purchase in exchange for the net income of the telegraph system for the next fifteen years.[99] If this proposition had been accepted, the later fiscal history of the nationalised system would have been a very different matter.

It is also a mistake to assume that Parliament was not involved in the decision-making process throughout the passage of the bill. Kieve has asserted that 'the direct negotiation between the Post Office and the companies, by-passing Parliament, and, in fact, presenting it with a virtual fait accompli, was damaging to the control it had over the spending of public money'.[100] This judgement unduly minimises the consideration of the proposal by MPs in two separate sessions under two different governments. In an early round of debate Ward Hunt had pointed out the essence of the situation facing Parliament. The two sides involved had simply come to an agreement and brought the agreement before Parliament for sanction or rejection. It could choose either, and Parliament had many opportunities to reject the terms,

---

97 Post 82/58, Scudamore to Hartington, 21 July 1872.
98 *Hansard's, Third Series*, vol. 192, 1216 and vol. 193, 755.
99 Post 30/488, E7036/1886, Stern Brothers to Post Office, 21 July 1868.
100 Kieve, p. 174.

such as Torrens's motion for a second select committee. In the final debate, Hartington reiterated that the government was not under any legal obligation to the companies and that 'the House was quite competent to repudiate the bargain if they thought it a bad one'.[101] Parliament did not pass the legislation as a result of being hoodwinked. Rather the easy passage with large favourable majorities on the amendments indicated a strong agreement among private lobbyists, civil servants, and MPs as to the necessity of nationalisation. This analysis should not be taken as a blanket approval of Scudamore and the government's handling of the pressures for nationalisation, pressures which in the case of Scudamore he helped to sustain and nurture. In retrospect, the passage of the bill may well have been too easy. As George Harrison said, the 'truth is, that we found such a unanimous concurrence of opinion on the part of the commercial public, that very possibly we did not go into the details as we should have done if there had been any opposition'.[102] In the negotiations with the companies and in the planning of the take-over, Post Office administrators faced a set of problems fundamentally different from any they had encountered previously. There appeared to be pressing reasons for each decision they made. There certainly was strong evidence that only a government take-over would cure the ills and destroy the inequities of the private system. In a country whose towns and villages were much more isolated and whose regions much more provincial than is now remembered, the nationalisation of the telegraphs seemed one way to unite its people into a common citizenry through commercial and social intercourse.[103]

One final question remains. Where does the nationalisation of the telegraphs fit into the wider context of Victorian administrative history? Some Englishmen believed that the enactment of nationalisation was part of a larger process which would redistribute power among the various classes. One petition received by the Post Office in 1868 went so far as to proclaim

> that Parliament has just passed a measure [the Second Reform Bill] which makes the users of our telegraphs the rulers of our state, the assumption of the [telegraph] system by the Executive is really a transfer of it to the people – virtually to make the customers of the wires the shareholders in the companies.[104]

101 *Hansard's, Third Series*, vol. 193, 759.
102 BPP, 1867–8, vol. 11, Select Committee on the Electric Telegraph Bill, p. 36.
103 For a study which provides much evidence of the regional complexity of the nation, see Keith Robbins, *Nineteenth-Century Britain Integration and Diversity* (Oxford, 1988).
104 Post 30/488, E7036/1886, Memorial, 17 June 1868. Given Scudamore's role in

But as the Reform Bill of 1867 did not signify the automatic triumph of democracy, the nationalisation of the telegraphs did not lead in straight-line fashion to state socialism. As has been emphasised earlier, Victorians – whether civil servants, economists, politicians or merely interested laymen – to a degree sometimes overlooked approached the question of government growth on a case by case basis. This is not to imply that such judgements were made on a completely rational basis or that personal ambitions did not influence the conclusions reached. Goschen was absolutely correct to note that 'the desire of the Post Office authorities for the acquisition of the telegraphs developed almost into a passion'.[105] But it was a passion which was grounded in a particular social vision. Undeniably ideology was actively at play shaping the dreams of Scudamore and Chadwick as well as the actions of Gladstone, Lord Stanley and their fellow politicians. This was not a measure passed in a fit of absence of mind. Rather a consensus had emerged that in this case nationalisation was the proper solution to the problems created by an industry which charged excessively high tariffs and which did not offer adequate service to the whole of the country.

Of course, the successful passage of the nationalisation of the telegraphs should not be understood as necessarily constituting an inevitable triumph of government over industry or revealing a great preference among all involved for public management over private initiative. Without the direct and enthusiastic support of pressure groups composed of businessmen and journalists neither Disraeli's government nor Gladstone's could have pushed the legislation through Parliament. Likewise, in the delicate matter of negotiations, Scudamore and Ward Hunt realised that the government simply lacked the power to impose its terms unilaterally. As Scudamore testified before the select committee, 'Parliament uniformly protects private enterprise.'[106] Therefore, any attempt to use political pressure to crush this particular private industry would have been rejected by Parliament as unacceptable. The recognition of this prevailing opinion by the government negotiators had been a critical consideration in the final determination of the purchase terms. The 1868–70 take-over of the telegraphs, then, may best be regarded as a significant case of government expansion which required some compromise on the part of politicians and civil servants as well as much support from groups usually committed to the ideal of the efficiency of capitalist private enterprise and the dogma of laissez-faire.

the promotion of such petitions, an intriguing, if unanswerable, question arises as to whether he wrote this particular passage.
[105] G. J. Goschen, *Addresses on Educational and Economical Subjects* (Edinburgh, 1885), p. 69.
[106] BPP, 1867–8, vol. 11, Select Committee on the Electric Telegraph Bill, p. 225.

5

The Trials of the Post Office Telegraphs, 1870–1914

We have taught the public that Government can beat private enterprise. . . . In two years we have done more work than the Companies did in ten years. – Frank Ives Scudamore to Lord Hartington, 21 July 1872, Post 82/58.

We are much exercised by the condition of the Telegraph, which threatens to become a heavy charge upon our finances. The revenue increases slowly and the expenditure rapidly. . . . The promises made when we took over the business have long since proved to be delusive. – Sir Stafford Northcote to Sir William Anderson, 8 March 1875, Iddesleigh Papers, Add. MS. 50052, fols. 105–105b.

With the transfer of the telegraphs to Post Office control on 5 February 1870 St Martin's le Grand faced its greatest challenge since Penny Post. It was not only a challenge to the department, but it was also an opportunity and a test for Frank Ives Scudamore, whose name had become irrevocably associated with the cause in the public mind. Scudamore in his position as second secretary was given a free hand to manage the telegraphs, and in the months after take-over he was a man driven to demonstrate the accuracy of his earlier predictions of his and his department's ability to operate a complex industry. After experiencing some initial difficulties arising from winter storms and antiquated equipment, which the companies had allowed to deteriorate, Scudamore and St Martin's le Grand embarked on a programme of remarkable expansion.[1] After all, Scudamore had promised that the Post Office system would be more widely distributed as well as cheaper than the service offered by the private companies. In an effort to fulfil these promises it was not unusual for the Post Office to open thirty new stations in a single week. In Liverpool, where there had been sixteen

---

[1] For the following, see Post 82/197, Scudamore to Postmaster General, January 1871 and BPP, 1871, vol. 38, Report by Mr Scudamore on the Reorganisation of the Telegraph System of the United Kingdom.

offices before nationalisation, there were thirty-three by the end of the
first year of Post Office management. Pains were also taken to distribute the offices more widely, whereas under the private system they
had usually been grouped in town centres. For example, in Manchester
new offices were established at Cheetham Hill to the north and Ru-
sholme to the south, while before the Queen's Hotel and the Oxford
Road railway station had been the northernmost and southernmost
points. Such expansion placed a great strain on Scudamore's employees. Accordingly, a school was established to train new telegraph
clerks. For the staff at St Martin's le Grand the mass of paperwork often
seemed overwhelming. In a single week in November 1870 Scudamore's own men dealt with 5,578 papers and wrote 786 letters which
ran to 1,272 pages.

By almost any standard the early results of these exertions were
encouraging. The average cost of a telegram dropped from 1s 7d under
the old system to 1s 1d. The number of telegrams rose by over 3 million
the first year to almost 10 million. In two years the number was twice
as large as under the private companies. The number of provincial
newspapers receiving news by telegraph increased from 144 to 365.
There were over 2,300 departmental stations open to the public as
opposed to half that number under the old system with 6,000 new
instruments joined by 40,000 miles of wire. Scudamore, as one might
expect, gloried in such statistics and relished informing his superiors
both in the department and in Parliament of the record. In a letter to
Gladstone, Scudamore claimed his system had reached a 'state of perfect efficiency'.[2] Other observers were equally enthusiastic. Seventeen
months after the transfer *The Times* pronounced the experiment in
nationalisation a success, which 'will soon make even the most invet-
erate grumblers cease to regret the disjointed and costly system we were
long content to bear with as a triumph of private enterprise, not to be
improved or impeached'.[3]

Yet even while these pronouncements were being made, serious
problems were already undermining the record of the Post Office telegraphs. In part these problems may be understood as the product of
Scudamore's drive to expand the system too rapidly and his refusal to
countenance any opposition in his path. Two crises illustrate this
point. The first came in the autumn of 1871, when employee unrest in
the telegraph department reached a momentary peak. The clerks who
had been transferred into the Post Office from the private companies
brought with them a militancy quite unusual in the mid-Victorian civil
service. The most visible fruit of this militancy was the Telegraphists'

---

[2] Post 30/215, E274/1872, Scudamore to Gladstone, no date, probably 1872.
[3] *The Times*, 26 July 1871, p. 9.

Association, organised in Manchester in October 1871. Many of these new employees believed that Scudamore had sacrificed their interests before the altar of departmental success. As an anonymous letter to *The Morning Advertiser* put it,

> If giving to the staff under his control salaries totally inadequate for the maintenance of their social position, and 30 per cent below that paid in any other branch of skilled labour, be the action of a real friend, Mr Scudamore can fairly claim to the title. If adding to this miserable pittance once in two years a sum varying from one to five shillings, compelling us to work Sunday duty without remuneration, setting in motion all the irritating machinery of official routine with a view of reducing us to mere machines, and deluding us from time to time with promises of a revision of salaries . . . be the action of a real friend, Mr Scudamore has well earned the title.[4]

In their efforts to correct alleged injustices and abuses, the discontented clerks had one advantage not ordinarily available to trade unionists. They could discuss grievances and make plans over the wires when ordinary messages were not being sent. By November Scudamore was so fearful of the possibility of a work stoppage that he ordered the wires tapped.[5] Through this method Scudamore learned the names of the ringleaders as well as details of their strike plans. He quickly drafted a contingency scheme in cooperation with the War Office to substitute telegraphists from the Royal Engineers. The precautions were justified, for in December over 200 telegraphists and messengers in Liverpool, Manchester, Edinburgh, Glasgow, Dublin, and Cork refused to work. The disturbance, however, was rapidly crushed. A majority of the men, aware that their leaders had been suspended from the Post Office and that strike breakers under Scudamore's command had arrived to operate the system, reluctantly returned to their jobs.

Behind Scudamore's rhetorical claims that he was only a civil servant serving the public's needs, there had always lurked a certain paternalistic strain, less apparent perhaps than the paternalism he criticised in the managers of Trustee Banks, but undoubtedly as real. What the 1871 strike did was to reveal one aspect of this inclination to believe that only he could direct the affairs of his department and that any opposition must be swept aside. No employee was allowed to resume work without first publicly recording 'his individual regret for his insubordination'.[6] Without consulting William Monsell the Postmaster General, Scudamore announced a salary increase for those

---

4 Post 30/215, E225/1874, *The Morning Advertiser*, 23 November 1871.
5 *Ibid.*, Scudamore to Monsell, 25 November 1871.
6 *Ibid.*, Scudamore to Monsell, 11 January 1872.

clerks who had remained loyal throughout the strike. (Scudamore later estimated it had cost £5,000 to break the strike.) For journalists and MPs much more controversial was his decision during the strike to delay four telegrams reporting the event, which had been addressed to newspapers, including *The Times*. Scudamore the former friend of the press had apparently become its enemy, and a storm of protest arose condemning, as the *Spectator* put it, Scudamore's 'despotic' methods.[7] *The Pall Mall Gazette*, although sympathetic to Scudamore's predicament, pointed out that 'In future Mr Scudamore will have to conduct his contests with Post Office clerks with such weapons as ordinary employers of labour can command.'[8]

Scudamore's defence against such criticism was that his actions had allowed loyal reserves to reach their duty stations before news of the strike spread and before the operation of the telegraph system was unduly disrupted. To Scudamore, the priority of maintaining service was more important than the irregularity of delaying the telegrams. In his handling of the strike Scudamore demonstrated that he had no conception of the distinction between his role as a subordinate civil servant and the ministerial responsibility exercised by the Postmaster General. Writing to Monsell, Scudamore explained

> I wished to relieve you and the Government of all blame or chance of blame and at the same time to show that what I did was for the Public Good. I apprehend if it be generally allowed that what I did was for the Public Good it will equally be allowed that I did not act contrary to my duty.[9]

Monsell did not accept Scudamore's explanation and officially censured him. As Monsell pointed out, 'There is no desire to cripple the power of the permanent Heads of the Department and thus to diminish their sphere of usefulness, but it must be plainly understood once and for all they are responsible not to the Public but to their political chief!'[10] The strike also revealed a growing disposition on Scudamore's part to feel misunderstood and unappreciated in his efforts to ensure the success of the departmental telegraphs. As he complained to Gladstone, 'I think I was very badly used in the last strike. I was abused by everyone, and helped by no one. The public and the Press were against me, and I was blamed because the strike had broken out, and for the means which I took to put it down and for what was called tyranny while the strike lasted, and for what was called mistaken leniency

---

7   *Spectator*, vol. 44, 1517.
8   Quoted by *The Times*, 30 January 1872, p. 6.
9   Post 30/215, E225/1872, Scudamore to Monsell, 10 January 1872.
10 *Ibid.*, Monsell's minute, February 1872.

when it was over.'[11] In January 1872 angered by Monsell's lack of support, Scudamore resorted to an expedient employed by all frustrated administrators, the threat of resignation. He remained in office, but the honeymoon period in the telegraphs department was clearly over.

Scudamore's tendency to place the welfare of his telegraph system above the niceties of constitutional practice led to a second, much more serious crisis in the spring of 1873. Of all the problems he faced in managing the telegraphs the financial arrangements proved the most complicated. From the very beginning of the push toward nationalisation much emphasis had been placed on the system's finances, and Scudamore had emerged as the government expert in this area. He had negotiated the purchase price with the companies, made the arrangements for transfer, and extended the system. In theory Scudamore's decisions and actions had been subject to Treasury scrutiny and approval. In practice there was no effective Treasury control. From 1869 to 1872 every Post Office request for funds for the telegraph received Treasury sanction. Not only was approval automatic, but it was given without any statistical justification from Scudamore. In 1869, for instance, the Treasury requested a detailed outline of the manpower required to operate the telegraph system. Yet Scudamore, claiming the press of time and business, was not able to furnish the information until June 1872. As the Treasury later admitted, 'In the meanwhile the votes taken for the pay of the establishment were practically granted on trust and placed for the time at the uncontrolled discretion of the Postmaster-General.'[12] Scudamore, intent on the future success of the telegraphs, paid little attention to normal procedures. During these years over 3,600 employees entered the telegraph service without the required civil service certificate. Moreover, as late as June 1873 Scudamore had failed to prepare for Parliamentary inspection the deeds and documents relating to the transfer of the property of the forty-five telegraph and railway companies as required by the 1868 act.

Given the laxity of Treasury supervision, the difficulties in launching a nationalised industry, and Scudamore's eagerness to expand the system, it was predictable that the Post Office would soon run through its Parliamentary grant. In June 1871 Scudamore informed Lowe the Chancellor of the Exchequer that the 1869 grant of £7 million had been exceeded by £610,000.[13] Although Scudamore still could not produce a precise statement of the telegraphs' financial situation, Lowe was understanding. Another £1 million was allocated. This sum proved inadequate, and in March 1872 Scudamore informed the Committee

---

11 *Ibid.*, Scudamore to Gladstone, no month, probably late 1871.
12 T1/7550A/20725, Confidential Report, no date, probably summer 1873.
13 Post 30/290, E1075/1876, Scudamore to Monsell, 27 March 1873.

of Public Accounts that the total grant of £8 million had been spent and that further funds would be necessary. In a private memorandum to Lowe, Scudamore estimated that £8.2 million had been spent, £6.64 million for purchase and £1.56 million for extensions and rearrangements.[14] Moreover, Scudamore requested an additional grant of £280,000, £150,000 for further extensions and £130,000 for current working expenses. Although two years had elapsed since the government take-over, he admitted that a financial statement on the telegraphs was not yet available, but promised to furnish one within three weeks. For the first time the Treasury refused to acquiesce. Lowe's private secretary, C. Rivers Wilson, informed Scudamore that

> the prospect of further large claims which you mention had both surprised and alarmed him [Lowe] and he feels that he will have great difficulty in inducing the House of Commons to pass any further measure for placing money at the disposal of the Post Office unless some more precise estimate is laid before it.[15]

No further Parliamentary grant was requested. During the next months the pressure of work continued to mount for Scudamore. He was involved in tasks ranging from handling complex railway reversionary interests to dealing with Lord Penrhyn's request that the telegraph wires on his Bangor property be placed underground so that grouse would not fly into them and kill themselves. In this hectic atmosphere he never bothered to submit an official letter stating that his funds were exhausted to the Treasury. More importantly, he did not suspend the enlargement of the system. By diverting funds from other sources, principally Savings Banks deposits on their way to the Bank of England, Scudamore without proper authority overspent his Parliamentary allocation by £812,000.

In March 1873 the Committee of Public Accounts revealed this situation to the nation, thus marking a fundamental turning point in the history of the Post Office and the later course of government expansion into other areas, such as the telephone. The revelation further weakened Gladstone's ministry, already damaged by the defeat of the Irish University bill. The irony of such large-scale misappropriations in a government which prided itself upon administrative excellence was not lost upon the opposition. Gladstone, who had championed Scudamore and nationalisation, was disheartened by the situation. As he wrote to Russell, 'The recent exposures have been gall and wormwood to me from day to day.'[16] The spring and summer of

---

14 *Ibid.*, Scudamore to Lowe, 19 March 1872.
15 *Ibid.*, Wilson to Scudamore, 21 March 1872.
16 Morley, vol. 2, 461.

1873 were difficult months not only for Liberal politicians in Westminster, but also for administrators at St Martin's le Grand. Scudamore, around whom the crisis swirled, offered a number of explanations for his overspending. First of all, he contended that the expenditure was justified because the extension of the telegraph system had been urgently demanded by both Parliament and the nation. As he pointed out,

> At the time of the transfer, and for long afterwards, nay even up to the present time, what has been the public cry? Has it not been continually? Give us more wires on existing lines! Give us extensions of wires to outlying places! Bring the offices of transmission and delivery closer to our doors![17]

Scudamore admitted that the 1868 act had not been specific on the question as to how far the system should be extended, but he argued that extension had been considered and tacitly approved by the select committee which deliberated on the bill. His confusion on this issue is a reminder how hazy the line between his activities as a social planner and his duties as an administrator was in his own mind. In reality Scudamore was looking back to neither the bill nor the report of the committee. Rather he was citing discussions on the need for rapid expansion of the telegraphs in the evidence presented to the committee, debates on the floor of the house, and comments in the press. The fact that he had played a major role in the creation of this demand for expansion rendered his argument somewhat circular. Promote the idea of an expanded telegraph system, have the idea discussed, and then later cite the discussions as justification for expansion. (The problem of overspending was further compounded by the fact that Scudamore spent money on extensions to places, the Isle of Man and the Channel Islands, and on projects, such as a new seven-wire cable to Ireland, which even he had not included in his earlier plans.) If an appeal to the public good was one bulwark of this general line of defence, another was the pragmatic consideration of potential revenue. Scudamore argued that, given the high cost of take-over, the system had to be expanded quickly in order to yield a profit. He estimated that over one quarter of the telegrams sent was directly attributable to the rapid extension of the system.[18]

Still the question was less a matter of vague references to the mood of the nation or the future revenue of the system than the specific authority Scudamore could cite for his £800,000 overrun. Concerning

[17] Post 30/290, E1075/1876, Scudamore to Monsell, 27 March 1873.
[18] *Ibid.*, Scudamore to Monsell, 28 July 1873.

this matter Scudamore offered two somewhat contradictory explanations. At times he claimed that the Treasury had been aware of the
drift of events in the telegraphs department and had sanctioned them.
After all, the Treasury had approved the general guidelines for extending the system in 1869, and subsequently the Post Office had submitted
reports in January and July 1871 and May 1872 on the progress of the
system. The key document in this line of explanation was Scudamore's
memorandum of 19 March 1872 to Lowe, which the Post Office administrator believed clearly indicated the need for additional funds.
However sincere this belief, an examination of the evidence indicates
that the Treasury had not sanctioned the expenditure and, indeed, had
no knowledge of it. On three occasions in 1872 the Treasury had
requested the Post Office to submit a detailed statement of the capital
expenditure on the telegraphs.[19] Scudamore repeatedly claimed that
the crush of work prevented the report's preparation, and an account
was not rendered until March 1873 when the Committee of Public
Accounts had already begun its investigation. Moreover, Scudamore
never officially informed the Treasury that the grants mentioned in the
semiprivate memorandum to Lowe would be needed. One could argue
that Lowe, having been informed, should have halted the expenditure
himself. Yet there are two things to be said in Lowe's favour. First, it
was primarily Monsell the Postmaster General's responsibility, not
Lowe's, to curb Scudamore's zeal. Secondly, as Reginald Welby of the
Treasury correctly pointed out, even Lowe could not have expected
Scudamore to spend over £800,000 after he had informed the Post
Office administrator that an allocation for a much smaller sum would
not pass without further justification.[20] In the end Scudamore was
forced to abandon this position and admit that the Treasury could not
have known of or have sanctioned the expenditure.

Yet he offered a still more intriguing second explanation for his
handling of the industry. He claimed that Treasury sanction of telegraph expenditure was neither possible nor necessary. Scudamore had
long regarded the Treasury clerks in Whitehall as obstacles to progress
just as the Post Office strikers of 1871 had been. He believed that the
Treasury had little knowledge of or sympathy for the complexities of
launching a nationalised industry. In Scudamore's view of the situation, 'you might as well expect a canary to hatch a setting of ostrich
eggs, as to expect the Treasury to drynurse the telegraph system'.[21]
Scudamore accurately pointed out that the expenditure for expansion

[19] T1/7550A/20725, Confidential Report.
[20] Monk Bretton Papers, Welby to J. G. Dodson, no date, probably December
1873.
[21] Post 30/290, E272/1876, Scudamore to Gladstone, no month, 1871.

had not come in large blocks, but rather in over 3,500 separate work orders. To have obtained Treasury approval for each of these would have overwhelmed the clerks in both St Martin's le Grand and Whitehall. Furthermore, there was some doubt as to what extent Treasury approval was even necessary. Regarding the final terms of purchase, the 1868 act had provided that the agreements were not valid without Treasury consent. However, in April 1870 Scudamore had consulted the law officers of the Crown on this question, and they had advised Treasury approval was unnecessary. (Typically Scudamore never informed the Treasury of this opinion, and, as a result, the Treasury later had to sanction in an *ex post facto* manner over £6 million in payments to the telegraph and railway companies.[22]) Similarly Scudamore asserted that no specific regulations had been drafted as to which other expenditures could be authorised at Post Office discretion. One should remember that in the early 1870s Post Office–Treasury relations were in a state of transition. While Treasury control over staff questions had increased, other items such as the £800,000 spent annually for the inland conveyance of mail were not yet subject to Treasury scrutiny. The telegraphs should be handled in a similar manner, as Scudamore saw no need to be tied down to bureaucratic requirements in the face of the urgent need for expansion. Writing to his political chief, Scudamore declared

> I have from the first supposed that all my superiors, either in the Department or out of it, were agreed in leaving to me a large discretion in the mode of carrying out the undertaking. If I had not been of this opinion, I should have hesitated to do much of what has been done, and assuredly if I had not been of this opinion, I would not have struggled against the unexampled difficulties which attended, and for a long time followed the transfer, and which I could not have overcome unless I had committed the irregularities to which exception is now taken.[23]

Scudamore further argued that his handling of the telegraphs was in line with a departmental trend which had begun much earlier in the century, even before the days of Penny Post:

> Year by year as the Post Office has been brought more and more into direct contact with the public – year by year it has been impelled by the requirements of the whole community to the utmost promptitude of action, it has become more and more necessary that the

22 T1/7530B/12390, Welby's memorandum, 25 August 1873.
23 Post 30/290, E1075/1876, Scudamore to Monsell, 27 March 1873.

Secretaries should from time to time act spontaneously and on their own responsibility, and then seek a covering responsibility from the Postmaster General, the Parliamentary chief.[24]

Of course, Scudamore had found an instrument of expansion unavailable to earlier Secretaries, the resources of the departmental Savings Banks.

There was some merit to this aspect of Scudamore's explanation. To be sure he had spent funds without Parliamentary or Treasury approval. Yet the subsequent efforts of the Treasury to tighten its control over the Post Office indicate that before 1873 existing guidelines were inadequate to regulate zealots like Scudamore in the administration of their departments. As Welby reluctantly admitted,

The great point is to be able to point to a rule, in print if possible, and when the offense happens, to be able to put one's finger on that rule, and say you have transgressed your duty – you knew it, and must take the consequences. The transgression of duty at the P.O. last year was notorious, but there was no written rule to which we could point as broken.[25]

The Treasury accordingly enacted a series of changes to bolster its control over St Martin's le Grand. As was seen in chapter two, a new position of Post Office financial secretary was established to oversee the allocation and expenditure of funds. The Post Office was further required to submit quarterly financial reports.[26] No Savings Banks balance larger than £10,000 was to be left under the control of the Post Office. The most important alteration was the decision to abandon the rapid expansion of the telegraph system. In future the Treasury would seek a guarantee from private citizens to cover losses from any new telegraph office which was not self-supporting. Predictably the number of stations slowly increased thereafter from 3,692 in 1874 to 3,992 in 1880. (After this date, expenditures on extensions began to rise once more.[27])

If the scandal marked a milestone in departmental history, it also had a profound impact on the lives of the politicians and administrators involved. Scudamore always maintained that the responsibility for the expenditure of funds was solely his. Monsell, his political chief, rapidly and completely agreed, claiming 'I was never completely in-

[24] BPP, 1873, vol. 7, Second Report from the Committee of Public Accounts, p. 41.
[25] T1/7425B/1630, Welby's memorandum, 19 February 1873.
[26] Ibid., Treasury minute, 31 December 1873.
[27] BPP, 1900, vol. 47, Return relating to Post Office Telegraphs.

formed that the expenditure which I was asked to sanction would overdraw my account. And no means of obtaining information was offered or suggested to me.'[28] On one level Monsell was correct. In managing the telegraphs Scudamore had consistently ignored the Postmaster General, never informing him, for example, of the March 1872 memorandum requesting more funds from the Treasury. However, all of Monsell's troubles were not of someone else's making. He was clearly not the 'Painstaking Irishman' *Vanity Fair*'s cartoonist had made him out to be. He had not learned from the 1871 strike that Scudamore's independence required curbing. Monsell had also failed to take notice when Lowe asked in March 1872 if St Martin's le Grand had spent more on the telegraphs than authorised.

Parliament did not accept the judgements of Scudamore and Monsell that the civil servant, not his political chief, should bear the responsibility in this case. In July 1873 Parliamentary deliberations of, to use Gladstone's description, 'a truly mortifying character' were conducted on the affair.[29] As Parris has shown, the reaction to the misallocation of funds marked a crucial juncture in the emergence of the concept of ministerial responsibility.[30] Only nine years earlier Lord Robert Cecil had argued that civil servants were directly responsible to Parliament. Now the consensus held that it was the political chiefs of the departments, not permanent civil servants, who should be ultimately answerable to Parliament for their administrations. Gladstone, for example, distinguished between the ability of a Parliamentary committee to question and criticise a civil servant and the duty of the House of Commons to hold the minister-in-charge liable for any misdeeds in his department. Indeed, Gladstone remained much more supportive of Scudamore than sympathetic to Monsell. In Gladstone's view of the administrative debacle, 'Mr Scudamore has committed a great error, but that great error is, in my judgement, balanced by still greater services; and upon the merits of this case I refuse to censure Mr Scudamore.'[31] Instead the wrath of Gladstone and the House of Commons fell upon the Postmaster General. Monsell's errors of judgement in failing to exercise any control over the operation of the Post Office and to halt the expenditure after being informed by Lowe that the grant was exhausted were extensively discussed by his fellow MPs. It was pointed out that only if the ministers were held responsible could Parliament exercise its proper control over the government.

[28] Gladstone Papers, Add. MS. 44152, fol. 203, Monsell's memorandum, July 1873.
[29] Morley, vol. 2, 461.
[30] Henry Parris, *Constitutional Bureaucracy* (London, 1969), pp. 103–5.
[31] *Hansard's, Third Series*, vol. 217, 1229, 29 July 1873.

Ralph Bernal Osborne, who as an MP had developed a certain reputation for indolence and unpredictability, was on this occasion at least on solid constitutional ground when he urged

> This House has nothing to do with Mr Scudamore. He is not responsible to us. We ought to look to the heads of Departments; for if we are to shuffle off these questions by saying a clerk in the Post Office, however distinguished and disinterested he may be, is to take the burden of blame on his shoulders, there is an end to Parliamentary government.[32]

It was, of course, not the end of Parliamentary government, but rather the end of Monsell's career at St Martin's le Grand. The matter had already been discussed at a cabinet meeting where it was agreed that Monsell would resign. Lowe's explanation that neither he nor the Treasury had any means of knowing of Scudamore's misallocations was accepted by the House of Commons, but in an attempt to improve the political situation Lowe, also under attack for his handling of a mail contract, left the Treasury and served his last days in the government as Home Secretary.[33]

On the surface the individual who had sparked the scandal emerged relatively unscathed. Having claimed total responsibility for the crisis, Scudamore continued to enjoy a reputation as a civil servant of ability and drive. While preparing a policy statement on the problem, Gladstone wrote

> As respects the irregularities in the Post Office I think we should now say (with Mr Lowe's approval) that we have read with satisfaction . . . [the] frank and manly statements from Mr Scudamore, that the services of Mr Scudamore have in our opinion given him a high place in the annals of British administration and that we should regard as a serious public loss either his removal from office or [an end to] relations of confidence towards him.[34]

This was more than simply an effort to shore up the sagging fortunes of the Liberal party, as Gladstone went on to add 'if you think this goes too far pray let me know, but I have had much official intercourse with Scudamore, and I place his . . . [merits] very high'. *The Times* shared this favourable appraisal in the post-scandal period, comparing

---

[32] *Ibid.*, 1223–4.
[33] For an account of Lowe's predicaments, see Winter, pp. 288ff. See also chapter eight for the Zanzibar imbroglio.
[34] Monk Bretton Papers, Gladstone to Dodson, 13 December 1873 for the following two statements.

Scudamore with Henry Cole as a capable administrator 'anxious to render his Department efficient, and confident that the end would justify the means'.[35] Scudamore remained head of the telegraphs, but the months after the revelation of the misappropriations were not happy ones for him. The sensitivity which the 1871 strike had revealed grew more pronounced, as he was convinced that government departments and their administrators were held to be guilty until proven innocent and for a long time after. Accordingly, he felt himself abused by the world outside St Martin's le Grand. There is a note of self-pity in some of his letters from this period, as he complained

> I have only too lively a recollection of the pressure put on the Department and for a long time after the transfer; a pressure which I alone had to bear, and which has left traces on me never to be effaced; a pressure which no consideration would induce me to encounter again.[36]

Angered by Treasury restrictions on his freedom of action over the telegraphs and weakened by deteriorating health, Scudamore resigned in 1875. His career as an a technocrat was not over. He accepted an offer from the Ottoman government to organise the Turkish post and telegraph system. He began a new life in the East and, as a result of his efforts, received the Order of the Medjidieh in 1877. Not surprisingly, however, he grew discouraged by the lack of progress there and resigned. Still he never lost his belief in the social and economic value of efficient communications, as one of his last letters to Gladstone attests.[37] He continued to live in Therapia where he died in 1884.

The irony of this entire episode (and, one might add, the tragedy of Scudamore's career) was that the misappropriations were probably unnecessary. Given the internal operation of the Post Office and his unchallenged direction of the telegraphs, Scudamore could have continued to dictate policy at St Martin's le Grand. Given the loose nature of Treasury control, he could have gained its approval for extensions by providing very minimal financial reports. Given his reputation among MPs and the general conviction that the telegraph system should cover the nation, he could have furnished very convincing statements to influence Parliament at least for a while longer. Real doubts as to the financial health of the telegraph system and, thus, harsher criticism of Scudamore's handling of nationalisation did not arise until 1875. Indeed, as late as March 1874 Chadwick was convinced that the nation-

[35] Post 16/15, *The Times*, 6 July 1874.
[36] Post 30/230, E1075, Scudamore to Monsell, 27 March 1873.
[37] Gladstone Papers, Add. MS. 44461, fol. 64, Scudamore to Gladstone, September 1879.

alised telegraphs were a 'brilliant success'.[38] Even after that point, Scudamore could have, as many others did, emphasised the social benefits provided by a state-owned system and minimised its financial problems. In the end Scudamore – one of those civil servants, described by Goschen, who had 'the keenest desire to add field after field to the region in which they labour' – was the victim of his own zeal.[39]

In less than a decade he had moved from the savings banks to life insurance to the telegraphs. Nevertheless, the journey was not made without a rationale. The intellectual origins of the rationale are unclear. No evidence has been found of Scudamore reading Bentham one night and expanding the telegraph system the next morning. Yet one can infer that Scudamore had been exposed to versions of Benthamite thought in discussions with Chadwick and in visits to the Political Economy Club.[40] Without question Scudamore was applying in a rough and ready manner some notion of utility in the pursuit of his goals of social service and increased revenue for the Post Office. It was a standard which cut two ways. On the one hand, nationalisation of the inland telegraphs was justified on financial as well as social grounds. On the other, Scudamore opposed Chadwick's and the Society of Arts' campaign for government purchase of the cable companies on the grounds that the clientele would be too limited.[41] Nonetheless, simply to invoke 'utility' as an explanation for Scudamore's actions is inadequate. For one thing, the term almost of necessity conveys the image of a dry calculator. Scudamore was never that. His many friends in the lower echelon of the London literary world are a reminder that he was not a narrow drudge. Moreover, the definition and application of the term 'utility' were, of course, susceptible to infinite interpretations. To a clerk in the Treasury, utility might be fulfilled only if each and every telegraph office operated at a profit, while Scudamore would have been satisfied if the entire system made a reasonable profit. Scudamore, in applying his notion of utility, had a remarkably broad and positive vision of the benefits possible through a wider role for his department. Indeed, Scudamore's bureaucratic approach with its somewhat disguised paternalism and its inevitable emphasis on planning and social engineering usually led him to place service to the public well before profit. Welby accurately described this outlook when he noted that 'Scudamore, I think, likes to drynurse the

[38] Post 30/47, Chadwick to Scudamore, 16 March 1874.
[39] Goschen, *Addresses*, p. 69.
[40] For an account of this organisation, see S. E. Finer, 'The Transmission of Benthamite Ideas, 1820–50' in G. Sutherland (ed.), *Studies in the Growth of Nineteenth-Century Government* (London, 1972), pp. 16–19. Post 30/47, Chadwick to Scudamore, 16 March 1874.
[41] Post 30/306, E8039/1876, Scudamore to Monsell, 28 July 1873.

British nation, and would like to manage [a] large Department (with the guarantee of the Consolidated Fund) to feed and manage us all.'[42] In this regard Scudamore was remarkably similar to Trollope's fictional clerk Curlydown, who 'would have expended the whole net revenue of the post-office – and his own – in improving the machinery for stamping letters'.[43]

Confirmation of the validity of this assessment comes not only from the record of Scudamore as a dynamic administrator, but also from his public addresses and private letters. For instance, in a speech before the Edinburgh Philosophical Institution in March 1873, the same month the telegraph scandal became known to the public, Scudamore praised the merits of what he termed a 'cooperative society'.[44] By this he meant a framework of public institutions planned so well and operating so efficiently and smoothly that social harmony and economic prosperity would inevitably result. The telegraph system as a forerunner of future experiments in state businesses would 'teach the people what they have achieved, and what far greater successes they may achieve if they will continue to work together'.[45] One side benefit of such operations would be a reduction – possibly the complete abolition – of the individual tax burden, as profits from telegraphs, mines, railways and other nationalised industries plus liquor taxes would come to finance government.[46] (The scope of his vision may be better gauged if one remembers that that in 1872 the government collected £9.1 million in property and income taxes.) Perhaps the most complete as well as the most enthusiastic statement of Scudamore's dreams for this new society is found in the following letter to Lord Hartington concerning that great laboratory for public administration, Ireland:

> If after the acquisition of the Railways in Ireland you can appeal not to the few but to the millions; if you can cheaply carry the peasant to his field and the artisan to his factory; if you can put the market next door to the produce; if you can carry the now wasted wealth of the coast to the hunger bitten poor of the great cities; if you can make the Railway minister still further than it does to the spread of intelligence; if you have a Telegraph to wait as a handmaiden on Trade, on the Post, and on the Railway; if through the Money Order Office which is a great state bank you aid the operations of retail

42 T1/7545A/4286, Welby to Northcote, 11 December 1874.
43 Anthony Trollope, *John Caldigate*, vol. 2 (1879, rpr. New York, 1911), pp. 166–7.
44 *The Times*, 11 March 1873, p. 4.
45 *Ibid.*
46 Post 16/13, *Spectator*, 24 December 1872, pp. 1619–20, reporting Scudamore's speech at Hull on 'The Nation Working for Itself'.

trade whilst through the Savings Bank you draw into close relations with the Government, all those who have a stake no matter how trifling it may be in order and tranquillity, if you thus bind together and guide them to one common end, what may you not do for Ireland? To increase her tranquillity and to make her tranquil is to attract to her shores the capital which shames disorder and the enterprise which riots tremble before.[47]

Without trying to establish more than rather vague parallels, one might do well to turn attention from Bentham and English antecedents and look to the continent as a possible source of inspiration for Scudamore's vision. He had, after all, studied the results of government expansion in Belgium and Switzerland. Furthermore, it should be remembered that the ascendancy of Scudamore coincided with the age of Napoleon III with its Saint-Simonian residues and its complex financial experiments, such as the Credit Mobilier.[48] Scudamore's version of the corporate state was sui generis, but it belonged to a wider European pattern. Troubled by the waste and inefficiency in certain areas of the Victorian economy, such as the telegraph companies and bubble life insurance firms, he regarded the state as a proper remedy. Once precise planning by public-minded administrators replaced the chaos of short-sighted individualism, other positive results would rapidly emerge. Prices would be lowered; profits would be maintained. Workers would dutifully emulate the industriousness of their superiors. Hierarchy would not disappear, but it would be founded on the more equitable basis of merit. Perhaps most important of all, as his statement on Ireland promised, social disorder and class tension would ease. Citizens would become joined in a greater whole. Scudamore's vision was a noble one, but it was also profoundly naive. It placed too much weight on the abilities of civil servants to plan and too much hope on the inclination of citizens to cooperate. In sum, the problems which destroyed Scudamore's career did not affect a passive individual driven forward by the mere force of events. They were the natural result of his active, almost emotional belief in the benefits – primarily social, but partly financial – which were possible through government expansion into the areas of the economy previously considered the domain of private effort.

The subsequent history of the Post Office telegraphs did not fulfil all Scudamore's hopes for a model state enterprise. By 1875, the year of his retirement, former advocates of nationalisation began to realise that

[47] Post 82/58, Scudamore to Hartington, 21 July 1872.
[48] See Rondo E. Cameron, *France and the Economic Development of Europe* (Princeton, 1961) for an analysis of this complex topic.

something was deeply wrong with the system and that the original projections of revenue and expenses were badly flawed. Jevons, for example, abandoned his earlier position and concluded that 'The accounts of the telegraph department unfortunately demonstrate what was to be feared before, namely, that a Government department cannot compete in economy with an ordinary commercial firm subject to competition.'[49] The situation which vexed Jevons, Northcote the Chancellor of the Exchequer, and others can be illustrated by a few statistics. In 1875 there were 228 telegraph offices in the United Kingdom which were operating with a deficit.[50] Equally importantly, the revenue from the other offices was not sufficient to offset this loss. The working expenses of the system were equal to 97.54 per cent of the total revenue. The remaining net revenue was only £28,145, while £293,706 still had to be paid as interest on the stock created for the original purchase. It is also clear that the financial problems of the system were not simply the result of Scudamore's post-nationalisation management, as the department continued to incur large deficits after his departure. (See table one.)

Table 1
The financial record of the Post Office telegraphs

Year	Total revenue	Total expenditure	Net revenue	Interest on stock created for purchase of telegraphs
1871–2	£ 754,634	£ 600,926	£153,708	£233,081
1875–6	1,287,623	1,106,912	180,711	294,906
1880–1	1,633,887	1,308,454	325,433	326,417
1885–6	1,787,264	1,832,401	– 45,137	326,417
1890–1	2,456,764	2,388,581	68,183	299,215
1895–6	2,879,794	2,920,341	– 40,547	299,888
1900–1	3,459,353	3,824,163	–364,810	294,860
1905–6	4,151,338	4,892,199	–740,861	271,691
1910–11	3,168,804	4,081,399	–912,595	271,691

Source: Annual reports of the Postmaster General.

[49] W. S. Jevons, 'The Post Office Telegraphs and their Financial Results', *The Fortnightly Review*, 18 (1875), 835.
[50] For the following see Post 30/290, E1075/1876, Post Office to Treasury, 23 December 1875 and BPP, 1900, vol. 47, Return relating to the Post Office Telegraphs. See also Reports of the Postmaster General for specific years. Care must be used in evaluating these statistics. The Post Office maintained that no accurate

In analysing the reasons for the deficits, some care must be taken in assigning responsibility. The explanation does not lie in the public's reaction to nationalisation. The telegraph was more widely used in England than in any continental country. The number of telegrams increased rapidly as a result of the lower, uniform tariff and the extension of the system to outlying areas, as table two illustrates.

Table 2
The expansion of telegraph usage

Year	Number of telegrams	Number per capita
1868–9	6,500,000	.21
1870–1	9,850,000	.32
1880–1	29,412,000	.84
1890–1	66,409,000	1.76
1900–1	89,577,000	2.14
1910–11	86,707,000	1.91

(These figures include foreign and press telegrams as well as inland telegrams.)

Source: Annual reports of the Postmaster General.

Part of this growth may be attributed to the need for rapid communication by the business community, which the Post Office met effectively. Jevons's 1875 judgement that the 'messages appear to be generally delivered with speed and regularity' would have found general agreement throughout the years before the First World War. If the public's reaction to a state system does not explain the continuing fiscal problems of the telegraphs, neither does the purchase price negotiated by Scudamore in June 1868. Departmental officials later liked to cite the supposedly excessive purchase price as an explanation for all their difficulties, but this masks a rather more complicated set of interrelated issues. After all, before 1914 there were 26 years in which telegraph revenue did not equal expenditure, much less cover the interest on the approximately £10 million worth of stock created for the purchase.

comparison between its performance and that of the companies was possible because of differences in accounting procedures. In the Post Office capital expenditure of one year was charged against the revenue of the same year, unlike the practice outside government. The Treasury maintained that this was a red herring. The financial performance of the telegraphs was so poor, that if the system had been operated in such a manner by a private firm, it would have been impossible to secure loans for capital expenditure: T1/8799A/1086, Treasury to Post Office, 23 February 1894.

Where, then, did the problem lie? There can be no doubt that Scudamore in his eagerness to conclude the nationalisation process had made concessions, which later proved costly. The low rate granted to the press, while serving a social need, did not help the department's balance sheet. Before nationalisation the private companies had sent a daily average of 6,000 words for the press during a Parliamentary session; the Post Office was sending over 20,000 by 1871.[51] By 1900 it was estimated that the Post Office was sending over 110 million words for the press at an annual loss of over £375,000. This sum alone would have radically reduced the annual telegraph deficit. Another aspect of the original agreement which later contributed to the poor financial health of the Post Office telegraphs was the right granted to the railways to send telegrams free. By 1890 the Post Office was sending almost 1.5 million such messages for railways without any compensation. Having made these terms with the press and the railways, the department found itself in the awkward position of the greater the aggregate business, the larger the aggregate loss.

However, the main source of the telegraph deficit was the high operating costs of the system. The Post Office was simply not able to save as much through a centralised administration as Scudamore had hoped – a problem recognised by a Treasury committee of inquiry as early as 1875.[52] It is important to note precisely where the increases in operating costs occurred. For the most part, the expensive growth in bureaucracy did not come at the highest levels of management.[53] In contrast to the nine secretaries and assistant secretaries and the fifty-three directors of the private companies, the Post Office telegraph branch in 1875 was managed by only one secretary and two principal clerks with the aid of assistants. Salary costs under the Post Office were comparatively smaller at this level of administration. The private companies, handling annually over 6 million telegrams, paid £15,000 a year in salaries to their eighty-six executive officers. The Post Office, while it processed three times as many telegrams, paid only £16,900 for the management in the Secretary's Office. Per capita salary costs in the accounting branch of the Post Office were also lower than under the private companies, although the total costs were higher because of the increase in the size of the staff to handle the larger work load. The increase in the government bureaucracy came primarily at the lower level. Only eight months after the Post Office take-over the total number of employees was twice as large as the staff of the private

---

51 Another estimate placed the 1903 press deficit at £500,000. See Post 30/947 and Kieve, p. 219.
52 Post 30/290, E1075/1876, Report of Treasury Committee, 17 July 1875.
53 Ibid., Post Office to Treasury, 23 December 1875.

companies.[54] It had been originally anticipated that the unified Post Office system would require only 1,528 clerks and 1,283 messengers in comparison to the 2,514 clerks and 1,471 messengers employed by the private companies. Nevertheless, 4,913 clerks and 3,116 messengers were hired by the Post Office in the initial rapid expansion of the system under Scudamore. Not only did the Post Office have a larger staff than the private companies, but it came to pay them higher salaries. The first significant increase was given in 1872 when a definite scheme of classification for the telegraph establishment was introduced. The cost of salaries, which was £313,591 in 1870–1, increased to £570,983 in 1872–3. The department already found itself in a dilemma from which it was not to escape. In the wake of the 1871 strike Scudamore described the difficulty when he complained 'The press and the public would probably [take] an impartial view of the difference between a Company and its servants, but if there were a difference between the Post Office and its servants, no such impartiality could be looked for. The first prescription would be inevitably against the Government Department.'[55] As employee agitation grew from the early 1870s on, the department found itself unable to stem the tide of rising salary scales. The average weekly salary of a male telegraphist in the central office in St Martin's le Grand increased from 28s 10d in 1885 to 50s 10d in 1910. Contributing to the problem was, of course, the fact of the over-all fiscal health of the Post Office. As long as the mail operations yielded large profits, employees on the telegraph side, which was losing money, felt entitled to their share of the spoils. The end result of this trend was that wages consumed an ever increasing percentage of total telegraph revenue. (See table three.)

Table 3
The pattern of wages in the telegraphs department

Year	Total wages	Percentage of wages to total revenue
1870–1	£ 313,591	39%
1880–1	719,289	44%
1890–1	1,506,219	61%
1900–1	2,343,769	68%
1910–11	2,701,490	85%

Source: Annual reports of the Postmaster General.

[54] For the following see BPP, 1900, vol. 47, Return relating to the Post Office Telegraphs and Post 30/290, E1075/1876, Report of Treasury Committee, 17 July 1875.
[55] Post 30/215, E274/1872, Scudamore to Monsell, 25 November 1871.

It is also evident that, as a government agency, St Martin's le Grand faced external pressures of a different kind and magnitude than had the telegraph companies.[56] For a brief period after 1878 net revenue in the telegraphs department began to rise from £119,913 in 1877 to £325,433 in 1881. Although the surplus was still not sufficient to cover the interest on the stock created for the purchase, at that time usually around £326,000 a year, many commentators and customers seized upon the increase in profits as evidence that telegraph rates were excessively high. Accordingly, in the summer of 1880 a lobbying campaign in which the Society of Arts and various Chambers of Commerce participated was launched. It won support inside the department. Henry Fawcett the Postmaster General agreed that

> any profit beyond what was necessary for the maintenance of the charges connected with the Telegraph service, including interest . . . must be regarded as taxation; and when the day came when they [the Post Office] secured this profit, it would be a question eminently deserving of the consideration of the Chancellor of the Exchequer whether a tax on telegrams was a desirable means of securing revenue, especially when taxation involved the maintenance of so exceptionally high a rate per telegram of 1s.[57]

Despite the opposition of Gladstone's government to any reduction, Fawcett pressed for one. When the motion for a change came up for a vote in 1883, the Postmaster General, as described by the *Morning Post*, 'not only did not contest the general soundness of this demand, but unmistakably manifested his sympathy with it'.[58] Although the official who replaced Fawcett, G. J. Shaw-Lefevre, sought to resist the change, nonetheless the tariff was reduced in 1885 to 6d for 12 words, including the address. This led to an immediate drop in the charge for the average telegram from 1s 1d in 1885 to 8d in 1886, as senders learned to condense the length of their messages.

It is clear, then, that the financial problems of the Post Office telegraphs had their origins primarily in the rates charged to the public and the press as well as in departmental staffing and salary policies. Moreover, given the efficiency of mail delivery and the 1896 purchase of the telephone trunk lines the department was to an extent compet-

---

[56] Such problems, of course, were to be a lasting feature of the history of the Post Office, which was an 'organisation charged with performing economic and service functions within a politically-determined environment': Eric Batstone, Anthony Ferner, and Michael Turner, *Consent and Efficiency: Labour Relations and Management Strategy in the State Enterprise* (Oxford, 1984), p. 275.

[57] *Hansard's, Third Series*, vol. 271, 428, 26 July 1882.

[58] Post 16/20, *Morning Post*, 30 March 1883.

ing with itself, thus compounding these problems. What is more difficult to assess is the significance of this continuing deficit and the
record of the telegraphs operation as a whole. It would be easy to
conclude, as Jevons did, that the state simply could not manage as well
as private companies. The Treasury, examining the situation, described
the record of this nationalised industry as 'a state of affairs which would
probably [be] regarded in the financial world as little less than desper-
ate'.[59] It would be equally easy to conclude, as one newspaper did on
the twenty-fifth anniversary of the government take-over, that the
Post Office had played only a minor role in developing the telegraph's
economic usefulness. Thus, to 'impute what is really due to a huge
increase in trade, in the semi-educated public, and in the purpose for
which the instrument was gradually found suitable – to impute this to
the action of a beneficent government in taking over the wires is surely
too absurd to need refutation'.[60] Still it is worth remembering that the
record of the private telegraph companies had not been an unbroken
series of triumphs. For example, between 1861 and 1865 the UKTC
charging the 1s rate had not been able to pay a dividend on its ordinary
shares. Moreover, the social benefits of the nationalised system should
not be minimised. *The Daily News* noted six years after the Post Office
began to operate the system that 'Cheap telegrams have become a
necessity of modern existence; and be they irksome or not, profits or no
profits, the public must have them.'[61] St Martin's le Grand supported
this approach that service to the public, not profit considerations, was
the most important criterion in decision-making. As one civil servant
argued,

The financial position of the [telegraph] department is not flourishing, but this is not necessarily [a] national loss. The public have
received in exchange for the deficit advantages that they may consider fully worth it. The whole question is one that can hardly be
settled except in accordance with the tendency of outdoor feeling,
and the . . . [Treasury] in regarding the matter purely as one of
equilibrium of accounts, appear to have taken a view that will not be
very generally endorsed.[62]

This outlook was evident in numerous aspects of departmental policy.
The Post Office remained committed to the need to bring the

---

59 T1/8799A/1086, Treasury to Post Office, 23 February 1894.
60 Post 16/33, *Globe*, 28 January 1895.
61 Post 16/15, *The Daily News*, 25 July 1876.
62 Post 30/306, E8039/1876, E. Graves's report to Tilley, 11 October 1875.

telegraphs to the wider society. Hence, the cost of extensions, which held fairly low for six years after the Scudamore scandal, increased after 1880 as table four demonstrates.

Table 4
The extension of the telegraph system

Year	Amount spent on extensions	Amount as percentage of total expenditure
1873–4	£ 23,928	2%
1877–8	28,041	2%
1880–1	103,488	8%
1885–6	154,021	9%
1890–1	109,735	5%
1895–6	80,102	3%
1900–1	148,118	4%
1905–6	257,704	5%
1910–11	271,668	7%

Source: BPP, 1900, vol. 47, Return relating to the Post Office Telegraphs; *Reports of the Postmaster General* (1908), p. 96 and (1913), p. 93.

The department sought to transmit all messages ten minutes after receipt, instead of the frequent one-hour delay of telegrams under the private companies. This effort improved service, but also added to operating costs since a larger staff was required. (Not unexpectedly, this was one area where the union leadership supported the departmental point of view.[63]) The Post Office also resisted attempts to close offices which had proven to be unprofitable. In the end neither the Treasury nor the Post Office was able to resist the pressures to maintain and expand the system. The guarantee system, which was designed to eliminate the losses from unprofitable offices, was gradually phased out through concessions granted in 1891, 1897, and 1906.

Without question the record of the Post Office telegraphs before 1914 was decidedly mixed.[64] St Martin's le Grand had fulfilled the

[63] Post 33/488, M523/1928, Union of Post Office Workers Report, 12 January 1928.
[64] Two recent articles have shown that the performance of public utilities in the nineteenth century was by no means always inferior to that achieved by private management. See J. S. Foreman-Peck, 'Natural Monopoly and Railway Policy in the Nineteenth Century', *Oxford Economic Papers*, 39 (1987), 699–718 and Robert Milward and Robert Ward, 'The Costs of Public and Private Gas Enterprises in Late 19th Century Britain', *Oxford Economic Papers*, 39 (1987), 719–37.

essence of Scudamore's promises in regard to public service, but fell short on the fiscal side. When two years after take-over Scudamore had proclaimed that government could defeat private enterprise, he of course misstated the question. It was not a contest in which both sides were playing by the same set of rules. For better and for worse the goals and circumstances of this departmental industry were different from those obtaining for the telegraph companies. This reality clouds the debate over the record of St Martin's le Grand during the era of Scudamore and after. Ideology had spurred the purchase, and ideology perforce has shaped any judgement of its impact. Hence, whether one applauds or condemns this experiment in nationalisation depends not only on the thousands of statistics gathered to chart the history of the telegraphs, but also on one's reading of those same statistics.

6

The Coming of the Telephone, 1876–92

In olden days a man of business could arrange his affairs for the day after the delivery of the morning post, and the perpetual arrival of telegrams has served to add new stings to existence. The case will surely be worse with verbal communications than with written ones. – The Times, 10 May 1879, p. 11.

In December 1880 The Sheffield Post applied to various government departments the Shakespearian adage that some are born to greatness, some achieve it, and some have greatness thrust upon them. The Foreign Office was the preeminent example of the first category, while the Treasury belonged to the second group. The Post Office was representative of the third type, as the newspaper noted that 'Everything seems to fall into its lap. It centralises, it concentrates, some would say monopolises.'[1] This insight serves as an appropriate text with which to begin a consideration of the Post Office's relationship with the telephone. With the introduction of Bell's new invention to the United Kingdom by William Thomson, the future Lord Kelvin, at the September 1876 Glasgow meeting of the British Association, a major issue had indeed fallen into the lap of St Martin's le Grand. The obvious problem was to determine what the proper departmental attitude toward this new means of communication should be. Both the telegraph and the telephone used electricity to convey messages, but there was an even more direct link between the two which demanded the Post Office's attention, the ABC telegraph. By means of this instrument, one could spell out messages with no knowledge of Morse or any other code. The Universal Private Telegraph Company had established a system of intercommunication between private customers using such instruments in Newcastle-on-Tyne in 1864, and the operation had been nationalised along with the rest of the telegraph companies in 1870. Hence, the Post Office was in the business not only of sending telegrams from one station to another, but also house-to-house through

1 Post 30/542, E13267/1889, The Sheffield Post, 24 December 1880.

what were termed private wires *before* the invention of the telephone. Commentators on Post Office history have complained that the department inhibited the use of the telephone out of an obsessive concern for the financial well-being of the telegraphs. So spoke *The Times* in 1880, and the Manchester *Guardian* in 1884. Kieve endorsed this criticism when he wrote 'from the beginning the telephone was regarded as a competitor to the telegraph and was so hampered in its growth. . . . The Post Office policy appeared to be a deliberate attempt to stand between the public and the full utilisation of a great scientific invention.'[2] As the following two chapters demonstrate, such an appraisal is seriously misleading in its failure to comprehend the complexities of the relationship between the Post Office and the telephone in the years between 1876 and 1912, the year which saw the completion of the complicated cycle of nationalisation.

In the months following the introduction of the telephone to Britain, the invention received a great deal of publicity. Demonstrations, such as the experiments conducted in London between the Queen's Theatre and Canterbury Hall, and Bell's lecture tour, which included an address to the Society of Arts, served to arouse interest. *The Times* reflected this attitude when it noted 'Few of the recent applications of science have attracted so much popular curiosity as the telephone, and few, perhaps, have been the subject of such extravagant and erroneous statements as the telephone. . . . Yet the invention is a most startling one – too remarkable, indeed to be discredited by any amount of exaggeration.'[3] Sharing this interest, St Martin's le Grand was not lethargic in its reaction to the coming of the telephone. By March 1877 the department had instructed William Preece its chief engineer to report on the telephone's capabilities, especially its practical utility. Studies were made of the state of telephone technology in America and Germany. The early reports were mixed. On the one hand, the telephone was held to pose no immediate threat to the telegraphs for long-distance communications. On the other hand, it seemed very suitable for use in certain private-wire situations where the ABC instrument was currently employed. As Preece who was a distinguished scientist of wide reputation reported,

---

[2] Post 16/17, *The Times*, 21 January 1880. Post 30/542, E13257/1889, the Manchester *Guardian*, 30 June 1884. Kieve, p. 214.
[3] *The Times*, 14 July 1877, p. 7. For other reactions, see Asa Briggs, 'The Pleasure Telephone' and C. R. Perry, 'The British Experience' in Ithiel de Sola Pool (ed.), *The Social Impact of the Telephone* (Cambridge, Massachusetts, 1977). F. G. C. Baldwin, *The History of the Telephone in the United Kingdom* (London, 1925) is invaluable in its treatment of the telephone's reception.

Although in its present form the telephone is not generally applicable, there are a great many instances where wires are carried on special poles or where they are carried on open lines, where the instrument is perfectly practicable, and it certainly will be generally demanded by our renters. More than that, I believe it will lead to a large accession of private wire business.[4]

Accordingly, the department entered into negotiations with Colonel W. H. Reynolds, Bell's representative in England, and by December 1877 an agreement was successfully concluded. The department proposed to act as an agent for Bell, leasing his telephones to the public at annual rents of £5 for short circuits and £10 for long circuits. As compensation the Post Office would receive 40 per cent of the gross rental income. Two aspects of this early agreement should be noted. First, the Post Office was taking no risk by purchasing telephones, as it continued to be somewhat sceptical as to their practicality. Lord John Manners the Postmaster General, for example, believed that the 'telephone could not be utilised on the public wires in any way, and it is only under certain conditions . . . that it can be rendered effective for private wire purposes'.[5] Secondly, the Post Office was not attempting to undersell private enterprise. The rate at which the department proposed to rent telephones to the public was the same as the tariff charged usually by Colonel Reynolds. Yet it is clear that the telephone evoked both fear and respect within the walls of St Martin's le Grand. In a May 1878 letter Manners informed the Treasury that the Post Office felt 'compelled' to adopt the telephone in order to protect its position in the market.[6]

The possibility of competition became a distinct reality one month later in June 1878 when the Telephone Company, Ltd was registered for the purpose of acquiring and working Bell's patent. From the very outset the relationship between St Martin's le Grand and this private firm was shaped by circumstances not usually present in the economic warfare waged by rival concerns. Each side enjoyed assets which were essential for a successful telephone system. The company held the patent, while the Post Office had the right to lay wire along public wayleaves. Between the summer of 1878 and the summer of 1879 the two sides conducted an extensive round of negotiations over this

4   Post 30/603, E4522/1892, Preece's memorandum, 19 September 1877. See also E. C. Baker, *Sir William Preece* (London, 1976). Preece was only one of a larger number of specialists influencing government policy in the latter half of the nineteenth century. Roy MacLeod (ed.), *Government and Expertise* (Cambridge, 1988) sets these administrators in context.
5   Post 30/603, E4522/1892, Post Office to Treasury, 20 February 1878.
6   *Ibid.*, Post Office to Treasury, 17 May 1878.

predicament. The Telephone Company was amenable to forming a close working relationship with St Martin's le Grand, a relationship which would have almost constituted a partnership. As one departmental negotiator observed after a May 1879 meeting, the company's basic strategy was that it 'had little to obtain from the Post Office as simple customers or agents, and that it was in the interest of [the company] to bribe the department into becoming its ally'.[7] Thus, the company proposed to supply the government telephones at cost price in return for the government's sanction of the company's right to put down pipes and wires. The Telephone Company did not long remain the sole private enterprise in the field. In August 1879 the Edison Company was established to work the rival patent of Thomas Alva Edison. The Lancashire Company, in reality a subsidiary of the Telephone Company, was also organised at the same time to open exchanges in Manchester and other towns in the northwest. Advertisements in newspapers promised other exchange systems similar to those already operating in the United States. The entry of these new firms into the rapidly developing industry only served to increase the number of difficult policy questions faced by administrators at the Post Office. Should one firm be favoured over others? Should the department enter the telephone field? How should legitimate considerations in regard to telegraph revenue be weighed against equally legitimate considerations concerning the nurturing of the telephone's social and economic usefulness? By September 1879 the department had decided to allow private initiative to develop the telephone locally under licence. Companies were to be allowed to operate systems which would serve areas not larger than a half mile radius from a central exchange. However, the government was to receive a fixed royalty of £100 a year and 25 per cent of the gross profits, and there was to be no interconnection between exchanges. Without question, the Post Office's policy at this stage was ambivalent. Departmental experiments with the telephone had not proved completely satisfactory, but the department did not want to 'put a stop to what may . . . prove to be a public convenience'.[8] At the same time administrators were concerned that the telephone, if successful, would cut into departmental revenue from local telegraph operations, worth at that point £75,000 a year in London alone.

The Treasury quickly sanctioned this policy, but the private companies proved less cooperative. The Edison Company, in particular, refused to acknowledge the necessity of applying for a licence from the Post Office. It contended that the monopoly established by the 1869

[7] *Ibid.*, Graves's memorandum, 27 May 1879.
[8] *Ibid.*, Post Office to Treasury, 22 September 1879.

Telegraph Act did not apply to the telephone, and, therefore, companies were at liberty to open exchanges without payment of royalties. St Martin's le Grand, predictably, disagreed. Legal proceedings were initiated against the Edison Company in November 1879 and against the Telephone Company one month later. The department received much criticism from the press and in Parliament for this action, but the overriding influence in this specific matter was the protection of its revenue interests. A decision in favour of the Post Office was rendered on 20 December 1880 after five days of proceedings. The basic definition of a telegraph, that is, 'any apparatus for transmitting messages by electric signals',[9] was found to be broad enough to cover the completely unforeseen telephone and subsequently the Marconi wireless. The decision was not greeted with universal approval. There was considerable fear that this line of legal reasoning would stifle individual effort and private enterprise. The old stereotype of an indolent government failing to appreciate the potential of new technological developments was revived. As the *Saturday Review* asked five days after the court decision, what were 'the future prospects of scientific invention and inventors in this country, if this is the encouragement they are to receive'?[10]

This assessment underestimated St Martin's le Grand's ability to develop the telephone's potential. Even before the court decision affirming the department's monopoly, the Post Office had begun to take a more positive, more aggressive outlook toward telephone development. With the replacement of John Tilley by Stevenson Arthur Blackwood as Secretary in May 1880, the department now had a senior permanent official much more enthusiastic as to the potential of the telephone. By December Blackwood was urging Fawcett the Postmaster General to take the offensive by establishing telephone systems under direct departmental ownership and management. Interestingly, Blackwood offered essentially the same justifications, public service and revenue potential, for a Post Office system which had been put forward in support of the private licensing system proposed only fifteen months earlier. But it cannot be emphasised too strongly that Blackwood was concerned with far more than simply threats to telegraph income. As he warned Fawcett, the companies were more interested in forcing the government to buy them out at inflated prices than in serving the needs of the public.[11] Rather than allow the companies to establish themselves, Blackwood proposed a surprisingly bold plan. The department should buy 5,000 telephones from Frederick A. Gower,

9   Post 30/489, E7036/1886.
10   *Saturday Review*, 25 December 1880, p. 803.
11   See Post 30/542, E13267/1889, Blackwood to Fawcett, 10 December 1880 for the following.

who was not connected with any private company and who held his own patent. Gower had offered the department a 25 per cent reduction from the usual charge for telephones, but the total cost still would have amounted to £45,000. Blackwood further estimated that another £15,000 would be necessary for pipes and wire and £13,000 for ordinary maintenance of the existing private wire systems. Thus, the former Treasury clerk, originally brought into the department to curtail spending, was proposing to spend initially a total of £73,000. (The calculations appear to have been made with no less haste and no more care than the telegraph estimates for which Scudamore had been earlier criticised.) Furthermore, no specific estimates of future profits appear to have been made at this point. Yet Blackwood felt the need to act in 'a wide and comprehensive manner' in order to outflank the opposition. He believed that telephone development would be best advanced by governmental, not private, initiative. His faith in departmental efficiency had clearly survived the telegraph troubles, and by 1880 he had emerged as a forthright advocate of expansion into new fields. As Blackwood sought to convince Fawcett,

> There can be no doubt that the Public would very much rather deal with the Post Office than Private Companies. In all the large towns the Postmasters are being asked why the Department does not establish Telephone Exchanges; many people say they would willingly pay a higher charge to the Post Office than to a private company; and many are waiting in the hope that the Post Office will before long enter the field.

For the moment the Postmaster General agreed with Blackwood's point of view, and Treasury sanction was accordingly sought. It should be made clear that the Post Office was not at this stage seeking to nationalise the private companies, but simply trying to cultivate its own system. The department was even willing to continue negotiations with the companies on the licensing procedures outlined in September 1879. The policy was a sound one. Public needs would have been met, and the question of government purchase of the private companies at inflated prices for goodwill would not have arisen. In addition, St Martin's le Grand could not be accused of seeking to destroy private initiative and competition.

Unfortunately, the Treasury did not view the matter in the same light. Until December 1880 there had been essential unanimity between the two departments over telephone policy, but the Treasury reply to the Post Office proposal marked the beginning of a sharp break. At first glance the decision appeared favourable.[12] The entire

---

[12] Post 1/68, Treasury to Post Office, 16 December 1880.

amount requested by the Post Office was approved. Nevertheless, the goal of the Treasury in sanctioning the request was totally opposed to that of St Martin's le Grand. The Treasury would allow the Post Office to establish a limited telephone exchange system, but only in order to force the private companies to negotiate more amicably for licences. The Post Office telephone system was not to have an independent life and purpose, but rather was to be only a ploy in a game of commercial diplomacy. The Treasury had opted for private initiative, rather than a government agency, to develop the telephone in England.

Civil servants at St Martin's le Grand were by no means as pessimistic and hesitant as their counterparts in Whitehall and did not regard the Treasury decision as the final word on the matter. The Post Office continued to press ahead for a departmental telephone system, but found itself caught in the middle between the Treasury and private industry. Relations with the latter also deteriorated during this period. On 20 December the department advertised its intention to establish telephone exchanges wherever public demand justified it. Annual charges in London would be £15 if the user was within one-half mile of the exchange, £19 between one-half and one and one-half miles, and so on. The United Telephone Company, which had been formed in May 1880 through the merger of the Bell Company and the Telephone Company, immediately protested, claiming that the Post Office was infringing the patent rights of the company. Blackwood firmly replied that consultations with the law officers of the Crown as well as private opinion had confirmed the department's right to buy telephones from Gower. Blackwood was resolute on this issue. No single company should have a monopoly of telephone patents. As he advised Fawcett, 'By purchasing from Mr Gower a large number of telephones which we propose, we shall . . . be able to checkmate them.'[13] Moreover, in almost Scudamore-like fashion, Blackwood pushed the enlargement of the department's telephone system. Between the advertisement of 20 December and late January the Post office received fifty applications for the establishment of exchange systems. Blackwood argued that the necessity of obtaining Treasury sanction for such exchanges could be postponed, as there were still funds available in the department's private wire account. On this issue Blackwood, it is clear, had become something of a zealot.

However, there were limits as to how far Blackwood could exercise his zeal. After all, the Treasury had decreed that the department negotiate with private companies on licensing terms, and soon the department would expend all allocated funds for its own telephone exchanges. From December 1880 to the following spring the general

13 Post 30/542, E13267/1889, Blackwood to Fawcett, 23 December 1880.

licensing philosophy and specific details were hammered out in discussions between the Post Office, the Treasury, and individual companies. The specific details were the easier of the two matters to clear up. Licences were to run for thirty-one years with a government option to cancel at the tenth, the seventeenth, or the twenty-fourth year. Exchanges were to operate within a two-mile radius, with London being an exception. The department was to receive 10 per cent of gross receipts. Determining whether competition between one company and another or between the Post Office and private industry was to be permitted proved much more difficult. In January 1881 *The Electrician* had insisted that 'It seems axiomatic to us that telephony must necessarily be a monopoly.'[14] Yet it was by no means clear who should hold the monopoly in a particular area. The problem arose in March when the National Provincial Telephone Company applied for a licence to work in the Midlands, Yorkshire, Scotland, and Ireland. The Post Office already had ABC private wire systems in several towns in these regions, which it was converting to telephone service. How should the department respond to a request to allow a competitor to invade its own territory? The answer proposed by Blackwood was eminently fair and again demonstrates that the Post Office was more willing than its critics have allowed to accommodate the demands of private industry as well as the needs of the public. Blackwood's formula was simple. Where the Post Office already had an exchange, any request from a private company to establish its competing system would be denied. Where a company already had an exchange, the department would refrain from competition and further would deny others the right to compete. In towns lacking telephone systems, Blackwood suggested that local opinion should be canvassed as to its preference for a government or a private system and a licensing decision so made.[15] Fawcett approved Blackwood's proposal, which would have eliminated wasteful competition in what many believed was a natural monopoly and which would have allowed the telephone industry to develop according to popular sentiment. The department also indicated its willingness to foster the expansion of telephony by agreeing to abandon all claims to royalties for the years preceding 1881 as well as to give up the court costs granted to it in the case against the companies. Once more revenue considerations were not an overriding concern in a revenue department.

The Treasury failed to appreciate the merits of Blackwood's plan.[16] It continued to prefer private initiative, rather than the state, as the chief

---

14 Post 30/603, E4522/1892, *The Electrician*, 8 January 1881.
15 Post 30/542, E13267/1889, Blackwood to Fawcett, 4 March 1881.
16 *Ibid.*, Treasury to Post Office, 3 May 1881.

means of telephone development. On learning that the Treasury was attempting to thwart the expansion of this Post Office project, Blackwood exploded in frustration. He insisted that the department had faithfully followed Treasury guidelines and went on to argue that the department should pursue an even more thrusting policy of telephone development. Emphasising the telephone's profit potential, Blackwood in May 1881 modified his earlier proposal and advocated that, in towns where there was the slightest indication of a demand for a telephone system, the Post Office 'should step in at once'.[17] In response the Treasury preferred to maintain its piecemeal policy of sanctioning the establishment of Post Office exchanges on an individual basis. Nevertheless, Whitehall refrained from adopting an overall telephone policy, and St Martin's le Grand was forced to continue the difficult round of interdepartmental negotiations in order to convince the Treasury of the wisdom of a Post Office telephone system. The contrast between the telegraph nationalisation and the history of the telephone is especially vivid in this regard. In the earlier campaign Scudamore had enjoyed the support of powerful politicians and friends as well as much of the press. He had also dealt with a complacent Treasury. Blackwood enjoyed none of these assets. Of necessity, then, his policy was more cautious. This was particularly evident in his concern not to establish telephone exchanges in towns where there was no hope for profit. Projections of income and expense were to be made before opening a system. In promising cities, however, Blackwood argued that the Post Office should move with vigour. As he predicted, 'the public in the great centres of trade will demand the establishment of a Telephone system, and the question, therefore, is not whether the system should be established, but whether the Department should have any share in its establishment'.[18]

At this point the department was involved in the telephone question in two crucial, yet somewhat contradictory ways, as a competing operator of exchanges and as the licensing agency for the entire industry. By 1882 the Post Office system included exchanges in Cork, Cardiff, Hull, Leicester, Limerick, Liverpool, Londonderry, Middlesbrough, Newcastle-on-Tyne, Newport, Sunderland, Waterford, and West Hartlepool, which charged the rates shown in table one.

---

17 *Ibid.*, Post Office to Treasury, 19 May 1881.
18 *Ibid.*, Blackwood to Fawcett, 31 May 1881.

Table 1
Rate structure of the Post Office telephones, 1882

Single wire not exceeding ½ mile	£14 10s
Single wire not exceeding 1 mile	18 0
Double wire not exceeding ¼ mile	14 10
Double wire not exceeding ½ mile	16 5
Double wire not exceeding 1 mile	21 10

Source: Post 30/1615, E29062/1908, unsigned memorandum, 7 January 1910.

Licences had also been granted to private companies in over seventy towns. The problem was somehow to reconcile these two conflicting roles. To what extent should the department encourage and foster the development of rival companies? On minor points the Post Office appeared conciliatory. It permitted private companies to connect customers' wires directly with telegraph offices. It also agreed to rent trunk lines between neighbouring towns to the companies. Yet in the mind of the public these concessions did not erase the image that the department was unfairly trying to restrict the growth of private systems. After all, connections with telegraph offices were to be allowed only in towns where there was no Post Office telephone system. Leases on trunk lines were also subject to termination on an annual basis, and the Post Office was to receive the entire revenue on these.

Further entangling the formulation of policy was the fact that on the fundamental issue of whether new licences should be granted there was no consensus within St Martin's le Grand. C. H. B. Patey, head of the telegraph branch, supported Blackwood's vision of a strong Post Office telephone system. Patey held that the telephone, like the telegraphs, was a natural monopoly. Only one agency could efficiently and profitably operate an exchange in a given area. Like Blackwood, Patey believed that many of the requests for new licences by private groups did not represent genuine efforts to develop exchanges, but were simply attempts on the part of unscrupulous businessmen to force previously established companies to buy up their licensing rights. Patey thus advocated the expansion of the Post Office system. If a private company failed to give adequate service, the Postmaster General should first demand that the company correct the situation. If it did not, then the department should provide the required service.[19] Earlier the department had followed this approach in connecting Manchester and Liverpool when customers were dissatisfied with the operations of the Lancashire and Cheshire Telephone Exchange Company. The

[19] Post 30/603, E4522/1892, Patey to Fawcett, 5 June 1882.

policy proposed by Patey and Blackwood was a bold one, formulated with an eye to both the needs of the public and the potential of a profitable return for the Post Office.

However, this was not the only view of decision-makers at St Martin's le Grand. Robert Hunter – who, as the recently appointed departmental solicitor, was deeply involved in the legal aspects of the telephone – saw the situation differently. He felt that the Post Office had no statutory power to discriminate among various applicants for licences or to enforce efficient service by existing companies. Hunter also stressed the difficulties of a government department carrying on such an industry, especially in the short run when private firms could offer 'greater facilities than the Government and at a cheaper rate'.[20] Hunter, in contrast to Blackwood and Patey, did not consider the telephone a natural monopoly. In his opinion the public interest would be best served by allowing several companies to compete in the same town. The disagreement which raged within the department was not simply a matter of esoteric economic theory, but rather a matter for departmental adjudication. Early in 1882 the London-Globe Telephone Company had applied for a licence to operate in the capital, where the United Telephone Company was already in business. The latter opposed, of course, the entry of any competitors.

The decision on this crucial request was made by Fawcett, and it again demonstrates that Postmasters General were by no means always nonentities who automatically approved the minutes of their permanent officials. Fawcett, who had been elected professor of political economy at Cambridge in 1863 against a field of rather weak candidates, had made it his life's work to disseminate economic theory as defined by John Stuart Mill, only without Mill's subtlety.[21] As a derivative thinker, Fawcett never satisfactorily reconciled his views on what might be termed competing social ideals – for example, the virtues of private property produced by capitalism as opposed to the appeal of cooperation. Although not completely against state intervention and government programmes which did not entail the expenditure of public funds such as self-supporting Post Office Savings Banks, he remained suspicious of proposals which smacked of socialism, however well-intentioned. As he insisted, 'any scheme will indefinitely increase every evil it seeks to alleviate, if it lessens individual responsibility by encouraging the people to rely less upon themselves and more upon the

---

[20] *Ibid.*, Hunter to Blackwood, 8 May 1882.
[21] C. J. Dewey, 'Cambridge Idealism', *The Historical Journal*, 17 (1974), 76. See also Phyllis Deane, 'Henry Fawcett: the Plain Man's Political Economist' in Lawrence Goldman (ed.), *The Blind Victorian: Henry Fawcett and British Liberalism* (Cambridge, 1989).

State'.[22] Fawcett had brought this mix of ideological predilections to St Martin's le Grand in 1880, and it led him to support Hunter, not Blackwood and Patey, on the all-important telephone licensing issue.[23] Competition was to be permitted not only between one private company and another, but significantly also between private industry and the department even in towns where the government had previously enjoyed a monopoly. Fawcett's decision stands as a reminder of the continuing attractiveness of the ideal of local autonomy for certain economic thinkers. In opposing competition, Blackwood and Patey believed that it would lead to an unnecessary duplication of plant, an excessive dislocation of streets because of the laying of extra wire, and problems of intercommunication between the customers of one company and those of another. (It goes without saying that in so arguing these two administrators were carrying on the national thrust of Scudamore's thinking on departmental policy.) Fawcett, an advocate of decentralisation, dismissed the difficulties arising from competition as questions not to be handled by bureaucrats in London, but rather by local authorities. Unfortunately what Fawcett's decision did was to fragment telephone policy even further by enlarging the number of groups involved in the decision-making process.[24]

The Treasury had no objection to Fawcett's proposed change in licensing procedure and indicated its concurrence with the view that competition between private companies ought to be encouraged. Yet it was less confident that the Post Office could effectively compete against private enterprise. Even Fawcett had believed that the department could and should compete in local communities with private enterprise. After all, this approach was the essence of open competition. The state and private industry would offer their services to the people, and the people would choose. The Treasury offered a number of objections, practical as well as ideological, to the plan. For one, there was the uncertainty as to the outcome of competition between the state and private industry and consequently the difficulty of making accurate financial estimates of the results. As a Treasury clerk complained, 'If the Postmaster General is to go into trade as a provider of telephones . . . it will be impossible for the Treasury to control or criticise transactions which are quite outside the usual duties of a

---

[22] Henry Fawcett, *State Socialism and the Nationalisation of Land* (London, 1883), p. 24.

[23] Post 30/542, E13267/1889, Fawcett to Patey, 4 July 1882.

[24] In writing that 'Theoretically, [Fawcett] . . . would have certainly applauded the privatisation of the telephone service, but his was the regime which set up the first state-run telephone exchanges', Harvie has oversimplified the alternatives faced by the Postmaster General and the choice he finally made: Christopher Harvie, 'Fawcett as Professional Politician' in Goldman, p. 186.

government office.'[25] Ironically, this uncertainty would never have been a problem if Blackwood's plan of limiting local service to one system, state or private, had been adopted. Moreover, there was the matter of canvassing for trade. The private companies were in the habit of appointing influential local businessmen to committees to publicise their services, and the Post Office believed that some sort of advertising campaign would be necessary to offset such efforts on the part of the companies. Throughout the summer of 1882 St Martin's le Grand repeatedly petitioned the Treasury for a canvassing staff. Equally repeatedly, the Treasury rejected the requests. As Lingen sniffed, 'If the system is accepted, the tout and the sandwich [board man] would seem to be legitimate members of the administration.'[26] There were, however, deeper worries at the Treasury than simply the social position of civil servants. The problem of paying a constantly growing Post Office staff which resembled a 'large army' frightened officials in Whitehall. To understand these disagreements, one needs to grasp the fact that by the 1880s the Treasury was operating from a different position than had been the case in the 1860s. Earlier it had been relatively open to suggestions for Post Office expansion. Now in a development critically important in shaping the relationship between the two departments the Treasury had grown more, not less, rigid in its preference for private initiative in economic affairs. In June 1883 Leonard Courtney reminded Fawcett that

> The sound principle in the opinion of My Lords is that the State, as regards all functions which are not, by their nature, exclusively its own, should, at most, be ready to supplement, not endeavour to supersede, private enterprise, and that a rough but not inaccurate test is not to act in anticipation of possible demand.[27]

The widening gulf which separated the two departments over this issue is well illustrated by the fact that, while the Post Office enjoyed a net return of 14 per cent on its £400,000 telephone investment, the Treasury was so intent upon limiting the system's expansion that it suggested raising fees charged in order to discourage new customers.

The increasing influence of the Treasury over the Post Office in this area, as reflected in the former's insistence on private development of the telephone, did not lead to extensive use of the invention. By the spring of 1884 St Martin's le Grand had established exchanges in only 17 towns, and its subscribers numbered only 748. The major opposition

25 T1/13910/1882, C. Barrington's memorandum, 13 August 1882.
26 Ibid., Lingen's note, 17 August 1882.
27 Post 30/603, E4522/1892, Treasury to Post Office, 25 June 1883.

was the United Telephone Company and its subsidiaries with exchanges in 66 towns and over 10,600 customers. Neither system blanketed the country, and by this point the public began to realise that something was badly amiss in the national development of the telephone. *The Times* was already publishing statistics to illustrate the dismal state of telephone use in England, one telephone for every 200 people in Chicago versus one for every 3,000 in London.[28] In this situation St Martin's le Grand, not the Treasury or private firms, received the brunt of criticism for supposedly restricting growth. The refusal to allow companies to erect their own trunk lines and the decision to limit exchange systems to small areas were seen as part of a Post Office plot. Furthermore, the department's insistence on the right to buy any patented instrument from any licensed company had discouraged companies from applying for new licences. The *Guardian*, which had supported the nationalisation of the telegraphs, now vehemently opposed any idea of a state-run telephone system.[29] The *Spectator* in comments which were not atypical complained

> The New Yorker of means is understood to be no more able to do without his telephone than the Englishman without his Penny Post. As we are the most letter-writing country in the world . . . it is most probable that had it not been for the hateful effects of state monopoly we should have been the most wire-speaking country in the world.[30]

Criticism was not limited to the press. The Liberty and Property Defence League, which was hard at work waving the banner of laissez-faire, protested Post Office ineptitude at its meeting at the Westminster Palace Hotel in June 1884.[31] And in the House of Commons E. Dwyer Grey, Chairman of the Telephone Company of Ireland, used Home Rule sympathies to attack the department.[32]

This external dissatisfaction with the state of telephone development contributed to an escalating policy debate within the department. Throughout the first half of 1884 Blackwood and Fawcett moved in opposite directions over the issue. Blackwood argued that St Martin's le Grand should be more stalwart in its posture vis-à-vis both

---

[28] *The Times*, 1 December 1882, p. 3.
[29] Post 30/542, E13267/1889, the Manchester *Guardian*, 30 June 1884.
[30] *Spectator*, vol. 57, 1167.
[31] *The Times*, 19 June 1884, p. 10. For an account of this conservative organisation, see N. Soldon, 'Laissez-Faire as Dogma: The Liberty and Property Defence League, 1882–1914' in K. D. Brown (ed.), *Essays in Anti-Labour History* (London, 1974).
[32] *Hansard's, Third Series*, vol. 288, 1052ff., 22 May 1884.

the Treasury and the individual companies. No concessions should be made in giving away Post Office privileges, such as the right to buy telephones from licensed companies. He pointed out that private initiative was not meeting the needs of the public and that cities such as Exeter, Falmouth, Limerick, Waterford, and West Hartlepool would have remained without telephone service but for departmental intervention. Blackwood specifically criticised the UTC for seeking only short-run profits, especially in its handling of subsidiary companies. The Secretary was profoundly disappointed with Fawcett's management of telephone policy and blamed him as well as the Treasury for the imbroglio in which the department found itself. Blackwood in a remarkably frank letter to his superior pointed out that 'I cannot help thinking that the absence of persistence on the part of this Department has its influence on the Treasury and accounts for much of their unwillingness to grant funds for private wire business.'[33] To Blackwood, Fawcett was, of course, responsible for the 'absence of persistence'. Blackwood's plea for a more forward policy was supported by other administrators such as Preece the engineer and John Charles Lamb, who had served under Scudamore and who was now emerging as a key departmental expert on the telephone. Both Preece and Lamb went so far as to suggest that the problem would be best solved by simply nationalising the companies.[34] It is clear that as late as the mid-1880s these civil servants were carrying on the self-confident approach of an earlier generation at St Martin's le Grand.

The Postmaster General once more disagreed.[35] Fawcett, whom Gladstone found a singularly difficult colleague, was proving an equally difficult political chief for his subordinates at St Martin's le Grand. He rejected nationalisation on the grounds that the government would be forced to buy costly patents which had only seven years to run. Moreover, much of the companies' wire was above ground, and after purchase the department would have to place it underground at great expense. After discussions with the companies, Fawcett instead of following Blackwood's advice chose the opposite course of abolishing many of the Post Office restrictions which had earlier been criticised. In effect he moved closer, if not all the way, to proposing a laissez-faire approach. Radius restrictions on the size of exchange areas were abolished, which allowed the companies to construct their own long-distance systems. The government's option to buy telephones from companies holding patents was also dropped. In return for these con

[33] Post 30/603, E4522/1892, Blackwood to Fawcett, 7 February 1884.
[34] Post 30/542, E13267/1889, Preece to Fawcett, 18 February 1884 and Lamb's memorandum, 22 May 1884.
[35] Ibid., Fawcett to Treasury, 28 July 1884.

cessions the government was to collect a simple 10 per cent royalty on the gross receipts of each company. New licences which would lapse in 1911 were to be issued, with the option on the part of the government to nationalise in 1890, 1897, or 1904. In fairness it should be added that, whatever the strengths and weaknesses of Fawcett's thinking on the telephone, in promoting his vision of competition the Postmaster General was concerned with much more than simply protecting telegraph revenue. He, like Blackwood with whom he fundamentally disagreed, was groping for the best means to develop the telephone's potential. Treasury reaction to Fawcett's proposals was positive. After all, Fawcett's policy views now closely resembled those of Lingen who urged

> My own opinion is against all government trading, as such, root and branch: Monopoly is not trading, and it follows, therefore, that . . . the Postmaster General should meddle with nothing where he is not prepared to assert his monopoly. I think his position . . . in regard to the telephones, where he competes while asserting his monopoly – to be essentially wrong and sure to produce the difficulties of all false principles in practice. I agree that all restrictions on the development of them [telephones] must be abandoned.[36]

After discussions with Gladstone, the policy was announced in the House of Commons on 7 August 1884. The alterations seemed to offer an end to a long period of uncertainty, and the liberalisation of licensing policy was generally applauded in the press. With the 1884 change in policy the first stage of the history of the telephone in Britain was at an end. The activist approach favoured by departmental administrators such as Blackwood had been rejected in favour of private development. Perhaps no other outcome could have been possible. The Treasury was decidedly unenthusiastic about the prospect of government development of the system. Moreover, the telephone companies, especially the UTC, had thwarted the Post Office by refusing to apply for licences and, therefore, preventing St Martin's le Grand from obtaining an adequate supply of telephones. The moment for a quick, clean nationalisation of the industry had passed, and in Blackwood's words, 'Mr. Fawcett was led to concede everything the companies desired.'[37] Without question, Fawcett's role in shaping telephone policy left a bitter legacy for two decades. If some outside the department felt that it had been unyielding in its treatment of the companies, some inside believed that too much had been given away to those same companies.

[36] T1/8119A/13025, Lingen's memorandum, 30 July 1884.
[37] Post, Telephone Policy 1879–1898, Blackwood to Raikes, 4 February 1890.

Indeed, the wrangling even at this early stage belies any assertion that a monolithic Post Office spoke with one voice on telephone policy.

The years following Fawcett's decision to institute a more open licensing policy to encourage competition among private firms were not productive ones for telephone development. On the one hand, the companies continued to regard the situation as unsatisfactory. Not only were they required to pay a royalty to the government, but they also were hampered by the fact that they lacked the same wayleave privileges which the Postmaster General enjoyed. The companies as private bodies were forced to negotiate with local authorities for permission to tear up streets and lay wire underground. In May 1885 the Select Committee on Telephone and Telegraph Wires recommended that such wayleave rights be granted to the companies, but attempts in 1885 and 1888 by the UTC to push such a bill through Parliament failed. On the other hand, there was growing disenchantment with the service offered by private firms. Between 1884 and 1889 a mounting tide of public opinion called for nationalisation of the telephone under the aegis of the Post Office. In 1886 and again in 1887 the Convention of Royal and Parliamentary Burghs of Scotland petitioned the Postmaster General to take such action. In 1888 the Associated Chambers of Commerce similarly voted for a national telephone system either under Post Office or private monopoly. As telephone development languished, *The Economist* abandoned its earlier position and now favoured the creation of a state monopoly.[38] The Duke of Marlborough, who was quite interested in telephone development and later promoted the New Telephone Company, made a similar suggestion in 1889.[39]

The fundamental source of this discontent stemmed from the fact that Fawcett's open policy had not fostered competition in the industry. The drift was in exactly the opposite direction. Despite objections from the Post Office in April 1889 a private monopoly covering virtually all of the country was established. The new company was the National Telephone Company, an amalgamation of the United, the National, and the Lancashire and Cheshire Companies. As a result of the formation of this monopoly, the hope that competition would bring lower prices and efficient service was not realised. Marlborough, for example, complained to Raikes the Postmaster General about the excessively high charges in London and the NTC's haphazard method of constructing lines. This period witnessed the continuation of what had become a leitmotif in press comments on the telephone, the inferiority of the domestic system in comparison to those of other nations. As *The*

---

[38] *The Economist*, 12 May 1888, p. 593.
[39] *Hansard's, Third Series*, vol. 337, 1432, 4 July 1889.

Economist pointedly asked in 1890, 'What hope was there of getting something like continental standards?'[40] The complaint was at least a decade old, but what was new was that such criticism was now directed as much at the NTC as at St Martin's le Grand.

The administrators at St Martin's le Grand once more were forced to consider what the solution to the growing monopoly of the NTC and its inadequate service should be. Again they took on a regulating function not usually associated with a department such as the Post Office. In assessing ways around the impasse, leading civil servants believed that there were only two choices, either active competition by the department or nationalisation. Each presented problems. Concerning the former there were both theoretical and practical difficulties. It was becoming more and more evident to men like Lamb that the telephone was a natural monopoly, whose efficiency depended upon the limitation of service to one system per area. Furthermore, the Post Office was prevented from competing actively by the fact that the department could obtain only 15,000 telephones outside the NTC's patent, an insufficient number for competition. The NTC also used promotional schemes which the department could not adopt in expanding its system. Often the company would distribute shares of stock among prominent businessmen or offer six months' free service as enticements for its system. Moreover, the belief that active competition was somehow beneath the dignity of civil servants continued to colour policy-making. For example, W. H. Smith, First Lord of the Treasury in Salisbury's second government and an individual whose family's fortune was based on the private touting of books and newspapers, drew the line at government advertising and canvassing.[41] If there were problems inherent in competition, there were also difficulties in nationalisation. The most obvious of these was the initial cost of take-over, with the possibility of the government having to pay large sums for the NTC's goodwill. Without question the telegraph take-over had cast a long shadow, as almost twenty years after his retirement Scudamore's name continued to be cited in Treasury memoranda as a reminder of the dangers of departmental and personal ambition.[42]

Still some decision was necessary, since the government did have the option to purchase the NTC in 1890. The consensus at St Martin's le Grand was that the government should not allow the NTC to aggrandise the profitable, larger cities, while neglecting the small towns and backwaters. The Post Office's solution to this dilemma, which was urged on the Treasury throughout the first months of 1890,

---

40 *The Economist*, 12 July 1890, p. 889.
41 Post 30/542, E13267/1889, Lamb's memorandum, 21 June 1889.
42 T1/8683B/1679B, Welby's memorandum, 10 November 1892.

was nationalisation.[43] Despite a thorough study of the question made by the Post Office's financial secretary, the Treasury refused to budge. Unlike other less important subjects on which Treasury resistance might be worn down, the telephone question was too large an issue to abdicate responsibility. The Treasury remained intransigent for several reasons. For one, it believed that the administrators at St Martin's le Grand were simply not up to the kind of hard bargaining required in complex business deals. As Welby somewhat caustically put it, the managers of the NTC could give their Post Office counterparts fifty yards in a hundred yard race and still win.[44] Furthermore, much of the Treasury opposition to nationalisation continued to be predicated on the belief that the Post Office could neither control its employees nor limit the pace of growth after take-over.

> My Lords are not prepared to embark upon another enterprise gigantic in itself, while the developments it might lead to are beyond their powers of prediction. It is certain, however, that besides the first cost of acquiring the business . . . it would place serious responsibility upon the government in connection with the increase in staff, enlargement of premises, and new works of various kinds.[45]

A note pencilled by an exasperated Post Office clerk in the margin of this letter – ' "My Lords' " powers of prediction are very limited. They cannot see beyond their noses at the present.' – is a good indication of the disappointment felt at St Martin's le Grand over this rebuff. Yet only two weeks after this letter was written Treasury fears were confirmed when a major labour confrontation occurred at the Mount Pleasant sorting office in London. A large number of staff, angered by the hiring of new employees whom they saw as potential strike breakers, threatened to walk off the job. Blackwood broke the resistance of the discontented men by suspending 435 workers, but the lingering suspicion at the Treasury was that the Post Office in its eagerness for new projects had, in Welby's assessment, created 'an empire over which they rule but do not govern'.[46]

Nonetheless, St Martin's le Grand continued throughout the autumn of 1890 to advocate immediate nationalisation. For example, Raikes and Blackwood presented their case to W. H. Smith, G. J.

---

[43] Post, Telephone Box File I, Raikes to W. H. Smith, 18 February 1890.
[44] T1/8683B/1679B, Welby's memorandum, 10 November 1892.
[45] Ibid., Treasury to Post Office, 27 June 1890.
[46] T1/8565B/8146, Welby's memorandum, 20 May 1891. For accounts of the Mount Pleasant confrontation, see Clinton, pp. 140ff. and H. A. Clegg, A. Fox, and A. F. Thompson, A History of British Trade Unions since 1889, vol. 1 (Oxford, 1964), p. 216.

Goschen the Chancellor of the Exchequer, and senior permanent Treasury officials at a meeting at the House of Commons in late November. In fact, the department was so persistent that Goschen became incensed that, as Blackwood later reported, the Post Office managers 'had not put their backs into an alternative policy; but had devoted themselves entirely to arguments in favour of purchase'.[47] Students of administrative paranoia should note the fact that, during these same months when the Post Office felt itself battered and abused by the Treasury and the public, the Treasury felt itself under such pressure from the Post Office and the public that Welby predicted that nationalisation would be forced on an unwilling government.[48] In an effort to prevent this occurrence Goschen, who it will be remembered had been a critic of Scudamore's handling of the telegraphs take-over, summarily ordered St Martin's le Grand to formulate a plan acceptable to Whitehall. Having found nationalisation rejected by his government, Raikes next attempted to implement the alternative, active competition on the part of the Post Office. Blackwood had estimated that such a programme would involve about an initial capital outlay of £1.5 million to establish an exchange network equal in extent to the existing private industry plus annual working expenses of about £0.2 million. He was encouraged, however, by the revenue potential of such a competing system. Even after deducting interest and the loss of about £38,000 a year in royalties from the private companies, Blackwood estimated an annual surplus of £92,000. Moreover, Blackwood hinted that much of the surplus might be used to reduce telephone charges, thus increasing the invention's usefulness. The Treasury was not moved by this line of reasoning. Goschen complained that 'the Post Office authorities are determined not to help towards the solution which I may call the policy of the Government, but we really must insist on their loyal endeavours to carry out the principle of licensing which seems to us to be the only way out of the difficulty'.[49] Raikes, who had long been in disagreement with his Tory colleagues, angrily replied that he was at a loss to comprehend the policy of the government and more importantly to see how it could offer a solution to the entangled telephone problem.

Two months later in August 1891 Raikes died. One of the most outspoken advocates of an aggressive departmental policy on the telephone was gone. His replacement, Sir James Fergusson, proved more amenable to Treasury guidance and much less likely to strike out on his

[47] Post, Telephone Bundle R, Blackwood to Raikes, 4 December 1890. Kieve is mistaken in his assertion that 'The Post Office did not consider the time was right for nationalisation': Kieve, p. 213.
[48] T1/8565B/8146, Welby's memorandum, 20 May 1891.
[49] Ibid., Goschen to Raikes, 22 June 1891; Raikes to Goschen, 25 June 1891.

own. Indeed, the transfer of office from Raikes to Fergusson accelerated a trend of a loss of nerve at St Martin's le Grand which was to continue for the next generation and beyond. (Blackwood's death in October 1893 only served to confirm this drift within the department.) How did this influence attitudes on the telephone question? Fergusson was more convinced of the merits of the private development than either Raikes or his advisors had been.[50] He completely disavowed any scheme of active competition by St Martin's le Grand. Rather his vision of proper policy was one of close cooperation, almost a partnership between the companies and the department. In effect, this Postmaster General favoured a return to the pre-1884 policy of one exchange system per local area, i.e. the establishment of small private monopolies. The department, in Fergusson's opinion, should withdraw as much as possible from local business. Instead it should encourage development by facilitating legislation to confer on private companies moderate powers to erect wires in towns. Hence, a distinction was to be made between local and national telephone administration. Local telephone operations were to be privately owned and managed. Fergusson proposed that on the national level the department purchase all trunk lines erected by the companies for long-distance communications and rent them back to the companies. The Postmaster General insisted that this approach would not only promote expansion of the telephone system, but would also protect departmental revenue by a reimposition of Post Office control over all forms of long-distance communication. For the remaining activists within the department who believed that the Post Office should be involved at both the local and the national levels of the telephone industry, Fergusson's policy was a major setback. Inside St Martin's le Grand a somewhat Machiavellian rumour circulated to the effect that as Fergusson sat for North East Manchester and that as Manchester was the home of the leaders of the NTC, they must have unduly influenced the Postmaster General's thinking.[51]

The implementation of Fergusson's policy of cooperation with the industry was not an easy task. It took over four years from his first outline of the plan in October 1891 to the purchase of the trunk lines by the government in April 1896. For once the Treasury was not the inhibiting villain. After the Post Office had assured Goschen of the scheme's sound revenue prospects, Whitehall's approval was almost immediate.[52] Rather the trunk line purchase was slowed by resistance from the industry itself, continued public agitation for complete nationalisation, and, as will be seen in chapter seven, a new unknown in

50 Post, Telephone Bundle F, Fergusson's memorandum, 16 October 1891.
51 Post, Telephone Box File I, unsigned memorandum, probably by Lamb.
52 Post, Telephone Bundle F, Treasury to Post Office, 21 December 1891.

an increasingly complicated situation – the possibility of municipally owned telephone companies. Concerning the first of these three factors, the private companies viewed the change of government policy as a propitious moment to win new concessions, such as the extension of the period of their licences. Moreover, with the limitation of business to one company per area, there was a scramble among the various companies to stake out as large a territory as possible. At this time the NTC was being challenged by the New Telephone Company headed by the Duke of Marlborough. The New Company was not widely established, but it did represent an obstacle to the NTC, especially after it acquired the Mutual Telephone Company in March 1892. Threatened by competition, the NTC sought government compensation for goodwill and loss of prospective profits on trunk line business as well as compulsory wayleave privileges. The latter were necessary, the company argued, since local authorities could still block expansion by refusing construction permits.

The implementation of Fergusson's plans was also delayed by increasingly widespread opinion outside St Martin's le Grand that the new policy was unwise on the premise that it surrendered too much to the private companies. There was also an increasing belief that the telephone problem could only be resolved through nationalisation by the Post Office. On 29 March 1892 this campaign reached a momentary climax in a House of Commons debate.[53] The leader of the pro-nationalisation MPs was Dr Charles Cameron, who had earlier been successful in forcing a reduction of telegraph rates. Cameron and allies such as Henniker Heaton, men at times critical of the Post Office, had come to regard government take-over as a way out of the confusing jumble of private companies licensed by a government department that was operating competing forms of communication. Indeed, it is telling that these men had more confidence in the Post Office than did the Postmaster General. Fergusson, adopting a view firmly held by the Treasury, opposed nationalisation because it would add to the already huge number of government employees, who constantly pressured Parliament for salary increases. Cameron's motion in favour of nationalisation was defeated 205–147. However, the point must be made that the defeat of the motion should not necessarily be taken as an indication of intransigent anti-nationalisation sentiment during this period. Many MPs would have agreed with the line of reasoning later proposed by *The Financial Times* that, while 'it is to the State that the telephones must belong', immediate purchase was not practical.[54]

Thus, the Post Office was forced to return to the difficult role of

---

[53] *Hansard's, Fourth Series*, vol. 3, 188 ff., 29 March 1892.
[54] Post 16/31, *The Financial Times*, 8 September 1893.

mediator between the Treasury and the telephone industry. The former remained insistent that the purchase of the trunk lines should be at the lowest possible price. Goschen, for example, threatened that the government would build its own lines if the companies refused to cooperate.[55] The latter viewed the negotiations as a chance to win new concessions from the state, particularly on the extension of their licences. St Martin's le Grand, caught in the middle, barred from either nationalisation or competition, sought to achieve two somewhat contradictory goals. First, telegraph revenue, much of it intercity in nature, was to be protected. Secondly, telephone development should be encouraged. The department's genuine commitment to development may be illustrated by its stand on the issue of intercommunication. St Martin's le Grand desired that a customer of one private company in, say, Manchester should be able to speak to subscribers of another company in London.[56] The NTC fought this proposal as it offered a threat to the company's monopolistic control over the industry. (In 1892 the NTC controlled over 90 per cent of the telephone business in the country.) In an effort to break this impasse and to balance the department's priorities, a telephone bill was introduced in the House of Commons in May 1892 to raise £1 million for the purchase of the companies' trunk wires and necessary extensions.[57] The following charges were established:

Trunk line charges

For any distance not exceeding 20 miles	3d
For any distance between 20 and 40 miles	6d
For every additional 40 miles or fraction thereof	6d

These tariffs, the department informed the Treasury, would allow a profit, although no estimate of the exact margin was made. A select committee, nonetheless, reported favourably on the proposal. The committee noted that, as there was no agreement between the government and the companies, the government should be free to negotiate as it thought best, with the one proviso that the terms of company licences should not be extended.[58] The act received the Royal Assent on 28 June 1892. The passage of the act signalled the end of the second stage of the history of the telephone in Britain. A certain caution should be exercised in assessing the significance of this milestone. The more avid proponents of the act believed that the policy of leaving

55 Post 30/708, E708/1896, Lamb's memorandum, 1 July 1892.
56 Ibid., Lamb to Fergusson, 6 April 1892.
57 Post 30/1615, E29062/1908, Treasury minute, 23 May 1892.
58 BPP, 1892, vol. 17, Select Committee on the Telegraphs Bill, p. iii.

local development to private initiative, while placing the trunk lines in the hands of the state offered a solution to the retarded state of the industry. In fact, it represented an inadequate response to the situation. As the history of the telephone after 1892 reveals, the take-over of the trunk lines by no means marked the end of difficulties for Post Office administrators grappling with what was an increasingly intractable mass of issues.

7

The Acquisition of the Telephone, 1892–1920

The thing to do is to make the best of it, to make ourselves, as of any other of the appliances of modern civilisation, its master and not its slaves. – *The Times*, 17 December 1905, p. 7.

Part of the difficulty in explaining the history of the relationship between the Post Office and the telephone is that the subject has a confusingly circular quality. As soon as one is convinced that a particular strategy or policy has been relegated to the scrap-heap, it emerges at the forefront of discussion and consideration. This characteristic was particularly evident in the 1890s when advocates of nationalisation as well as supporters of the ideal of competition once again clamoured for changes in government policy regarding the telephone. In August 1892 a preliminary agreement was signed by representatives of the telephone industry and St Martin's le Grand to implement the nationalisation of the trunk lines. The NTC and its subsidiaries, which had previously been reluctant to consummate the relationship, were moved to cooperation by three considerations. For one, the Post Office agreed to pay an extra 10 per cent above the book cost of the trunk wire plant.[1] Secondly, the NTC's fear of private competition dissipated in July, when the NTC and the New Company entered into a working agreement, again establishing a virtual monopoly of private telephony in the country. (By December 1892 the New Company was in essence amalgamated with the NTC.) Finally, and most importantly, the possibility of municipally owned and operated systems drove the NTC into a defensive posture and agreement with the Post Office.

As historians have long recognised, the late Victorian period marked a high point in the popularity of municipal trading.[2] Gas works and tramway companies had been taken over, and it was inevitable

---

1   Post 30/1615, E29062/1908.
2   For accounts of this phenomenon, see M. Falkus, 'The Development of Municipal Trading in the Nineteenth Century', *Business History*, 19 (1977), 134–61 and Lowell, vol. 2, 233ff.

that the telephone would attract the attention of those who believed in the Civic Gospel. The NTC was more fearful of municipal competition than that from other private firms because municipalities could block construction of telephone lines through the denial of wayleave privileges. The likelihood of municipal competition loomed very large in 1892 when A. M. Provand, MP for Glasgow, intimated that the Glasgow corporation was contemplating applying for a telephone licence.[3] In February 1893 W. E. L. Gaine, General Manager of the NTC, suggested that the Post Office and his company enter into a secret agreement to block the growth of municipal exchanges.[4] The response of the Post Office was crucial, for the entire thrust of Fergusson's policy had been one of joint action between state and private industry. Lamb, the departmental expert on the telephone, had long opposed any idea of competition in the industry. Yet he advised rejection of Gaine's proposal and advocated that the Postmaster General retain his option to grant licences to municipalities. Lamb, of course, was not in favour of municipal development of the telephone. Rather he feared that any agreement between St Martin's le Grand and the NTC to block the growth of municipal exchanges would only increase the company's net worth and, therefore, increase the government's expense in the event of nationalisation. During this same period when the NTC was increasing its pressure on the Post Office, the municipalities were also stepping up their activity. In July 1893 the Association of Municipal Corporations passed a recommendation opposing the granting of wayleave rights to any private telephone company. If such a recommendation were enacted, the intent of Fergusson's policy would almost inevitably be frustrated. The next month Glasgow took the step of applying for its own licence. Something of a triangular situation had emerged with the Post Office, the NTC, and the municipalities struggling for control of telephone policy and management.

The upshot of these difficulties was to allow those in favour of complete and immediate nationalisation to present their case once again. Lamb as before was the leading activist pushing for take-over. In May 1894 he outlined nationalisation's dual advantages of protecting telegraph revenue at the same time as assuring efficient telephone service. The NTC, in his opinion, would never be able to provide the latter, as it would be constantly impeded by municipal and local authorities. Quick and decisive action was essential because, as Lamb wrote, the company would 'not hesitate to use every act to bring pressure to bear

[3] H. R. Meyer, *Public Ownership and the Telephone in Great Britain* (New York, 1907), p. 139.
[4] Post, Telephone Bundle M, Interview between Gaine and Lamb, 23 February 1893.

on the Government as they did in the early days to secure the concessions which were granted by Mr Fawcett'.[5] The price was as low as it would ever be. Hence, the government should move with determination. It should be further stressed that Lamb did not envisage nationalisation as a step toward lower charges for the telephone customer. In contrast to Scudamore's hopes for the state-managed telegraphs, Lamb favoured take-over because it would lead to improved service, not because customers' bills would necessarily be lowered.

At the Treasury Lamb's argument was considered by Sir Francis Mowatt the Permanent Secretary. He accepted the Post Office estimate that £5 million would be a reasonable price to pay for the company. The NTC's market worth was calculated to be £4,223,349, while subsidiary companies were worth about £320,000. In other words, Lamb and Mowatt were willing to pay approximately 10 per cent above the market price. However, Mowatt did not expect that telephone revenue would be as large under government management as under private control, as he anticipated both pressures for some reduction of charges as well as increased expenses from an enlarged Post Office staff. (Mowatt estimated that Post Office salaries were about 10 per cent higher than those for comparable jobs in private industry.) Hence, nationalisation with an inevitably larger Post Office staff 'will constitute a real risk to its control and discipline by a single department'. Mowatt further predicted that the government might initially lose as much as £27,000 per year on the telephone and even more as extensions were carried out. A distinction, obviously, should be made between the preconceptions of Lamb and Mowatt. The former was much more hopeful as to the financial results of a state-run telephone system than the latter. Yet, despite these fears Mowatt, like Lamb, supported nationalisation. He believed the government had to step in given the fact that

> the control of the whole system by one central authority is essential, if the country is to enjoy the full benefit which can be derived from telephonic communication, and (which is more to the point) that pressure in and out of Parliament will ultimately compel the Government to purchase.[6]

Mowatt was without question correct on a number of points. In the end the pressure for a government system proved irresistible. One must not, however, underestimate the continuing impediments to nationalisation in the 1890s. The problem of buying out the companies before

---

5 Post 30/1615, E29062/1908, Lamb's memorandum, 25 May 1894.
6 T1/8982A/17448/95, Mowatt's memorandum, 9 June 1894.

their licences expired and, thus, paying a large sum for goodwill was not a minor issue. In July 1894 J. S. Forbes of the NTC demanded as compensation the entire capital cost of his company's plant plus a 50 per cent premium.[7] The Treasury was naturally wary on this point, as conventional wisdom in that department held, as Murray later phrased it, 'The greatest administrative blunder of the last generation was the price paid for the telegraphs. Let us, if we can, save the present generation from making another like unto it.'[8] There was another less apparent, but equally important, reason for hesitancy. Twenty years after the introduction of the telephone many policy-makers at St Martin's le Grand, Whitehall, and Westminster continued to regard the instrument as either a toy or a somewhat irritating machine to be answered by servants, but certainly not an essential part of modern life. Arnold Morley the Postmaster General was not alone in believing that unlike necessities such as gas and water, the telephone was something of an extravagance, especially in the home. To Morley, 'It was no use trying to persuade . . . [ourselves] that the use of telephones could be enjoyed by the large masses of people in their daily lives.'[9]

Although Morley's myopic vision may seem lamentable today, one should remember that the country then enjoyed the most efficient mail and telegraph systems in the world. Furthermore, the high rates charged for a telephone in the early 1890s did limit its clientele. After all, weighed against the cost of employing a housemaid for around £20 a year, paying £8 for the Post Office tariff for unlimited service in a provincial town was not much of a bargain.[10] Such considerations contributed to the difficulty of forming any consensus among administrators and politicians as to what should be done. Indeed, the convoluted history of the telephone is to some degree a result of the fact that few individuals consistently maintained the same approach. Spencer Walpole, who had replaced Blackwood as Secretary of the Post Office in 1893, is a case in point. In December 1895 he was in favour of allowing municipalities to develop the telephone. Less than one year later he advised nationalising the companies, but leasing their plant back to them until the expiration of their licences. In this muddle there was no single Post Office or Treasury or even party view. Lamb and Mowatt favoured Post Office management; Walpole and at this stage Murray did not. One Conservative Postmaster General, Fergusson, had advocated cooperation with the NTC; another Conservative

7   Post, Telephone Bundle N, Forbes to Morley, 13 July 1894.
8   T1/9133B/4495C, Murray to Lamb, 27 January 1896.
9   *Hansard's, Fourth Series*, vol. 31, 207, 1 March 1895.
10 For a revealing analysis of middle-class budgets in these years, see M. Laski, 'Domestic Life' in S. Nowell-Smith (ed.), *Edwardian England* (London, 1964), pp. 166ff. Post 33/1582, M9196/1925 gives a history of telephone charges.

Postmaster General, the Duke of Norfolk, did not. The situation was further complicated by the growing realisation on all sides that the government had painted itself into a corner on the telephone question and, hence, no alternative was completely attractive. When Norfolk, for example, endorsed nationalisation, he termed it 'the least unsatisfactory course to pursue'.[11]

During these months when alternative policies were so indecisively discussed, St Martin's le Grand had continued to negotiate with the NTC for the purchase of the trunk system. This, like much the Post Office did during the 1890s, was a policy which attracted many critics. Some, like Henniker Heaton the Conservative MP from Canterbury who made the Post Office the focus of his Parliamentary career, regarded the established approach as surrendering the essence of the telephone market to an inefficient private industry. As he put it, 'it was plain that a grosser blunder was never perpetrated. It was a good illustration of dividing the oyster, the Government taking the shell and leaving the oyster to the Companies.'[12] When a draft trunk line agreement was presented to the House of Commons in August 1894, such vehement opposition arose that the Postmaster General was forced to postpone its final implementation.[13] In November the Association of Municipal Corporations moved a resolution against conferring wayleave powers on private companies. In February 1895 a deputation from Scottish cities urged Morley to license municipalities. A major debate on the question took place in March when J. W. Benn, MP for Tower Hamlets as well as a member of the London County Council, attacked the proposed trunk line purchase. He predicted that its enactment would lead to an unrestricted private monopoly, the frustration of municipal competition, and increased charges to the public.[14] Morley was forced to agree to the formation of the select committee called for by Benn, and the committee took evidence in the spring of 1895. However, its deliberations were cut short by the close of the session and the fall of Rosebery's Liberal government. No report was made, but it became known that Morley, who believed that the threat of competition would be sufficient to goad the NTC into providing adequate service, had drafted a report sanctioning the idea of granting licences to municipalities.[15] The deliberations of the select committee had the intended effect of defusing opposition to current telephone policy long enough for the trunk line purchase to be completed after a delay of four years. In March 1896, after the price had been ascertained by two

11 T1/9133B/4495C, Norfolk to Hicks Beach, December 1896.
12 *Hansard's, Fourth Series*, vol. 17, 1644, 19 September 1893.
13 *Ibid.*, vol. 28, 1250, 16 August 1894.
14 *Ibid.*, vol. 31, 207, 1 March 1895.
15 Cab 37/38, Morley's memorandum, 23 February 1895.

experts, the government paid £459,114 for 29,000 miles of trunk lines. As Murray at the Treasury earlier had pointed out, the arrangement sanctioning local operations by the NTC with the department connecting their exchanges 'practically established a partnership between the Post Office and the National'.[16]

To many the partnership was a less than acceptable solution to the telephone problem. There were those inside the Post Office, Lamb being the most prominent, who continued to call for nationalisation, by arbitration if necessary. St Martin's le Grand approached the Treasury with this request only to be rebuffed in March 1897. If the Treasury could withstand this sort of interdepartmental pressure, it could not resist the renewed chorus of discontent and criticism which was rising outside Whitehall. At the heart of the matter was the government policy of denying licences for municipal systems. The Glasgow Corporation had requested a licence in July 1896 and again in March 1897, but each time the Post Office had refused. Government policy at this point was based on the belief that telephony was best organised on the basis of one system per area, i.e. no competition was to be permitted. However, to the world beyond St Martin's le Grand this same policy appeared to coddle the NTC's monopoly without providing adequate public safeguards. On 2 April 1897 yet another debate on the state of telephone service took place in the House of Commons, and the government was led to institute inquiries into the existing situation. An investigation was begun in August when the Treasury appointed Sheriff Andrew Jameson to examine the Glasgow case. His report illustrated the basic predicament in the semi-private, semi-public circumstances of the telephone industry of the 1890s.[17] Jameson concluded that the service provided by the NTC in Glasgow was inadequate. Yet he went on to stress that much of the blame lay with the Glasgow Corporation, which refused to allow the company to place its wires underground along public wayleaves. (A similar situation existed in London, where the Commissioners of Sewers had attempted to block the NTC's laying of wire.) Jameson believed the only solution to the deadlock was either the establishment of a Post Office exchange or the licensing of a Glasgow Corporation system.

Whitehall remained hesitant to sanction competing systems. For example, George Gleadowe, a Treasury clerk, contemplated the possibility of additional Post Office exchanges and did not find it a pleasing prospect. Claiming that Post Office employees were not famous for either their celerity or their courtesy in dealing with the public, he questioned the ability of the senior Post Office officials to run a profit-

[16] T1/8982A/17448, Murray's memorandum, 4 December 1895.
[17] Meyer, *Telephone*, pp. 133–4.

able telephone system.[18] Such a view of course went far beyond the relatively simple matter of the cost of undertaking a state-run system to long-term considerations of the quality of Post Office management and the reliability of its staff, considerations which would not have arisen thirty years earlier. If the option of departmental telephone operations was not attractive, neither was the alternative of municipal competition. There was no certainty that weaker or smaller town governments would be able or willing to provide adequate service. Hence, in March 1898 the request of the Glasgow Corporation for a licence was again refused. (The only exception to the government's refusal to license municipal systems before 1898 was a licence granted to Guernsey in December 1897 for essentially political reasons.)

The wisdom of this policy was more and more attacked. In a motion in the House of Commons in April 1898 James Caldwell, Liberal MP for Lanark, described the government's refusal to issue municipal licences as misguided and certain to inhibit the establishment of a cheap, widely available telephone service. Such an argument was not new, but the response of the government was. In a most significant development, the Parliamentary spokesman for the Post Office, R. W. Hanbury the ambitious Financial Secretary to the Treasury, joined in the condemnation of the NTC. Instead of defending the recent policy of allowing the NTC to dominate local development of the telephone, Hanbury insisted that the absence of competition had led to excessively high rates and inadequate service in London, Glasgow, and other cities. The remedy to this situation according to Hanbury was competition – competition by municipalities, not St Martin's le Grand.[19] He predicted that the municipalities with their wayleave powers might prove formidable rivals to the NTC. What lay behind this shift in Treasury policy? As recently as November 1897 Hicks Beach the Chancellor of the Exchequer had preferred that, if competition had to come, it should come from the Post Office, not from municipalities. It has been suggested that, in supporting the case for municipal development, Hanbury was simply seeking wider political popularity.[20] It is true that the lobbying efforts of the municipalities in public forums and by more private means were strong in the spring of 1898. There were meetings, for example, at the London County Hall on the question. These would have inevitably influenced the formulation of policy. But in Whitehall there was another rationale for sanctioning municipal development. It would not constitute a financial drain on the Post Office budget. This fact had been recognised by certain administrators

18 T1/9220B/17570, Gleadowe's memorandum, 8 December 1897.
19 *Hansard's, Fourth Series*, vol. 55, 1732, 1 April 1898.
20 Meyer, *Telephone*, p. 3.

such as Murray, who long argued that, if the municipalities wished to waste their own money on exchanges which would probably not succeed, the national government should not stand in their way.[21]

The shift in government policy led to the convening of a select committee which sat between May and August 1898 and which thoroughly covered the telephone question. Very little new information or few strikingly innovative points of view were brought forward by the witnesses. Instead, the various sides – the Post Office, the NTC, and the municipalities – simply went over old ground. Lamb, for example, continued both to emphasise the potential of the telephone for public benefit and to insist that a complete Post Office monopoly offered the best means to fulfil its potential:

> In the postal and telegraph systems the whole of the country is treated as one, and the richer districts lend support to those which are not so prosperous; but if, in the telephone exchange business, the prosperous cities and towns be empowered to establish exchanges for their own benefit, who is to find the money for the development of the system in the rural districts?[22]

Spokesmen for private initiative also opposed any kind of competition, although for different reasons. James S. Forbes, chairman of the NTC, and Sir James Fergusson, now on its board after leaving the Post Office, both argued that a partnership approach – the NTC taking the local business, while the Post Office handled the long-distance lines – offered the best formula for development.[23] Once again the distinction between private initiative and state intervention was proving a blurred concept in the minds of these businessmen. In the end, however, the committee concluded that the telephone as currently developed by the NTC was of no practical benefit to the country and was never likely to be so as long as the company enjoyed a virtual private monopoly. Particularly singled out for criticism was the fact that the NTC structured its rates on the principle of a single annual subscription, which entitled the customer to unlimited use of his telephone. The committee favoured a smaller annual fee with an additional charge per call as a means to attract a larger clientele to the telephone. (Forbes of the NTC frankly admitted that his company was not interested in attracting such business and, indeed, would accept no new accounts after 1904 in order to reduce capital expenditures and maximise profits.) Much was also made of the contrast between the poor state of service

---

21 T1/9133B/4495C, Murray to Lamb, 27 January 1896.
22 BPP, 1898, vol. 12, Select Committee on Telephones, p. 410.
23 *Ibid.*, pp. 103, 304, 327.

in London and the more efficient exchanges on the continent. For example, in London there were only 237 call offices available for a population of over 6 million, while in Stockholm there were 700 for a population of only 250,000. The committee in contrast to its condemnation of the NTC's local service praised the Post Office owned and operated trunk systems as the most extensive in Europe. It is readily apparent that the committee's analysis raised many of the same themes on the telephone which had been emphasised by Scudamore and others in regard to the telegraphs thirty years before, i.e. the limitation of its use to the urban business classes, unnecessarily high rates, the superiority of systems in foreign countries, and the lack of vision on the part of private management.

If the diagnosis of the telephone problem was remarkably similar to that pertaining to the telegraphs before 1870, there were also critical differences. For one, anxiety concerning the inadequate state of British telephone development as compared with that of foreign systems was more profound than had been the case with the telegraphs. The telephone was now only one of many areas from defence to social welfare in which the nation seemed to be slipping behind, and complaints about the industry's shortcomings formed part of a wider mosaic of national self-doubt which had emerged by the end of the nineteenth century.[24] For another, the prescription for the solution of the problem offered by the 1898 select committee differed. Instead of advocating immediate take-over, the committee concluded that competition was both expedient and necessary for the extension of the country's telephone system. In a sense the committee was urging a return to the policy of the early 1880s when Fawcett advocated first competition by the Post Office and then competition among private firms as a means to foster telephone development. Still it is noteworthy that the Post Office, not municipalities, was considered the best source to provide such competition. The Council of the Association of Municipal Corporations, a conference of London local authorities, and the committee itself viewed the telephone as a national problem best handled by a national organisation. However, in the event of the Post Office failing to offer competition, the committee concluded that local municipalities should be allowed to compete. After all, ten corporations had made application since 1893, and by 1898 twenty-five others had

---

[24] See, for example, A. H. Hastie, 'The Telephone Tangle and the Way to Untie It', *The Fortnightly Review*, 70 (1898), 893. The political context of such fears is explored in G. R. Searle, *The Quest for National Efficiency* (Oxford, 1971) and Aaron L. Friedberg, *The Weary Titan Britain and the Experience of Relative Decline 1895–1905* (Princeton, 1988). For a discussion of analogous concerns in another industry, see Leslie Hannah, *Electricity Before Nationalisation* (London, 1979), pp. 36–7.

passed formal resolutions endorsing the general principle of municipal exchanges.[25]

How did the government react to the committee's recommendations? At St Martin's le Grand one line of thought held that, if competition were to be instituted, it should be an active, vigorous programme throughout the entire country. As table one indicates, the Post Office went on to estimate the costs of such an approach over a four-year period at £2 million.

Table 1
Post Office estimate of cost of active competition with the NTC over a four-year period

London	£1,300,000
Towns where the Post Office had exchanges	560,000
Towns in areas in which neither the Post Office nor the NTC had exchanges	140,000
	£2,000,000

Source: T1/9346/2251, Post Office to Treasury, 6 February 1899.

In Whitehall there was rather less enthusiasm for competition between the Post Office and the NTC. Hicks Beach expressed doubts as to the department's ability to compete against the NTC 'without a specially qualified staff, working with a free hand'.[26] There was also in the Chancellor's mind the sombre prospect of a financial venture which 'can hardly be profitable in view of the certain demands of the public for low rates and of the employees for high wages'. One gets the distinct impression from the letters and memoranda of this period that politicians such as Hicks Beach, unimpressed by the potential of the telephone, wished that the problem of control would somehow go away. As he put it,

> for the present the rural districts can very well wait, and if we admit smaller local authorities than city burghs, the towns will be able to take care of themselves. If they try, and succeed, I should much prefer that they should go on with the work after 1911, instead of all of it being undertaken by the P.O.[27]

The government, then, only partially accepted the recommendations

---

[25] BPP, 1898, vol. 12, Select Committttee on Telephones, p. 520.
[26] Cab 37/48, Hicks Beach's memorandum, 30 December 1898.
[27] T1/9377/7800, Hicks Beach to Hanbury, 17 April 1899.

of the select committee. To be sure, competition was to be encouraged, but not the widespread Post Office competition which the committee favoured as the best approach to efficient service. The decision was made that the Post Office would undertake competition in London on a trial basis, while the responsibility fell on municipal authorities for any competition in the rest of the country. In June 1899 Hanbury introduced a bill (62 and 63 Victoria c. 38) in the House of Commons to enable local bodies to raise funds for establishing exchanges. They were to be licensed by the Postmaster General and to pay a 10 per cent royalty, as the NTC did.

Yet from the point of view of some officials at the Post Office the prospect of competing with the NTC in London, or anywhere else for that matter, was less than attractive. The company enjoyed expertise developed over almost two decades and had 100,000 subscribers all over the country. In contrast the department had only about 1,000 subscribers, the majority of whom were in Newcastle-on-Tyne and Cardiff.[28] Thus, entering the London market against an established firm appeared a daunting venture. Further complicating the situation was the fact that competition to the death was not regarded by administrators at St Martin's le Grand as a necessarily fruitful policy. Denial of concessions, such as the use of departmental wayleaves, might hurt the NTC, but it would also diminish the public benefit of the telephone. The most difficult problem associated with competing telephone systems remained intercommunication, i.e. allowing the subscribers of one system to speak to those of a competing system. On this issue the NTC refused to budge, as it already had 19,000 customers in London and reasoned that to allow intercommunication would only undermine its position there. Beyond such matters, there was another obstacle to active Post Office competition. By the turn of the century St Martin's le Grand was a much less optimistic organisation than it had been forty years earlier. Instead of eagerly seeking new challenges, officials were ambivalent about adopting bold policies. This outlook is perhaps best illustrated by George Murray, who was appointed Secretary to the Post Office in 1899. Murray, who had the reputation of being particularly quick of mind, came to St Martin's le Grand as a man who was in the literal sense of the word an 'outsider'. Still he was by no means unfamiliar with the department, having been involved in the formulation of Treasury policy on the Post Office for years. Thus, Murray brought with him judgements as to the specific strengths and weaknesses of St Martin's le Grand as well as more general preconceptions about the proper role of government in the larger economy. Concerning both areas Murray revealed none of the pride which had

28 Post, Telephone Box File C, unsigned memorandum, June 1911.

characterised the mid-century generation. In Murray's view, 'There is a general incapacity of a Government Department to compete with outside enterprise.'[29] Such was the result of two disadvantages. First, a government business could not resort to tactics used by private firms. Secondly, a government business was peculiarly open to pressure from customers for lower prices and employees for higher wages. (Quite obviously, Hicks Beach and Murray shared the same fears as to the prospects of Post Office competition with private firms.)

The implications of such assessments merit comment. Murray, moving logically forward from his negative appraisal of the department's position on the telephone, did not conclude that some expansion was necessarily unwise. In this case he proposed that the NTC's London operations be taken over by the state, while leaving the municipalities free to compete with the company in the provinces. At first glance this might appear to be the plan of, if not a zealot like Scudamore, then at least a moderately aggressive administrator. After all, Lamb and other managers had recommended nationalisation for over a decade. However, they had done so in the belief that the Post Office could operate the telephone efficiently and profitably. Murray was not so confident. He advocated nationalisation not out of a sense of trust in the abilities of his department, but rather to protect it from the challenges of the market place. In an interesting reversal of stereotypical roles, some at the Treasury were more sure of the Post Office's abilities than its permanent head. Hanbury the Financial Secretary, for instance, found Murray's timidity 'incredible' and urged that the Post Office should take the offensive against the NTC in London.[30] From the summer of 1900 to June 1901 the Post Office and the NTC were locked in a stalemate over the London market. The department declined to allow the NTC to lay wires under the streets, effectively blocking any expansion since to string wires across rooftops exposed them to the weather and required expensive payments for right-of-way privileges to estate owners. The NTC continued to reject intercommunication between its customers and the department's. It was clear that this impasse injured both parties as well as potential users of the telephone and that some way out of the situation had to be found.

In May 1901 St Martin's le Grand once again petitioned the Treasury for a major alteration in policy. The proposal was based on an examination of the telephone question by Murray, which proved to be perhaps the most important and the most persuasive departmental

---

[29] Post, Telephone Box File C, Murray's memorandum, 3 May 1900. Such values also coloured his thinking on the sale of Post Office life insurance, as was shown in chapter three.
[30] *Ibid.*, Hanbury to Hicks Beach, 6 July 1900.

analysis produced since the early 1880s. His starting point was that, as the company's licence would expire at the end of 1911, the NTC faced a troubled financial future. At that time it would have essentially no assets to offset liabilities on share and loan capital, which at par had a value of £7 million. Given this situation the company found it impossible to raise new capital for expansion and, thus, there were over 10,000 people awaiting the installation of telephones, which the company could not furnish. Murray argued that the Post Office had to act to alleviate this situation, for 'So long as the provision of telephonic communication is part of a State monopoly, the Government cannot stand aside.'[31] Again, the contrast with the nationalisation of the telegraphs is evident. In that case Scudamore eagerly sought their acquisition, and the monopoly came only as an afterthought. With the telephone it was the monopoly which drew the department more and more into involvement. Still it is revealing that even a slightly cynical and decidedly reluctant man like Murray had by 1901 come to believe that government 'must be prepared either by itself or its agents to . . . provide telephones for all who want them and are prepared to pay for them'. Murray went on to add that, if public service were the only consideration, immediate nationalisation offered the best answer to the question of development. But he recognised that the Treasury would not depart from its policy of not acquiring the NTC before its licence expired. Thus, another solution, albeit a temporary one, was proposed – cooperation between the NTC and the Post Office. Although this suggestion ran directly against the 1898 select committee's report, Murray saw it as advantageous to both sides. For the Treasury it offered the additional attraction of fiscal safety through the avoidance of the uncertainties of competition. Chamberlain the Postmaster General and Hicks Beach the Chancellor of the Exchequer were both easily won over to the plan. As the latter pointed out, a 'friendly competition' might reveal how well the Post Office would do against the NTC. Contributing to Hicks Beach's tentative approach to the question of expansion was his continuing assumption that the telephone had limited value and, as he put it in a memorable phrase, was certainly not an invention 'desired by the rural mind'.[32] Once again, civil servants and politicians had arrived at the same policy, cooperation with the NTC, having come from different starting points, Murray from the position that something must be done to develop the telephone's potential, Hicks Beach from the opinion that the telephone did not have much potential.

For the first time in almost two decades, Post Office administrators

31 See T1/9740A/18574, Murray's memorandum, 31 May 1901 for the following.
32 Post, Telephone Box File C, Hicks Beach to Chamberlain, 11 June 1901.

were formulating telephone policy instead of simply implementing decisions made at higher levels. The results were quickly evident. A series of negotiations between the NTC and St Martin's le Grand opened in late June 1901, and by 8 August heads of agreement were signed. The department agreed to buy the London plant of the NTC at the end of 1911 at its value *in situ,* that is, the cost of reconstruction less allowances for depreciation and any unsatisfactory state of repair. In the meanwhile the London market was to be parcelled out with the NTC taking the eastern areas, the Post Office the west, and both working the central districts. Each side benefited from such an approach. The Post Office gained through the NTC promise to allow intercommunication between the subscribers of both systems. The NTC's operation was strengthened by the Post Office commitment to provide underground wires for the company, thus, eliminating any wayleave problems. The NTC and the Post Office also agreed to charge the same rates, which are found in table two.

Table 2
London telephone rates

Type of service	Rates
Unlimited service	£17 per year
	£14 per year for additional lines
Message rate service	£6 10s* per year within County of London
	£5 10s* per year in outer London

* These figures include £1 10s worth of calls. Calls were charged at 1s or 2s, depending on distance.

Source: Post, Telephone Rates Committee, 1920, p. 5.

With the approval of the agreement by the Treasury in November 1901, another turning point in the history of the department's acquisition of the telephone had been reached. Murray, who had engineered the retreat from competition, believed that, given the limited number of policy choices, the Post Office had adopted the best possible course.[33]

Many others were not convinced. These critics believed that expediency, not the needs of telephone customers, had warped the decision-making process. In a speech at the City Liberal Club J. W. Bebb attacked the new rates as 50 to 70 per cent too high. Later at a meeting

[33] T1/9740A/15972, Murray to Chamberlain, 29 December 1901.

of the London County Council he also stressed the point that the government in coming to terms with the NTC had betrayed the trust of municipal authorities. At a meeting at the Guildhall on 13 January 1902 Alpheus C. Morton took up the attack. 'It was an old tale. For 200 years the Post Office had always opposed progress. Every reform had to be forced on them from without. The well-paid officials had stood out against reform, and so it would be in this case.'[34] The subject came up again the same month when Sir Joseph Dimsdale, Conservative MP for the City of London, moved an amendment to the address. Dimsdale argued that, although the 1899 bill had called for strenuous competition in London, the Post Office was unwisely lapsing into a partnership with the NTC.[35] This relationship had only served to throw London further behind other cities in the use of the telephone. (At this point there was one telephone for every 82 people in Berlin and one for every 132 people in Vienna as opposed to one for every 433 people in London.)

As has been noted earlier, there were many parallels between these complaints and earlier rhetoric on the telegraphs. A key difference in 1902 was that the Post Office, unlike the telegraph situation in 1868, did not enjoy the advantage of being dissociated from the shortcomings of telephone service, but rather was held to be primarily responsible for them. It had had to walk the tightrope between its function as a licensing agency and its function as a provider of telephones, at all times juggling the revenue considerations and the needs of the public. Austen Chamberlain, then Financial Secretary to the Treasury, argued in response to Dimsdale's motion that there was no alternative to a policy of cooperation. As he insisted, 'it would have been criminal for the Post Office or the Treasury to consent to a needless cut-throat competition of rates at the expense of the country'.[36] Chamberlain further pointed out that, if the Post Office had refused the NTC way-leave rights, the NTC's customers as well as the company would have been injured in the end. Hanbury, moving away from his earlier preference for competition, also defended the agreement on the grounds that only the rich in London were complaining and that the government, in establishing a measured rate service, had made the telephone available to a wider range of customers. The motion was defeated 237 to 139.

However, the victory in the House of Commons did not lull either Whitehall or St Martin's le Grand into believing that a final solution to the telephone problem had been reached. For one thing, it was

---

34 *The Times*, 14 January 1902, p. 6.
35 *Hansard's, Fourth Series*, vol. 101, 981, 27 January 1902.
36 *Ibid.*, 994.

becoming evident that municipal competition would not offer a satisfactory alternative to the NTC in the provinces. Municipalities certainly had not leapt at the chance to undertake telephone development. Of 1,334 local bodies only 56 sought information from the government on the matter. Of these only 13 ever applied for licences, and only 6 ultimately opened exchanges. (See table three.)

Table 3
Municipal development of the telephone

Town	Date of licence	Date of expiry of licence	Date of opening	Result
Glasgow	1 and 6 Mar. 1900	31 Dec. 1913	June 1901	Sold to Post Office June 1906
Tunbridge Wells	30 Apr. 1900	30 Apr. 1925	June 1901	Sold to NTC Nov. 1902
Brighton	30 Apr. 1901	30 Apr. 1926	Nov. 1903	Sold to Post Office Apr. 1910
Swansea	27 Sept. 1902	31 Dec. 1920	Aug. 1903	Sold to NTC Mar. 1907
Portsmouth	21 Sept. 1901	30 June 1926	Nov. 1902	Sold to Post Office Oct. 1912
Hull	8 Aug. 1902	31 Dec. 1911	Oct. 1904	Remained in operation after 1912

Source: Post, Telephone Box File C, 7.

The Times declared the outcome of the experiment in municipal competition to be a 'ludicrous result to those who recall such magnificent declamation about securing to the public the splendid possibilities of a new discovery'.[37] Murray's 1896 prediction of municipal failure had been confirmed, and one possible remedy for the telephone problem, thus, was eliminated. Compounding development difficulties was the poor financial condition of the NTC. The 1901 London agreement had enabled the company to raise with great difficulty £1 million in new capital. As soon as this sum was exhausted, it would not be able to

[37] *The Times*, 10 August 1905, p. 7.

provide service for new customers demanding telephones. At the annual meeting in February 1904, its General Manager noted that there were approximately 3,300 people waiting for service in London and another 7,700 people in the provinces.[38]

There was a general consensus, therefore, that some further adjustment in policy was necessary, but it was still debated within the government exactly where the adjustment should be made. Both sides within the Post Office, optimists such as Lamb as well as pessimists such as Murray, were now committed to a telephone network centralised in the hands of state. Yet it was unclear how and when nationalisation should occur. There was, in short, no easy progression from the 1901 London agreement to the 1905 accord, which dealt with the entire country. Austen Chamberlain, who had become Postmaster General in July 1902, considered piecemeal purchase of the NTC, but rejected it on the grounds that it would strengthen the company's bargaining power by the time that the last districts were acquired.[39] Purchase by arbitration in 1904 was discarded on the grounds that the government could not afford to pay arbitrator's terms to an unwilling seller. The option of building a provincial system that would be capable of taking over the National Telephone Company's subscribers was dismissed on the grounds that the construction would needlessly duplicate an existing telephone system. Hence, it was decided to opt for complete government take-over in 1912 on the expiration of the NTC's licence. The Tory Chamberlain and the economically orthodox Murray saw this as the best, i.e. least expensive, escape route from a generation of misconceived policy toward the telephone, not as an opportunity to expand the corporate state.

Formal negotiations between the Post Office and the NTC opened in March 1904. At that time the company controlled 90 per cent of the telephone industry in the country with 1,079 stations, 3,671 public call offices, and 283,580 telephones.[40] As with the telegraph take-over, an elaborate game of diplomacy was played between the two sides. In this case, however, the department felt the constraints of the purse much more strongly. Murray warned a Post Office negotiator that the recent rise in the price of NTC shares might convince some in Parliament that the Post Office was too generous and accommodating: 'We simply cannot afford to make a bargain which looks too good for the Co.; because we couldn't carry it.'[41] It is beyond question that in this series of negotiations the Treasury was much more deeply involved

---

38 *The Economist*, 26 March 1904, p. 524.
39 Post 30/1615, E29062/1908, Chamberlain's memorandum, 25 March 1903.
40 Post 30/1216, E13364/1905, NTC to Post Office, 6 May 1904.
41 Post, Telephone Box File I, Murray to Smith, 16 June 1904.

than in the telegraphs acquisition. Murray had left the Post Office to become Permanent Secretary to the Treasury in the autumn of 1903. Yet he essentially directed St Martin's le Grand from his new post in Whitehall. He was insistent, for instance, that the 1901 agreement serve as the basis for a national agreement and convinced H. B. Smith, the new Secretary of the Post Office, on this point. By this stage it is, of course, misleading to speak of a Treasury or Post Office telephone policy *per se*. After all Murray had gone from the Treasury to Inland Revenue to the Post Office and back to the Treasury and Smith from Treasury to the Post Office. Moreover, Murray and Smith shared many of the same ideological concepts, the fear of large masses of government employees being one of the most obvious points in common. The two departments now tended to think alike, at least at the top.

Negotiations proceeded fairly smoothly throughout the summer of 1904, and by 15 August an informal agreement had been signed by Henry Fowler, President of the NTC, and Lord Stanley, then Postmaster General. The accord was provisional. No financial terms were settled, and Parliamentary approval was still necessary. St Martin's le Grand was to nationalise the NTC at the end of 1911 at tramway terms. Accordingly, the Postmaster General would pay a price based on the simple cost of replacing the NTC's current plant in 1911 with allowances for depreciation due to wear and unsuitability of existing equipment. The NTC would receive no compensation for goodwill, compulsory purchase, or loss of future profits. In the interim the Post Office would lay wire underground and rent it to the NTC. In return the company would grant free intercommunication between its customers and the Post Office's everywhere in the country and charge maximum and minimum rates set by the Postmaster General. All in all, the negotiations went much faster and much more easily for the government than in the telegraph take-over. Murray at the Treasury judged the agreement as 'extremely favourable to the Post Office'.[42] The explanation for this difference lies not so much in the skill of the negotiators at St Martin's le Grand as in a profoundly different set of circumstances. Instead of having to deal with numerous telegraph and railway companies, Smith had only one adversary about which to worry. Moreover, the NTC was in a much weaker position than the telegraph companies, as the expiration of its licence in 1911 would have destroyed its worth. The department also had been dealing with the telephone issue for years and was much more knowledgeable and experienced than Scudamore had been with the telegraphs. The Post Office wisely refused to make predictions of exactly how much nationalisation would cost, although a figure of £9–10 million was offered as a

[42] T1/10945/14169, Murray to Chamberlain, 11 August 1904.

rough guess. Hence, the pattern of constantly changing estimates of purchase price and future gross and net revenue which characterised the 1868–9 deliberations was not repeated.

After a formal agreement was signed by the Post Office and the NTC on 2 February 1905, a select committee sat to consider the wisdom of nationalisation. Among supporters of the agreement there was much less elation than had accompanied the telegraph take-over. No rosy future of a utopian state system was predicted by even the most idealistic proponents. The most obvious reason for the absence of excitement was the fact that nationalisation of the telephone was never associated with the promise of an assured reduction in rates. The previous December the Treasury had made this point very clear when it warned

> telephone capital is intended to be spent on remunerative business only. The telephone service will thus be wholly paid for by the telephone users. My Lords cannot admit that there is any force in the contention that the expenditure should be distributed proportionately in the several parts of the United Kingdom; the only proper rule for the course of development being that the places where it is remunerative should be chosen first.[43]

There was, then, no equivalent to Scudamore's rhetoric of quickly providing all social classes with an instantaneous means of communication and no counterpart to his imagery of linking small hamlets with major urban areas to unify the country. Indeed, at this time the department did not contemplate uniform telephone rates for the entire country in contrast to mail and telegraph charges. The spokesman for St Martin's le Grand justified nationalisation on rather different grounds. H. B. Smith argued that the telephone was a natural monopoly because the operation of one unified system reduced engineering costs and promoted efficiency. This being the case, only a public monopoly would meet public needs. The timing and the manner of nationalisation were also justified on equally pragmatic grounds. By waiting until 1912 the department would avoid paying a higher price for compulsory purchase. Smith emphasised the revenue aspects of nationalisation and, directly linking the telephone to the telegraphs, argued that the Post Office had the obligation to consider the shifting market shares of each industry – the former rising, the latter declining – in setting communications policy. In point of fact, Smith and the other witnesses for the department saw no need to offer new justifications for nationalisation or to launch a campaign for it, as Scudamore had done

[43] T1/10204/19802, Treasury to Post Office, 15 December 1904.

with the telegraphs. By this time all other alternatives had been tried and found wanting. Smith even went so far as to state that the burden of proof lay not with the Post Office, but with the opponents of nationalisation.

There was opposition to nationalisation from several witnesses before the select committee. It was not based on ideological objections to government intrusion into the private economy. Instead it came primarily from spokesmen for municipalities who wanted to expand their local empires. Daniel Macaulay Stevenson, Subconvener of the Glasgow Telephone Committee, argued that municipalities, if they so chose, should continue to work local exchange systems after 1911.[44] J. W. Southern, Alderman of Manchester, voiced a similar fear of the inefficiency of the national government: 'We feel that we could do better . . . locally than any central body in London would be likely to do.'[45] Critics of the agreement also claimed that rates, too high under NTC management, would continue to be prohibitive, if the Post Office nationalised the company. At that time, for example, the Glasgow Corporation charged £5 5s for unlimited service versus £17 charged in London. (What such comparisons failed to address were the differences in the cost of living and doing business in the two cities as well as profit considerations.)

The select committee, in assessing the wisdom of nationalisation, essentially endorsed the government's policy. No fundamental criticism was made of either the general schedule for take-over or the terms granted the company. W. E. L. Gaine of the NTC emphasised the fact that St Martin's le Grand had driven a hard bargain. After all, the company had to pay for all the initial mistakes involved in launching a new industry as well as £1.85 million in royalties to the Post Office.[46] Still the committee was slightly hesitant to place complete responsibility for telephone development in the hands of the Post Office. It suggested, therefore, that the option of granting new municipal licences be retained. (The government chose not to adopt this recommendation.) The last major issue considered by the committee concerned the disposition of the NTC's employees after nationalisation. The government, particularly Chamberlain at the Treasury, had earlier been hesitant to make any commitments to the employees. The telegraph employees taken on after 1870 had proven both more troublesome in their union activities and more expensive to pay than anticipated. Yet

44 BPP, 1905, vol. 7, Select Committee on Post Office (Telephone Agreement), p. 58.
45 Ibid., p. 81.
46 Ibid., p. 48.

the committee urged that all NTC employees with more than two years' service be taken on by St Martin's le Grand.

When the agreement came up for discussion in the House of Commons on 9 August 1905, the government once again had a comparatively easy time of it. Much of the government's support came from MPs highly critical of private enterprise. William Field, an Irish MP, argued that 'In this country we have the worst telephonic system of the whole world, the reason being that instead of its being taken over by the State, private individuals were allowed to control it.'[47] Chamberlain agreed that Fawcett had made a fundamental error in believing that competition and private initiative would develop the telephone's potential. The Post Office's position, moreover, was strengthened by Lord Stanley's willingness for political reasons to adopt the select committee's recommendation regarding the NTC's staff. Much of the opposition to nationalisation appeared to collapse after Stanley assured the House of Commons that the government would treat the employees fairly and even generously, up to the point of giving them pensions before they had served ten years under the department. Thus, John Burns the labour leader welcomed the prospect of adding thousands of employees to the state.[48] The anticipation of Murray and Smith on this matter was doubtlessly not as warm.

The agreement was finally approved by the House of Commons 187–110. After over two decades of wrong turns and haggling, the government was committed to the second significant case of nationalisation in British history. As one might expect, the decision to nationalise did not mark the end of the Post Office's problems with the telephone. Simply determining the price to be paid for the company's plant proved vexing. Although the process began in 1908, the department and the company were still haggling over the price in 1911. Complicated questions arose over how much should be allowed for depreciation, for compensation, for supervision of construction by NTC employees, and for the cost of raising capital by the company. Furthermore, the NTC would not agree to value its inventory on the basis of a representative sample. The process became so complex and extensive that at one point over 600 men were engaged in the task. Despite this commitment of manpower, the sides could not agree on what the proper purchase price should be. As a result, arbitration by the Railway and Canal Commission was necessary. The NTC submitted a claim of £18,350,307, while the Post Office contended that £9,381,048 was a fair amount.[49] In January 1913 the court issued its

[47] *Hansard's, Fourth Series*, vol. 151, 862, 9 August 1905.
[48] *Ibid.*, 849–50.
[49] Post 30/2487, E11888/19123.

decision that £12,515,264 would be the price. (The department and the NTC later slightly reduced the figure through mutual agreement.) St Martin's le Grand took pride in the fact that no chorus of criticism ever arose over the magnitude of the purchase price, as had been the case with the telegraphs.

Another difficulty, which was handled much less satisfactorily, was the transfer of the NTC's employees to government service. The task of implementing Stanley's decision – fitting the employees into the department and determining their responsibilities, salaries, and pension status – was not a simple one. A committee worked on the problem from March 1910 to July 1912. Upon the transfer of ownership to St Martin's le Grand virtually all the employees, except those earning £700 or more, were hired. Ultimately 19,000 workers were added to the Post Office staff.

The results were not encouraging to those who had believed that the state could run a business as cheaply as a private company. As one irritated Treasury clerk observed in December 1911, 'the gain to individuals taken over (as a whole) will be very considerable, and the transaction will demonstrate once more what we have [previously] learned . . . how much lower the market rates of wages are than those paid by the Post Office'.[50] For example, the weekly salary range for NTC provincial operators had been 6 to 14 shillings, while the Post Office paid 10 to 26 shillings. In addition to higher salary and pension benefits, the new employees enjoyed additional fringe benefits, such as a longer annual leave. About 9,300 people worked a shorter week for the Post Office than they had for the NTC, while 2,250 people worked a longer week. Such differences quickly mounted up, as table four indicates.

Moreover, salary costs rose dramatically in the first decade after nationalisation. This fact was partly due to normal expansion of the system and partly due to a large war bonus granted by the government. In 1913–14, telephone wages amounted to £2,472,091. By 1918–19, the sum had grown to £2,572,175 – which when combined with the war bonus of £1,198,118 amounted to £3,770,293.[51] As with the telegraphs, salary costs were to be a continuing problem for the managers of the telephone system.

[50] T1/11341/2061, R. Wilkins's memorandum, 6 December 1911.
[51] BPP, 1920, vol. 8, Select Committee on Telephone Charges, p. vi. By 1921 the war bonus would reach £4.2 million.

Table 4
Comparison of labour costs under
NTC and Post Office management

	NTC	Post Office
Mean salary cost of staff transferred to Post Office*	£1,228,953	£1,327,726
Authorised posts vacant at transfer	4,178	4,388
Costs of proportionate increase of staff to balance shortage, due to reduced hours, longer holidays, and more favourable sick pay privileges		67,138
Average commission earnings of contract officers	1,605	
Compensation to contract officers for loss of commission		1,483
Pension charges	13,853	165,000
Total	£1,248,589	£1,565,735
Increase under Post Office management		317,146

* This figure does not include Post Office employees engaged in telephone work before 1912 or new non-NTC employees hired after 1912.

Source: Post 30/3446, E15561/1915, Post Office to Treasury, 28 September 1915.

Establishing the purchase price and administering the ever-growing number of employees were internal problems at St Martin's le Grand, which seldom attracted much outside scrutiny. The same cannot be said for the rate structure and the system's efficiency. Severe criticism of these two aspects began before formal take-over. On the issue of rates, many individuals naturally desired a standard charge for an un-limited number of calls. The NTC and the Post Office, nonetheless, concluded that such a schedule offering unlimited use was unprofitable. Moreover, they believed it unfair for one customer making numerous calls to pay the same amount as another making little use of his tele-phone. In 1907 both institutions withdrew the option of unlimited service in the provinces for new subscribers, although old customers were allowed to continue under the former schedule. The decision brought forth a barrage of complaints from the general public, es-pecially the business community. In February 1908 Sydney Buxton the Postmaster General received a large group of protesting lobbyists, who claimed to represent sixty Chambers of Commerce, twenty county and town councils, the Association of Municipal Corporations, the County

Boroughs Association, the Trade Protection Society, and other business groups.[52] The deputation, led by Herbert Shaw of the Newcastle Chamber of Commerce, demanded the convening of a select committee to study the rate structure and the future policy of telephone development. To these men high telephone rates, which might yield large departmental profits, were wrongheaded because they interfered with trade and, thus, lowered their own profits. St Martin's le Grand, nevertheless, resisted the request. According to Buxton, the flat rate inevitably promoted profligate telephone use, which injured the system as a whole.

The department's critics were not satisfied. Laws Webb, an ardent campaigner for rapid telephone development, attacked the Post Office at a meeting of the British Constitution Society in London.[53] Webb argued that the Post Office monopoly of telephony to be established in 1912 would always be inefficient and inhibited by the Treasury. As a remedy he suggested the establishment of a National Telephone Authority, modelled on the London Port Authority, to operate the telephone system properly. The Association of Chambers of Commerce also refused to drop the issue. Throughout 1910 it continued to lobby for the restoration of the unlimited rate, and a resolution was passed on the subject at its London meeting in March 1911. Parliamentary criticism of the department further escalated throughout the pre-war period. For example, Leo Amery criticised the Post Office's lack of sophistication in business and engineering matters. Amery claimed that 'the attitude of the Post Office toward the engineering side is still to regard it as a routine department for installing and mending things – a base mechanic adjustment, a kind of glorified plumbing and gasfitting department'.[54] Other MPs voiced the familiar refrain that competition was necessary for efficient operation of any enterprise. The point was also made that there was no automatic correlation between the Post Office's past success in carrying mail and its future performance in furnishing telephone service. During these years a leader of the Parliamentary critics of St Martin's le Grand was C. S. Goldman, Conservative MP for Penryn and Falmouth. Goldman could always be relied upon to make much of the abuses and inefficiencies in the telephone system. An attack in July 1914 was typical:

My complaint against the system is that it has not expanded to half the extent that it would if the Post Office recognised their responsi-

---

52 Post 30/1616, E29062/1908, notes of meeting, 18 February 1908.
53 For the following, see Post 30/2223, E6813/1912, F. E. Milne's memorandum, no date.
54 *Hansard's, Fifth Series*, vol. 64, 771, 3 July 1914.

bilities and duties towards the great commercial community. Let us take the case of an expanding country like the United States. What has been done there last year? They increased their service by 700,000 telephones in one year – more than the whole system of the United Kingdom – and the longest time it takes for applicants to have telephones installed is seven and a half days in Buffalo – less than half the time it takes in London. [The] Post Office is not armed with the activity necessary for the development of the service, and the result is that instead of going ahead, we are going backward.[55]

It is difficult to judge the validity of such complaints and to distribute the responsibility for the situation. Beyond doubt there was some truth in Goldman's charges. When the Post Office took over the management from the NTC in 1912, there was very little excess capacity in the existing plant. As a result, new equipment had to be installed. Delays in supplying new telephone service resulted. (See table five.)

Table 5
Average time to connect a new subscriber in 1914

London	18½	days
Birmingham	51	days
Liverpool	26	days
Manchester	40	days
Edinburgh	18	days
Belfast	40	days

Source: Post 30/3112, E18875/1914, A. F. King's memorandum, 7 April 1914.

Even after the transition period was over, telephone usage as compared to other countries remained low. In 1921 there was one telephone for every forty-seven people in the United Kingdom as opposed to one for every eight in the United States and one for every ten in Canada.[56] Nevertheless, it is open to debate how much that lag was a function of the shortcomings of the Post Office rather than other variables such as per capita income, the size of the country, and the relative efficiency of other means of communication. On other points the available evidence pertaining to the efficiency of the Post Office telephone system after acquisition is also susceptible to conflicting interpretations. In

[55] *Ibid.*, 720.
[56] BPP, 1922, vol. 6, Select Committee on the Telephone, p. 9.

1914 Goldman conducted a survey of 1,500 subscribers in London, and approximately one-half reported that service had deteriorated since state management began. However, St Martin's le Grand polled 128,000 subscribers with the rather leading question 'Is your line working all right?' and 87 per cent of the respondents expressed full satisfaction.

Even if one accepts the more critical appraisal, the question of determining the Post Office's long-term responsibility for the situation remains unresolved. The department had only been in control of the nationalised system for two years when the war intervened to disrupt any hope of quick progress. A committee studying possible improvements in the organisation and management of the telephone was forced to disband. Thirteen thousand of the twenty thousand employees in the Post Office's engineering department joined the armed forces. Expansion of exchanges and trunk lines after 1915 was radically cut back. If one considers these problems as well as the additional strain which the war bonus imposed on wage costs, then it would not be an exaggeration to assert that the war delayed the development of the telephone in England almost as much as the long period of uncertain public policy between 1880 and 1905. Of course, this is not to say that the Post Office forged boldly ahead once the war ended. It did not. Evelyn Murray, Secretary 1914–34 and son of the earlier Secretary who had done more than any other civil servant to shape telephone policy, was like his father in believing the Post Office should go no further than to meet existing demand for telephones and should take no active role in the creation of new demand through advertising or canvassing.[57]

As in other areas, the crucial problem encountered by St Martin's le Grand was juggling the priorities of public service and the demands of the Exchequer. Here not only was the general public involved, but also the Treasury. In contrast to Scudamore's efforts to lower telegraph tariffs, the administrators of the Post Office now placed efficiency, not lower rates, at the top of their list of objectives. As Herbert Samuel told a deputation from a conference of local authorities in February 1911, 'It is a false policy to pay low fees, if the result of low fees should be a service which is slow, untrustworthy, and troublesome; and both Trunk and local service must be maintained at the highest level of speed and accuracy.'[58] Samuel, hence, argued that rates should be set at such levels as to yield a moderate profit in order that the system would be business-like and independent. One should, however, not assume that the Post Office and the Treasury were always in agreement over

[57] Post 33/1562, M9196/1925, E. Murray's memorandum, 23 March 1923.
[58] Post 30/3281, E288812/1914, Samuel's note, 27 February 1911.

the precise course to pursue on the profit question. On the nuances of expanding the system there was no unanimity. The Post Office at times sought to open exchanges, which would not yield an immediate profit. The Treasury disagreed, insisting that the telephone was not a necessity. Hence, unlike postal or telegraphic services which might properly be provided by the state at a loss, exchanges should be profitable from the outset or not opened at all.[59] The largest concession that the Treasury would grant was to allow exchanges to be opened where the deficit was projected at 3 per cent or less. There were similar disagreements over the rate schedule. Here again it was a difference of opinion measured in degrees, not in absolutes. In the period immediately after nationalisation the Post Office constantly feared that, if the charges were too high and profits too large, an unremunerative schedule would be forced upon it by Parliament. Such a reduction in telegraph rates had been rammed down the government's throat in 1885. The Treasury also hoped to resist any fundamental reduction until a few years had elapsed and a more accurate picture of the telephone accounts could be drawn. In April 1913 Lloyd George, then Chancellor of the Exchequer, informed Samuel that

> I think it is most important that no promise of reduction [of rates] or of a Select Committee should be given. The information available with regard to the State of the telephone account is admittedly incomplete. I understand that you are likely to approach us with a further demand for expenditure on staff, part of which will fall on the telephone account, and unless we are careful we shall find a deficit on telephones as well as telegrams. The question is of considerable importance from the point of view of the revenue, and I do hope that no definite action will be taken until the matter can be considered in all its bearings by the Estimates Committee of the Cabinet.[60]

The argument proved persuasive. In March 1914 the Post Office considered reducing the rates, but refused to do so on the grounds that the profit of over £300,000 for 1912–13 was justified. When in 1915 the rate schedule was revised, the trend was upward. Long-distance charges were increased by one-third, and local schedules were redrafted, eliminating many obsolete rates held over from the period of NTC management. (See appendix, table seven.) Unfortunately this revision did not eradicate the system's fiscal difficulties, as table six shows.

---

[59] *Ibid.*, Conference of Post Office–Treasury officials, 20 October 1911.
[60] T1/11636/9077, Lloyd George to Samuel, 24 April 1913.

Table 6
Profit and loss in the nationalised telephone

Exchange system

	1912–13	1914–15	1916–17	1918–19	Estimated 1919–20
Expenditure	£4,579,191	£5,277,777	£5,523,667	£6,579,773	£8,820,000
Income	4,897,482	5,420,880	5,762,779	6,415,330	7,120,000
Profit*	318,291	143,103	239,112		
Loss*				164,443	1,700,000

Trunk system

	1912–13	1914–15	1916–17	1918–19	Estimated 1919–20
Expenditure	£964,452	£1,306,710	£1,500,944	£1,753,534	£2,180,000
Income	949,504	1,052,589	1,463,561	1,881,716	1,930,000
Profit*				128,182	
Loss*	14,948	254,121	37,383		250,000

Exchange and trunk systems combined

	1912–13	1914–15	1916–17	1918–19	Estimated 1919–20
Expenditure	£5,543,643	£6,584,487	£7,024,611	£8,333,307	£11,000,000
Income	5,846,986	6,473,469	7,226,340	8,297,046	9,050,000
Profit*	303,343		201,729		
Loss*		111,018		36,261	1,950,000

* After providing for depreciation and interest on capital.

Source: BPP, 1920, vol. 8, Select Committee on Telephone Charges, p. ix.

Clearly the problems of telephone administration had only begun, as the number of select committees devoted to the problem in the 1920s and after demonstrates.[61]

At this point it is necessary to place the Post Office's involvement in telephone policy and development in a wider context. In many ways the story of the government's handling of the invention must be pronounced a lost opportunity. Approach after approach proved inadequate to develop the telephone's potential. After an initial period of doubt and uncertainty Fawcett in accord with the Treasury in 1884

[61] See Douglas C. Pitt, *The Telecommunications Function in the British Post Office* (Westmead, 1980).

chose a policy of development by private firms in a competitive market. This strategy, as has been shown, did not establish competition, but instead contributed to the growth of a monopoly under the NTC. In the 1890s two piecemeal remedies for this monopoly were tried. The purchase of the trunk line system, accomplished after much delay in 1896, left the real problem – local telephone development – unresolved. Moreover, encouragement of municipal systems to take up the fight against the NTC did not spark sufficient interest in that expedient. Thus, St Martin's le Grand and Whitehall were forced to address the problem once again. Even then the approach taken was not direct: first competition, then cooperation, and then nationalisation of the telephone in London were tried before the final policy of a complete government take-over was implemented. At each stage the inadequacy of one policy led to a growing involvement of the government in the next round. Beyond question this erratic policy history contributed to the limited impact of the invention in Britain both before and after nationalisation, which table seven illustrates.

Why did the nationalisation of the telephone diverge so radically from the pattern seen in the telegraphs' acquisition? A temptingly brief answer would be that there was no Scudamore to promote the telephone. Lamb – who was a capable civil servant, although not to the same degree as Scudamore – sought to carry on the expansive, optimistic vision of his former chief, but failed. Murray was certainly Scudamore's equal as advocate and administrator. He was perhaps the most able man of the prewar generation at St Martin's le Grand. But he operated from a different intellectual position in an economic and political environment which had changed fundamentally since the 1860s. Thus, no entrepreneurial administrator emerged to transform the situation. It should also be remembered that, unlike the telegraphs case, administrators grappling with the telephone found little support or interest among leading politicians. For example, Lord Salisbury, Prime Minister for much of this period, was without question fascinated by electricity and even went so far as to have a telephone installed at Hatfield House. But as Briggs has pointed out, when Salisbury addressed the first dinner of the Institution of Electrical Engineers in 1889 on the social potential of electricity, the Conservative leader failed to mention the telephone even once.[62] As with the telegraphs, ideological preconceptions and pragmatic concerns were crucial. How-

---

[62] Asa Briggs, *Victorian Things* (London, 1988), pp. 373, 389. Salisbury's indifference to the development of government policy on the telephone is also reflected in Post Office records where his presence is not noticeable. For a judicious overview of the role of the state in industrial affairs during this period, see Sidney Pollard, *Britain's Prime and Britain's Decline The British Economy 1870–1914* (London, 1989), chapter 4.

Table 7
Number of telephones in Great Britain, 1890–1920

	Post Office	NTC	Guernsey	Hull	Other Municipalities	Total	Total as percentage of population
1890	5,000	40,000				45,000	0.12
1895	7,000	92,000				99,000	0.25
1900	8,800	200,200	1,000			210,000	0.51
1905	54,100	362,500	1,400	1,900	18,100 a	438,000	1.02
1910	121,000	534,000	1,900	3,100	2,500 b	662,500	1.48
1915	804,000		2,100	11,400		817,500	1.85
1920	970,000		2,600	13,200		985,800	2.11

a	Glasgow	12,300	b	Portsmouth
	Portsmouth	2,500		
	Brighton	1,900		
	Swansea	1,400		
		18,100		

Source: BPP, 1921, vol. 7, Select Committee on the Telephone Service, p. 302.

ever, here they tended to reduce, not increase, the appeal of nationalisation for W. H. Smith, Chamberlain, and H. B. Smith as well as for Murray. Doubts over the wisdom of adding to the Post Office's staff, the fear of having to pay an unnecessarily high purchase price before the NTC's licence expired, concern over the ability of the Post Office managers to administer the system, problems already existing with the telegraphs, uncertainties about the proper role of government in the economy – each undercut interest in a take-over. (By now it should be abundantly clear that protecting telegraph revenue was only one, and at times a somewhat minor one, of many priorities shaping telephone policy.)

These worries and barriers might have been swept aside if national opinion had been more unanimously positive in its assessment of the telephone, particularly its potential utility for non-business uses and its potential appeal for the working classes. From 1876 on the invention had unquestionably attracted much interest among the general public. However, it was one thing to be amused by hearing Kate Field sing 'Comin' Thro' the Rye' over a telephone at Osborne House.[63] It was quite another thing to commit government funds and energies to an industry about which there existed so many contradictory opinions. Not surprisingly, there had been a good deal of initial scepticism concerning the telephone outside and inside the Post Office. In 1880, for instance, Tilley likened what he heard over a telephone to the noise from a bad Punch and Judy show.[64] What needs to be stressed is that such impressions, even if they were less than accurate, persisted much longer than one might have anticipated. The negative attitudes of Morley and Hicks Beach accurately reflected wider societal perceptions. Hence, 'the telephone, usually inconveniently located in the flower-room, in a corner of the hall, or in a lobby between the smoking-room and the gentlemen's lavatory, was seldom used for chats'.[65] Moreover, the efforts of businessmen and pressure groups, such as the Association for the Protection of Telephone Subscribers, to convince the public of the necessity of telephone expansion were not successful. Unlike the campaign for the nationalisation of telegraphs, a strong press–business coalition on the telephone never emerged. When, for example, the London County Council complained in 1902 of high rates which inhibited use of the telephone, The Times was less than sympathetic:

63 The Times, 16 January 1878, p. 9.
64 Post 30/398, E3497/1880, Tilley to Manners, 13 January 1880.
65 Laski, 'Domestic Life', p. 190.

[After] all is said and done the telephone is not an affair of the million. It is a convenience for the well to do and a trade appliance for persons who can well afford to pay for it. For people who use it constantly it is an immense economy even at the highest rates charged by the telephone company. For those who use it to merely save themselves trouble or add to the diversions of life it is a luxury. An overwhelming majority of the population do not use it and are not likely to use it at all, except perhaps to the extent of an occasional message from a public station.[66]

Such statements serve as a reminder of the point that inventions and the businesses which seek to develop them, like ideas, seldom encounter a neutral climate. Steven Tolliday has recently argued that the 'determinants of . . . [a firm's] development are social and institutional as well as market and technical'.[67] The history of the Post Office's difficult relationship with the telephone supports Tolliday's insight. In Victorian Britain the telephone ran up against an array of obstacles, cultural in the broadest sense of the word, which was not necessarily connected to the specific technological characteristics of the invention. Laws Webb was groping toward this point when in 1907 he argued 'The financial and administrative difficulties are much greater than the technical; telephone engineering has become fairly standardised, but rapid development is mainly a question of large capital development, and high efficiency of service is mainly a question of sound and efficient organisation.'[68] In the end what may be termed external barriers proved paramount, and the 'financial and administrative difficulties' which the Post Office sought at times energetically and at times reluctantly to overcome became part of a larger set of self-fulfilling prophecies. The telephone cannot be used. The telephone will not be used. The telephone should not be used. As a result, the telephone was not used to its potential during the years of delay and hesitation before the First World War.

---

[66] *The Times*, 14 January 1902, p. 7. For a similar argument, see *Edinburgh Review*, 199 (1904), 73.
[67] Steven Tolliday, *Business, Banking, and Politics. The Case of British Steel, 1918–1939* (Cambridge, Massachusetts, 1987), p. 16.
[68] *The Times*, 21 August 1907, p. 8.

PART THREE
COMPLICATIONS OF GROWTH

8

Railway Contracts

This is the Night Train crossing the Border,
Bringing the cheque and the postal order,

Letters for the rich, letters for the poor,
The shop at the corner, the girl next door.
                                    – W. H. Auden, 'Night Mail'

When the Post Office commissioned Auden to write a poem for a film
marking the 1938 centenary of the use of travelling post offices to sort
mail on railways, a much more important centenary was on the horizon
– that of Penny Post. Indeed, from 1840 forward the department and
the railways had entered the nineteenth-century revolution in government linked together. Before that time, despite the efforts of able
officials such as Sir Francis Freeling, Secretary 1798 to 1836, the Post
Office had remained a creaky machine excessively committed to its
tax-collecting functions. In the 1830s a pressure group of fundamental
importance emerged to challenge the old ways of doing business at St
Martin's le Grand. The leader of this movement was, of course,
Rowland Hill, who had made a career out of reform in areas from
empire to education. What needs to be stressed initially about Hill's
campaign for Penny Post is its close similarity to other reform move-
ments of that same generation, such as the Anti-Corn Law League.
Working from an Utilitarian insistence on efficiency and economy,
Hill argued that the old system of charging the recipient of a letter
postage based on the distance conveyed and the number of sheets the
letter contained was an impediment to the expansion of trade and
ideas. An indefatigable collector of statistics, Hill marshalled much
evidence to demonstrate that the Post Office revenue had not kept
pace with the growth of the population. A simplified system of charging the sender on the basis of weight, one penny for the first half
ounce, was the obvious solution. Two additional points should be made
about Hill's attack on St Martin's le Grand. First, as has been convincingly argued, Hill's grasp of the complexities of departmental finance
was far from sound, based more on 'mere guesses' than accurate com-

prehension.[1] Not surprisingly, the insiders at St Martin's le Grand, most notably Maberly, had a better understanding than Hill of the relative elasticity of demand for mail services and the size of staff required to operate the system. This leads to a second point. Hill's success, and his enshrinement in departmental hagiography, rests more on his energetic skill as an advocate and gadfly, both words apply, than on his sophistication as an economist. More than anyone else, he recognised the need for a well-orchestrated campaign to convince Melbourne's government of the validity of his suggestions. He coordinated and stimulated support among MPs, most importantly Robert Wallace who had long been interested in postal reform. Wallace, as chairman of a select committee examining Hill's proposals, reciprocated by asking key witnesses leading questions, which drove the issue of reform home.[2] Outside Parliament Hill found allies among likeminded ideologues, such as Edwin Chadwick, business groups such as the Mercantile Committee – formed in February 1838 and led by Henry Cole – and the press. On 10 January 1840 Hill's campaign bore fruit with the inauguration of the Penny Post. All in all, it was a result in which men of liberal ideals could take some pleasure, for it symbolised the march of progress. To John Stuart Mill, 'Only in a popular government (setting apart the accident of a highly intelligent despot) could Sir Rowland Hill have been victorious over the Post Office.'[3] It goes without saying that Mill's decidedly Whiggish division of the world into forces of light and darkness did not do justice to the realities of the situation, for St Martin's le Grand took up the task of implementing the Penny Post with more interest and ability than Hill liked to admit.

The new postage rates contributed, as table one indicates, to a remarkable rise in the number of letters handled by the department. Behind these statistics lay ever present demands to accelerate the delivery of mail and to extend service to small villages all over the country. Occasionally the source of this pressure was political. Such was the case in 1885 when Hicks Beach the Chancellor of the Exchequer approved an acceleration of the Dublin–Galway mails despite his own department's insistence that the increased expense was 'indefensible' on financial grounds.[4] More often it was businessmen who lobbied for improvements in the system to facilitate trade. For

---

[1] Daunton, *Royal Mail*, p. 35. See also D. Graham, 'Victorian Reform as a Family Business: the Hill Family' in A. S. Wohl (ed.), *The Victorian Family* (London, 1978).
[2] See, for example, BPP, 1837–8, vol. 20, q. 3508.
[3] John Stuart Mill, *Considerations on Representative Government* (1861, rpr. New York, 1958), p. 90.
[4] T1/8185A/13069, Barrington's memorandum, 7 August 1885.

Table 1
Letters delivered

	1839	1840	1860	1881	1901	1911
England and Wales (millions)	65	132	462	981	1977	2606
Number per capita	4	8	22	38	61	73
Scotland (millions)	8	18	54	105	202	265
Number per capita	3	7	17	29	47	56
Ireland (millions)	9	19	48	79	144	177
Number per capita	1	2	8	15	32	40

Source: *The Sixty-first Report of the Postmaster General on the Post Office* (London, 1916), p. 35.

example, in 1857 a memorial was received from Liverpool, Manchester, Huddersfield, Bradford, Hull, and Sheffield on the need for a late mail train to London which would allow these northern towns more time to prepare their correspondence. Hill thoroughly studied the request and devoted four pages of the annual report of 1858 to a prospectus for improved service for these towns.[5] Such an attentive response was by no means atypical. After all, the organisation of the inland mails was the pride of St Martin's le Grand. With the implementation of Penny Post, the department's reputation for efficiency and celerity had been established. Indeed, the average citizen judged the department more on the basis of the quality of the mail service than on any other criterion. Another reason for administrative celebration as well as watchfulness lay in the fact that the domestic mails provided the annual surplus crucial to good relations with the Treasury. In 1900, for example, the postal side of the department's business contributed over £3.7 million to the Exchequer, while the telegraphs operated at a deficit of £.6 million.

From the first use of the Liverpool and Manchester Railway in 1830, the Post Office had turned rather quickly away from coach companies to railways for necessary aid in the conveyance of the increasing volume of mail. One measure of this increasing reliance was the steep rise in payments to the railways during the Victorian and Edwardian peri-

5 *Report of the Postmaster General on the Post Office* (London, 1858), pp. 68ff.

ods – £2,000 in 1838, £1.2 million in 1910. Such an outcome was the result of literally thousands of individual decisions made by departmental administrators on matters such as the establishment of timetables, problems of punctuality, arrangements for the transfer of mail from one line to another, and payments due to the various companies. One can get some idea of the intricate and frequently tedious nature of such problems from an 1885 letter requesting Treasury sanction for changes in the Highland mail route:

> The train which now leaves Inverness at 2 p.m. will start at 12.10 p.m., and instead of arriving at Wick at 8 o'clock at night, will be due there at ten minutes past six, thus largely extending the opportunity for the preparation of replies by the return mail which leaves Wick shortly after midnight. Corresponding improvements will be made at Thurso where mails will arrive at 6.50 instead of 7.50 p.m. At Strome Ferry, there will even be a greater acceleration: the mails will arrive there at 3.30 p.m. instead of 5.40 p.m., and I hope to be able to carry on this improvement to Stornoway by an earlier dispatch of the Mail Steamer from Strome Ferry.[6]

Such arrangements were made repeatedly by the administrators in charge of the inland mails.[7] In 1859 twenty-one separate railway contracts were necessary to carry one letter from Land's End to John O'Groats. In 1870 the department had thirty-two contracts with English railway companies, fourteen with Irish, and eleven with Scottish. (See appendix, table nine for a description of part of this complex system.) It was a matter which demanded more and more of the clerks' time. In 1881 approximately 1,400 pages of letters were written to railways by the Home Mails Branch of the Secretary's Office. Ten years later such letters filled almost 4,000 pages.

However, it is necessary to consider more than numbers, if one is to understand the nature of Post Office–railway relations. In some ways the problems involved would appear much more straightforward than those faced by Scudamore with the telegraphs or by Lamb and Murray with the telephone. Rarely did the inland mails form a subject for lengthy Parliamentary debate. In contrast to the overseas mails, questions of foreign policy or national interest did not so often intervene to complicate what was basically a business arrangement between the department and the railways. The Post Office was, therefore, able to negotiate with minimal outside interference from more powerful government departments, such as the Foreign Office. Even the Treas-

---

6 T1/8172B/8224, Post Office to Treasury, 12 May 1885.
7 For the following, see the appropriate Postmaster General's Report and Baines, vol. 2, 207.

ury presented fewer difficulties. In fact, it was not until 1884 that the Treasury began to study proposed railway contracts and consider their financial results before any final arrangements were concluded.[8] Even after that date Treasury authority was as a rule easily won. At times such compliance resulted from the inability of the Treasury to fathom the implications of the detail involved in railway arrangements. When, for example, a Treasury clerk considered the request for the acceleration of the Highland route quoted above, he admitted bafflement as to its ramifications.[9] The general line of argument employed by the Post Office was that improved facilities or increased speed of delivery, while costly, would ultimately be offset by increased use and, therefore, by increased revenue. Beyond this, St Martin's le Grand had great difficulty offering an exact estimate of the financial results of any change in the railway timetable. In January 1890 John Kempe, principal clerk of the Treasury, considered a Post Office request for an acceleration of the London–Weymouth mails, which would increase the cost by £1,750. Kempe expressed displeasure that 'This [an assessment of the proposed acceleration's financial results] the P.O. cannot give us. . . . Yet they manage to collect curious and much more useless statistics to embellish their Annual Report. . . . [The] P.O. regard the matter as a sort of action of political economy requiring no proof.'[10] Nonetheless, it is revealing that the changes in the Highland mails and the London–Weymouth mails were both sanctioned.

Perhaps the major characteristic of postal–railway relations which distinguished them from other types of department activity arose from the fact that the statutory powers of the Postmaster General over this industry had been laid out in great detail. After 1838 the legal authority of the Post Office was defined and enlarged by a number of Parliamentary acts.[11] The Postmaster General could order any railway company on notice of twenty-eight days to carry mails, guards, or other postal employees by either ordinary or special trains at such hours, speed, and making stops of any length required, provided the speed did not exceed a safe maximum. He could require railways to outfit separate carriages or even to add an entire train, if necessary. Upon paying

8 Post 10/31, Treasury to Post Office, 13 February 1884.
9 T1/8172B/8224, Barrington's memorandum, 15 May 1885.
10 T1/8489B/1435, Kempe to Welby, 20 January 1890.
11 The Railway (Conveyance of Mails) Act, 1838 (1 and 2 Vict. c. 38) and the Regulation of Railways Act, 1873 (36 and 37 Vict. c. 48) were the chief acts. These were supplemented by the Railway Regulation Act, 1844, the Post Office (Duties) Act, 1847, the Regulation of Railways Act, 1868, the Railway and Canal Traffic Act, 1888, and the Conveyance of Mails Act, 1893. See Henry Parris, *Government and the Railways in Nineteenth-Century Britain* (London, 1965) for the broader context of this important relationship.

just compensation he could immediately terminate a service, and he could terminate on six-months' notice with no compensation whatsoever to the company. In cases of disagreement over the compensation to be paid, standard procedure with one arbitrator chosen from each side and an umpire was followed.

From these circumstances – less outside interference, frequently lax Treasury control, and specific powers of authority – one might assume that Post Office–railway relations ran fairly smoothly. In fact, they were bitterly strained during the 1840s and 1850s. Both sides found the situation unsatisfactory. The Post Office considered the statutory powers granted by Parliament to be of little use. In Tilley's estimation, 'the power of the Post Office to insist on regularity is very indefinite, – and we have a wholesome dread of the uncertainty of legal proceedings'.[12] St Martin's le Grand's anger over this awkward state of affairs was acute, and in 1856 Edward Page the Inspector General of Mails used the department's annual report as a platform to attack both the weaknesses of existing legislation and the high fees charged by the railways.[13] Harking back to a supposedly golden age of free trade and competition among mail coach companies, Page claimed that the introduction of railways essentially destroyed competition and placed dangerous monopolies in the hands of a few companies. To minimise this danger for the travelling public, Parliament had taken the precaution of ensuring moderate charges for passenger conveyance by special provision in each railway act. However, similar provisions covering remuneration for mail services had been overlooked, as it was deemed sufficient to specify that the remuneration should be 'reasonable'. To Page, this was regrettably a most indefinite term, which had given rise to a variety of opinion. Particularly distressing to the Post Office was the inconsistency of rates paid to various companies. The department, for example, paid 2s per mile on a Dublin to Drogheda route and 4s per mile on a Dublin to Cork run. These charges were outrageous compared to Page's estimate of 15d per mile as the cost of running an entire train. Not only was the cost of railway conveyance of mail high, but it could be dramatically higher than the cost of mail conveyance by coach. One estimate held that the average charge per mile for railway conveyance was 9.75d versus 2.34d for coach.[14] (Such estimates, of course, failed to take speed of conveyance or the greater capacity of railways into consideration.) Irish costs were especially high, and St

---

12 Post 101, Tilley's memorandum, 13 December 1853.
13 *Second Report of the Postmaster General on the Post Office* (London, 1856), pp. 49ff.
14 *Third Report of the Postmaster General on the Post Office* (London, 1857), p. 3.

Martin's le Grand felt the pinch between accommodation and revenue there more than in any other part of the United Kingdom.

Arbitration procedure, to which the Post Office resorted 139 times between 1839 and 1866, offered no automatic solution to these problems. Often the arbitrators lacked the essential data upon which to base an equitable judgement. Hence, the department engaged in a constant game of guessing whether arbitration was a good option. In 1864, for instance, Tilley predicted that, if a dispute involving the Midland Railway went to arbitration, the award might be £4,000 more than the company's original demand.[15] The process was also exceedingly slow. As one administrator complained, every 'effort on the part of the Post Office fails to obtain an award till one or two years after the service has commenced, when it is perhaps discovered that the cost of the service is far greater than the convenience will justify'.[16] Another circumstance complicating the arbitration process was that the more important trains were under the direct control of the department. In such circumstances the Post Office was not simply an ordinary customer, but rather the basic reason for the existence of a particular service and timetable. Such complications inevitably increased the cost of mail conveyance by the railways. As late as 1874 Tilley advised that the Post Office should avoid this problem by never putting trains under notice: 'We should take the trains as we find them, and then decide which is best, inconvenient trains or the road.'[17] The upshot of this situation was, in the opinion of many at the Post Office, intolerable. It is difficult to assess how much the high costs actually inhibited postal expansion during the middle third of the century. Hill complained that the railways' superior position meant that improvements in service were withheld.[18] Accordingly the Post Office sought to keep costs as low as possible by massing correspondence on a small number of main trunk lines. (Treasury insistence to the contrary, Post Office administrators did regard revenue considerations to be of significance when contemplating a new service.[19]) There was another reason for the department's, or more accurately Hill's, antagonistic outlook toward the railways. Hill believed that the high cost of railway contracts constituted the chief reason why his predictions as to the recovery of revenue after the establishment of Penny Post had proven inaccurate.[20] Caught between demands for improved mail service and financial considerations, administrators at St Martin's le Grand blamed the railways.

15 Post 30/252, Tilley's note, 20 July 1864.
16 Post 30/175, E2985/1866, Post Office to Treasury, 18 February 1856.
17 Post 101, Tilley to W. R. Mitford, 12 August 1874.
18 Post 30/138, E2324/1860, Hill to Postmaster General, 21 December 1859.
19 See, for example, Post 101, Tilley to Welby, 23 May 1864.
20 Post, Hill's Journal, 28 March 1851.

The railways had their own reasons for complaint. The introduction of the Book Post in 1848 was regarded by the industry as an unwarranted intrusion into their own sphere of private enterprise. A select committee which examined the situation in 1854 found that a large number of parcels had indeed been removed from the traditional means of conveyance and that the Post Office had become a competitor with the railways. The committee felt no qualms about this competition by a public department, for they believed 'that incalculable advantages are derived from it [the Book Post] by the public . . . particularly in the diffusion of literature and knowledge in county districts, which could not be approached with equal facility by other means'.[21] Unfortunately, the railways were not as enthusiastic over the new services offered by St Martin's le Grand. In 1856 Robert Stephenson used the occasion of his presidential address before the Institute of Civil Engineers to attack the department. Citing the establishment of the Book Post, Stephenson predicted that, if the Post Office continued to expand its services, 'it would be brought into absolute antagonism with the Companies'.[22] He went on to complain about what he considered the regrettably low compensation received by the railways for the conveyance of mail, and, touching a nerve at St Martin's le Grand, insisted that it was only the use of the railways which made the Penny Post possible.

The give-and-take in this war of words is less important than the question as to who dominated the bargaining process in the middle decades of the nineteenth century. Undoubtedly it was the railways which had the upper hand, as was demonstrated by repeated efforts on the part of departmental administrators to change the rules of the game. In considering these efforts, two points should be kept in mind. The first is the extent to which some civil servants at St Martin's le Grand felt that the state was justified in regulating, even controlling, private industry. The second is the ambivalent role played by the Treasury, which at best was hesitant to support the Post Office. For example, in the summer of 1848 Rowland Hill became incensed over the high cost of conveyance in Ireland.[23] His anger was compounded by the fact that the Great Southern and Western Railway Company, to which the department paid large sums, had recently secured a loan from the government. Hill, therefore, suggested that the government should pressure Irish railway companies which were receiving loans to lower their charges to the Post Office as a prerequisite for a loan. The

21 BPP, 1854, vol. 11, Select Committee on Conveyance of Mails by Railways, p. xv.
22 See Stephenson's address in Samuel Smiles, The Life of George Stephenson (London, 1857), pp. 524–5.
23 Post 100, Hill to Clanricarde, 11 July 1848.

Treasury refused to act upon this bold plan, and the scheme was dropped. Hill next sought to have a clause establishing a general schedule of charges for carrying the mails written into any new railway bill.[24] He regarded a 5 per cent profit plus cost as reasonable. Although this criterion failed to win support, Hill continued to press for some established standard on which to base railway payments. In 1850 a Treasury-appointed committee considered the question, and its recommendations are noteworthy. The Treasury concluded a rate of 2d per cwt. per mile was fair. This was four times higher than that recommended by Hill.[25] In contrast to their positions on many other issues, Whitehall in this instance was more generous than St Martin's le Grand. An exact tariff, however, was not established.

Hill continued to lobby for almost any bill which would clarify the rate situation. In 1852 he proposed a schedule that would in certain circumstances have increased the sums payable to the railways for trains run at Post Office request. The Select Committee on Railway and Canal Bills devoted only one paragraph of its report to Hill's suggestion. However, it did agree that 'the companies should afford to the Post Office, at the same charge as would be paid by private individuals for similar services, every assistance which might add to the convenience of the Public'.[26] Thus, a company which failed to cooperate in postal matters was not fulfilling its civic obligation. What the committee did not sufficiently realise, however, was that there was no consensus as to what constituted 'similar services'. The railways continued to oppose any departmental effort to establish a statutory rate schedule. In 1857 the power of the railway interest, which according to Hill included ninety-six MPs, destroyed an attempt to pass such a bill.[27] Two years later the Treasury refused to support another measure, which would have abolished all arbitration procedure and substituted in its place set rates. In this case the department was even prepared to guarantee the railways the existing remuneration as a minimum. Given the continuing state of frustration, it is not surprising that as late as 1866 Hill's brother Frederic drafted a memorandum outlining in detail the benefits, such as savings through 'avoidance of competition' and the end of 'petty opposition', which would accrue both to the public and the Post Office if the railways were nationalised.[28]

[24] *Ibid.*, Hill to Clanricarde, 1 November 1848.
[25] Post 30/174, E2985/1866.
[26] BPP, 1852–3, vol. 38, Fifth Report of Select Committee on Railway and Canal Bills, p. 16. A copy of Hill's proposed bill is included with the report.
[27] The significance of the railway interest may easily be overestimated. According to Alderman, the efficient inner core consisted of thirty-seven MPs in 1857: Geoffrey Alderman, *The Railway Interest* (Leicester, 1973), p. 25.
[28] Post 30/175, E2985, F. Hill's memorandum, no date, probably April 1866.

The situation began to improve slowly in the mid-1860s. The retirement of Rowland Hill in 1864 removed a major source of irritation. In 1866 the Post Office advised against reviving the aborted 1857 bill.[29] In some years there were even decreases in the cost of railway conveyance of the mails, dropping from £620,235 in 1861 to £526,966 a year later. More importantly, the weight of the mails conveyed by the railways could rise rapidly without a proportionate increase in payments to the railways, as contracts once made did not allow for later adjustments. In 1874 the department estimated that railway payments had risen on the average only 15 per cent, while some companies were carrying twice as much mail. This trend continued throughout the rest of the century much to the benefit of St Martin's le Grand. The number of arbitration cases also diminished, a sign of increasing harmony between the Post Office and the industry. To be sure, there were always complaints over punctuality of mail trains and petty squabbles with certain companies. In 1874, for example, Tilley complained that a Scottish railway had suggested that innkeepers not stable coach horses as a means to coerce the Post Office into using the railway.[30] In 1890 Blackwood similarly bemoaned the power of the Highland Railway Company, which 'has got a complete control of all the public bodies north of Perth. They only have to pass the word in order to deluge the Post Office with memorials and petitions from town councils, and letters of remonstrance from members of Parliament.'[31]

Such complaints were to be heard less and less frequently as the nineteenth century drew to a close. In part, this change may be related to what T. R. Gourvish has described as a general weakening of the railway interest over a wide range of issues.[32] In part, it must be attributed to two specific developments which enhanced the Post Office's position. The first, and the less important of the two, was the 1893 Conveyance of Mails Act which gave the department and the railways the power to call on the Railway and Canal Commission for arbitration. With this mechanism available the process was streamlined and made more predictable. The second improvement came as a result of increasingly effective vigilance on the part of both the Treasury and the Post Office concerning railway issues. In 1894 a Treasury committee was convened to study contract questions and to find an alternative to the old system, where the 'amount [paid by the Post Office] simply represents the result of haggling and, as might be

[29] Post 30/175, E2985/1866, Post Office to Treasury, 3 May 1866.
[30] Post 101, Tilley to Smith, 10 August 1874.
[31] Post 32/68, Scot1544/1893, Blackwood to Raikes, 20 March 1890.
[32] T. R. Gourvish, *Railways and the British Economy* (London, 1980), p. 56.

expected, the result so far as principle is concerned has been chaos'.[33] This system, according to Treasury analysis, had led to wildly erratic settlements. Eight railway contracts were judged against 'test principles', i.e. a fair price to be paid by the government.[34] Actual payments made by the Post Office ranged from 61 per cent above the ideal rate to 11 per cent below it. Put another way, on these contracts the Post Office was spending £302,165 when £263,939 would have been a reasonable amount. Such conclusions confirmed Welby's guess that the Post Office 'is far from getting the consideration which a good customer usually gets'.[35] In order to alleviate this problem, the committee recommended that the Post Office should pay only 50 per cent of the ordinary parcel rates charged to private customers. If Post Office staff instead of railway officials guarded the mails, the rate should be only 40 per cent of the standard charge. Such reductions were justified on the grounds of the magnitude and the regularity of Post Office business. For those trains under the Postmaster General's control, the committee endeavoured to tighten procedures on the extra payments made in compensation for departmental interference in a railway's operations. In the past this extra sum had been lumped into the actual conveyance cost in a haphazard manner. In the future such cost breakdowns would give the Post Office an advantage in bargaining with a company or presenting its case before the Railway Commission.

It was all fine and well to establish these general principles. What was more difficult, of course, was to put them to actual use. A case illustrating these difficulties can be found in a crucial series of negotiations with the Great Western Railway. In February 1899 the GWR wrote to the department demanding that its compensation for the conveyance of mails be raised to £182,000.[36] This figure represented a substantial increase over the previous year's payment of £126,564. The company argued that, since the last contract agreement was signed in 1883, the weight and the number of mails conveyed had dramatically increased. The company was also troubled by the fact that during the same period Post Office payments to other railways had risen rapidly. In a most interesting line of argument the GWR claimed that it should share in the profits of the Post Office, as if something of a *de facto* partnership existed between the government and the company. According to the GWR, only its cooperation had allowed the Post Office to handle its 'rapidly growing' business. Thus, in a strategy

33 Post 11/49, Report of Committee, 12 July 1894.
34 T1/8844B/11697, Kempe's memorandum, 12 July 1894.
35 T1/8622A/18753, Welby's memorandum, 19 April 1892.
36 Post 30/1037, E17033/1903, Great Western Railway to Post Office, 20 February 1899.

similar to that employed by some of the unions in demanding higher wage scales, the GWR was seeking what it believed was its rightful share of the growing departmental pie. The reaction of the Post Office to these demands was negative. It could not accept any notion of partnership. The payments to any railway should not be calculated on the basis of department profits. Without any mutually accepted standards the contract bargaining evolved into a three-year duel of power politics. Each side, for example, continually sought to determine the rationale for the evidence presented by the other in justification of its demands. The department attempted to separate the consideration of trains run under the authority of the Postmaster General from discussions of ordinary trains, while the GWR sought in the more traditional manner to negotiate all services under one lump sum. For over a year letters were exchanged without result. Finally, in March 1900 the company wrote that their basis of calculation for trains running under absolute control of the Postmaster General was 2s 9d per train mile, and, therefore, a sum of £195,000 per year was the minimum acceptable to the railway.[37] The postal officials who were handling the case could not have regarded this offer as a step forward, as the GWR had originally asked for £182,000.

The new demand was rejected out of hand, and the round of diplomacy continued. St Martin's le Grand sought information on the railway's receipts on its various trains. The company refused to supply the information, but it instead sought particulars from the government as to the weight of the mail sent over its lines and general department philosophy on the division of payments for mails sent by ordinary trains and those sent by special trains. At one point the company offered to run trains exclusively for St Martin's le Grand at 5s per train mile. (The estimated cost of such a train was 2s 9d per train mile.) In May 1900 the Post Office disclosed the basis for its calculation as somewhere between one-third and one-half of ordinary parcel rates plus an allowance for special trains, a standard in line with the recommendation of the 1894 committee.[38] Despite some progress the two sides remained far apart for another two years. The width of the gulf was revealed in a January 1902 interview between G. H. Murray and J. L. Wilkinson, the GWR's General Manager. Wilkinson contended that the Post Office should pay full parcel rates for ordinary conveyance, and 4s per mile for special trains, while Murray argued that one-third of parcel charges for ordinary conveyance and 3s per mile for special trains was quite sufficient. Murray wrote that the interview was not

---

[37] *Ibid.*, GWR to Post Office, 13 March 1900.
[38] *Ibid.*, Post Office to GWR, 28 May 1900.

a very promising one as regards the ultimate result of negotiations, as I have no doubt that the Co. will build up quite as high a claim on the basis which we have suggested to them as they did on their own basis; and I doubt if they will accept much less than they have claimed without going to Court.[39]

Murray was correct in perceiving that the two sides were drifting farther apart. The Post Office reduced its estimate of an equitable figure to £79,170 for the conveyance of mails, while the GWR raised their demands to £264,821. The case went before the Railway and Canal Commission in September 1902. The commission accepted the Post Office's reasoning that any award should be based on the specific value of each service rendered by the railway, not on any vague notions of partnership. Thus, after three years of difficult negotiations, the commission's award of £135,855 represented an increase of less than £10,000 over the payment in 1898.

Sir Robert Hunter the solicitor at St Martin's le Grand concluded that the case was the 'heaviest litigation (or quasi-litigation) which I have had to conduct in the twenty-one years which I have served the Post Office'.[40] The GWR case marked something of a turning point in contract deliberations. For one thing, it instilled in the railway companies a healthy fear of arbitration before the commission.[41] Guidelines had been established, which clarified the bargaining process. The favourable outcome also stiffened the vigour with which the Post Office approached negotiations. Administrators at St Martin's le Grand consistently refused to accept any sort of partnership with the railways in the conveyance of letter mails, and this refusal helped to keep costs down. It was always a difficult process, because the department had to rely on a handful of railways to carry the bulk of the mails. (See table two.) Nevertheless, the reliance on a few railways by no means implied subsidization of the railways. Unlike the relationship with the steamship companies, the Post Office ultimately received good value for the money it spent on the railways. The advantages of the situation were described in great detail in a 1911 memorandum by Assistant Secretary W. J. Gates. By this time the charges for the conveyance of the mails on ordinary trains were securely based on private freight rates with substantial reductions for the quantity and regularity of the mails.[42]

---

39 *Ibid.*, Murray's memorandum, 9 January 1902.
40 *Ibid.*, Hunter's memorandum, 4 May 1903.
41 Post 23/2543, M1968/1929, confidential memorandum, no date.
42 Post 11/11, Gates's memorandum, 14 January 1911.

Table 2
Principal railways employed by the Post Office, 1889–90

	Railway	Amount paid for mail conveyance
England	London and North Western	£173,920
and	Great Western	117,600
Wales	Midland	53,820
	North Eastern	44,500
	Great Northern	33,500
Ireland	Great Southern and Western	40,640
	Midland Great Western	29,070
Scotland	Caledonian	67,825
	Highland	55,526
Total		£616,401

Percentage of total spent for the conveyance of mail by all railways: 68%

Source: BPP, 1890, vol. 46, Revenue Department Estimates, pp. 91–3.

For trains running at times fixed by the Post Office, previously the most difficult area, the system was eminently fair. The Post Office paid the actual cost for the working of the train, a percentage of profit at the average rate obtained by the company on its ordinary trains, and a small sum for interference with the company's operations. The efforts of Post Office negotiators in addition to the work of the 1894 Treasury committee had borne fruit in the establishment of an equitable working relationship between the Post Office and the railways, which is reflected in table three.

Table 3
Post Office payments to railways for mail conveyance

Year	Amount	Percentage of total expenditure on postal services
1860–1	£620,235	20
1880–1	713,055	16
1900–1	1,088,850	11
1910–11	1,199,990	8

Source: Reports of the Postmaster General and BPP, Revenue Department Estimates.

Contracts for the conveyance of the letter mails constituted only part of the responsibility of Post Office administrators dealing with the railways. The parcel post was the other major area of concern. How-

ever, it presented a fundamentally different set of issues and considerations. The growing use of railways for mail conveyance had developed
on an ad hoc basis, and contracts had been negotiated with individual
companies. The expansion of the Post Office into the business of
conveying parcels required conscious decision and resolve on the part
of the bureaucrats at St Martin's le Grand as well as an agreement with
the entire railway industry represented by the Railway Clearing House.
It was an exercise of considerably greater difficulty, as the Post Office
was pushing into an area previously controlled by private industry. This
fact helps to explain the protracted period which elapsed between
Hill's suggestion of such a service in 1837 and its implementation in
1883.[43]

Throughout the middle decades of the century a wide range of
professional economists, business associations, newspapers, and philanthropic groups lobbied for the establishment of a parcel post. In 1853,
for example, James Elmes, who was Vice President of the Society for
Diffusion of Knowledge and Practice of the Fine Arts and an associate
of Joseph Hume and William Ewart, broached the topic with Gladstone. Another lobbyist better known, but equally representative of the
Benthamite approach to government was Edwin Chadwick who cam-
paigned for a parcel post at public meetings, such as that of the Social
Science Association in Belfast in 1867. Not surprisingly, Chadwick
held the parcel post to be part of a larger technocratic scheme of
government administration. Chadwick argued that as 'a question of
administrative improvement . . . the conveyance of letters, telegraphic
messages, passengers, and goods should be combined under one chief
and responsible public authority'.[44] Through this consolidation of management large savings would result, because the Post Office's more
extensive network of offices would enjoy economies of scale not available to private railways. In 1868 Chadwick, with his usual lack of tact,
pressured Scudamore to act immediately on the matter. He pointed out
that 'I believe it will produce much larger effects than you even or most
persons who have not considered it specifically can be made aware. A
policy would be to do it at once before . . . opposition can be got up.'[45]
Business groups, such as the Manchester Home Trade Association, sent
memorials to the Post Office urging the establishment of a small parcels delivery system.[46] Another advocate of a parcel post was W. S.

---

[43] BPP, 1837, vol. 39, Ninth Report of Commissioners appointed to inquire into
the management of the Post Office, pp. 458–9. See also BPP, 1843, vol. 8, Select
Committee on Postage, p. 34.
[44] Edwin Chadwick, 'On Railway Reform in Connection with a Cheap Telegraphic Post and a Parcel Post Delivery', *Journal of the Society of Arts*, 15 (1867), 726.
[45] Post 30/431, E1551/1883, Chadwick to Scudamore, 14 August 1868.
[46] Post 30/207, E1153/1871, Petition of 21 July 1870.

Jevons, who argued that the Post Office would be successful in managing the system, if it kept capital expenditures at a minimum. The department would contract with the railways, which would supply the equipment. Hence, a repetition of the debacle of the telegraph purchase would be avoided, and the benefits of the Post Office's distribution network would be fully available. To Jevons, 'A universal parcel post would be the harbinger of universal free trade.'[47] As in the case of the Post Office Savings Banks, government expansion was necessary to strengthen private capitalist institutions. Supported by some Post Office administrators, social reformers, and segments of private industry, a state parcel post was clearly an idea around which divergent interest groups coalesced.

Unlike the fairly rapid take-over of the telegraphs, the over forty-year period between Hill's proposition and its final enactment suggests that the theoretical arguments of Chadwick and Jevons and the lobbying of Hill and business groups were not sufficient in themselves to carry the day. Part of the difficulty, obviously, lay with resistance to the programme from the railways. As Bagwell has rightly pointed out, the Railway Clearing House, which coordinated goods traffic for the companies, further served to consolidate and focus the opposition of the industry.[48] Indeed, the fear of negative railway reaction inhibited even usually bold men like Hill from pushing the establishment of a parcel post, although he was convinced of the country's need for it.[49] At times the railway interest was so formidable as to lead the Post Office to withdraw from previously established enterprises. Such considerations were present in the intradepartmental debate over the Sample Post. Originally designed as a means to mail small samples of goods to customers, the Sample Post had grown from its origins in 1863 into a *de facto* parcel post for all manner of items through the mail. Should the department tolerate or even encourage this trend? The positions of Scudamore and Tilley on the question clearly illustrate the two directions in which the nineteenth-century Post Office was pulled by its administrators. On the one hand Scudamore, with his characteristic concern for social improvement and his equally characteristic disregard for small points of law and bureaucratic procedure, advocated that the Post Office ignore the rule limiting the service to genuine samples. He thought that it 'would be serious misfortune to the Public if the rule could be enforced. . . . [If] you go on with this rule, you will close up the bowels of the Nation and Alderman Nealis's fields will

---

[47] W. S. Jevons, 'A State Parcel Post', *The Contemporary Review*, 34 (1879), 229.
[48] Philip S. Bagwell, *The Railway Clearing House in the British Economy, 1842–1922* (London, 1968), p. 119.
[49] See, for example, the attack on Hill in *The Railway Times*, 7 November 1857.

become barren.'[50] On the other hand, Tilley the pragmatist was worried about both the financial difficulties which the railways might cause if the trend continued and the absence of any statutory authority for a parcel post. Tilley prevailed, and in 1871 the Sample Post was abolished.

Yet the reluctance of administrators to establish a parcel post was shaped by more than fear of railway reaction. There had always been legitimate doubt as to how far government should expand into the economy. In 1853 Hill had predicted that the public at large would view the venture as 'unjustifiable interference with private enterprise'.[51] Tilley was further aware that one effect of such government intrusion was to favour certain firms – in this case large concerns in London or Manchester over 'tradesmen of small towns, who would lose much of their retail business'.[52] Both men, much more than Scudamore, were concerned to maintain as far as possible what might be called the economic neutrality of the department by avoiding the use of its power in supporting one set of competitors against another.[53] The parcel post, then, was not a case of government expansion which came upon bureaucrats unaware of both the theoretical considerations and the long-range implications of the change. Blackwood's 1880 letter to the Treasury, for example, addressed these points:

> The first question which will naturally occur to your Lordships is whether a service of this description should not be left to private enterprise; and if it were practicable for ordinary Carriers to afford the Public the accommodation which is here contemplated you would doubtless object to its being undertaken by any Department of the State.[54]

The emergence of a Parcel Post act in 1882 was, then, less a function of a change in attitude on the part of the railways than a result of a renewed belief on the part of the Post Office that a parcel post was needed and that it could at least break even on expenses. Particularly influential was the 1878 Postal Congress in Paris, where it was announced that a conference of the principal European countries would be convened in 1880 to consider the establishment of an international parcel post. Moreover, lobbying pressure from the Association of

50 Post 30/207, E1153/1871, Scudamore to Tilley, 19 October 1870.
51 Post 30/no number assigned, E683/1853, Hill to Clanricarde, 5 February 1853.
52 Post 30/431, E1151/1883, Tilley to Monsell, 7 March 1871.
53 Of course, Hill was much more dogmatic on this point than Tilley, who on other issues, the overseas mails being the most obvious example, leaned the other way.
54 Post 30/431, E1153/1883, Post Office to Treasury, 11 May 1880.

Chambers of Commerce remained strong, as businessmen naturally envied the services in Germany where parcels as heavy as 140 pounds were delivered by the Post Office and where parcels of under 20 pounds were carried free of charge by the railways. Important also were newspaper reports that twenty-five railway companies contemplated the establishment of their own parcel service, possibly with the help of the Post Office in delivery. Tilley considered such an arrangement unworkable, but it did encourage him to study the matter further. Dropping his earlier reservations, Tilley came to conclude that such a service was needed and that 'no other machinery is available except the Post Office, which . . . penetrates into the remotest parts of the country'.[55] Accordingly, in 1879 the Post Office opened negotiations with the Railway Clearing House on the following terms. There was to be a two-tiered rate structure. Parcels under two pounds would be carried for six pence and parcels two to four pounds for one shilling. Government parcels were to be sent free, and the railways were to receive 50 per cent of the receipts. Most important, the Post Office was to maintain complete control of management.

However, negotiations had barely begun before there was a change of government and Gladstone's second cabinet entered office. As with the formulation of telephone policy, the role of Fawcett the new Postmaster General in this endeavour was crucial. How would he react to this proposed expansion into the economy? Given Fawcett's preference for laissez-faire, one might expect him to oppose the programme. After all, during his tenure at St Martin's le Grand he would campaign against the nationalisation of land and even question the wisdom of state-funded education, as it tended to discourage parental responsibility.[56] Such beliefs were part of a larger ideological vision, in which Fawcett exalted individual autonomy and denigrated socialism:

> Unlike the Socialists of former days, those who are at the present time under the influence of socialistic sentiment are beginning to place their chief reliance upon State intervention. They seem to think that if individual efforts have been unable to achieve success, this provides the most cogent argument in favour of an appeal to the State. This is the reason which induces me to ascribe such grave importance to Modern Socialism.[57]

Yet, Fawcett, who liked to cite Bentham on the utility of efficient communications, regarded his department as a necessary component of

[55] Ibid., Tilley to Manners, 30 November 1878.
[56] Henry Fawcett, *State Socialism and the Nationalisation of Land* (London, 1883), p. 24.
[57] Henry Fawcett, *Essays and Lectures* (London, 1872), p. 12.

free trade, not as an example of the socialism he deplored.[58] He further had maintained that 'Error and confusion are sure to result if we seek to lay down some rule as applicable to every proposed case of Governmental intervention.'[59] Hence, as was seen in chapter six, Fawcett's belief in the efficiency of competition ultimately led him to favour private development of the telephone. In this instance, the same faith encouraged him to support Post Office competition with the railways for the parcels trade. After a departmental study of the operation of foreign parcel post systems was made, Fawcett became even more convinced that the Post Office, as he later put it, 'has nothing to fear'.[60] The fact that the parcel post promised to be a revenue-earning enterprise as opposed to a revenue-spending one was the crowning feature of the arrangement. Fawcett perceived an insidious and dangerous aspect of state intervention to be the demands 'for the aid of a central authority to enable one section of the community to levy contributions for its own advantage from the rest of the nation'.[61]

Fawcett's position as an academic economist urging an expansion of government services is an interesting point for consideration. More germane for Post Office administrators was the paradox that, in seeking to establish a parcel post, the government was forced to negotiate with its chief competitor, the railways, in order to perform an essential part of the service. Moreover, the situation was further complicated by the Post Office's decision not to seek any monopoly on the conveyance of parcels. This move supposedly eliminated any claims to compensation on the part of private firms which might lose business.[62] It also assuaged Fawcett's dislike of the principle of monopoly. Nevertheless, the decision raised a whole range of questions as to how the parcel post should be established. What were the rights of the Postmaster General? How far could he coerce the railways? What was the proper time period for an agreement between the Post Office and the railways? Most crucially, what role would the railways themselves play in the administration of the service and the establishment of rate schedules?

Not only were these questions matters of central importance to the Post Office and the railways, but the Treasury was very much involved in the bargaining process. Whitehall's interest may in part be attributed to the fact that the parcel post represented the first major expansion of St Martin's le Grand since the nationalisation of the telegraphs. The Treasury simply did not wish to be burned again. In December 1878 Sir Stafford Northcote the Chancellor of the Ex-

---

58 Henry Fawcett, 'Postal Telegrams', *Journal of the Society of Arts*, 28 (1880), 736.
59 Fawcett, *Essays and Lectures*, p. 33.
60 Post 30/427, E606/1883, Fawcett to L. Courtney, 7 June 1882.
61 Fawcett, *Essays and Lectures*, p. 41.
62 *Hansard's, Third Series*, vol. 267, 465, 9 March 1882.

chequer had approved the concept of the parcel post subject to the stipulation that it would cover costs.[63] However, despite imploring letters from Blackwood in which he stressed the inadequate railway service and the needs of the public, doubts lingered as to the wisdom of government intervention in an area already served by private industry. As one Treasury clerk asked, 'If no such demand exists, why not wait until it arises?'[64] On the other front, the situation was no easier for the Post Office. Although the companies represented in the Clearing House had accepted the principle of a state-run parcel post, difficulties arose. The railways demanded 60 per cent of all receipts and a different scale of charges (from four pence for one pound to one shilling for five pounds). Moreover, in exchange for their cooperation in allowing the Post Office to invade their trade, they desired a perpetual partnership with the Post Office. In the spring of 1881 the Railway Clearing House, instead of considering a memorandum on a draft bill on the parcel post submitted by the Post Office, seized the initiative and drew up their own bill and returned it to St Martin's le Grand. The reaction to this bill, which would have virtually established a partnership between the Post Office and the railways on a permanent basis, divided St Martin's le Grand into conflicting camps. The assistant Parliamentary counsel insisted that the railways' bill destroyed the existing powers of the Postmaster General in respect to conveyance of the mails. Arguing that it was framed with the interests of the stockholders, not the public, in mind, the departmental solicitor also objected vehemently to the proposal. The railways, according to his view of their draft bill, would acquire a major voice over the administration of the parcel post and still be able to compete against the Post Office.[65] Fawcett disagreed and, in his eagerness to come to a settlement with the Clearing House, pressed ahead on the matter. In essence, he accepted the railways' line of reasoning. Writing to the Treasury, the Postmaster General argued that

> It is true that I have been unable to gain the consent of the Companies to the main principle that the Parcel Post should be established under the statutory powers of the Postmaster General, and that the agreement shall be confined strictly to the mode in which they should be remunerated. They contend that the weight of the parcels which they are to convey and rate of charge to be levied, of which they are to receive half, are matters in which they should

---

63 Gladstone Papers, Add. MS. 44156, fol. 118, A. Bentham's memorandum, no date.
64 T1/7860B/12266, C. J. Barrington's memorandum, 20 May 1880.
65 Ibid., Watson to Blackwood, 30 March 1881.

have a voice, and as it would be impossible for financial reasons at all events to give the Public the advantage of a Parcel Post to which I attach much importance without the concurrence of the Railway Companies . . . it appears to me that the objections which exist to the admission of this principle [of railway involvement almost to the point of partnership] should be waived. Any attempt to obtain an act at variance with the views of the Railway Companies would certainly be resisted by them, and probably with success.[66]

Treasury reaction to this capitulation was swift and negative.[67] In no manner should the traditional rights of the Postmaster General be infringed. Conveyance of parcels had to be conducted on the same constitutional basis as conveyance of letter mails. If the railways insisted on a partnership arrangement, the failure to reach an accord would be their responsibility. The Post Office was, thus, forced unwillingly to argue the Treasury line in ensuing negotiations with the railways. Although the railways protested over the lack of consideration given to their position and rights by the government, an agreement was finally reached through a process of accommodation. The Post Office would not ask the railways to carry official government parcels free in exchange for Clearing House concurrence that the railways would receive payments only for the parcels which they carried and not for any conveyed by road or sea. The rate of payment to the railways was set at 55 per cent of receipts on rail-borne parcels, a compromise advocated by both sides. Although the Treasury preferred that the agreement run only ten years, it sanctioned a twenty-one-year period on the recommendation of the Post Office.[68] Despite some opposition from MPs who objected to 'the general principle of allowing Governments to undertake business for the sake of profit', the bill had an easy passage through Parliament and received the Royal Assent in August 1882.[69] The service began one year later.

As with the telegraphs take-over, the settlement reached by the Post Office has received criticism. According to Bagwell, the 55 per cent proportion given to the railways was much too generous in comparison to the 40 per cent share allowed by continental governments.[70] While this assessment is accurate as far as it goes, it does not sufficiently take into account the ambiguities of the Post Office's position on the mat-

---

66 *Ibid.*, Post Office to Treasury, 27 May 1881. By this point the railways had temporarily lowered their demand to one-half of all receipts.

67 T1/7906A/9706, Treasury draft.

68 Post 30/432, E1551/1883, Treasury to Post Office, 24 June 1882. The rate scale was up to 1 lb. 3d; up to 2 lbs. 6d; up to 5 lbs. 9d; up to 7 lbs. 1s.

69 *Hansard's, Third Series*, vol. 272, 2116, 27 July 1882.

70 Bagwell, p. 113.

ter. From the beginning the Post Office had not been a free agent in its expansionist course. If the Post Office had tried to force the parcel post upon an unwilling industry, the results might have disrupted other aspects of the Post Office–railway relationship. In June 1881 Fawcett had outlined his fears on this possibility in a letter to Gladstone.

> The Railway Companies have the power of terminating every existing mail contract by notice, and in the event of the Post Office not being able to agree to terms, these terms have to be submitted to arbitration. Although within the last 13 years I believe it is a moderate estimate to say that the weight of the mails has increased threefold, the amount we pay the Railway Companies has increased by 15 per cent, and . . . if the present negotiations fell through and we attempted to obtain compulsory powers, the Railway Companies would retaliate by giving notice to terminate all their existing contracts – a course which would be sure to result in the Department having to make . . . largely increased payments.[71]

It should further be remembered that, although revenue considerations were not uppermost in the minds of departmental administrators, an estimate made immediately before the agreement was signed still foresaw a profit of £340,277, essentially derived from road-borne parcels.[72] Hence, the prediction that rail-borne parcels might only break even was not considered to be of great consequence. Finally, it was also hoped that the 55 per cent share, later criticised as unnecessarily high, would actually serve as a hedge against future requests to raise payments.

Post Office fear of the railways' influence and power did not end with the successful completion of an agreement in 1882, as it was unclear how the rights of the Postmaster General to administer the parcel service as he saw fit would actually work in practice. To be sure, no absolute partnership was established by the Parcel Post Act. The Postmaster General could alter the weight and rate scale at any time without railway approval. However, if this occurred, the railways were free to reopen the question of their remuneration. Less than three years after the institution of the parcel post, the administrators at St Martin's le Grand found themselves in exactly such a situation. The loss on the

[71] Gladstone Papers, Add. MS. 44156, fols. 106ff., Fawcett to Gladstone, 5 June 1881.
[72] Post 30/427, E606/1883, Baines's memorandum, 6 June 1882. One problem with Baines's estimate was that it was based on the thriving German parcel post and, hence, he overestimated the number of packages to be sent. The department lowered its estimate of the volume of business after the agreement between the government and the railways had been signed.

first year's operation had been over £86,000. The Post Office had originally estimated a volume of 27 million parcels a year at an average charge of 7d per parcel.[73] In the early years of service the actual figures ranged from 20 to 25 million per year at an average fee less than 5.5d per parcel. By January 1884 Gladstone was so discouraged by the situation that he was considering dropping the entire programme.[74] The deficit was attributed to several factors. At the Treasury the argument was made that the losses stemmed partly from the fact that the Post Office paid higher wages to an established staff as opposed to the railways which could more easily reduce expenses by hiring temporary workers.[75] This was especially troubling, given the fact that the parcel post was regarded as a possible precedent for future Post Office trading experiments, such as the telephone. The parcel post's problems also contributed to the deepening conviction at the Treasury that the Post Office should expand only if it acquired a monopoly of the particular service, an outlook which was maintained throughout the late-Victorian and Edwardian periods. Furthermore, Fawcett's original hope for stimulating competition had been realised with the lowering of rates by the railways for their own parcel system, but this also had reduced the departmental system's attractiveness. The Post Office prohibition on packages over seven pounds was cited as another reason for the disappointing financial performance of the service.

It would appear that the Post Office's next move should have been to recoup some of their losses by changing the weight scale. However, there existed real fears concerning the railways' reaction, especially at the Treasury, which delayed action on a Post Office request for a change in its scale. In February 1885 John T. Hibbert of the Treasury wrote that

> Assuming for a moment that the [railway] Companies were to defeat the P.O. and secure a percentage above 55 p.c. as compensation for diminished rates on parcels not exceeding 7 lbs., and for encroachment on their business between 7 and 11 lbs., My Lords would be glad to learn within what limits such a defeat of the P.M.G. would be financially fatal in these proposals.[76]

Once more the Post Office found itself in the middle between the Treasury and the railways. In spite of the statutory right of the Post-

---

[73] Post 25/6, Shaw-Lefevre to Treasury, 9 February 1885.
[74] D. W. R. Bahlman (ed.), *The Diary of Sir Edward Hamilton* (Oxford, 1972), p. 546. Without question the record of the parcel post damaged the already difficult Fawcett–Gladstone relationship.
[75] T1/8183B/8465, Lingen's memorandum, 19 December 1884.
[76] Post 30/490, E7087/1886, Treasury to Post Office, 19 February 1885.

master General to change the scale without the industry's approval, the railways were consulted on the proposed alterations. The companies demanded 65 per cent of receipts on parcels above seven pounds as compensation for the new rate schedule. There was no obvious detour around this obstacle. Blackwood favoured independent action through the issuance of a Treasury warrant changing the rate structure, but he also feared the end of 'cordial relations' with the railways if the Post Office could not somehow win their approval.[77] A compromise was again reached, as both the Post Office and the Treasury gave way before railway opposition. The government agreed to give the industry 60 per cent of receipts on parcels above seven pounds. In the end, only a technicality prevented this alteration from being enacted. The original Parcel Post Act had stipulated that only the railways had the right to claim the first revision of the percentages, but either the Post Office or the railways had the power to ask for subsequent changes. The managers at the Clearing House decided to let the percentage remain at 55 in order to retain the trump card of the right to call for the first revision in their position.[78] Unfortunately, this small victory for St Martin's le Grand and the subsequent revision of rates in 1886 did not lead to any significant improvement in the financial results of the parcel post. The service continued to run at a deficit. It was difficult to ascertain exactly how great the deficits were, as mail and parcels expenses tended to become intermixed. Nonetheless, estimates made in 1913 placed the parcel loss at somewhere between £0.9 and £1.5 million. Such results occurred despite efforts to reduce expenses by shifting part of the service to road contractors, using lighter bags instead of heavy wicker baskets to pack the parcels and thus reduce the payments made to the railways, and two further revisions of the parcel post rates in 1897 and 1906.

In 1910 Matthew Nathan described the relationship between the Post Office and the railways as of 'a somewhat intimate character'.[79] Yet it is instructive to note how radically different the mail and parcel contracts as aspects of government growth were. After the initial failure to establish a set of tariffs by Parliamentary means, the department was able slowly to establish an equitable basis for remuneration for the conveyance of mails. There was, to be sure, close cooperation between the Post Office and the railways, but the threat of a virtual partnership with any one railway never materialised. With the parcel post, however, the government faced not merely individual companies, but the combined bargaining strength of an entire industry already in

---

[77] *Ibid.*, Blackwood to Manners, 3 July 1885.
[78] Post 30/2384, E26265, undated, unsigned memorandum.
[79] Post 30/227, E7855/1872, Nathan to Board of Trade, 22 March 1910.

the business of conveying parcels. The high payments to the companies and their very real voice in the subsequent revision of the scale should be viewed as rather predictable and necessary compensations for the industry's collaboration. Rather more notable were the willingness of the Post Office and the compliance of the Treasury in sacrificing revenue to permit the continuation of the parcel post. Partly this was a function of the overall fiscal health of the department, which led many to overlook losses in one area if they were covered by profits in another. Partly this stemmed from the difficulty of eliminating a service which *The Times* ten years after service began termed 'an adjunct of daily life'.[80] Unlike the Post Office life insurance programme – a case of departmental competition with private industry which elicited a small response and which could be easily dropped – the public's reliance on the parcel post was measured in the tens of millions of packages sent. (See appendix, table ten.) As Blackwood had correctly pointed out, once such a programme established momentum, there was no turning back.

[80] Post 16/31, *The Times*, 19 August 1893.

9

Shipping Contracts

The fleets over which the Postmaster General exercises control are faster, better found than any which obey the bidding of the First Lord of the Admiralty. – Henry Cecil Raikes quoted in Henry St John Raikes, *The Life and Letters of Henry Cecil Raikes* (London, 1913), p. 358.

Throughout the nineteenth century the Post Office increasingly relied upon a second private industry, the merchant shipping companies. Such a result was the necessary consequence of the expansion of British trade around the world and the enlargement of the Empire. It was the task of St Martin's le Grand to bind the outposts of British interests together through an efficient communications network. Of course, when Raikes stated that a Postmaster General 'controlled' fleets, he was engaging in misleading, if forgivable, boosterism. The Post Office was never securely in charge of the management of overseas mails, as a much more difficult set of circumstances and problems was encountered here than in the case of the railways. The British shipping industry had traditionally enjoyed a privileged position among private industries. Moreover, the blossoming of the free trade movement symbolised by the repeal of the Navigation Acts in 1849 never seriously threatened the special status of the shipping industry. Indeed, the growth of commerce along with the demands of Imperial defence and foreign policy only served to confirm Victorians, even those who usually preached the virtues of free trade and laissez-faire, in their belief in the necessity of a robust merchant fleet. Some idea of the magnitude of this belief may be gained by placing the British record in an international context. Pollard has estimated that in 1901 British and colonial subsidies to shipping lines totalled almost £1.2 million as opposed to £1.8 million in France, £0.44 million in Germany and £0.35 million in the United States.[1]

This situation caused grave concern at the Post Office, which was

---

[1] S. Pollard, 'Laissez-Faire and Shipbuilding', *The Economic History Review*, second series 5 (1952–3), 114.

the main channel for such support. Large sums were expended, and large losses incurred on the international mail network, as table one demonstrates.

Table 1
The financial record of the overseas mails

	Cost of packet services	Cost as percentage of postal expenditure	Estimated deficit on sea postage
1860–1	£1,041,743	34%	£466,200
1880–1	724,621	16%	341,009
1900–1	771,293	8%	505,604
1910–11	722,249	5%	362,833

Source: Annual reports of the Postmaster General.

These figures must be assessed on several levels. It is true that packet expenses, like payments to railways, accounted for a decreasing percentage of department budgets. However, they should be understood in a rather different light. After all the overseas mails accounted for a disproportionate share of departmental costs far beyond their place in the overall volume of correspondence. For example, in 1896 over 2 billion letters and post cards flowed through the inland mail system in comparison to 52 million dispatched abroad. Thus, railways carried almost forty times as much mail as did the shipping lines. Yet, the amount expended for conveyance of mail by railways, £1,009,386, was less than twice as much as that spent on packet services, £717,641. The situation was, of course, made even more difficult by the fact that the department faced and at times succumbed to pressure to lower overseas postage rates, as in the 1898 establishment of an unremunerative Imperial penny rate.[2] Hence, in 1905 the cost of conveying a colonial letter was estimated to be 1.3d, which entailed a loss of 0.3d on each letter handled. For many Post Office administrators such revenue complications merely served to compound concern over the magnitude of shipping contracts in overall departmental expenditure.

The comparatively large costs of the overseas mails partly stemmed from the government's inability to alter the oligopolistic nature of the shipping industry. Approximately three-fourths of the annual subsidies went to three companies, the Peninsular and Oriental, the Royal Mail, and Cunard.[3] Earlier writers, moralising over the evils of this arrangement, have echoed the views of Lyon Playfair, who after a brief tour as

2 See Daunton, *Royal Mail*, pp. 147–54.
3 For an overview of the situation, see Freda Harcourt, 'British Oceanic Mail

Postmaster General 1873–4 found two great drawbacks in the subsidy system. The first was the obvious damage to competition inherent in the situation:

> Now, there is, rightly or wrongly, much apprehension among ship-owners trading to the East. They do not fear a fair and open competition with the Peninsular and Oriental Company, but they ask us not to allow our mail subsidy to be used for an unfair competition in regard to passengers and cargo. Mail steamers have precedence . . . [over] ordinary steamers in the Canal.[4]

Secondly, there was the insistence that subsidies inhibited the techno-logical progress of the industry. The most significant improvements in ship design – the use of iron, screw propellers, and compound engines – had not been developed by subsidized companies. For Playfair an eco-nomic truism was at stake. 'Subsidies promote conservatism in naviga-tion – free competition leads to reforms and improvements.'[5] This somewhat doctrinaire approach, stressing economic theory, did not adequately take into consideration the complications of contract allo-cation and the limitations of the Post Office position. It is in this imperfect world of administration and contracts that the important questions concerning Post Office–shipping industry relations stand out in clearer relief. What were the reasons behind the subsidies? What was the role of lobbying pressure? How did the various government departments involved – the Treasury, the Admiralty, the Foreign Office, and the Post Office – influence the formulation of policy? How much control did Parliament exercise after a tender had been ac-cepted? This chapter seeks to answer these questions through both a general consideration of shipping contracts and a detailed study of one particular case, the establishment of a packet service to Zanzibar.

The management of the overseas mails had traditionally been a problem for postal officials. Inefficiency and outright graft were charac-teristics of the system well into the nineteenth century. In some measure this state of affairs may be attributed to the fact that until the mid-1830s the government relied heavily upon its own packets, not upon private companies, for the conveyance of the mails. The Post Office employed agents at various ports – Liverpool, Dover, Harwich, and Holyhead, among others – to oversee the packet service. These agents were at best loosely supervised by St Martin's le Grand. In 1836

Contracts in the Age of Steam, 1838–1914', *The Journal of Transport History*, 9 (1988), 1–18.
[4] *Hansard's, Third Series*, vol. 221, 1319, 4 August 1874. See, for example, Royal Meeker, *History of Shipping Subsidies* (New York, 1905), p. 20.
[5] *Hansard's, Third Series*, vol. 221, 1323.

the agent at Liverpool was dismissed for fraud, and, when his books were examined, it was found that he had intermixed Post Office accounts with those of his private business. During the same period an agent at Holyhead had permitted ships stores to be sold to private individuals. Under such lax supervision the Post Office operated the packet service at a loss of £150,000 between 1832 and 1836.[6] Given this situation, it is not surprising that the entire packet service was transferred to the Admiralty in 1836. The Post Office continued to play an advisory role in the policy-making process, with the Treasury ostensibly exercising ultimate control over the packets. (Part of the rationale behind the transfer lay in the belief that the overseas mail system offered the means to subsidize a peacetime fleet which would be available in the event of war.) While the Admiralty appears to have been able to eliminate much of the petty graft which marred the service in the 1830s, it was totally unprepared for the great upheaval in the overseas mail services during the nineteenth century which was caused by the rise of privately owned steamship companies.

The potential of the steamship was convincingly demonstrated in 1838 by the north Atlantic crossing of the 'Great Western' in 14½ days. Private companies demanding large subsidies for the costs and risks involved in these operations began to lobby the government for contracts. The most conspicuous of this new breed of shipping entrepreneurs was the Nova Scotian Samuel Cunard, whose career represented a triumph of determination over adversity. In spite of a lack of adequate ships and financial resources, in 1839 Cunard won a contract for a North American mail run.[7] In the following years the government departments, the Treasury, the Admiralty, and the Post Office, which faced the collective efforts of Cunard and other ship owners were slow to develop the necessary procedures to consider the issues inherent in contract allocation. As an 1860 select committee noted,

> in making and modifying such contracts, there has been a want of concert, and an absence of a clear and well-defined responsibility . . .; the respective functions and provinces of the Treasury and the Admiralty have not always been duly adhered to; and . . . the Treasury has been led to endorse very important contracts without having the elements necessary for a right determination.[8]

[6] For the above, see BPP, 1836, vol. 28, Sixth Report of the Commissioners appointed to inquire into the Management of the Post Office Department, pp. 3–17.

[7] For the rise of Cunard, see F. E. Hyde, *Cunard and the North Atlantic 1840–1973* (London, 1975).

[8] BPP, 1860, vol. 14, First Select Committee on Packet and Telegraphic Contracts, p. iii.

Given this chaotic situation, anomalies were bound to occur, and outside pressures took on increased importance in the allocation process.
At one point, for example, the Treasury approved an extension of the
substantial West Indian contract for two years without prior consultation with either the Admiralty or the Post Office.[9] There was also the
case of a contractor for the Dover–Calais service who offered political
influence in the form of fifty-two votes to help elect a Lord of the
Admiralty from Dover, while his bid for an extension of the contract
was under consideration at the Treasury.[10] Such political chicanery was
unusual. But it is less clear whether the involvement of Parliamentary
agents in the lobbying process did not lead to frequent manipulation of
the system. Certainly it is evident that such agents were playing a
significant role in contract negotiations. One interesting case was revealed to the public in a curious manner. J. O. Lever, the head of a
steamship company, engaged G. O. Irwin and T. K. Holmes, Parliamentary agents, to help him procure a subsidy for an American mail
service and a trial run of an 'Indian Empire' packet. The agents busied
themselves with the task at hand. They drafted memorials on the
merits of the proposed services to be signed by prominent individuals.
Irwin visited two friends at St Martin's le Grand and contacted Lord
Clanricarde, a former Postmaster General. Holmes met his intimate
friend Lord Lonsdale, also a former Postmaster General, to discuss the
proposal. G. A. Hamilton the Financial Secretary to the Treasury was
also contacted. After these efforts it is not surprising that the agents
were successful in obtaining a subsidy for Lever.

What was unforeseen was Lever's refusal to honour his earlier agreement with the two agents. Thus, the details of the arrangement were
revealed only as a result of a lawsuit brought by Irwin and Holmes
against Lever. The select committee which reviewed the history of the
case doubted how effective such agents actually were. However, the
magnitude of the fees paid to Parliamentary agents indicated that
others found them to be useful. Lever, after all, had promised to pay
Irwin and Holmes £10,000, if the proposed subsidy of £172,840 were
obtained. Moreover, the committee itself revealed a fear of the influence of such lobbyists in its judgement that 'the agreement is in itself
deserving of the strongest reprobation; and the allowance of such
undertakings would present a temptation to corrupt practices, and
open a door to evils most injurious to the public service'.[11]

9 *Ibid.*, p. iv.
10 BPP, 1859, vol. 6, Select Committee on Mail and Telegraphic Contracts, pp.
ii–iv. See also John W. Cell, *British Colonial Administration in the Mid-Nineteenth
Century* (New Haven, Connecticut, 1970), pp. 243–53.
11 For the above, see BPP, 1860, vol. 14, Second Select Committee on Packet and
Telegraphic Contracts, p. iv.

Such sentiments were by no means new in 1860. For over fifteen years there had existed a growing awareness that the administration of mail subsidies demanded closer supervision. After a controversy arose in 1846 over the fact that contracts for the American mail service were being let to Cunard on a private basis with no public competition, Parliament began to take a more active interest in the question. One of the earliest manifestations of this concern was the committee headed by Viscount Canning in 1852–3, which set down general guidelines for administering shipping contracts: the government should deal only with responsible parties; contracts should be let only at public bidding and be terminable at notice; and companies should be held only to the frequency and speed of the service and be allowed to establish their own horsepower and tonnage figures to carry out the schedule.[12] These principles proved to be of little use, however, to administrators handling the day-to-day problems of the service. While concurring with the general drift of the report, the Treasury strongly held to the position that informed decisions made by the government were superior to any abstract principles. As one Treasury clerk insisted, 'the responsibility must rest mainly with the Executive Government and be decided in each instance upon its own merits with a view of arriving at the best result for the public service under the existing circumstances'.[13] Clearly the struggle for the ultimate control of packet contracts was by no means over. After loud protests and criticism arose in 1858 over a Conservative government's decision to approve an early extension of the Cunard contract, further attempts were made to bring the system under Parliamentary control. A resolution was passed making any contract invalid until it lay on the table of the House of Commons for thirty days.[14] The Treasury appeared to accept this change. In a minute of 16 April 1860 it further promulgated general guidelines that postal contracts should be self-supporting and long contracts should be avoided.[15] In point of fact, these principles were never closely followed, partly because the Treasury continued to resent any attempts by Parliament to influence its decisions. As Robert Lowe the Chancellor of the Exchequer was to argue in 1873,

it is extremely undesirable . . . that the House should take upon itself the dealing with these [contract] questions. The House is not a responsible body; the Executive Government is; and the consequence is, that if you take these things out of the hands of the

---

12 BPP, 1852–3, vol. 95, Committee on Packet Contracts, p. 6.
13 Post 51/92, Treasury to Post Office, 15 March 1860.
14 *Hansard's, Third Series*, vol. 160, 135ff., 15 March 1860.
15 BPP, 1868–9, vol. 6, Select Committee on Mail Contracts, p. 36.

Executive Government, and put them into the hands of the House, you take them away from responsible people and put them in the hands of irresponsible people.[16]

At least one ambiguity was removed in 1860. It had become abundantly clear that the original justification for Admiralty involvement in the packet service – the premise that such operations might be performed by government vessels or vessels adaptable for naval use – had been superseded by the use of private steamships. There was, thus, a sense of relief at the Admiralty when the administration of mail contracts was transferred to the Post Office in April 1860. Although Lord Elgin the Postmaster General enthusiastically accepted the return of this responsibility, the problems and vexations of packet administration did not vanish as a result of the change. Disagreements over whether Whitehall or Parliament should exercise ultimate control, and whether general principles or the pragmatic demands of the moment should be followed remained a recurring feature of packet administration throughout the nineteenth century.

As one might expect, there was no unanimity within the Post Office as to the proper strategy for mail contracts.[17] The Hill family – Rowland as Secretary before 1864 and meddler in departmental affairs after retirement, his brother Frederic who was in charge of packet contracts after 1860, and Rowland's son Pearson who was Frederic's private secretary – argued that subsidies and long contracts were an avoidable evil and that free trade and open competition would ensure low ocean postage rates and a profit for the Post Office. Such thinking was in line with their insistence that each service undertaken by the department should stand on its own and their equally strong adherence to the corollary that under no circumstances should profits from one branch cover losses in another. The Hills had always believed in a somewhat unreal ideological world in which the line between truth and error was clear and in which human beings and their institutions reacted predictably to inexorable economic laws. Tilley and Scudamore, who represented a different school of thought, saw principles as useful guidelines, but still held that each contract should be judged on its own merits. Tilley's approach emphasised the need to recognise the realities of the shipping industry and to admit the limits of departmental power. As he noted in regard to one such quandary,

[16] BPP, 1873, vol. 9, Select Committee (Cape of Good Hope and Zanzibar Mail Contracts), p. 109.
[17] BPP, 1868–9, vol. 6, Select Committee on Mail Contracts, pp. 14–15, 63.

There is no other line in the South Pacific but the Pacific Navigation Co. Line, and we therefore did not think it advisable to give
notice. Notice can be given now at any time, but there would be no
competition. We did not get much . . . by our new contract with the
P & O and we might not do better with the Pacific.[18]

Although Scudamore arrived at the same conclusion as Tilley, he took
a slightly different route. Of all the leading departmental administrators, Scudamore had always been the one most concerned with serving
the public and least concerned about spending money to do so. Hence,
arguing successfully for a subsidy to the P & O, Scudamore pointed out
'For the sake of keeping up such a communication with the East as the
Nation requires . . . [we] must set commercial principles at defiance and
cost what it may, the Nation must pay what they lose or forego the
communication.'[19] The departmental controversy over contract policy
reached a climax in 1867, when Frederic's responsibility for packet
administration was withdrawn and he was transferred to the Money
Order Office. Furthermore, Pearson was later censured for giving testimony before a select committee in which he exposed errors in Post
Office estimates of revenue on the American packet service. Rowland
Hill expressed his bitterness at these events in his journal:

Scudamore and his tools deliberately . . . [misled] the late Government by erroneous statements as to the earnings of the American
packets, etc., and attempt in like manner to mislead the Packet
Committee of this year; while Pearson in his evidence, exposes the
errors (to use a mild term). For doing so he is punished both by the
P.M.G. and by Tilley, while the misleaders go unscathed.[20]

This bureaucratic squabble was by no means an isolated event. The
important victory over the Hill family was part of a larger pattern in
the history of the nineteenth-century Post Office, in which the 1860s
marked a fundamental break between generations – the decline of the
Hills and the ascendency of Tilley and Scudamore –, the establishment
of a more expansive departmental ethic with less emphasis on revenue
considerations, and a more ready acceptance of new programmes and
responsibilities, including savings banks and the telegraphs.
    Beyond difficulties of personal rivalry and differing outlook, the
overseas mails were also a problem because they involved issues which

18 Post 101, Tilley to C. W. Stronge, 8 April 1870.
19 Post 29/143, Pkt.10T/1868 quoted by Daunton, *Royal Mail*, p. 170. See also
Scudamore's testimony in BPP, 1868–9, vol. 6, Select Committee on Mail Contracts, pp. 63ff.
20 Post, Hill's Journal, 17 August 1869.

were only tangentially related to the conveyance of mail. For example, some MPs regarded the department's contracts as a means of pressuring ship owners into furnishing better passenger accommodations on both mail and non-mail steamers. Adopting a similar strategy, Havelock Wilson, Labour MP for Middlesbrough and Secretary of the Merchant Seamen's League, believed that the Post Office should use its leverage to force lines to provide better working conditions.[21] Pressure came not only from Parliament, but also from the commercial communities of ports desirous of the prestige and prosperity associated with the establishment of a packet line. One such competition was waged between Falmouth and Plymouth in 1874 for designation as a packet port.[22] Of course, the Post Office was frequently the target of attack from allies of shipping companies. Such was the case in 1886 when the Liverpool Chamber of Commerce came to the aid of Cunard in a dispute with the department.[23] More important, and more difficult, were the questions of foreign policy, trade, and nationalism which were inherent in postal subsidies. Here St Martin's le Grand was drawn into problems and functions well beyond its competence. The inevitable question arose as to how far postal contracts should be used to encourage commerce. Clearly there was no consensus. But the large annual losses on the mails to areas outside the formal Empire, such as the United States and South America, indicated an inclination on the part of the government to use the contracts to stimulate trade. Accordingly, as early as 1840 the Pacific Steam Navigation Company received a subsidy for carrying mails between Central and South American ports. In these circumstances a related question arose as to whether contracts should be signed with foreign shipping companies. The answer of Victorian governments was often negative. Foreign companies rightly accused the Post Office of applying a double standard. As Thomas Wallis, agent for North German Lloyds, testified before a select committee,

Last year, in 1868 . . . it was distinctly stated that tenders sent in precisely in the form issued by the Post Office would secure more attention than those with any alteration; upon that our directors sent the tender in expressly as it was printed, without making any alteration whatever; and they were somewhat surprised to find afterwards that large subsidies had been given to Messrs. Cunard, and

21 *Hansard's, Fourth Series*, vol. 82, 845, 4 May 1900.
22 *Hansard's, Third Series*, vol. 221, 1303–6, 4 August 1874.
23 T1/8264A/18490, memorial from the Liverpool Chamber of Commerce, 26 November 1886.

different times and length of voyage given Mr Inman; those parties who tendered upon different terms had therefore better terms than those who did not alter the form.[24]

Such double standards did not offend some in the press. Reviewing an 1879 debate over a West Indian contract, *The Times* insisted 'The question involved was whether in years to come our colonies were to remain part of the British Empire or to be handed over to their neighbours across the Atlantic.'[25] On top of these outside complications the simple mechanics of establishing a mail service and later overseeing the operation presented problems to postal officials. Deciding how to advertise for bids, negotiating the phrasing of contracts, and winning both Treasury and Parliamentary approval could take a number of months. Shipping companies frequently complained that the time required to negotiate contracts made the financing of their operations very difficult. It could also lead to awkward situations such as the one in which the Royal Atlantic Navigation Company began a service two months before Parliamentary approval.[26] After a service was underway, the two most frequent problems for the Post Office were the enforcement of penalties for late arrival and the companies' substitution of ships that did not meet government specifications.

However bothersome the process was to postal administrators, the end product was the same. The growth of trade and Empire demanded more and more mail routes and, therefore, more packet subsidies. The Post Office and the private shipping companies became increasingly intertwined. Especially for lines to South America and the Orient, postal contracts 'were of profound consequence in bridging the gap between the known high cost of steamship operation and the commercial revenue obtainable'.[27] Thus, it was essential that the government be informed concerning companies' financial condition. In 1867 the Royal Mail Company suffered 'unparalleled losses' in a hurricane.[28] The Post Office refused to call for new tenders for the West Indian service out of fear that this move would destroy the company. The Post Office continued to watch the situation closely, and confidential reports on the company's financial health were submitted to the Treasury. Even established firms, such as the P & O, would not have been able to establish fast, regular passenger services without government contracts, which at times amounted to quasi-partnerships. In 1867,

24 BPP, 1868–9, vol. 6, Select Committee on Mail Contracts, pp. 24–5.
25 Post 16/16, *The Times*, 19 March 1879.
26 BPP, 1861, vol. 12, Select Committee on Royal Atlantic Steam Navigation Company, p. iv.
27 R. H. Thornton, *British Shipping* (Cambridge, 1959), p. 26.
28 *Fifteenth Report of the Postmaster General on the Post Office* (London, 1869), p. 9.

reacting to the recommendation of a select committee, the Post Office terminated the P & O contract for the East Indian and China mails and called for new tenders.[29] However, as was frequently the case, only one tender was submitted and that by the P & O. Departmental administrators, handicapped by the lack of competition, opened the usual bargaining process with the company. They were successful in forcing the P & O to lower its bid from £500,000 per year to £400,000. Still this reduction was not the most significant aspect of the contract. The Post Office further agreed that, if the P & O dividend fell below 6 per cent, the government would increase its payment to the company up to £500,000. Conversely, if the dividend rose above 8 per cent, the government would reap one-quarter of the excess in the dividend fund. Although this contract increased packet expenses, Montrose the Postmaster General felt it to be the best one possible given the prospect of competition from French ships and the fact that many military and government passengers were now travelling on Admiralty vessels. Certain MPs were less pleased over the prospect of the government entering into a partnership with a private shipping firm. In the debate over the contract A. S. Ayrton, the outspoken defender of laissez-faire, charged that the arrangement practically amounted to the nationalisation of the company by St Martin's le Grand.[30] Even though the contract was approved, the suspicion lingered that the Post Office had not negotiated an appropriate agreement. For one thing, the terms were proving advantageous to the P & O, as the maximum amount of £500,000 was paid for fourteen months. The sliding scale of payments with its concomitant connotation of partnership also proved to be a source of embarrassment. A new round of bargaining was begun, and the P & O agreed to drop the fluctuating clause in return for an additional £50,000 subsidy each year.[31] All in all, this contract demonstrates how complicated relations between state and private industry could become in conveying mails overseas.

As a means of better illustrating the problem of packet administration, a detailed examination of a longer-lived subsidy may be helpful. The establishment of a mail service to Zanzibar in 1872 and the subsequent contract permutations offer the opportunity to explore the dynamics of the process over five decades. The monetary amounts involved, to be sure, were never as large as the Cunard or P & O subsidies. But as will be argued at the conclusion of this chapter, the issues and problems encountered in the Zanzibar case were by no

---

[29] *Fourteenth Report of the Postmaster General on the Post Office* (London, 1868), pp. 14–15.
[30] *Hansard's, Third Series*, vol. 190, 455ff., 29 November 1867.
[31] *Report of the Postmaster General* (London, 1871), p. 9.

means atypical. This is clearly evident in the essentially defensive posture which the Post Office was forced to adopt at the beginning, since the earliest pressure for such a service came not from the Post Office, but from the Foreign Office. In 1860 Colonel C. P. Rigby the Consul at Zanzibar requested a regular English steamship service to the port. Rigby based his argument on commercial grounds. A consul had resided for almost twenty years in Zanzibar, and almost the entire trade passed through the hands of British Indian subjects. Nevertheless, not a single British merchant shared in this trade, which was dominated by Germans and Americans. No British merchant could compete with this opposition, Rigby maintained, unless the postal service were improved. The Treasury found the argument less than compelling, and the request was rejected.[32] Four years later the subject was again brought forward, but for different reasons. The Senior Officer in command of the ships on the Cape station suggested that a regular steamship service would be helpful in eradicating the slave trade which continued to exist in east Africa. The Post Office rejected this proposal on the grounds that the present monthly service from Mahe was more than adequate to handle the limited volume of correspondence.[33] Indeed, this position was resolutely maintained at St Martin's le Grand for forty years. The fact that a subsidy for the Zanzibar mails was also maintained until the eve of the First World War provides a hint of the next twist in the story.

In the spring of 1870 the Post Office received an extract from a report of a committee on the slave trade. The committee contended that postal communications with Zanzibar were unsatisfactory and suggested a regular service between Mahe and Zanzibar be established to connect with the regular French service to and from Aden. Tilley opposed the proposal on the grounds that the port produced only £50 postage each year.[34] The Foreign Office countered that it intended to make Zanzibar the centre of its anti-slave trade operations and, therefore, a regular mail service was justified. More importantly, the Foreign Office also forwarded a copy of an offer from William Mackinnon's British India Steam Navigation Company to provide a direct steam service between Aden and Zanzibar.[35] Having bypassed the established

---

32 T1/6305/9563, E. Buckland's memorandum, 17 October 1861.
33 Post 51/96, E. Francis's memorandum, 1 October 1898. See R. Coupland, *The Exploitation of East Africa* (London, 1939); Suzanne Miers, *Britain and the Ending of the Slave Trade* (New York, 1975); and Raymond Howell, *The Royal Navy and the Slave Trade* (New York, 1987).
34 Post 29/167, Pkt.534W/1871, Tilley to Hartington, 26 March 1870.
35 See the following: John S. Galbraith, *Mackinnon and East Africa 1878–1895* (Cambridge, 1973); J. Forbes Munro, 'Shipping Subsidies and Railway Guarantees: William Mackinnon, East Africa and the Indian Ocean, 1860–93', *Journal of*

Treasury and Post Office channels, the Foreign Office had taken charge of the negotiations and never lost the initiative. As befitted its lowly status, the Post Office yielded to this pressure. Tilley, attempting a holding tactic, suggested that the matter should be submitted to the Treasury. He also noted that an Imperial contribution to the scheme would be justified if the Indian government, not the British Post Office, agreed to accept Mackinnon's offer. Lowe the Chancellor of the Exchequer pushed ahead and instructed the Post Office to make guarded inquiries as to the probable cost of the enterprise. Two offers were received. The Union Steamship Company proposed a monthly Cape of Good Hope–Zanzibar service for £29,000 per year on a seven-year contract. The BISN Company tendered a plan for a four-weekly service between Aden and Zanzibar for £11,050 and between Zanzibar and the Cape for £16,315 on a ten-year contract. The Post Office forwarded these tenders to Lowe's private secretary on 19 December 1871. It is indicative of the state of administrative channels in this case that no acknowledgement of their receipt was ever received by the Post Office.

Throughout the fall of 1871 the Foreign Office had continued its lobbying campaign for the steamer service. Its view of the situation was well expressed in a confidential memorandum:

> The opening of the Suez Canal, and the discovery of the diamond fields in South Africa, seem to offer an opportunity for Steamers from Aden or the Cape of Good Hope along the East Coast of Africa. It is stated that the Sultan of Zanzibar would lose a large amount by the entire abolition of the transport Slave trade; but that it would be derogatory on his part were he to accept a money payment in consideration of this loss. This establishment of a mail service . . . might be considered as a recompense – if we admit that he deserves any – for the loss which the Sultan would sustain. We should enter into negotiations for the abolition of slavery with more influence if we had something of this sort to offer in return for compliance with our wishes.[36]

Reacting to such Foreign Office pressure and reports of the horrors of the slave trade by Livingstone, the Reverend Horace Waller, and Sir John Kirk, Gladstone's government came to accept the need for a regular steamship service to Zanzibar. However, it was the Treasury, not the Post Office, which undertook the negotiations. In August 1872 the

African History, 28 (1987), 209–30; and Stephanie Jones, *Two Centuries of Overseas Trading* (London, 1986).

[36] Post 29/167, Pkt.534W/1871, Foreign Office minute, printed 27 November 1871.

Treasury forwarded a joint tender from the Union and BISN Companies for a Cape–Aden service for £25,000 per year on a ten-year basis.[37] (The Union Company would receive £15,000 for a Cape–Zanzibar service, and the BISN Company £10,000 for a Zanzibar–Aden service.) The Post Office was also instructed to consider an extension of the Union Company's England–Cape contract. Although the Treasury paid lip service to the philanthropic and commercial benefits of such a combined service, the real advantage of the arrangement was that it represented the cheapest method to carry out the task at hand. As Lowe wrote to Gladstone,

> I think we had better go on with the Zanzibar Ocean Steam Contract. We shall get money from India and Natal . . . – £6,000 from India, £2,500 from Natal out of £25,000. The extra cost of this [Admiralty] Squadron alone was £50,000. I think the contract must be made with the Post Office and if so the expenditure must be borne on the Post Office estimates. It would never do for the Treasury to make the contract.[38]

It is indicative of Lowe's poor perception of the entire situation that not only did other governments never contribute to the service, but he misunderstood the respective roles of the departments in the granting of the contracts. It was not a Post Office matter. Rather the power of the Foreign Office and the concurrence of the Treasury had presented St Martin's le Grand a *fait accompli*. One result of the incident was a lingering feeling of departmental bitterness toward the Treasury in general and Lowe in particular. As Tilley complained,

> The upshot of the Zanzibar question (which by the way the Treasury sanctioned the instant they got our letter) lead[s] me to doubt the wisdom of going on with the fight. It is clear that in that case Mr Lowe was in no other way influenced by Mr Gladstone's interference than to be made angry. [From] . . . the remarks which were made the other day at the Treasury when Mr Page . . . [saw] the Chancellor of the Exchequer about the West African Contract there was evidently a good deal of irritation. The source of the evil is that Mr Lowe will do everything himself instead of trusting small matters to the Secretary to the Treasury who must always be more accessible than the Chancellor of the Exchequer and that his Lieutenant, the permanent Secretary [Lingen] is a Pedant who can only look at matters and write upon them in a pedantic fashion.[39]

37 Post 29/176, Pkt.99Y/1873, Treasury to Post Office, 13 August 1872.
38 Gladstone Papers, Add. MS. 44403, Lowe to Gladstone, 28 October 1872.
39 Post 101, Tilley to Monsell, 1 November 1872.

From the beginning the contracts had been shaped by outside lobbying pressures. At this point public opinion intervened again to alter the course of the negotiations. Administrators at the Treasury early on had recognised that the Union Company's primary interest in the entire arrangement was the profitable western route from England to the Cape. In bidding for the eastern contract the company, which had won a contract to carry mail to the Cape in 1857, hoped to be able to extend the existing western contract without submitting a new tender and facing possible competition. However, colonists at the Cape offered strong objections to the extension, as it ensured the continuation of the existing heavy postage charge of one shilling per half ounce.[40] The Chambers of Commerce in Cape Town and Port Elizabeth as well as several London merchants protested the fact that neither the Treasury nor the Post Office had consulted the Secretary of State for the Colonies concerning the renewal. They further argued that open competition would have reduced the amount of postage by half, especially if the shipping line headed by Donald Currie won the contract.[41] Although Lingen rejected this line of argument, the Treasury was hesitant to face a fight in the House of Commons over approval of the contract. Hence, the agreement extending the Union Company's western service was dropped, but the government was not yet out of the mire of the affair. The Union Company protested that its offer of £15,000 for the Cape to Zanzibar service was inseparably connected with the abandoned contract. The Treasury had yielded to public opinion, and now it was to demonstrate the same acquiescence toward the Union Company management. Tilley summarised the situation in a semi-official note to Lowe:

Sir B. Phillips [Chairman of the Union Company] came to see me this morning – I think they will consent to be quiet if you will give the terms originally asked for the Zanzibar service . . . and let them take a third mail a month to the Cape under the terms of the old Contract. They will thus get in the shape of compensation £120,000 during the continuance of the two contracts.[42]

On 8 May 1873 the Post Office signed a new contract with the Union Company for a service between the Cape and Zanzibar for £26,000. Lowe as before took charge of the arrangements. As this contract ran for eight years instead of the seven in the earlier bid, it represented an additional expense for the Post Office and Gladstone's government.

[40] Howard Robinson, *Carrying British Mail Overseas* (New York, 1964), p. 181.
[41] For Currie's role, see Andrew Porter, *Victorian Shipping, Business, and Imperial Policy* (New York, 1986), pp. 61ff.
[42] Post 101, Tilley to Lowe, 2 May 1873.

Notorious for his eagerness to pick fights, Lowe had approved a more expensive contract partly out of a desire to avoid a confrontation.[43] Unfortunately the House of Commons did not share the same attitude, and six weeks later a select committee was appointed to inquire into the circumstances under which the 8 May contract had been made. The evidence revealed problems concerning general contract procedures as well as specific matters of Treasury–Post Office relations. On the former difficulty, Tilley reported that 'there is no fixed rule; sometimes the companies come to us and ask for a contract; sometimes we ask for public tenders; and sometimes we negotiate with certain companies; but we always submit all the facts to the Treasury, and ask for their instructions'.[44] As for the latter, it quickly became clear that there still existed no set of instructions or memoranda outlining the two departments' areas of responsibility. Rather a vague 'understanding' was the only basis for handling contracts. One ramification of this situation was the fact that the Post Office was not aware that the Union Company's low bid on the Zanzibar route was contingent on winning an extension of the western contract. Moreover, as has been shown above, in this case even this loose procedure was not followed. The tenders for the Zanzibar route were received by the Treasury, not the Post Office. Monsell, the Postmaster General, was not consulted on the £26,000 version of the contract, and he remarked that Tilley had acted more like a Treasury official than a Secretary of the Post Office in his negotiations on Lowe's behalf.[45] Lowe, of course, was the focus of the committee's attention, and he attempted to brush aside criticism by placing the blame elsewhere. According to Lowe, the consolidated tender of the two companies

> ought not to have been sent to us; it ought to have been sent to the Post Office. It is no part of the duty of the Treasury to receive tenders or to make contracts; for this reason, if other departments make contracts the Treasury can look after them; but if the Treasury makes contracts, who is to look after the Treasury? Therefore it was perfectly irregular that it [the consolidated tender] should be sent to us.[46]

Who, then, was responsible for the contract and the ensuing debacle? It should be remembered that the Zanzibar mails crisis peaked during the same period the Scudamore telegraph scandal broke. As was

43 See Winter, pp. 290–1.
44 BPP, 1873, vol. 9, Select Committee (Cape of Good Hope and Zanzibar Mail Contracts), p. 5.
45 *Ibid.*, p. 86.
46 *Ibid.*, p. 104.

noted in chapter five, Parris has correctly singled out the Scudamore case as marking the beginning of the implementation of the concept of ministerial responsibility. However, in the actions of politicians and administrators in the Zanzibar entanglement, one can see how vague and indefinite this concept remained. Tilley had essentially forsaken his responsibility to the Postmaster General in his service to Lowe. At the Treasury the situation was equally complex. W. E. Baxter, the Financial Secretary, and, thus, next to Lowe the most important politician in that department was an outspoken champion of free trade in contract allocation wherever possible. He, therefore, had opposed the extension of the Union Company's western contract on the grounds that competition might offer the government better terms. He, nevertheless, had signed minutes drawn up under Lowe's direction with which he disagreed. Baxter's excuse was that these minutes were 'merely ministerial'. Lowe correctly attacked this line of reasoning, arguing there

> is no such thing as signing such papers ministerially; when you see a letter signed by Mr Law, the assistant Secretary, for instance, it only authenticates that letter; but I am not aware of any practice of initialing such a thing as this ministerially. Your initials convey that it is the proper thing to go forward. If the Secretary of the Treasury can really sign things without being responsible for them, then there is no check at all, because a vast quantity of business must be signed either by the Permanent Secretary or by the Financial Secretary, and never reaches the Chancellor at all. . . . [Baxter] has exactly inverted the case. He says that he is not responsible, and I am. The truth is, that he is and I am not.[47]

However, as the report of the select committee confirmed, Lowe was ultimately responsible for the contracts both ministerially and in point of fact. He had sanctioned the linkage of the two dissimilar contracts – the western for postal purposes and the eastern one for philanthropic and political purposes – in order to lower the cost. It was this linkage which first aroused opposition at the Cape. It was this linkage which forced the Treasury to accept a £26,000 subsidy instead of one of £15,000. Thus, the Chancellor of the Exchequer was also responsible for the committee's recommendation that the contract should not be confirmed. In his haste to complete the arrangement, Lowe had forgotten the fact that the BISN Company had previously offered to perform a similar Cape–Zanzibar service for £16,315 per year. Lowe's mishandling of the negotiations had now led to a third contract. The select

47 *Ibid.*, p. 113.

committee advised, that given the erratic course of the bargaining, the Union Company should be allowed to submit a lower bid before throwing the competition open to all comers. The company did so, and on 1 August 1873 a contract for a Cape–Zanzibar service for £20,000 per year was successfully concluded. Reviewing the course of these negotiations, one sees little evidence of the overriding demand for economy which is said to characterise Robert Lowe's administrative philosophy. To be sure the method of employing a postal subsidy was cheaper than the maintenance of an Admiralty squadron. Still the final settlement was by no means the cheapest possible. Lowe admitted as much, but he claimed that the government had an obligation to the Union Company to complete the contract as the firm had already invested £350,000 in new ships for the Zanzibar service.[48] In a wider context, this episode along with the Scudamore scandal should be understood as contributing to the general unravelling of Gladstone's first government and the specific events of August 1873 when W. E. Baxter resigned as Financial Secretary to the Treasury and Lowe went to the Home Office and was replaced as Chancellor of the Exchequer by Gladstone. Given the earlier troubles, the Treasury's unsuccessful efforts to pressure other governments to contribute to the cost of the anti-slave trade subsidy marked a fitting conclusion to this stage of the story.

Thus, by August 1873 there existed two services to Zanzibar – the Union Company's southern route from Table Bay at £20,000 per year and the BISN Company's northern route from Aden at £10,000 per year. (The latter had encountered no substantial Parliamentary opposition and won approval easily.) The Union Company's contract was the first to come under consideration for renewal. Between 1873 and 1880 the Post Office had collected about £100 per year on sea postage on the southern route, and, therefore, St Martin's le Grand was eager to terminate the contract. The Treasury adopted a similar attitude, but it was still more concerned with the opinion of the Foreign Office than with that of the Post Office. The Treasury did argue that, since the telegraphs had practically superseded mail service as a means for suppressing the slave trade, the contract should not be renewed.[49] The Foreign Office accepted this suggestion, as there still existed the BISN Company to provide communication between Zanzibar and other ports. The Union Company's contract, therefore, was allowed to lapse on 9 February 1881.

The efforts of both the Treasury and the Post Office to eliminate the northern service were less successful. This route earned only £250 per year in sea postage against a £10,000 subsidy, and in December 1881

---

48 *Hansard's, Third Series*, vol. 261, 1198, 19 June 1873.
49 Post 51/96, Francis's memorandum, 1 October 1898.

the Post Office advised its discontinuance. However, a major shift of emphasis occurred at this point. The original justification for the mail subsidy had been the philanthropic motive of destroying the slave trade. It was this idea that had first convinced Gladstone's cabinet of the wisdom of the scheme. Mackinnon, the Chairman of the BISN Company, had earlier professed to be interested in the plan for motives which were not primarily pecuniary.[50] By 1882, however, the subsidy had come to be valued more for economic and political reasons. As concern about the slave trade diminished, lobbyists for the BISN Company and Foreign Office officials began to emphasise the importance of the subsidy for British trade and strategic purposes. Initially the Treasury supported the Post Office's view that the contract should be allowed to lapse, as Lingen insisted that it was 'retrograde policy' to subsidize a service which should be provided by private initiative, if provided at all.[51] Nonetheless, the losses on the mail service and the fact that a French steamship service would help to cripple the slave trade as well as a British one would were not sufficient arguments in face of the widespread opinion that the subsidy was essential for political and commercial dominance in Zanzibar. S. B. Miles, Acting Consul and Political Agent at Zanzibar, effectively summarised this point of view:

> There can be little doubt that the French would be eager to seize a fair opportunity to take up and subsidize a mail line from Zanzibar in the event of our relinquishing it. . . . They are not ignorant that the possession of the Post Office is one of the causes that has given us our present commanding position at Zanzibar, and they would not be sorry to deprive us of it.[52]

The lobbying campaign proved effective, and in December 1882 the Treasury sanctioned the extension of the contract for a total of nine months. More importantly, in the following spring the government invited tenders for a five-year service. The Post Office, however, won a small and rare victory when the Treasury agreed not to charge the costs of the subsidy to the Post Office Vote.

The involvement of St Martin's le Grand was by no means over. Again only one company – the BISN Company – responded to the government's call for tenders. The company submitted three different schemes, and the longest and most expensive one – an Aden–Lindi

---

[50] BPP, 1873, vol. 9, Select Committee (Cape of Good Hope and Zanzibar Mail Contracts), pp. 94–5.

[51] T1/8462B/13228, Lingen's memorandum, 25 September 1882.

[52] Post 29/346, Pkt.3231/1883, Miles to Granville, 24 June 1882.

route at £7,950 per year – was accepted.[53] Once more the Treasury negotiated the contract with the Post Office only serving as a channel for the tenders and as the signatory for the government. In June 1888 the Post Office was requested by the Treasury to advertise again for tenders for a Zanzibar service with the extension to Lindi omitted since that port was now in the German zone. Only Mackinnon expressed an interest in the service, and he began to press the Treasury for a longer, more costly London to Zanzibar contract. Mackinnon, seeking the support of the Foreign Office, argued that the old route from Aden to Zanzibar had been made obsolete by a through service from Marseilles recently established by the Messageries Maritimes Company of France. He further predicted that a London connection might strengthen British influence in East Africa.

The Treasury was well aware that a London–Zanzibar service had none of the philanthropic justifications summoned up for the 1883 Aden–Zanzibar contract. As George Gleadowe wrote to Sir Reginald Welby,

> Sir W. Mackinnon assumes that the object of the Aden–Zanzibar subsidy was all along to assist and develop British trade. This may have been its effect but I cannot find that we ever regarded its object as anything but the suppression of the Slave Trade, though no doubt the development of legitimate Trade would . . . [help] to bring this about. The F. O. affected to believe that the subsidy was given on postal grounds.[54]

This line of reasoning was also very clearly expressed to the Foreign Office when the Treasury urged that it was 'unsound commercial policy' to subsidize a particular line in its struggles with foreign rivals.[55] Nevertheless, the Foreign Office and particularly Salisbury supported Mackinnon and his idea of a London–Zanzibar service on political, if not economic, grounds. The end product was the same. Recognising that the case involved what one clerk termed 'considerations of *haute politique*', the Treasury once again yielded.[56] In February 1890 a two-year contract at £16,000 per year was granted. Only two months after the signing of the agreement the entire question of subsidizing merchant shipping for the purpose of suppressing the slave trade was again hotly debated in the House of Commons.[57] The Treasury gave way under criticism of this practice and promised that the £16,000 annual

---

53 *Ibid.*, Treasury to Post Office, 10 July 1883.
54 T1/8462B/13464, Gleadowe to Welby, 16 August 1889.
55 *Ibid.*, Treasury to Foreign Office, 29 August 1889.
56 T1/8462B/20234, the phrase is George Ryder's, 15 January 1889.
57 *Hansard's, Third Series*, vol. 243, 1447ff., 25 April 1890.

cost would be shifted from the Vote for the Suppression of the Slave Trade to the Post Office Estimates. Raikes, the Postmaster General, entered a protest over the inclusion of a service which earned a paltry £300 annually, but to no avail. The expense was transferred to the Post Office. Once again the Zanzibar mails were proving a drain on departmental income.

There remains only one more major alteration in the contract to be discussed. After 1890 it became apparent that the London–Zanzibar service was a financial failure for the BISN Company, while the assumption of protectorate authority over Zanzibar by Britain had removed much of the political justification for the subsidy. Moreover, Salisbury had become interested in the establishment of a regular line of communications with the Mozambique ports and the Zambesi. Such a change was predicated upon the fact that the creation of a British protectorate in Nyasaland and the penetration of the British South African Company into the Upper Zambesi had increased British interest in that area.[58] Hence, the Treasury instructed the Post Office to sound out the BISN Company on this proposal with the view of using funds from the London–Aden route for the new service recommended by the Foreign Office. The company continued to insist that a return to the Aden–Zanzibar branch line would throw nearly the entire trade between Europe and East Africa into foreign-subsidized through-services, for shippers would not risk the transfer of cargo at Aden. Nevertheless, two tenders were submitted – one a £13,000 offer for the Aden–Zanzibar route and another a £19,000 offer for services to Chinde and Delagoa Bay from Zanzibar. Although the latter subsidy was not established, this discussion did divert pressure from the Treasury long enough to allow St Martin's le Grand to cancel the expensive London–Zanzibar service. After consultation with the Post Office, the Treasury did decide to continue the Aden–Zanzibar subsidy in spite of the fact that it earned less than £300 annually.

The tender ultimately accepted by the Treasury was for the slowest, cheapest mail service that the BISN Company offered to conduct – £9,000 subsidy at 7½ knots. The Treasury was aware that service under these terms was 'miserably slow and so uncomfortable that no East African official will travel by it'.[59] However, it had one redeeming characteristic. Its existence served as a bulwark against more expensive and elaborate plans to subsidize other routes. As Wilkins astutely pointed out,

58 Post 51/96, Francis's memorandum, 1 October 1898.
59 T1/10978/16484, Wilkins's memorandum, 1 September 1905.

If once the Colonial Office and Protectorate officials can induce us to terminate this small subsidy – which to be quite frank, is indefensible on the merits – they will have a very fair fighting case for pressing us to give a more ambitious service – something like £50,000 or £60,000 a year if not more. An ideal government might terminate the present subsidy and refuse to give another. But, in practice, – considering the divergent views which have been taken about the All-Red Route – it would perhaps be wiser for ministers not to expose themselves to too great temptation. . . . I think we had better tell the P.O. in the usual way not to give notice to terminate the contract with the British India S. N. Co.[60]

Employing this line of reasoning, the Treasury continued to approve the extension of the contract each year until 1913, when the subsidy was finally replaced by an arrangement which paid the shipping company strictly on the basis of the number of items carried.

In conclusion, some effort should be made to assess the significance of the lengthy history of the Zanzibar mail service. For the purposes of this study its significance rests primarily in its typicality. The issues, pressures, and responses involved here were by no means unique in the administration of packet contracts. Rather the difficulties and obstacles met by the administrators at St Martin's le Grand in the Zanzibar case were encountered time and time again. Take the role of the colonies. Even though the Post Office in London was responsible for Imperial communications, the colonies, not the mother country, could critically influence the decision-making process. In the Zanzibar case, South African business interests objected to the original contract with the Union Company. A similar pattern can be seen in the history of the West Indian mail service. In 1890 two tenders were being considered for this contract. The tender of the Atlas Company was £5,000 lower than that of the Royal Mail. Yet, the Treasury was forced to accept the more expensive bid at the urging of colonists since 'a large preponderance must necessarily be allowed to the [West Indian] opinion whatever direction it might fall'.[61] Moreover, the involvement of Parliament rejecting one contract and forcing another on an unwilling government was not unusual. The large number of select committees and debates over shipping contracts indicates that the great expansion in the overseas mail network was not pushed through a sleeping Parliament by faceless civil servants. MPs were acutely aware of the situ-

---

[60] T1/10978/16347, Wilkins's memorandum, 13 September 1907.
[61] Treasury memorandum quoted by R. G. Greenhill, 'The State Under Pressure: the West Indian Mail Contract 1905', *Business History*, 11 (1969), 125. See also BPP, 1890, vol. 41, Contract for the Conveyance of the West Indian Mails.

ation. The fact that more contracts were not rejected or altered was not due to weakness or negligence on the part of Parliament, but rather to the fact that MPs shared the same ambiguities and differences of opinion toward shipping subsidies as did civil servants at the Post Office and the Treasury. An 1869 debate on the American mail contracts is one example of such division. Outrage on the part of some MPs over the costs of the Cunard contracts was offset by the usual pleas from other MPs that the government was doing as well as possible. Hence, an inconclusive resolution that the government should consider lowering postage rates to America appeased both sides and closed the affair.[62]

The role of the Foreign Office was of fundamental importance in shaping the history of the Zanzibar service. Its early support of the scheme, its agreement that the Union Company's contract should be cancelled in 1881, its continued support of the BISN Company, all of these were crucial. Such interference by other government departments in the Post Office's operations was common. In this regard, there was the 1879 case when St Martin's le Grand recommended Alfred Holt of Liverpool for a packet contract. However, the India and Colonial Offices intervened at the Treasury on behalf of the P & O, and the Post Office was forced to deal with the latter firm.[63] It should also be evident that the Treasury's part in the allocation process was central. The administrators at St Martin's le Grand did not exercise any sort of final authority. Clerks at the Treasury, such as Gleadowe and Wilkins, were more influential than their counterparts at the Post Office, who at times did little more than submit the various tenders for selection by the Treasury. Of course, even the control exercised by Treasury civil servants was by no means supreme in the process of contract allocation. In 1886 one of them complained about the 'side issues' involved in the management of the north Atlantic route including threats by Cunard to lay up some of their fast steamers and to cease calling at Queenstown, which would lead to 'serious representations as to the injury inflicted on the south of Ireland'.[64] One should also not forget that the Treasury, like the Post Office, could fall victim to the force of interdepartmental alliances. When, for example, Murray, the Permanent Secretary at the Treasury, studied a Royal Mail contract in 1907, he concluded that better terms might be reached, if it were not for 'the combination of Col. Office and the Post Office; so I suppose we must acquiesce'.[65] In the final analysis the granting of mail contracts

---

62 *Hansard's, Third Series*, vol. 196, 1128ff., 1 June 1869.
63 *Ibid.*, vol. 249, 507ff., 8 August 1879.
64 T1/8264A/18490, W. L. Jackson's memorandum, 6 November 1886.
65 T1/10733B/21992, Murray's memorandum, 19 April 1907.

was often a political question which involved issues beyond the control of permanent officials either in Whitehall or St Martin's le Grand. It is misleading to argue, as one MP did in 1887, that

> the permanent officials are really the parties who manage all these contracts, and that the heads of Departments are merely tools in the hands of permanent officials. When once a contract has received the sanction of the permanent officials, I do not care who the Chancellor of the Exchequer may be or to what Government he may belong, he will form his views according to the views, facts, and statistics presented to him by the permanent officials.[66]

Lowe's influence over both Treasury and Post Office administrators as well as Salisbury's subsequent role refute this argument.

Ultimately, however, the most telling argument for the typicality of the Zanzibar case is that it illustrates the limited options available to the Post Office in contract allocation. Indeed, a review of the history of the case presents the definite impression that the department tried to stay out of the battle. As perhaps in no other area of its responsibility, St Martin's le Grand simply lacked influence over the course of events. Once it had been decided that a particular mail service was necessary for imperial, commercial, or simply postal reasons, the universe of choices open to the Post Office was a limited one. Sir Spencer Walpole, a former Secretary of the Post Office and a member of the Cobden Club, made this clear when he testified before a select committee that 'the weak point of the Post Office position and the difficulty is, that the great lines of trade are in the hands of such powerful companies that practically there is not the free competition which I confess I would like to see'.[67] Cases demonstrating the validity of Walpole's observation frequently arose. In 1876, for example, the department launched a major campaign to institute a more competitive policy for the North American mails.[68] Subsidies were to be replaced by payments based on the weight of mail carried. As a result of this change, the cost of the service in 1877 fell from £105,000 the previous year to £28,000. However, the Liverpool shipping ring, consisting of the Cunard, White Star, and Inman Companies, soon joined together to demand a monopoly of the service at a rate of 4s 8d per pound for letters. The Post Office was able to reduce the rate to 4s, and expenses rose to £50,000. It is true that St Martin's le Grand had won something

---

[66] *Hansard's, Third Series*, vol. 316, 1719–20, 4 July 1887.
[67] BPP, 1902, vol. 9, Select Committee on Steamship Subsidies, p. 157.
[68] Robinson, *Carrying British Mail Overseas*, pp. 248–51. *Hansard's, Third Series*, vol. 237, 318ff., 22 January 1878.

of a victory as costs were now lower than before. It is equally true, however, that the leading firms were able to consolidate their position over the north Atlantic route. Thus, according to a Treasury assessment, the introduction of pure competition 'having been tried in the most favourable case, that of the North American mail service, must be pronounced a failure'.[69]

Such outcomes were to be seen time and time again. The overseas mail system continued to be characterised by long contracts held by a few large firms and large annual deficits. If one examines the contract situation in 1913 – over seventy years after the rise of the private steamship carriers – one is struck with how little the basic arrangements had changed. (See table two.)

Table 2
Major foreign and colonial packet services, 1913

Service	Commencement	Payment	Cost borne in respect of mails from the United Kingdom
Dover and Calais and Folkestone and Dover	23 October 1908	£40,000	£40,000
America:			
Cunard	7 August 1902	68,000	114,621
White Star	1 August 1902	72,573	
West Indies	18 Jan. 1911	62,900	34,413
Brazil and River Plate	1 Sept. 1876	18,895	13,077
West Coast of Africa	1 Jan. 1899 and 1 Jan. 1888	15,355 7,213	15,521
Brindisi and Bombay Shanghai and Adelaide	1 Feb. 1908	305,000	148,665

Source: *Report of the Postmaster General* (London, 1913), pp. 56–7.

Lengthy contracts, such as the seven-year P & O contract signed in 1908, were still being made. Even the cases in which the Post Office appeared to have been successful in reducing the longevity of contracts are misleading. To be sure, the service for the Brazil and River Plate route was terminable on six-months' notice, but the contract had been

---

[69] T166/62, Treasury memorandum, no date.

in existence since 1876. Other contracts, which are not shown in the table, were equally terminable at short notice, but had been in operation for periods ranging from twelve to twenty years. The costs borne for all these services continued to undercut the department's net revenue and its contributions to the Exchequer.

In the end, these deficits should not necessarily be seen as manifestations of maladministration. Rather they were the outcome of the realistic policies which Tilley and Scudamore had advocated. Such an approach recognised that there were gains as well as losses in any overseas mail contract. For example, long contracts at fixed amounts were easy to condemn, but at times they could also benefit the department. This was the case with the 1903–27 Cunard contract, which paid a set amount of £68,000 to carry mail over the North American route.[70] There the volume of mail increased so rapidly that the department came to regard the contract as something of a bargain.[71] To more perceptive civil servants it was evident that a fiercely economical approach toward the contracts might not achieve other desired ends. Even at the Treasury there could be a pragmatic acceptance of these trade-offs. As John Hibbert admitted in 1884,

> under the present circumstances it would be quite impossible to abolish subsidies on the mail lines to the East and to secure the same speed and regularity as at present. It would doubtless be possible to obtain greater frequency . . . at less cost, but the commercial classes . . . would seriously condemn any change which . . . did not give them equal or better speed and regularity.[72]

What, then, does the history of the overseas mails reveal about the nature of the department's growth? The enterprise developed, and the responsibilities increased, oftentimes despite the wishes of the civil servants at St Martin's le Grand. Without question ideology and ambition helped to shape the policy decisions of the departmental managers, as the defeat of the Hills reminds us. But what must be stressed is that these forces played a more limited role here than in any other area of the Post Office's activities. After all, the administrators handling the overseas mails were usually on the defensive – reacting to outside pressures from Parliament, other government departments, colonies, and shipping companies. They were men forced to choose from among

[70] For background see Vivian Vale, 'The Government and the Cunard Contract of 1903', *The Journal of Transport History*, new series 5 (1979), 36–45.
[71] Post 33/2573, M4002/1929, Mail contracts at fixed amounts in force, 1890–1930.
[72] T1/8141A/19911, Hibbert to Spring Rice, 19 December 1884.

a number of less than perfect options in a place and time that bears little resemblance to what used to be called the Age of Laissez-Faire. The best they could do, as a departmental letter to the Colonial Office accurately observed, was not to be in the forefront of overseas expansion, but simply to keep pace with it.[73]

[73] Post 33/2570, M4002/1929, Post Office to Colonial Office, 21 July 1917.

PART FOUR
EPILOGUE

10

A Pattern of Government Growth?

Ministries come and Ministries go; the Department remains. – W.
S. Jevons, 'Postal Notes, Money Orders, and Bank Cheques', *The
Contemporary Review*, 38 (1880), 161.

The fundamental role played by the Post Office in the nineteenth-century revolution in government is beyond debate.[1] The expansion of its services and responsibilities, the nationalisation of two private industries, deepening entanglements with two others – all were aspects of the dramatic growth which took place during the decades after Hill's campaign for the Penny Post. The magnitude and rapidity of this growth may be gauged by placing the department in the larger context of government budgets. In 1839, the year before Penny Post, Post Office expenditure constituted 1.5 per cent of gross public expenditure; by 1910 it constituted 12 per cent.[2] Moreover, as table one shows,

[1] The literature on the nineteenth-century revolution in government is extensive. See J. B. Brebner, 'Laissez Faire and State Intervention in Nineteenth-century Britain', *The Journal of Economic History*, 8 Supplement (1948), 59–73; Oliver MacDonagh, 'The Nineteenth-Century Revolution in Government: A Reappraisal', *The Historical Journal*, 1 (1958), 52–67; Henry Parris, 'The Nineteenth-Century Revolution in Government; A Reappraisal Reappraised', *The Historical Journal*, 3 (1960), 17–37; David Roberts, *Victorian Origins of the Welfare State* (New Haven, Connecticut, 1960); J. Hart, 'Nineteenth-Century Social Reform: A Tory Interpretation', *Past and Present*, no. 31 (1965), 39–61; W. O. Aydelotte, 'The Conservative and Radical Interpretations of Early Victorian Social Legislation', *Victorian Studies*, 11 (1967), 225–36; A. W. Coats (ed.), *The Classical Economists and Economic Policy* (London, 1971); W. C. Lubenow, *The Politics of Government Growth* (Hamden, Connecticut, 1971); R. M. MacLeod, 'Statesmen Undisguised', *The American Historical Review*, 88 (1973), 85–112; A. J. Taylor, *Laissez-Faire and State Intervention in Nineteenth-Century Britain* (London, 1972); W. H. Greenleaf, *The British Political Tradition*, vols. 1 and 2 (London, 1983). This is a field in which case studies abound. See, for example, Peter Dunkley, 'Emigration and the State, 1803–1842', *The Historical Journal*, 23 (1980), 353–80 and P. W. J. Bartrip, 'State Intervention in Mid-Nineteenth Century Britain: Fact or Fiction?', *The Journal of British Studies*, 23 (1983), 63–83.
[2] Mitchell and Deane, *British Historical Statistics*, pp. 396–8.

Table 1
The growth of government expenditure
(in £000,000s)

Year	Works and Buildings	Salaries etc. of Public Departments	Law and Justice	Education, Art, and Science	Colonial, Consular, and Foreign	Army and Ordnance	Navy	Post Office
1839	0.24	0.72	1.42	0.20	0.48	8.2	4.4	0.8
1850	0.48	0.94	2.28	0.37	0.41	8.9	6.2	2.1
1860	0.68	1.47	3.44	1.27	0.42	14.1	10.8	2.9
1870	0.94	1.64	4.25	1.62	0.55	12.1	9.4	3.6
1880	1.4	2.2	6.5	4.0	0.6	15.0	10.2	5.2
1890	1.5	2.1	5.2	5.8	0.7	17.4	15.3	8.3
1900	2.0	2.1	4.2	12.2	1.7	43.6	26.0	12.8
1910	3.1	3.0	4.6	17.9	1.9	27.2	35.8	18.7

Percentage of Increase 1839–1910:

	1291%	417%	324%	8950%	396%	332%	814%	2337%

Source: Mitchell and Deane, *British Historical Statistics*, pp. 396–8.

departmental expenditure at St Martin's le Grand had grown faster than almost any other major component of government spending.

One could further argue that Post Office expansion had a greater impact on the life of the nation than many other cases of government growth which have been more extensively studied, such as the role of factory inspectors, the procedures of poor law guardians or the methods of emigration officers. After all, these activities affected only a relatively small percentage of the total population. When all is said and done, there is more than a grain of truth in the quip that for the average Victorian the policeman, the tax-collector, and the postman constituted the state.[3] Of the three, the postman in his blue coat with scarlet collar was the most ubiquitous and usually the most welcomed. As *The Times* correctly pointed out, 'The Post Office comes into closer and more constant contact with all grades of the community than perhaps any other department of the public service.'[4]

If it is clear that the empire ruled by St Martin's le Grand grew dramatically after 1840, questions remain as to how and why the process developed in the way it did. For instance, perhaps the most striking impression arising from the history of the department is the relative ease with which expansion occurred, at least until the 1880s. Of the major experiments in expansion, only the telephone nationalisation took a protracted period. In the other cases surveyed, the rapidity of growth was notable. Once the civil servants at St Martin's le Grand became committed to a project, whether it was the Savings Banks or the telegraphs, the period of delay before implementation was usually minimal. Thus, the first question to ask is how did the Post Office usually avoid obstacles, both philosophical and political, which often blocked or delayed growth in other areas of government.

To begin with the most important point, there existed a fundamental conviction among the public, or certainly that part of the public Bagehot termed the 'educated ten thousand', that the work of the Post Office was necessary and that the department for the most part handled its tasks efficiently and economically. In order to substantiate this claim, it may be helpful to look at the attitudes of three intellectuals – Adam Smith, Jeremy Bentham, and Alfred Marshall – concerning the Post Office. While no assertion is made that these three were typical of their particular eras, they were at least representative of some broader currents of thought. Indeed, what is especially notable is the

---

[3] *The Times*, 16 August 1881, p. 9. According to F. M. L. Thompson, 'It would not be far wrong to argue that the postman was the only representative of authority encountered in ordinary daily experience who was generally regarded as benign and helpful': *The Rise of Respectable Society* (Cambridge, Massachusetts, 1988), p. 358.
[4] *The Times*, 13 October 1891, p. 7.

continuity of outlook on the Post Office which they reflect. Smith held the Post Office to be an exception to any general dicta about laissez-faire. In *The Wealth of Nations* he had insisted that

> The Post Office is properly a mercantilist project. The Government advances the expense of establishing different offices and of buying or hiring the necessary horses or carriages, and is repaid with a large profit by the duties upon what is carried. It is perhaps the only successful mercantile project which has been successfully managed by . . . every sort of Government. There is no mystery in the business. The returns are not only certain, but immediate.[5]

There was, then, no theoretical underpinning in the work of the greatest classical economist which opponents of the Post Office, at least on the question of the conveyance of mail, could use. It is significant that Smith's outlook was not that of a dogmatic ideologue, but rather that of a reasonable pragmatist. His confidence in the Post Office was based on the simplicity of its operations and the predictability of the results. Bentham had a slightly different perspective. Instead of emphasising the practical side of the question, he was more concerned with the intellectual and moral benefits which accrued from the Post Office. He believed that 'liberty of the press' and 'liberty of the Post Office' would help to establish 'the perfectly unrestrained communication on every subject within the field of government'.[6] The difference in emphasis between the two is revealing. Smith liked the Post Office because it worked. Bentham saw it as a necessity for a free society. Yet they were in agreement as to its utility, economic as well as philosophic. Writing near the end of the nineteenth century, Marshall was more reserved in his praise of the Post Office than Smith and Bentham. This difference may be explained by two influences, one historical and the other theoretical. First, like Jevons, Marshall had observed the department stumble in its management of the telegraphs. Thus, its record was no longer unblemished, and a certain caution was in order before praising the Post Office too enthusiastically. Secondly, as a vigorous foe of monopoly, Marshall was particularly sensitive to what he termed 'the consumers' net loss, which results from fettering the actions of those who are endeavouring to perform services for the public'.[7] To Marshall, then, some consideration of modifying the department's monopoly of mail conveyance in certain cases was justified. Nonetheless, Marshall found both the Parliamentary and permanent officials at St Martin's le

---

5 Adam Smith, *An Inquiry into the Nature and Causes of the Wealth of Nations*, vol. 2 (1776, rpr. Oxford, 1880), p. 405.
6 Bowring (ed.), *Bentham*, vol. 2, 287.
7 *The Times*, 6 April 1891, p. 13.

Grand to be 'able men' and concluded that to suggest private enterprise could better handle the ordinary work of the department 'would not be the act of a sane man'.[8] Of course, this is not to say that there were not vocal critics of the Post Office and of the theory behind a government-operated business in the nineteenth century. Herbert Spencer most readily comes to mind. He insisted that privately owned and managed companies would flourish, if only the government would forego its monopoly.[9] Yet Spencer on the Post Office is as extreme and atypical of his age as Spencer on any number of issues. The favourable analysis developed by Smith and supported by other writers and economists held the intellectual high ground.

The assessment of the department by the press on the whole reflected this fact. As one might expect, the press always had something of a love–hate relationship with St Martin's le Grand. Accordingly, it is not difficult to find articles dripping with the most fulsome praise as well as pieces full of bitter denunciations of the stupidity and short-sightedness of the department at almost any time during the nineteenth century. What is rather more revealing is the relative distribution of such judgements. In the early years of the century the overall image of the department in the press tended to be negative. For example, in 1807 John Walter II, chief proprietor of *The Times*, battled with Francis Freeling, the Secretary at St Martin's le Grand, over what Walter regarded as an intolerably inefficient overseas mail service.[10] Press relations remained strained until the establishment of Penny Post, when the department began to enjoy a better reputation. Indeed, the outlook of James Wilson, who founded *The Economist* in 1843, serves as a reminder that confidence in the Post Office was not limited to the esoteric intellectual circles of Smith, Bentham, and Marshall. Wilson was a committed advocate of laissez-faire, a man who regarded government interference in the economy as misguided and foolish. The one exception to this doctrinaire opposition was his support of the Post Office.[11] Wilson enthusiastically welcomed Hill's reforms and predicted that great benefits would result from the reductions in postal rates. Wilson was not alone in his appraisal of St Martin's le Grand. Positive assessments such as the following panegyric from *The Birmingham Mail* frequently appeared during the decades after 1840.

> The Post Office is a great co-operative undertaking. It is worked by the nation for the nation's benefit. The principle upon which this is

8   *Ibid.*
9   Herbert Spencer, *Social Statics* (1851, rpr. New York, 1873), pp. 440ff.
10 *The History of the Times*, vol. 1 (London, 1935), chapter 7.
11 Scott Gordon, 'The London *Economist* and the High Tide of Laissez Faire', *The Journal of Political Economy*, 63 (1955), 486.

done would, no doubt, have shocked some of the older political economists whose favourite theory was that the State must not compete in the slightest way with private trade. . . . But the modern theory is the right one, after all; and proof of that is the success which has attended . . . [the Post Office Savings Banks and Annuity programmes]. They are national benefits; and whatever is for the national good is based upon a sound system of political economy.[12]

As this passage suggests, the widespread confidence in the Post Office was based to a large degree upon its record, which was displayed in great statistical detail in the annual reports of the Postmaster General. Success in one area, like the Penny Post, tended to breed enthusiasm for other projects in totally unrelated fields, such as life insurance. Although such analogies were open to criticism, they nevertheless contributed to the pace at which the department grew. Unlike some other partners in the vanguard of government growth, the bureaucrats at St Martin's le Grand did not face a hostile society. Hence, in 1876 *The Times* applauded the department's 'immense invasion of spheres which were once believed to be proper for private enterprise alone'.[13] The nation as a whole accepted the idea of a state-operated communications system and applauded, rather than opposed, its expansion.

Another factor contributing to the rapid growth of the department arose from the specific condition of the enterprises and the nature of the tasks which it took up. They were industries, like the telegraphs, or philanthropies, like the Trustee Banks, which were not flourishing. They were schemes, like the overseas mails, which no private corporation could manage efficiently – a consideration which found its way into the work of, among others, Alfred Marshall.[14] In brief the apparent strength of the Post Office was also a function of the real weaknesses of the opposition. Efficient, thriving industries were never nationalised. Furthermore, when the department faced an entrenched competitor, such as the railways over the parcel post, the process of expansion proved much more difficult. All in all, the Post Office did not challenge the conventional wisdom that private enterprise was to be preferred to state management. The department's activities were usually understood as means to shore up weak spots in the existing economic structure rather than as frontal attacks on the entire edifice. Without question a recurring and crucially important theme in the history of the nineteenth-century Post Office is this compatibility of a firm belief in capitalism, competition, and individual initiative with an

12 Post, *The Birmingham Mail*, 18 December 1872.
13 Post, *The Times*, 8 September 1876.
14 Alfred Marshall, *Industry and Trade* (London, 1923), p. 428.

equally firm advocacy of state intervention in support of such ideals. Such an outlook was evident in an 1880 review article written by Gladstone. Gladstone, who had favoured the Post Office Savings Banks and the nationalisation of the telegraphs, argued that the material progress of Victorian England had been based on two factors. The first was the 'Improvement of Locomotion', a not unexpected sentiment in the age of rail and steam. Perhaps more surprisingly, the second was the 'Liberation of Intercourse'. As he explained,

I rank the introduction of cheap postage for letters, documents, patterns, and printed matter in the category of what is commonly termed Free Trade Legislation. Not only thought in general, but every communication, and every publication, relating to matters of business, was thus set free. These great measures, then, may well take their place beside the abolition of prohibitions and protective duties, the simplifying of revenue laws, and the repeal of the Navigation Act as forming together the great code of Industrial emancipation. Under this code, our race, restored to freedom in mind and hand, and braced by the powerful stimulus of open competition with the world, had upon the whole surpassed itself and every other and has won for itself a commercial primacy more evident, more comprehensive, and more solid than it had at any previous time possessed.[15]

As Gladstone would have readily admitted, competition between business firms for trade and competition between ideas for acceptance had both been facilitated by the 'Liberation of Intercourse'. These themes of economic and intellectual freedom were central to a Victorian creed which went far beyond the rhetoric of a single party. Indeed, the same year Gladstone's article appeared Disraeli argued in a similar vein that

It is difficult for us who live in an age of railroads, telegraphs, penny post and penny newspapers, to realise how limited in thought and feeling, as well as in incident, was the life of an English family of retired habits and limited means, only forty years ago. The whole world seemed to be morally, as well as materially, 'adscripti glebae'.[16]

An examination of such attitudes helps to establish the societal framework within which the department grew, but cannot of itself locate the impetus behind the growth or measure the direction and pace of change. There was undeniably a momentum in the expansion

15 W. E. Gladstone, 'Free Trade, Railways, and the Growth of Commerce', *The Nineteenth Century*, 7 (1880), 370.
16 Benjamin Disraeli, *Endymion* (New York, 1880), p. 48.

of the nineteenth-century Post Office. Involvement in one project almost of necessity demanded expansion into other areas. The establishment of the Savings Banks led to the formation of the Annuity and Insurance programmes. The take-over of the telegraphs was followed by the nationalisation of the telephone. The carrying of books and samples expanded into the parcel post. Perhaps most important of all, the volume of mail both domestic and overseas relentlessly grew. At first glance the process appears to correspond closely to a larger pattern of government growth described by Professor MacDonagh. According to MacDonagh, administration 'may be . . . creative and self-generating. . . . It may gather its own momentum; it may turn unexpectedly in new directions; it may reach beyond the control or comprehension of anyone in particular.'[17] Nonetheless, three additional points – in ascending order of importance – need to be kept in mind, if the history of St Martin's le Grand is to be properly understood. First, it would be incorrect to assume that in the Post Office administrative momentum was of a general amorphous type, which encompassed all individual examples. Rather there were significant nuances in the separate cases and radical variations in the specific patterns of expansion. For example, the enthusiastic nationalisation of the telegraphs was justified on the premise that prices would be lowered and service improved. The somewhat reluctant nationalisation of the telephone was justified on the basis of only the latter, never the former. Secondly, Post Office administrators were never completely free agents in the pursuit of new roles and responsibilities. They were very much dependent upon outside forces. They relied heavily on public opinion, the press, and politicians both to supply new ideas and to support proposals for expansion. Consider the difference between the record of the Savings Banks and that of the Insurance programme. The idea of Post Office Savings Banks was widely supported before it came into being, and the system quickly succeeded. Post Office Life Insurance was a scheme hatched within the department – with insufficient attention to public opinion or wants – and was an abysmal failure. Furthermore, the civil servants at St Martin's le Grand were also influenced and occasionally restrained by their superiors both in Parliament and at the Treasury, particularly after the Scudamore scandal. The very nature of the Post Office's work did not allow planning to be done undercover. It was conducted very much in the public eye and was subject to wider debate and consideration. Expansion at St Martin's le Grand, therefore, was never completely 'self-generating'. Thirdly, the department's administrators were to a notable degree cognisant of the theoretical implications of the particular programmes

17 MacDonagh, 'The Nineteenth-Century Revolution in Government', p. 53.

they promoted as well as the pertinent justifications for refusing to support other policies. In short, momentum did not take the department beyond the 'comprehension of anyone in particular'. Of course, the Post Office's civil servants never unanimously shared the same vision. After all, St Martin's le Grand was an ideological house in which there were many mansions. This was necessary in order to accommodate the rather narrow Utilitarianism of the Hills, the more pragmatic economic assumptions of Tilley and Trollope (a self-described conservative Liberal[18]), the articulate, well-developed social philosophy of Scudamore, and the reserved, almost austere thinking of patricians such as Murray and Smith.

This great ideological diversity merits attention and emphasis if one is to grasp sufficiently the implications of the fact that Rowland Hill's vision of reform with its concomitant assault on the department, although the most studied area of Post Office history, does not constitute the totality of the ideological pressures which affected St Martin's le Grand. Hill, it cannot be denied, did a remarkably effective job of proclaiming that improvements could come only from outsiders such as himself, untainted with the sins of bureaucratic sloth and self interest. In some circles this assumption became a commonplace. Thus, six decades after Penny Post an MP could urge, 'It was a well known fact that the Post Office permanent officials were always against any reform of any sort whatsoever. Every improvement . . . for the last one hundred years had to be forced on the officials from the outside.'[19] The problem with this line of argument, obviously, is that it ignores important civil servants who, as insiders during the middle decades of the century, welcomed the opportunity to increase the department's usefulness and to further their own careers. Take Anthony Trollope, who in 1834 entered the department through jobbery. Trollope was not a man specifically trained for his position. He was not a man to ignore the comforts and pleasures of the good life. He was not a man to avoid feuds with superiors. (Indeed, of the many adjectives which might accurately describe Trollope as a civil servant, 'Weberian' is not one.[20]) Yet these circumstances did not prevent him from becoming an effective civil servant firmly committed to his departmental duties. In 1851 he was put in charge of revising the network for rural mail delivery. It was a task which so occupied his energies that even he was unable to write and, thus, his novel The Warden was delayed. As he later re-

18 Trollope, An Autobiography, p. 291.
19 Hansard's, Fourth Series, vol. 159, 419, 21 June 1906. The MP was Sir Alpheus Morton. Herbert Spencer also attributed the efficiency of the department to 'pressure from without': Spencer, Social Statics, p. 440.
20 H. H. Gerth and C. W. Mills (eds.), From Max Weber: Essays in Sociology (Oxford, 1958), pp. 198ff.

flected on his vision of the proper role of the department, 'It is amusing to watch how a passion will grow upon a man. During those two years [1851–2] it was the ambition of my life to cover the country with rural letter-carriers.'[21] The epitome of the obsessive permanent official eager to extend the range of the department's services, of course, was not Trollope, but Scudamore. The establishment of savings banks and life insurance, the reorientation of policy on the overseas mails, and the nationalisation of the telegraphs, each was nurtured by this remarkable administrator. In the 1860s Scudamore helped to change not only the direction and rate of the department's expansion, but also its very sense of purpose. The dynamic ethic of St Martin's le Grand during the optimistic era of his predominance certainly does not conform to the general image of 'administrative quiescence', which was once said to characterise these years.[22] It marks, rather, a crucial phase in the department's evolution and an equally important era in the wider revolution in government. Unfortunately, Scudamore's mishandling of the telegraph allocations and his self-imposed exile in Turkey precluded any place in the Victorian administrative pantheon for this visionary civil servant. As a result, he and the projects he promoted have been regrettably ignored.

Sometime between 1885 and 1895 this middle period, characterised by an eager willingness within St Martin's le Grand to take on new projects, began to come to an end. The Post Office started to lose confidence in itself. Scudamore's dreams of a technocratic bureaucracy uniting the country in harmony and prosperity faded. Expansion no longer seemed to solve all problems and, it could be argued, often created more than had existed previously. The department grew wary of accepting new responsibilities. What had brought about this change in attitude? Certainly something of a generational shift in outlook among activists outside government and administrators within the civil service had occurred. Issues and rhetoric – the urgency to establish a rapid mail train or the need to encourage thrift – which earlier had been compelling now seemed slightly stale, as the enormity of social and economic problems facing the country – problems which were well beyond the ability of the Post Office to ameliorate – became clearer. Hence, within the broad spectrum of government officials the few Post Office men such as Lamb still ardently seeking expansion and new programmes found themselves in a situation analogous to that occupied by temperance advocates in the greater reform movement,

[21] Trollope, An Autobiography, p. 89.
[22] Valerie Cromwell, 'Interpretations of Nineteenth-Century Administration: An Analysis', Victorian Studies, 9 (1966), 254.

i.e. 'no longer *avant garde*'.[23] The more forward position in the civil service was now held by administrators such as Llewellyn Smith at the Board of Trade.[24]

In analysing this generational shift at St Martin's le Grand, it is also tempting to focus upon the new breed of departmental Secretaries who came into office beginning in 1880 with Blackwood and then followed by Walpole in 1893, Murray in 1899, and H. B. Smith in 1903. These men were neither agitators like Hill nor insiders such as Scudamore who had worked their entire careers at St Martin's le Grand. They were generalists who had advanced through the civil service from department to department. All were graduates of distinguished public schools, and three were university graduates. Did they as mandarins in a state-owned industry evidence the gentlemanly outlook inculcated by that educational world which, according to Wiener, allowed 'little attention or status to industrial pursuits'?[25] In the case of Blackwood, the answer is clearly no. He was eager to move into the telephone field and was held back only by Fawcett's preference for private development of the industry and resistance in Whitehall. His years at Eton, Trinity College, Cambridge, and the Treasury had certainly not destroyed his taste for expansion and competition. As for the others, summary judgement is more difficult. They were not as interested as Blackwood in forging ahead, but why? The case could be made that by the end of the nineteenth century Post Office managers lacked the necessary skills to operate complex technological enterprises, such as the telegraphs or telephone, or to appreciate new developments, such as the wireless. Something of a division in the mind of the department appeared to open, as the engineering branch came to feel thwarted and mistreated by the generalists in the Secretary's Office. Thus, Lieutenant Colonel Walter O'Meara, who served as Engineer-in-Chief between 1907 and 1912, complained bitterly about 'the contempt in which the Engineer-in-Chief and his Staff are held by officers in the Secretary's Office'.[26] He further lamented that

> If the Post Office had taken the precaution to obtain for the Engineering Department only fully qualified officers, there would not have been the necessity for passing over officers and imposing examinations on officers late in life. I think you will agree that the results of the examination of Sub-Engineers for Second Class Engineerships

23 Brian Harrison, *Drink and the Victorians* (London, 1971), p. 405.
24 Roger Davidson, 'Llewellyn Smith, the Labour Department and Government Growth 1886–1909' in Sutherland, pp. 227–62.
25 Wiener, p. 24.
26 Nathan Papers, fol. 412, O'Meara to Nathan, 1 September 1910.

has proved, without a doubt, that the class of officer drafted into this Department in the past has been considerably below the required standard.[27]

However, one should not hastily assume that statements such as O'Meara's definitively substantiate a precipitous decline circa 1890–1910 in the understanding of and sympathy for technical and business problems on the part of administrators in the Secretary's Office. After all, Scudamore knew little of the engineering aspects of the telegraphs, and Tilley underestimated the potential of the telephone. Hence, to attribute the hesitant attitudes of the post-Blackwood leadership concerning technology and departmental growth entirely to their social origins or educational experience places much too heavy a superstructure of interpretation on too slight a factual foundation.

In the end the decline of optimistic zeal in the Secretary's Office was more the result of a new understanding concerning the changing economic and labour context in which St Martin's le Grand was operating at the close of the century than a function of the backgrounds of individual civil servants. It was this altered situation more than any other single circumstance which contributed to a growing tendency of departmental administrators to dwell on the Post Office's disadvantages. For example, in 1898 when testifying before a select committee on the telephone, Walpole argued that a government department could not compete as effectively as a private concern which was spurred on by a 'pecuniary interest'.[28] In such judgements Walpole was joined by others. Without doubt the most influential civil servant shaping departmental policy and at the same time lowering departmental expectations during the prewar era was Sir George Murray. First as a Treasury clerk, later as Post Office Secretary 1899–1903, and finally as Permanent Secretary to the Treasury 1903–11, Murray repeatedly and persuasively emphasised the difficulties and ambiguities of the Post Office's role in the larger economy.[29] Perhaps the most extensive statement of Murray's pessimistic perception of the situation is found in a 1900 memorandum:

> Personally I hold rather strongly to the view that the State should not undertake any business which private enterprise can do, unless it has a monopoly such as the P.O. possesses in the carriage of letters and telegrams.

[27] Ibid.
[28] BPP, 1898, vol. 12, Select Committee on the Telephone, p. 474.
[29] As shown in chapter seven, the impact of Murray's influence stemmed more from the acuity of his vision and the force of his argument than from the particular departmental position he occupied, either at the Post Office or the Treasury.

When it takes to competing with private enterprise, it goes beyond its proper functions, and what is more important – it is almost certain to fail. *Ceteris paribus*, I believe a private company will almost always beat a Gov't Dept. The latter cannot use methods open to the former. It must treat everybody alike; it cannot push its business by favouring one class of customers and neglecting others; nor can it very well go round and tout for custom. It is also exposed to two different kinds of pressure which it is much less able to resist than a body of Directors or Shareholders. On the one side the public will be demanding a better service and lower charges. On the other its employees will be demanding more privileges and higher wages.[30]

Two further points should be made. First, Murray's assessment did not necessarily establish one unchanging strategy for departmental policy. It might lead to retrenchment as in the case of life insurance or to a somewhat self-protecting expansion as in the case of a telephone monopoly. It did, nonetheless, set a very different tone in the Edwardian period than had been the case before. Secondly, as Murray and others found to their regret, the disadvantages of government-operated businesses did not vanish when a monopoly was established. The absence of competition did not prevent the public from pressing for unprofitable, but nonetheless socially desirable, changes. The 1885 reduction of telegram charges and the 1898 lowering of Imperial postage rates are but two examples of changes forced upon government in areas where it held a monopoly. Equally, government employees in a monopoly at times seemed no less aggressive in their demands for better wages and employment conditions than their fellow workers in private industry. As was shown in chapter two, neither the Post Office nor the Treasury developed an adequate strategy in response to the growth of unions inside the department. Two results emerged. First, the Secretaries and other important administrators devoted more and more of their time and energy to staff issues, the preparation of statistics for Parliamentary inquiries, and conferences and negotiations with union leaders. Indeed, to H. B. Smith the difficulties of managing government employees increased 'not merely in direct proportion of the increase of numbers, but in an increasing ratio'.[31] Accordingly, there was less opportunity to oversee other aspects of the department's current operations, much less contemplate new programmes. Secondly, wages consumed an increasing portion of the department's expenditure, and the escalation appeared unstoppable.

[30] Post 30/145, E29062/1908, Murray's memorandum, 10 April 1900.
[31] Post 30/1699, E14099/1909, Smith's testimony before the Farrer Committee, 29 April 1907.

Outside observers, noting this trend, were sometimes given to over-reaction. In 1890, for example, after the strike at the Mount Pleasant office, *The Economist* gloomily predicted: 'The community has grad-ually become free, but its freedom is now menaced with a new attack. Its servants are combining in every direction to extort more than market wages under penalty of the public . . . being exposed to grave loss as in the case of the postmen and dockers.'[32] Such sentiments were to be repeated over and over in the period before the First World War. In 1906 Henniker Heaton the Conservative MP from Canterbury examined the threat of unions in government departments. He was by no means a loyal spokesman for St Martin's le Grand, having made a career out of pestering and criticising St Martin's le Grand over a broad range of issues. Yet on the labour question Heaton strongly supported a hard line from the Secretary's Office:

A postman or dockyard hand finds that he can win promotion and increased pay only by strenuous hard work, just as if he were a mere artisan or shop assistant. But the agitators point out that he can attain an equivalent result by bullying the local M. P., and so he joins the league or union formed for the purpose.

Where is this to stop? The late Sir W. Harcourt wrote (to me) that the demands of the postal employees reached such a depth or abyss which no plummet could fathom. We know now that they claim the postal surplus, which amounts to nearly five millions. Since 1881 they have secured increases of pay amounting to 1½ millions. There are 192,000 of them, and of these probably 100,000 have votes. Adding to these the dockyard, arsenal, and stores factory hands, and other Government employees, we have a political force that may turn the scale at a General Election.[33]

Given the fear which such a spectre could evoke, it is no wonder that the civil servants both at the Post Office and the Treasury drew together and began to question the desirability of adding to an already huge bureaucracy, which had become highly unionised. (By 1912, there were over 78,000 union members in the manipulative ranks, which constituted the lower echelons of the department. These in-cluded 86 per cent of all postmen, 82 per cent of the London sorters, and 70 per cent of the sorting clerks and telegraphists.[34])

---

32 Post 16/27, *The Economist*, 12 July 1890.
33 J. Henniker Heaton, 'Wanted! An End to Political Patronage', *The Nineteenth Century and After*, 59 (1906), 571–2.
34 Clinton, p. 646.

All in all, there was a change in both the style of the behaviour of civil servants at St Martin's le Grand as well as the substance of their thinking. Previously, statesmen-in-disguise, such as Hill, Scudamore, or Chetwynd, could and did lobby forthrightly for changes and new programmes. By the Edwardian period strict neutrality or at least anonymity was more the order of the day. In 1911, for example, a Post Office union became interested in promoting certain reforms, such as a half-penny local post and changes in the investment procedure for Savings Bank funds. Herbert Samuel, the Postmaster General, firmly opposed their methods and quashed their proposals. Writing to Asquith, he maintained 'officers of a Government Department . . . ought not to be allowed to advocate by public propaganda administrative measures which may not form part of the policy of the head of the Department'.[35] Administrative timidity and the accompanying hesitancy to consider new ideas, like administrative zeal, can gather momentum. The cautious role played by the Post Office in the founding of the BBC in 1922 stands as one more piece of evidence for this generalisation.[36] As Coase has pointed out, a broadcasting monopoly was supported by the Post Office not as a means to develop the potential of radio, but rather as a solution to internal management problems. The 'view that monopoly was better for the listener was to come later'.[37] Obviously, the defensive preference for monopoly voiced by Sir George Murray continued to shape a wide range of policy decisions during the administration of his son Sir Evelyn Murray, departmental Secretary 1914–34.

By the turn of the century, then, there existed a widespread conviction both in and out of government that the department had grown too large, had taken on too great a variety of tasks, and was not managing some of these tasks very well. In 1902 The Daily Mail described the situation as going from bad to worse and pointedly asked the question 'Has it really got too much to do?'[38] Over a decade later Sir Harry Lawson, MP and managing proprietor of The Daily Telegraph, summed up the matter in the following way:

> My belief is, that at the present moment the fabric of the Post Office has entirely outgrown its frame. It is weak in the head, but strong in the body. . . . [There] is [not] any definite line between labour

---

[35] Samuel Papers, A/37, Samuel to Asquith, 8 September 1911.
[36] Asa Briggs, The Birth of Broadcasting (London, 1961), part three.
[37] R. H. Coase, 'The Origin of the Monopoly of Broadcasting in Great Britain', Economica, 14 (1947), 210.
[38] Post 16/42, The Daily Mail, 1 January 1902.

questions, commercial questions, and the scientific questions with which it has to deal, and I am quite sure that while there is too much centralisation at one end, so there is too little control at the other.[39]

However, as was shown in chapter one, such criticism failed to spark the necessary reforms in the administrative structure of the department. Thus, complaints grew. For instance, a deputation from the executive council of the Association of British Chambers of Commerce met departmental leaders in 1924 to drive home the point that 'The general impression abroad today is that the Post Office is not holding its own.'[40] Thus, within the Secretary's Office a certain siege mentality was further encouraged.[41]

In the context of the question posed by the title of this chapter – whether there was a pattern to Post Office growth – one must answer that there were three. An external assault upon the department launched by Rowland Hill in the 1830s constituted the first. The second emerged during the 1850s and 1860s when a fruitful alliance between departmental zealots such as Scudamore, able administrators such as Tilley, politicians such as Gladstone, and the public encouraged St Martin's le Grand to take up new responsibilities. Finally, by the 1880s a fundamental reassessment of the Post Office's ability to manage a large, overly centralised department and to reconcile the conflicting priorities of revenue and service led to a decline in enthusiasm for expansion. Obviously, these patterns were by no means totally distinct and removed from each other. They tended to overlap, as in the nationalisation of the telephone. That is why the history of the Victorian Post Office is so convoluted and at times cloudy. What is clear is that by 1914 the third trend had become predominant. One temporary pattern of government growth had given way to another.

---

[39] *Hansard's, Fifth Series*, vol. 64, 743–4, 3 July 1914.
[40] Post 33/1228, M3807/1924, Deputation of the British Association of Chambers of Commerce, 5 March 1924.
[41] The results of such thinking may be seen in the 1969 reorganisation of the Post Office, when it ceased to be a department of state, the 1981 division of posts and telecommunications into separate corporations, and the 1984 sale of 51 per cent of British Telecom stock to private investors. Much of the thrust of recent policy has to been to take apart what the Victorians put together. For a review article on the larger subject, see Martin Chick, 'Privatisation: The Triumph of Past Practice over Current Requirements', *Business History*, 29 (1987), 104–17.

APPENDIX

Table 1
Postmasters General 1835–1915

	Date assumed office	
Earl of Lichfield	30 May	1835
Lord Lowther (Earl of Lonsdale)	15 Sept.	1841
Earl of St Germans	2 Jan.	1846
Marquess of Clanricarde	14 July	1846
Earl of Hardwicke	6 May	1852
Viscount Canning (Earl Canning)	8 Jan.	1853
Duke of Argyll	30 Nov.	1855
Lord Colchester	13 Mar.	1858
Earl of Elgin and Kincardine	24 June	1859
Duke of Argyll again	11 May	1860
Lord Stanley of Alderley	28 Aug.	1860
Duke of Montrose	19 July	1866
Marquess of Hartington	30 Dec.	1868
William Monsell (Lord Emly)	24 Jan.	1871
Lyon Playfair (Lord Playfair)	13 Nov.	1873
Lord John Manners	4 Mar.	1874
Henry Fawcett	14 May	1880
George J. Shaw-Lefevre (Lord Eversley)	7 Nov.	1884
Lord John Manners again	29 June	1885
Lord Wolverton	10 Feb.	1886
Henry Cecil Raikes	5 Aug.	1886
Sir James Fergusson	21 Sept.	1891
Arnold Morley	19 Aug.	1892
Duke of Norfolk	5 July	1895
Marquess of Londonderry	10 Apr.	1900
J. Austen Chamberlain	15 Aug.	1902
Lord Stanley	9 Oct.	1903
Sydney Buxton	11 Dec.	1905
Herbert Samuel (Viscount Samuel)	21 Jan.	1910
C. E. H. Hobhouse	12 Feb.	1914
Herbert Samuel again	28 May	1915

Source: Post Office establishment books.

Table 2
Post Office Secretaries 1836–1914

	Date assumed office
Colonel W. L. Maberly	29 Sept. 1836
Sir Rowland Hill*	22 Apr. 1854
Sir John Tilley	15 Mar. 1864
Sir Stevenson Arthur Blackwood	1 May 1880
Sir Spencer Walpole	10 Nov. 1893
Sir George H. Murray	10 Feb. 1899
Sir H. Babington Smith	1 Oct. 1903
Sir Matthew Nathan	17 Jan. 1910
Sir Alexander King	7 Aug. 1911
Sir G. Evelyn P. Murray	24 Aug. 1914

* Secretary to the Postmaster General 1846–54.

Source: Post Office establishment books.

Table 3
Some personnel of the British Post Office
1836–1914

Ashurst, W. b. 1819; became a Solicitor 1843; Solicitor to Post Office 1862; father had been active as a Parliamentary agent for the Mercantile Committee on Penny Post; a friend of Garibaldi and Mazzini; d. 1879.

Baines, F. E. b. 1832; entered Post Office 1855; Surveyor General for Telegraph 1873; Assistant Secretary 1880; Third Secretary 1889; CB 1885; d. 1911.

Blackwood, Sir Stevenson Arthur b. 1832; educ. Eton, Trinity College, Cambridge; Clerk in Treasury 1852–74; Financial Secretary to the Post Office 1874–80; Secretary 1880–93; great Evangelical leader; President of Civil Service Prayer Union; General Post Office Abstinence Society; CB 1880; KCB 1887; d. 1893.

Crabb, Edward b. 1853; educ. Manchester Grammar School; entered Post Office 1876; Assistant Secretary 1905; Second Secretary 1911; d. 1914.

Forman, H. Buxton b. 1842; educ. Teignmouth; entered Post Office 1860; Assistant Secretary 1893; Joint Second Secretary 1905 and Controller of Packet Services; author of many works on Shelley and Keats as well as his own poetry; d. 1917.

Gates, W. G. b. ?; educ. King's School, Canterbury; entered Secretary's Office 1881; Assistant Director, Investigation Branch 1892; Director 1900; Assistant Secretary for Home Mails 1910–21; d. 1936.

Hill, E. B. Lewin b. 1834; educ. Bruce Castle School; entered Secretary's Office 1855 on nomination by Lord Canning; Assistant Secretary 1892–9; CB 1897; d. 1915.

Hill, Sir Rowland b. 1795; 3rd son of Thomas Wright Hill; educ. Kidderminster; established Hazelwood System of School Management 1812; invented a rotary printing press; Secretary to South Australian Commissioner 1835–9; published *Post Office Reform, its Importance and Practicability* 1836; attached to Treasury 1839–42; dismissed by Peel 1842; Director of London & Brighton Railway 1843; Chairman 1845–6; presented by public subscription £13,000 17 June 1846; Secretary to Postmaster General 1846; Permanent Secretary of Post Office 1854–64; £20,000 grant from Parliament 1864; d. 1879; buried in Westminster Abbey.

Howe, L. T. b. 1860; educ. Grammar School, Newport, Shropshire, St John's College, Cambridge; entered Post Office 1883 as Clerk (grade 1) in Secretary's Office; Private Secretary to Sir George Murray 1899–1903; Assistant Secretary 1911; d. 1939.

Hunter, Sir Robert b. 1844; educ. University of London; Solicitor 1867; JP for the County of Surrey; Solicitor to the Post Office 1882; an important figure in the founding of the National Trust; d. 1913.

King, Sir Alexander Assistant Secretary 1903–5; Joint Second Secretary 1905–7; Second Secretary 1907–11; Secretary 1911–14.

Lamb, Sir John b. 1845; entered Post Office 1864; Assistant Secretary 1889; Third Secretary 1896; Second Secretary 1897–1905; participant in many conferences and committees on telegraphy; Chairman of Council Royal Society of Arts; wrote *The Lifeboat and its Work*; CMG 1890; CB 1895; Kt. 1905; Knight of Grace of St John of Jerusalem 1911; d. 1915.

Maberly, William L. b. 1798; Lt. Col. 76 Foot; MP Northampton, 1820–30; Shaftesbury 1831–2; Chatham 1832–4; Clerk of the Ordnance 1833–4; Commissioner of Customs 1834–6; Secretary of Post Office 1836–54; Commissioner of Board of Audit 1854–66; d. 1885.

Murray, Sir George H. b. 1849; educ. Harrow, Christ Church, Oxford; entered Foreign Office 1873; transferred to Treasury 1880; Private Secretary to Gladstone and Rosebery when they were Prime Minister; Chairman of Board of Inland Revenue 1897–9; Secretary to Post Office 1899–1903; Permanent Secretary to Treasury 1903–11; KCB 1899; GCVO 1920; GCB 1908; d. 1936.

Nathan, Matthew b. 1862; entered Royal Engineers 1880; Brevet Lt. Col. 1907; served in the Nile Expedition 1885; Secretary, Colonial Defence Committee 1895–1900; administered government Sierra Leone 1899; Governor Gold Coast 1900–3; Governor Hong Kong 1903–7; Secretary to Post Office 1910–11; Chairman Board of Inland Revenue and member Pacific Cable Board 1911–14; PC (Ire.) 1914; GCMG 1908; KCMG 1902; CMG 1899; LLD (Queensland Univ.) 1925; d. 1939.

Ogilvie, Sir Andrew b. 1858; educ. University College, London; Private Secretary to successive Postmasters General 1891–9; Assistant Secretary 1903; Third Secretary 1911–14; Joint Second Secretary 1914–19; Col. (Retired) Royal Engineers (TF); CB 1912; KBE 1918; d. 1924.

Preece, W. H. b. 1834; educ. King's College, London; appointed to Electric and International 1853; joined Post Office 1870 as Divisional Engineer; Engineer-in-Chief and Electrician 1892–9; several publications on telephone telegraphy; JP for Carnarvonshire; FRS; LLD; President Institution of Civil Engineers; KCB 1899; d. 1913.

Scudamore, Frank Ives b. 1823; son of a Solicitor; educ. Christ's Hospital; entered Post Office 1840; Chief Examiner of Receiver and Accountant General's Office 1852; Receiver and Accountant-General 1856; involved in savings banks and telegraph administration; Second Secretary 1868. The D. N. B. obliquely refers to the telegraph scandal as follows: his 'eagerness for progress and impatience of obstacles led to some conflict of opinion, which was terminated by his resignation in 1875'. Worked on Turkish Post Office reform 1875–7; author of a lecture on fairies 'People Whom we have Never Met' 1861 and 'The Day Dreams of a Sleepless Man'; wrote in *Punch*, the *Standard*, the *Scotsman* and the *Comic Times*; d. 1884; buried in English cemetery in Scutari.

Smith, Sir Henry Babington b. 1863; educ. Eton, Trinity College, Cambridge; Double First in Classical Tripos (parts I and II); member of the Apostles; Chancellor's medal; Examiner in Education Department 1887; Principal Private Secretary to the Chancellor of the Exchequer (Goschen) 1891; served at numerous conferences on finance; Secretary to Post Office 1903–9; later was a Director of the Bank of England; CB 1905; KCB 1908; GBE 1920; d. 1923.

Tilley, Sir John b. 1813; son of a London merchant; entered Post Office as a clerk 1829; Assistant Secretary 1848; Secretary 1864–80; retired on full pay; CB 1871; KCB 1880; related by marriage to Anthony Trollope; d. 1898.

Turnor, Algernon b. 1845; educ. Eton, Christ Church, Oxford; entered Treasury 1867; appointed Private Secretary to Permanent Secretary and in 1874 to the Prime Minister; Financial Secretary of the Post Office 1880; resigned 1896; d. 1921.

Walpole, Sir Spencer b. 1837; educ. Eton; Clerk in War Office; Inspector of Fisheries; Lt. Governor of Isle of Man; Secretary to the Post Office 1893–9; numerous publications including *The History of Twenty-Five Years*; KCB 1898; Hon. DL Oxford and LLD Edinburgh; d. 1907.

Sources: Frederic Boase, *Modern English Biography*, 6 vols. (New York, 1965); *Who Was Who 1897–1915* (London, 1920); *Who Was Who 1916–1928* (London, 1929); *Who Was Who 1929–1940* (London, 1941); *Dictionary of National Biography*, 63 vols. and supplements (London, 1885–1937); *The Dictionary of Business Biography*, 5 vols. (London, 1985–6).

Table 4
The treatment of labour issues

The following must be read with the understanding that there was a continuing debate within and outside the Post Office during the nineteenth century as to the exact legal, political, and economic status of its employees. Were they civil servants, enjoying the privileges of that position, and thus rightfully expected to exercise a 'proper reserve and reticence', as one memorandum phrased it? Or, should the employees be free in bargaining and other matters to use all of the weapons available in the arsenal of their fellow trade unionists? It must also be emphasised that there was equal disagreement concerning the results listed below. To some the drift of events constituted a very unfortunate decline in good government. To others the concessions gained, although just, were frequently seen as inadequate and partial and, hence, represented only a first stage in a longer process toward equitable labour relations.

1866   Rule established prohibiting letter carriers from meeting to discuss official questions.

1868   Restrictions against Post Office civil servants voting lifted by Parliament.

1880   Telegraphists meet to discuss official questions. No action taken by Fawcett the Postmaster General.

1881   Fawcett, against Blackwood's advice, receives deputation from telegraphists.

1890   Raikes the Postmaster General allows staff to discuss official questions at meetings under certain conditions and accepts *fait accompli* in recognising right to form unions.

1892   Fergusson the Postmaster General warns the staff against extracting promises from Parliamentary candidates on wage issues.

1893   Morley the Postmaster General removes all restrictions on meetings. However, he and the next two PMGs adhere to the policy of refusing to receive deputations which include men not currently employed by the department, i.e. union officials.

1895–7 Tweedmouth Committee, including civil servants from other departments, studies wages and staff conditions in the Post Office. Morley the Postmaster General believed such an interdepartmental committee was preferable to 'the appointment of a Select Committee . . . [which] would be . . . a severe blow to our system of government, constituting as it would, an appeal on matters of discipline and administration from the Executive to the Legislature'. (Cab 37/38, A. Morley's memorandum of 14 March 1895.)

1899   Norfolk the Postmaster General permits memorials from the staff to be sent through normal channels.

1903   Chamberlain the Postmaster General allows such memorials to be sent directly to him, thus circumventing normal channels.

1903–4   Bradford Committee, including businessmen, Charles Booth the social investigator, and Thomas Broderick of the Co-operative Wholesale Society, studies wages and staff conditions in the Post Office. Murray's comments on the committee's report: 'This is an amazing document; and will, I fear, give us a great deal of trouble in the future.' (T1/1035B/14045, Murray to A. Chamberlain, 11 May 1904.)

1906   Buxton the Postmaster General 'frankly' recognises unions and agrees to receive deputations including men not employed by the department, i.e. union officials. Later a union leader comments on the usefulness of such meetings: 'I am a great believer in these interviews. They sometimes enable us to put the Postmaster General in an awkward corner; it does our Associations and the general cause good.' (G. H. Stuart, National Joint Committee in executive session, 16 February 1914.)

1906–7   Hobhouse Committee, the first of the Parliamentary inquiries, studies wages and staff conditions in the Post Office. Buxton reasoned that 'From a Parliamentary point of view . . . it would seem almost hopeless (even if we desired) to resist the appointment of a Parliamentary Committee.' As revenue was 'in a most flourishing condition', such a committee might be appointed as an act of grace. (Cab 37/82, Buxton's memorandum of February 1906.)

1912–13   Holt Committee, another Parliamentary select committee, again addresses the question of labour in the Post Office. One estimate held that, if all the staff requests to the committee had been granted, £10 million per year would have been added to departmental expenses.

1914   Gibb Committee, a small ad hoc group including two representatives from the unions, considers questions left unresolved by the Holt Committee. Wilkins's comments: 'For the first time in the history of English public life the staff take a hand in administrative questions. This they have long coveted in vain.' (T1/11928/13311, memorandum of 13 June 1914.) The age of Whitleyism was about to begin.

See Post 30/4344, E10983/1919 for much of the above.

Table 5
The pattern of departmental salaries

Class	1885		1891		1897		Average Weekly Pay 1903		1905		1908–9		1910	
	s	d	s	d	s	d	s	d	s	d	s	d	s	d
LONDON														
Sorters (Male)	28	5	32	10	35	10	40	8	45	8	49	7	50	7
Telegraphists, Central Telegraph Office (Male)	28	10	32	4	37	6	40	2	44	10	49	3	50	10
Telegraphists, Central Telegraph Office (Female)	22	10	23	9	22	5	24	0	25	10	29	0	29	8
Counter Clerks and Telegraphists (Male)	34	5	36	1	39	5	42	6	45	3	48	2	49	0
Counter Clerks and Telegraphists (Female)	21	11	23	6	25	7	26	10	27	8	30	1	31	9
Telephonists	–		–		–		13	5	15	1	not ascertained		19	9
Postmen	25	1	25	1	26	7	29	1	30	0	32	10	33	1

REST OF UNITED KINGDOM

Sorting Clerks and Telegraphists (Male)	27 2	28 7	33 1	33 2	35 5	37 9	38 2
Sorting Clerks and Telegraphists (Female)	19 10	19 3	21 0	22 1	23 3	25 9	25 9
Telephonists	–	–	–	15 9	16 11	not ascertained	19 5
Postmen	19 10	22 5	23 5	24 6	25 9	not ascertained	27 5

Source: Post 33/2142, M15635/1927.

Table 6
Post Office Savings Banks statement of business

Year	Deposits			Withdrawals			Interest credited to Depositors	Average Amount standing to credit of each open account	
	Number	Average Amount		Number	Average Amount			Active	Dormant
		£ s d			£ s d		£	£ s d	s d
1862	592,582	3 5 9		94,427	4 11 5		21,763	9 12 4	—
1870	2,135,993	2 16 1		787,172	6 0 11		337,961	12 15 3	—
1880	3,755,689	2 14 5		1,465,331	6 7 7		777,985	15 8 11	—
1890	8,776,566	2 7 10		2,892,006	6 3 10		1,553,355	14 0 3	—
1900	14,969,849	2 14 2		5,406,347	7 1 5		3,145,978	16 1 3	—
1910	19,975,375	2 6 3		10,058,009	4 11 2		3,949,461	20 2 7	2 2

Source: *Report of the Postmaster General on the Post Office* (London, 1913), pp. 70–1.

Table 7
Telephone rate structure 1915

London

Unlimited Service: £20 for the first line; £17 for each additional line.

Message Rate: £6 10s in the County of London; £5 10s in outer London, including in each case £1 10s for calls.

Provinces

Unlimited Service: £8 for private residences only.
£12 for business premises for the first line and £10 for each additional line (restricted to contracts made before 1907)

Message Rates: Tariff 'A' £5 covering 500 calls; additional calls per 100

> 501–1,000 – 8s
> 1,001–2,000 – 6s
> 2,001–4,600 – 4s

Tariff 'B' £6 covering 500 calls; additional calls per 100

> 501–1,300 – 7s 6d
> 1,300–4,600 – 4s

Source: Post 84, Report of Telephone Rates Committee, 1920.

Table 8
Post Office telephone revenue

Year	Trunk telephones	London telephones	Provincial telephones	Royalties from NTC and other licensees	Total receipts
1882				£6,702	£6,702
1885				18,825	18,825
1890				40,676	40,676
1895	£9,702 *			71,499	81,201
1900	198,792			129,950	328,742
1905	372,658	£186,037	£45,115 **	200,725	804,535
1910	651,638	564,036	214,044	320,590	1,750,308

* Receipts from continental calls. The inland trunk system was not taken over until 1896.
** Provincial telephone receipts were not separated from telegraph receipts until 1905.

Source: *The Post Office an Historical Summary* (London, 1914), p. 127.

Table 9
The mail-train network

It would be virtually impossible to give a satisfactory picture of the entire mail-train network. The system was never static. New trains and stops were always being added. However, one can get some idea of the system by examining a small part of it at one particular time – the English night-mail network in the early 1890s. Every night the Northumbrian 'up' night mail started from Newcastle-on-Tyne at 7.08 p.m., passing through York making for Normanton, ten miles southeast of Leeds. There the Midland Railway took over from the North Eastern and carried the mails southward through Sheffield, Chesterfield, Derby, and Burton-on-Trent. At Tamworth it received the mails from the 'up' night-mail train from Scotland. Passing through Birmingham and Gloucester, it reached Bristol at 4.36 a.m. There a branch train carried a portion of the mails into Wales, and the Great Western Railway carried the rest on to Devon and Cornwall.

In the opposite direction there was a similar train as well as one from Plymouth which ran via Hereford and Shrewsbury to Crewe. Also heading toward Crewe were the Irish mail train, which left London at 8.20 p.m., and trains from Leamington, Bristol, and South Wales. As the following table indicates, they and others converged upon Crewe near midnight.

	Arrival at Crewe
The mails from Birmingham	11.33 p.m.
The mails from North Wales	11.33 p.m.
The mails from the West of England	11.35 p.m.
The mails from the Potteries	11.45 p.m.
The mails from London for Ireland	11.48 p.m.
The mails from Manchester	11.50 p.m.
The 'Down' night mail from London	11.54 p.m.

At midnight the Irish mails were dispatched, and five minutes later the mails for Scotland. The system was further facilitated by cross-post trains, which prevented mails from being sent unduly out-of-the-way. For example, there was a spur from Normanton via Leeds to Carnforth, a station north of Lancaster. This spur prevented letters from York or Hull for places north of Carnforth being sent unnecessarily via Staleybridge.

Source: F. E. Baines, *Forty Years at the Post Office*, vol. 2 (London, 1895), pp. 179ff.

Table 10
The record of the parcel post

Year	Number of parcels	Number per capita	Gross revenue amount	Amount paid to railways for rail-borne parcels	Post Office share
1890–1	46,228,000	1.22	£1,035,773	£ 499,913	£ 535,860
1895–6	60,527,000	1.54	1,372,577	648,825	723,752
1900–1	81,017,000	1.95	1,699,994	801,236	898,758
1905–6	101,682,000	2.34	2,138,673	996,449	1,142,224
1909–10	118,190,000	2.63	2,371,928	1,085,932	1,285,996

Source: Annual reports of the Postmaster General.

Bibliography

Primary Manuscript Sources

Bodleian Library, Oxford
Monk Bretton Papers, the papers of J. G. Dodson, First Lord Monk Bretton.
Nathan Papers, the papers of Sir Matthew Nathan.

British Library, London
Gladstone Papers, the papers of W. E. Gladstone.
Iddesleigh Papers, the papers of Sir Stafford Northcote, First Earl of Iddesleigh.

House of Lords Record Office, London
Samuel Papers, the papers of Herbert, First Viscount Samuel.

Post Office Records Office, London
Rowland Hill's Journal, 1839–69.
Post 1, Treasury Letter Books.
Post 11, Railway Records.
Post 16, Newspaper Accounts.
Post 29, Zanzibar Mail Service Records.
Post 30, Postmaster General minutes and memoranda, 1794–1920.
Post 51, Cape of Good Hope and Zanzibar Mail Service Records.
Post 60, Staff Questions.
Post 65, Associations.
Post 82–3, Telegraph Records.
Post 100, Rowland Hill Papers.
Post 101, John Tilley Papers.
Post 151, Railway Letter Books.
Post, Report of G. Chetwynd and F. I. Scudamore Upon the Arrangements which they proposed to be made for Putting the Post Office Savings Bank into Operation, 26 July 1861.
Post, Report of the Committee on Savings Banks Funds, 1896.
Post, Telephone Records, 4 Box Files, 10 Bundles, uncatalogued, 1876–1913.
Post, Report of Telephone Rates Committee, 1920.

Public Record Office, Kew
Cabinet 37, Cabinet Papers, 1880–1914.
Treasury 1, Original correspondence, minutes, reports, etc.
Treasury 19, Treasury–Post Office correspondence, 1850–1920.

Union of Communication Workers Archives, Clapham, London
Papers of the early Post Office Unions.

University College Library, London
Chadwick Papers, the papers of Sir Edwin Chadwick.

Primary Printed Sources

British Parliamentary Papers (listed in chronological order)
1836, vol. 28, Fourth Report of the Commissioners Appointed to Inquire into the Management of the Post Office Department.
———— Sixth Report of the Commissioners Appointed to Inquire into the Management of the Post Office Department.
1836–7, vol. 20, Select Committee on Postage.
1837, vol. 34, Eighth Report of the Commissioners Appointed to Inquire into the Management of the Post Office Department.
1837, vol. 50, Returns of the Post Office, Dublin.
1843, vol. 8, Select Committee on Postage.
1852–3, vol. 38, Fifth Report of Select Committee on Railway and Canal Bills.
1852–3, vol. 95, Committee on Packet Contracts.
1854, vol. 11, Select Committee on Conveyance of Mails by Railway.
1857–8, vol. 16, Select Committee appointed to inquire into the Acts Relating to Savings Banks and the Operation thereof.
1859, vol. 6, Select Committee on Mail and Telegraphic Contracts.
1860, vol. 14, First Select Committee on Packet and Telegraphic Contracts.
———— Second Select Committee on Packet and Telegraphic Contracts.
1861, vol. 12, Select Committee on Royal Atlantic Steam Navigation Company.
1867–8, vol. 11, Select Committee on the Electric Telegraph Bill.
1867–8, vol. 41, Memorandum in Support of the Expediency of the Telegraphic Communication being Placed in the Hands of Her Majesty's Government.
———— Report of Committee appointed by the Chamber of Commerce to consider the present condition of Telegraphic Communication throughout the United Kingdom.

———— A Report to the Postmaster General Upon Certain Proposals which have been made for Transferring to the Post Office the Control and Management of the Electric Telegraphs Throughout the United Kingdom.

———— Returns of the names of all railway companies in the U.K. who construct or use electric telegraphs as part of their undertaking.

———— Supplementary Report of the Postmaster General upon the Proposal for Transferring to the Post Office the Control and Management of the Electric Telegraphs Throughout the United Kingdom.

———— Thomas Allan's Reasons for the Government Annexing an Electric Telegraph System to the General Post Office.

1868–9, vol. 6, Select Committee on Mail Contracts.

1870, vol. 48, Revenue Department Estimates.

1871, vol. 37, Report by Mr Scudamore on the Reorganisation of the Telegraph System of the United Kingdom.

1873, vol. 7, First Report of Committee of Public Accounts.

———— Second Report of Committee of Public Accounts.

1873, vol. 9, Select Committee (Cape of Good Hope and Zanzibar Mail Contracts).

1873, vol. 22, Friendly Society Committee.

———— Third Report of Friendly and Benefit Society Commissioners.

1876, vol. 13, Select Committee on Post Office (Telegraph Department).

1880, vol. 40, Return of all Taxes and Imposts from the Imperial Revenue of the United Kingdom.

1882, vol. 12, Select Committee on Annuities and Life Assurance.

1888, vol. 18, Select Committee on Revenue Department Estimates.

1890, vol. 41, Contract for the Conveyance of the West India Mails.

———— Return of all Taxes and Imposts from the Imperial Revenue of the United Kingdom.

1890, vol. 46, Revenue Department Estimates.

1892, vol. 17, Select Committee on the Telegraphs Bill.

1897, vol. 49, Interdepartmental Committee on Post Office Establishments.

1898, vol. 12, Select Committee on Telephones.

1900, vol. 47, Return of all Taxes and Imposts from the Imperial Revenue of the United Kingdom.

———— Return Relating to the Post Office Telegraphs (Revenue and Expenditure).

1901, vol. 44, Appropriation Accounts of Sums Granted for Civil Services and Revenue Accounts.

1902, vol. 9, Select Committee on Savings Bank Funds.

———— Select Committee on Steamship Subsidies.

1904, vol. 33, Committee on Post Office Wages.

1905, vol. 7, Select Committee on Post Office (Telephone Agreement).

1907, vol. 7, Report of the Select Committee on Post Office Servants.

1910, vol. 59, Return of all Taxes and Imposts from the Imperial Revenue of the United Kingdom.

1911, vol. 62, Revenue Department Estimates.

1912–13, vol. 9, Report from the Select Committee on Post Office Servants.

1914–16, vol. 32, First Report of the Committee Appointed to Examine Issues Arising out of the Report of the Select Committee of the House of Commons on Post Office.

1920, vol. 50, Appropriation Accounts of Sums Granted for Civil Services and Revenue Accounts.

1920, vol. 8, Select Committee on Telephone Charges.

1921, vol. 7, Select Committee on the Telephone Service.

1922, vol. 6, Select Committee on the Telephone Service.

1931–2, vol. 12, Report of the Committee of Enquiry on the Post Office.

Hansard's Parliamentary Debates, Third Series, vols. 31–356.
Hansard's Parliamentary Debates, Fourth Series, vols. 1–199.
Hansard's Parliamentary Debates, Fifth Series, vols. 1–68.

Historical Summaries of the Post Office Services to 30th September 1906, London, 1906.

Reports of the Postmaster General on the Post Office, London, 1855–1914.

Newspapers and Periodicals
The Economist
Journal of the Society of Arts
Saturday Review
Spectator
The Times

Contemporary Accounts, Articles, and Memoirs
Bahlman, D. W. R. (ed.), *The Diary of Sir Edward Hamilton*, Oxford, 1972.

Baines, F. E., *Forty Years at the Post Office*, 2 vols., London, 1895.

Blackwood, Harriet S., *Some Records of the Life of Stevenson Arthur Blackwood*, London, 1896.

Booth, Charles (ed.), *Life and Labour of the People in London*, 5 vols., London, 1903.

Bowring, John (ed.), *The Works of Jeremy Bentham*, 11 vols., New York, 1962.

Chadwick, Edwin, 'Life Assurances', *Westminster Review*, 9 (1828), 384–421.

—— 'On Railway Reform in Connection with a Cheap Telegraphic Post and a Parcel Post Delivery', *Journal of the Society of Arts*, 15 (1867), 720–6.

David, Edward (ed.), *Inside Asquith's Cabinet from the Diaries of Charles Hobhouse*, New York, 1977.

Davies, H., 'The Jubilee of Post Office Savings Banks', *St Martin's le Grand*, 21 (1911), 342–50.

Defoe, Daniel, *Giving Alms No Charity*, London, 1704.

Disraeli, Benjamin, *Endymion*, New York, 1880.

Fawcett, Henry, *Essays and Lectures*, London, 1872.

—— *Manual of Political Economy*, London, 1874.

—— 'Postal Telegrams', *Journal of the Society of Arts*, 28 (1880), 735–9.

—— *State Socialism and the Nationalisation of Land*, London, 1883.

Forman, H. Buxton, 'Sir Arthur Blackwood', *St Martin's le Grand*, 4 (1894).

Gladstone, W. E., 'Free Trade, Railways, and the Growth of Commerce', *The Nineteenth Century*, 7 (1880), 367–88.

Goschen, G. J., *Addresses on Educational and Economical Subjects*, Edinburgh, 1885.

Hastie, A. H., 'The Telephone Tangle and the Way to Untie It', *The Fortnightly Review*, 70 (1898), 893–900.

Heaton, J. Henniker, 'Wanted! An End to Political Patronage', *The Nineteenth Century and After*, 59 (1906), 571–80.

Hill, Arthur, 'Government Telegraphs', *Edinburgh Review*, 129 (1860), 154–69.

Hill, G. B., *Life of Sir Rowland Hill and History of Penny Postage*, 2 vols., London, 1880.

Holcombe, A. N., *Public Ownership of Telephones on the Continent of Europe*, Boston, 1911.

Hyde, J. W., *The Royal Mail*, Edinburgh, 1885.

Jevons, W. S., *Methods of Social Reform*, London, 1883.

—— 'The Post Office Telegraphs and Their Financial Results', *The Fortnightly Review*, 18 (1875), 826–35.

—— 'Postal Notes, Money Orders, and Bank Cheques', *The Contemporary Review*, 38 (1880), 150–61.

—— 'A State Parcel Post', *The Contemporary Review*, 34 (1879), 209–29.

Johnston, R. W., 'Early Telegraph Days', *St Martin's le Grand*, 4 (1894), 259–73.

Kempe, J. A., *Reminiscences of an Old Civil Servant 1846–1927*, London, 1928.

Lewins, William, *A History of Banks for Savings*, London, 1866.

Marshall, Alfred, *Trade and Industry*, London, 1923.

Marvin, Charles, *Our Public Offices*, London, 1882.

Matthew, H. C. G. (ed.), *The Gladstone Diaries*, vols. 5–9, Oxford, 1978–86.

Meeker, Royal, *History of Shipping Subsidies*, New York, 1905.

Meyer, Hugo R., *The British State Telegraphs*, New York, 1907.

———— *Public Ownership and the Telephone in Great Britain*, New York, 1907.

Mill, J. S., *Considerations on Representative Government*, 1861, rpr. New York, 1958.

Murray, Evelyn, *The Post Office*, London, 1927.

Raikes, Henry St John, *The Life and Letters of Henry Cecil Raikes*, London, 1898.

Ricardo, J. Lewis, *The Anatomy of the Navigation Acts*, London, 1847.

Samuel, Herbert, *Memoirs*, London, 1945.

Smiles, Samuel, *The Life of George Stephenson*, London, 1857.

Smith, Adam, *An Inquiry into the Nature and Causes of the Wealth of Nations*, 1776, rpr. 2 vols., Oxford, 1880.

Smyth, Eleanor C., *Sir Rowland Hill*, London, 1907.

Spencer, Herbert, *Social Statics*, 1851, rpr. New York, 1873.

Swift, H. G., *A History of the Postal Agitation*, London, 1900.

Taylor, George, 'The Substitution of Savings Banks for Poor Laws', *Quarterly Review*, 36 (1827), 484–96.

Trollope, Anthony, *An Autobiography*, 1883, rpr. New York, 1950.

———— *John Caldigate*, 1879, rpr. 2 vols., New York, 1911.

———— *Marion Fay*, 1882, rpr. Ann Arbor, Michigan, 1982.

West, Algernon, *Private Diaries*, London, 1922.

Wolmer, Viscount, *Post Office Reform*, London, 1932.

Woolf, Leonard, *Sowing*, New York, 1960.

Wynter, Andrew, 'The Electric Telegraph', *Quarterly Review*, 95 (1854), 118–64.

Yates, Edmund, *Recollections and Experiences*, 2 vols., London, 1884.

Reference Works

Boase, Frederic, *Modern English Biography*, 6 vols., New York, 1965.

Butler, David and Jennie Freeman, *British Political Facts*, New York, 1963.

Dictionary of National Biography, 63 vols. and supplements, London, 1885–1937.

Jeremy, David (ed.), *The Dictionary of Business Biography*, 5 vols., London, 1985–6.

Mitchell, B. R., and Phyllis Deane, *Abstract of British Historical Statistics*, Cambridge, 1962.

Who Was Who 1897–1915, London, 1920.
Who Was Who 1916–1928, London, 1929.
Who Was Who 1929–1940, London, 1941.

Secondary Sources

Secondary Authorities directly related to the British Post Office
Baker, E. C., *Sir William Preece*, London, 1976.
Baldwin, F. G. C., *The History of the Telephone in the United Kingdom*, London, 1925.
Batstone, E. et al., *Consent and Efficiency: Labour Relations and Management Strategy in the State Enterprise*, Oxford, 1984.
Bealey, Frank, *The Post Office Engineering Union*, London, 1976.
Clinton, Alan, *Post Office Workers*, London, 1984.
Daunton, M. J., *Royal Mail*, London, 1985.
Goldman, Lawrence (ed.), *The Blind Victorian: Henry Fawcett and Victorian Liberalism*, Cambridge, 1989.
Greenhill, R. G., 'The State Under Pressure: The West Indian Mail Contract 1905', *Business History*, 11 (1969), 120–7.
Harcourt, Freda, 'British Oceanic Mail Contracts in the Age of Steam, 1838–1914', *The Journal of Transport History*, 9 (1988), 1–18.
Hemmeon, J. C., *The History of the British Post Office*, Cambridge, Massachusetts, 1912.
Kieve, J. L., *Electric Telegraph*, Newton Abbot, England, 1973.
Perry, C. R., 'Frank Ives Scudamore and the Post Office Telegraphs', *Albion*, 12 (1980), 350–67.
———— 'The General Post Office's Zanzibar Shipping Contracts, 1860–1914', *The Mariner's Mirror*, 68 (1982), 57–67.
Pitt, Douglas C., *The Telecommunications Function in the British Post Office*, Westmead, 1980.
Pool, Ithiel de Sola (ed.), *The Social Impact of the Telephone*, Cambridge, Massachusetts, 1977.
Robinson, Howard, *Britain's Post Office*, New York, 1953.
———— *The British Post Office*, Princeton, 1948.
———— *Carrying British Mail Overseas*, New York, 1964.
Super, R. H., *Trollope in the Post Office*, Ann Arbor, Michigan, 1981.
Vale, Vivian, 'The Government and the Cunard Contract of 1903', *The Journal of Transport History*, new series 5 (1979), 36–45.

Secondary Authorities of a more general nature
Alderman, Geoffrey, *The Railway Interest*, Leicester, 1973.
Annan, Noel, 'England's Intellectual Aristocracy' in J. H. Plumb (ed.), *Studies in Social History*, London, 1955.

Aydelotte, W. O., 'The Conservative and Radical Interpretations of Early Victorian Social Legislation', *Victorian Studies*, 11 (1967), 225–36.

Ayerst, David, *The Manchester Guardian Biography of a Newspaper*, London, 1971.

Bagwell, Philip S., *The Railway Clearing House in the British Economy 1842–1922*, London, 1968.

Barry, E. Eldon, *Nationalisation in British Politics*, London, 1965.

Bartrip, P. W. J., 'State Intervention in Mid-Nineteenth Century Britain: Fact or Fiction?', *The Journal of British Studies*, 23 (1983), 63–83.

Brebner, J. B., 'Laissez Faire and State Intervention in Nineteenth-Century Britain', *The Journal of Economic History*, 8 Supplement (1948), 59–73.

Briggs, Asa, *The Birth of Broadcasting*, London, 1961.

—— *Victorian Things*, London, 1988.

Burn, W. L., *The Age of Equipoise*, New York, 1964.

Cameron, Rondo E., *France and the Economic Development of Europe*, Princeton, 1961.

Cell, John W., *British Colonial Administration in the Mid-Nineteenth Century*, New Haven, Connecticut, 1970.

Checkland, Sydney, *British Public Policy 1776–1939*, Cambridge, 1983.

Chester, Norman, *The English Administrative System, 1780–1870*, Oxford, 1981.

Chick, Martin, 'Privatisation: The Triumph of Past Practice over Current Requirements', *Business History*, 29 (1987), 104–17.

Clapham, J. A., *An Economic History of Modern Britain*, 3 vols., Cambridge, 1930–8.

Clark, G. S. R. Kitson, 'Statesmen in Disguise', *The Historical Journal*, 2 (1959), 19–39.

Clegg, H. A., Alan Fox, and A. F. Thompson, *A History of British Trade Unions Since 1889*, vol. 1, Oxford, 1964.

Coase, R. H., 'The Origin of the Monopoly of Broadcasting in Great Britain', *Economica*, 14 (1947), 189–210.

Coats, A. W., ed., *The Classical Economists and Economic Policy*, London, 1971.

Coleman, D. and C. MacLeod, 'Attitudes to New Techniques: British Businessmen, 1800–1950', *Economic History Review*, second series 39 (1986), 588–611.

Coupland, Reginald, *The Exploitation of East Africa, 1856–1890*, London, 1939.

Cromwell, V., 'Interpretations of Nineteenth-Century Administration: An Analysis', *Victorian Studies*, 9 (1966), 245–58.

Crossick, Geoffrey, *An Artisan Elite in Victorian Society*, London, 1978.

Daunton, M. J., ' "Gentlemanly Capitalism" and British Industry', *Past and Present* 122 (1989), 119–58.

Davidson, Roger, *Whitehall and the Labour Problem in Late-Victorian and Edwardian Britain*, London, 1985.

Dewey, C. J., 'Cambridge Idealism', *The Historical Journal*, 17 (1974), 63–78.

Dunkley, Peter, 'Emigration and the State, 1803–1842', *The Historical Journal*, 23 (1980), 353–80.

Edsall, Nicholas C., *Richard Cobden Independent Radical*, Cambridge, Massachusetts, 1986.

Elbaum, Bernard and William Lazonick (eds.), *The Decline of the British Economy*, Oxford, 1986.

Falkus, M., 'The Development of Municipal Trading in the Nineteenth Century', *Business History*, 19 (1977), 134–61.

Finer, S. E., *The Life and Times of Sir Edwin Chadwick*, London, 1952.

Foreman-Peck, J. S., 'Natural Monopoly and Railway Policy in the Nineteenth Century', *Oxford Economic Papers*, 39 (1987), 699–718.

Friedberg, A. L., *The Weary Titan. Britain and the Experience of Relative Decline*, Princeton, 1988.

Galbraith, J. S., *Mackinnon and East Africa 1878–1895*, Cambridge, 1973.

Gerth, H. H. and C. W. Mills (eds.), *From Max Weber: Essays in Sociology*, Oxford, 1958.

Gordon, Scott, 'The London *Economist* and the High Tide of Laissez Faire', *The Journal of Political Economy*, 63 (1955), 461–88.

Gosden, P. H. J. H., *Self-Help*, New York, 1974.

Gourvish, T. R., 'British Business and the Transition to a Corporate Economy: Entrepreneurship and Management Structures', *Business History*, 29 (1987), 18–45.

—— *Railways and the British Economy 1850–1914*, London, 1980.

Graham, D., 'Victorian Reform as a Family Business' in A. S. Wohl (ed.), *The Victorian Family*, London, 1978.

Greenleaf, W. H., *The British Political Tradition*, vols. 1 and 2, London, 1983.

Hamer, D. A., *Liberal Politics in the Age of Gladstone and Rosebery*, Oxford, 1972.

Hanham, H. J., 'Political Patronage at the Treasury 1870–1912', *The Historical Journal*, 3 (1960), 75–84.

Hannah, Leslie, *Electricity Before Nationalisation*, London, 1979.

—— 'Managerial Innovation and the Rise of the Large-Scale Company', *The Economic History Review*, 27 (1974), 252–70.

Harrison, Brian, *Drink and the Victorians*, London, 1971.

Hart, J., 'Nineteenth-Century Social Reform: A Tory Interpretation of History', *Past and Present*, no. 31 (1965), 39–61.

Hennock, E. P., *British Social Reform and German Precedent*, Oxford, 1987.

The History of the Times, 5 vols., London, 1935–52.

Hollis, Patricia (ed.), *Pressure From Without in Early Victorian England*, London, 1974.

Horne, H. Oliver, *A History of Savings Banks*, London, 1947.

Howell, Raymond, *The Royal Navy and the Slave Trade*, New York, 1987.

Hume, L. H., *Bentham and Bureaucracy*, Cambridge, 1981.

Humphreys, B. V., *Clerical Unions in the Civil Service*, London, 1958.

Hyde, F. E., *Cunard and the North Atlantic 1840–1973*, London, 1975.

Johnson, Paul, 'Credit and Thrift and the British Working Class, 1970–1939' in Jay Winter (ed.), *The Working Class in Modern British History*, Cambridge, 1983.

—— *Saving and Spending*, Oxford, 1985.

Jones, Stephanie, *Two Centuries of Overseas Trading*, London, 1986.

Lambert, R., *Sir John Simon, 1816–1904, and English Social Administration*, London, 1963.

Laski, M., 'Domestic Life' in S. Nowell-Smith (ed.), *Edwardian England*, London, 1964.

Lazonick, William, 'Competition, Specialization, and Industrial Decline', *The Journal of Economic History*, 41 (1981), 31–8.

Lowell, A. L., *The Government of England*, 2 vols., New York, 1908.

Lubenow, W. C., *The Politics of Government Growth*, Hamden, Connecticut, 1971.

MacDonagh, Oliver, 'Delegated Legislation and Administrative Discretion', *Victorian Studies*, 2 (1958), 29–44.

—— *Early Victorian Government*, New York, 1977.

—— 'The Nineteenth-Century Revolution in Government: A Reappraisal', *The Historical Journal*, 1 (1958), 52–67.

—— *A Pattern of Government Growth*, London, 1961.

McGraw, Thomas K. (ed.), *The Essential Alfred Chandler Essays Toward a Historical Theory of Big Business*, Boston, 1988.

MacLeod, R. M. (ed.), *Government and Expertise*, Cambridge, 1988.

—— 'Statesmen Undisguised', *The American Historical Review*, 88 (1973), 1386–1405.

Mack, M. P., 'The Fabians and Utilitarianism', *Journal of the History of Ideas*, 16 (1955), 76–88.

Mather, F. C., 'The Railways, the Electric Telegraph, and Public Order During the Chartist Period, 1837–1848', *History*, new series 38 (1953), 40–53.

Matsumura, Takao, *The Labour Aristocracy Revisited: The Victorian Flint Glass Makers*, Manchester, 1983.

Matthew, H. C. G., 'Rhetoric and Politics in Great Britain, 1860–1950' in P. J. Waller (ed.), *Politics and Social Change in Modern Britain*, London, 1987.

Midwinter, E. C., *Social Administration in Lancashire*, Manchester, 1969.

Miers, Suzanne, *Britain and the Ending of the Slave Trade*, New York, 1975.

Milward, Robert and Robert Ward , 'The Costs of Public and Private Gas Enterprises in Late 19th Century Britain', *Oxford Economic Papers*, 39 (1987), 719–37.

Mokyr, Joel, 'On the (Alleged) Failures of Victorian Britain', *The Journal of British Studies*, 28 (1989), 89–95.

Morgan, Kenneth O., 'The Rise and Fall of Public Ownership in Britain' in J. M. W. Bean (ed.), *The Political Culture of Modern Britain: Studies in Memory of Stephen Koss*, London, 1987.

Morley, John, *The Life of William Ewart Gladstone*, 3 vols., New York, 1904.

Munro, Forbes, 'Shipping Subsidies and Railway Guarantees: William Mackinnon, East Africa, and the Indian Ocean, 1860–1893', *Journal of African History*, 28 (1987), 209–30.

Parris, Henry, *Constitutional Bureaucracy*, London, 1969.

——— *Government and the Railways in Nineteenth-Century Britain*, London, 1965.

——— 'The Nineteenth-Century Revolution in Government: A Reappraisal Reappraised', *The Historical Journal*, 3 (1960), 17–37.

Pellew, Jill, *The Home Office, 1848–1914*, East Brunswick, New Jersey, 1982.

Perkin, Harold, 'Individualism versus Collectivism in Nineteenth-Century Britain: a False Antithesis', *The Journal of British Studies*, 17 (1977), 105–18.

——— *The Origins of Modern English Society*, London, 1969.

——— *The Rise of Professional Society*, London, 1989.

Pollard, Sidney, *Britain's Prime and Britain's Decline. The British Economy 1870–1914*, London, 1989.

——— 'Laissez-Faire and Shipbuilding', *The Economic History Review*, second series 5 (1952–3), 98–115.

Porter, Andrew, *Victorian Shipping, Business, and Imperial Policy*, New York, 1986.

Robbins, Keith, *Nineteenth-Century Britain Integration and Diversity*, Oxford, 1988.

Robbins, Lionel, *The Theory of Economic Policy in English Classical Political Economy*, London, 1965.

Roberts, David, 'Jeremy Bentham and the Victorian Administrative State', *Victorian Studies*, 2 (1959), 193–210.

—— *Paternalism in Early Victorian England*, New Brunswick, New Jersey, 1979.

—— *Victorian Origins of the British Welfare State*, New Haven, Connecticut, 1960.

Roseveare, Henry, *The Treasury*, London, 1969.

Rydz, D. L., *The Parliamentary Agents*, London, 1979.

Sandberg, L. G., 'The Entrepreneur and Technological Change' in R. Floud and D. McCloskey (eds.), *The Economic History of Britain since 1700*, vol. 2, Cambridge, 1981.

Searle, G. R., *The Quest for National Efficiency*, Oxford, 1971.

Soldon, N., 'Laissez-Faire as Dogma: The Liberty and Property Defence League' in K. D. Brown (ed.), *Essays in Anti-Labour History*, London, 1974.

Spinner, T. J., *George Joachim Goschen*, Cambridge, 1973.

Supple, Barry, 'Legislation and Virtue' in Neil McKendrick (ed.), *Historical Perspectives: Studies in English Thought and Society*, London, 1974.

Sutherland, G. (ed.), *Studies in the Growth of Nineteenth-Century Government*, London, 1972.

Taylor, A. J., *Laissez-Faire and State Intervention in Nineteenth Century Britain*, London, 1972.

Thompson, F. M. L., *The Rise of Respectable Society*, Cambridge, Massachusetts, 1988.

Thornton, R. H., *British Shipping*, Cambridge, 1959.

Tolliday, Steven, *Business, Banking, and Politics. The Case of British Steel, 1918–1939*, Cambridge, Massachusetts, 1987.

Wiener, Martin J., *English Culture and the Decline of the Industrial Spirit*, Cambridge, 1981.

Winter, James, *Robert Lowe*, Toronto, 1976.

Wright, Maurice, *Treasury Control of the Civil Service 1854–1874*, Oxford, 1969.

Zimmeck, Meta, 'Jobs for the Girls: the Expansion of Clerical Work for Women, 1850–1914' in Angela V. John (ed.), *Unequal Opportunities: Women's Employment in England 1800–1918*, Oxford, 1986.

Index